reader's choice

fourth canadian edition

kim flachmann

CALIFORNIA STATE UNIVERSITY, BAKERSFIELD

michael flachmann

CALIFORNIA STATE UNIVERSITY, BAKERSFIELD

alexandra maclennan

BMO FINANCIAL GROUP INSTITUTE FOR LEARNING

PEARSON

Prentice
Hall

Toronto

National Library of Canada Cataloguing in Publication

Flachmann, Kim
    Reader's choice / Kim Flachmann, Michael Flachmann, Alexandra
MacLennan.—4th Canadian ed.

First-3rd ed. written by Kim Flachmann ... et al.
Includes bibliographical references and index.
ISBN 0-13-039792-X

    1. College readers. 2. English language—Rhetoric. I. Flachmann,
Michael II. MacLennan, Alexandra, 1964– III. Title.

PE1417.R42 2003   808'.0427   C2003-901318-9

ISBN 0-13-039792-X

Vice President, Editorial Director: Michael Young
Acquisitions Editor: Marianne Minaker
Marketing Manager: Toivo Pajo
Developmental Editor: Adrienne Shiffman
Production Editor: Avivah Wargon
Copy Editor: Susan McNish
Production Manager: Wendy Moran
Page Layout: B.J. Weckerle
Permissions Research: Beth McAuley
Art Director: Julia Hall
Interior Design: Arlene Edgar
Cover Design: Jennifer Federico
Cover Image: Peter Leverman/firstlight.ca

4 5   08 07 06 05

Printed and bound in Canada.

RHETORICAL CONTENTS

CHAPTER 2

NARRATION: *Telling a Story*   77

CHAPTER 3

EXAMPLE: *Illustrating Ideas* 125

ANITA RAU BADAMI *My Canada* 136
What constitutes *your* Canada? In this essay from the *Imperial Oil Review*, Anita Rau Badami uses a multitude of examples to make her Canada come alive and to explain why it is now her home.

SHARON BUTALA *The Myth: The Prairies Are Flat* 145
Prairie writer Butala tackles a common misperception about her region of Canada.

CECIL FOSTER *Why Blacks Get Mad* 150
Using strongly affective examples drawn from his own and his family's lives, Foster speaks forthrightly and personally of the insidious presence of racism in everyday life in Canada.

BARBARA KINGSOLVER *Life Without Go-Go Boots* 160
What fashion item was essential to you when growing up? Barbara Kingsolver discusses the role of fashion in her life.

CHAPTER 4

PROCESS ANALYSIS: *Explaining Step by Step* 167

PAUL QUARRINGTON *Home Brew* 178
What golden beverage is a Canadian institution? How do you make this product yourself? The answers to these and other questions are amusingly offered for your enjoyment in Quarrington's essay.

CHAPTER 5

DIVISION/CLASSIFICATION: *Finding Categories* 211

PREFACE

Accurate thinking is the beginning and fountain of writing.

—Horace

Reader's Choice is based on the assumption that lucid writing follows lucid thinking, whereas poor writing is almost inevitably the product of foggy, irrational thought processes. As a result, our primary purpose in this book, as in previous editions of *Reader's Choice*, is to help students think more clearly and logically—both in their minds and on paper.

Furthermore, we believe that college and university students should be able to think, read, and write on three increasingly difficult levels:

1. *Literal*, characterized by a basic understanding of words and their meanings;

2. *Interpretive*, consisting of a knowledge of linear connections between ideas and an ability to make valid inferences based on those ideas; and

3. *Critical*, the highest level, distinguished by the systematic investigation of complex ideas and by the analysis of their relationship to the world around us.

To demonstrate this vital interrelationship between reader and writer, this text provides prose models that are intended to inspire students' thinking and writing. Although studying rhetorical strategies is certainly not the only way to approach writing, it is a productive means of helping students become better writers. These essays are intended to encourage students to improve their writing through a partnership with some of the best examples of professional prose available today. Just as musicians and athletes richly benefit from studying the techniques of the foremost people in their fields, students will, we hope, grow in spirit and language use from their collaborative work with the writers in this collection.

HOW THE TEXT IS ORGANIZED

Each chapter of *Reader's Choice* begins with an explanation of a single rhetorical technique. These explanations are divided into six sections that move from the effect of this technique on our daily lives to its integral role in the writing process. Also, in each introduction we include a student paragraph and a student essay featuring each particular rhetorical strategy under discussion. The essay is highlighted by annotations and underlining to illustrate how to write that type of essay and to help bridge the gap between student writing and the professional selections that follow.

The essays that follow each chapter introduction are selected from a wide variety of contemporary authors. Of course, "pure" rhetorical types rarely exist, and when they do, the result often seems artificial. Therefore, although each essay in this collection focuses on a single rhetorical mode as its primary strategy, other strategies are always simultaneously at work. These selections concentrate on one primary technique at a time in much the same way a well-arranged photograph highlights a certain visual detail, though many other elements function in the background to make the picture an organic whole.

In introducing each reading selection, we offer some material to focus attention onto a particular writer and topic before the essay is read. This "prereading" segment begins with biographical information about the author and ends with a number of questions to whet the reader's appetite for the essay that follows. This section is intended to help readers discover interesting relationships among ideas in their reading and then anticipate various ways of thinking about and analyzing the essay. The prereading questions forecast not only the content of the essay, but also the questions and writing assignments that follow.

The questions after each reading selection are designed as guides for thinking about the essay. These questions are at the heart of the relationship represented in this book among thinking, reading, and writing. They are divided into four interrelated sections that move readers smoothly from a literal understanding of what they have just read, to interpretation, and finally to analysis.

After students have studied the different techniques at work in a reading selection, a specific essay assignment provides an opportunity to practise all these skills in unison and encourages the discovery of even more secrets about the intricate and exciting details of effective communication. Three "Ideas for Discussion/ Writing" are preceded by "prewriting" questions to help readers generate new ideas. Most of the Discussion/Writing topics specify a purpose (a definite reason for writing the essay) and an audience (an identifiable person or group of people that should be addressed in the essay) to help students focus their work as precisely as possible. The word *essay* (which comes from the Old French *essai*, meaning a "try" or an "attempt") is an appropriate label for these writing assignments, because they all ask students to wrestle with an idea or problem and then try to give shape to their conclusions in some effective manner. Such "exercises" can be equated with the development of athletic ability: The essay itself demonstrates that students can put together all the various skills they have learned; it proves that you can actually play the "sport" of writing.

Finally, the websites listed at the end of each selection will lead the reader to sites on the World Wide Web that will provide more information about reading. Students can visit the *Reader's Choice* webpage at **www.pearsoned.ca/flachmann** to find a glossary of useful terms as well as a collection of websites that offer more information about the readings. This might be information about the author, the original source of the piece of writing, or the topic of the essay being read.

WHAT IS NEW

We have made some changes in the fourth edition of *Reader's Choice* that reflect the responses of reviewers from many different types of colleges and universities all over Canada and the United States.

• *The fourth edition of* Reader's Choice *contains 16 new essays.*

We have updated some of the selections, added new authors, and introduced new topics, including overwork, genetic engineering, hockey and opera, Hanukkah, the naming of sports venues, organic farming, racist language, and Canada's ability to influence global issues.

• *Chapter 10 contains a new, Canadian, student essay*

"Language for a New Age," a new, award-winning student essay by Dave Kendall, is now included in the chapter on documented essays.

- *The fourth edition of* Reader's Choice *is accompanied by a new Instructor's Manual.*

The new Instructor's Manual will supplement the text by offering the following key features: discussion of the some theoretical approaches to the teaching of composition, techniques for responding to student writing, and vocabulary and content quizzes for each of the reading selections.

- *Author biographies have been updated.*

The biographical information for the authors of essays from previous editions of *Reader's Choice* has been updated.

- *Weblinks have been updated and made available online.*

The weblinks following each essay selection have been updated and are now also available online at **www.pearsoned.ca/ flachmann** for easy access to relevant supplementary information.

Kim Flachmann
Michael Flachmann
Alexandra MacLennan

ACKNOWLEDGMENTS

I would like to acknowledge a number of people who helped in the preparation of this edition of *Reader's Choice*. At Pearson Education Canada, for their guidance, patience, and support, I would like to thank Marianne Minaker, Acquisitions Editor; Adrienne Shiffman, Developmental Editor; Avivah Wargon, Supervising Editor; and Susan McNish, Copy Editor.

I would also like to thank the following reviewers for their feedback during development: Judith Carson, Melanie Rubens, and Allison McNaught, Seneca College; Mary Gossage, Dawson College; Kay Oxford, George Brown College; and Kathy Woodward, Grant MacEwan College. Finally, I would like to thank my colleagues for their ongoing support, feedback, and advice about *Reader's Choice*.

Alexandra MacLennan

INTRODUCTION

Thinking, Reading, and Writing

Have you ever had trouble expressing your thoughts? If so, you're not alone. Many people have this difficulty—especially when they are asked to write their thoughts down. The good news is that this "ailment" can be cured. We've learned over the years that the more clearly students think about the world around them, the more easily they can express their ideas through written and spoken language. As a result, this textbook intends to improve your writing by helping you think clearly, logically, and critically about important ideas and issues that exist in our world today. You will learn to reason, read, and write about your environment in increasingly complex ways, moving steadily from a simple, literal understanding of topics to interpretation and analysis.

Part of becoming a better writer involves understanding that reading and writing are companion activities that engage people in the creation of thought and meaning—either as readers interpreting a text or as writers constructing one. Clear thinking, then, is the pivotal point that joins these two efforts. Although studying the rhetorical strategies presented in *Reader's Choice* is not the only way to approach writing, it provides a productive means of helping students improve their abilities to think, read, and write. Inspired by the well-crafted prose models in this text and guided by carefully worded questions, you can raise the level of your thinking skills while improving your reading and writing abilities on three progressively more sophisticated levels:

1. *The literal level* is the foundation of all human understanding; it entails knowing the meanings of words—individually and in relation to one another. In order to comprehend the sentence "You must exercise your brain to reach your full mental potential" on the literal level, for example, a person would have to know the definitions of all the words in the sentence and understand the way those words work together to make meaning.

2. *Interpretation* requires the ability to make associations between details, draw inferences from pieces of information, and reach conclusions about the material. An interpretive understanding of the sample sentence in level 1 might be translated into the following thoughts: "Exercising the brain sounds a bit like exercising the body. I wonder if there's any correlation between the two. If the brain must be exercised, it is probably made up of muscles, much as the body is." None of these particular "thoughts" is made explicit in the sentence, but each is suggested in one way or another.

3. *Thinking, reading, and writing critically,* the most sophisticated form of rational abilities, involves a type of mental activity that is crucial for successful academic and professional work. A critical analysis of our sample sentence might proceed in the following way: "This sentence is talking to me. It actually addresses me with the word *you.* I wonder what *my* mental potential is. Will I be able to reach it? Will I know when I attain it? I certainly want to reach this potential; it will undoubtedly help me succeed scholastically and professionally. The brain is obviously an important tool for helping me achieve my goals in life, so I want to take every opportunity I have to develop and maintain this part of my body." Students who can take an issue or idea apart in this fashion and understand its various components more thoroughly after reassembling them are rewarded intrinsically with a clearer knowledge of life's complexities and the ability to generate creative, useful ideas. They are also rewarded extrinsically with good grades and are more likely to earn responsible jobs with higher pay, because their understanding of the world around them is perceptive and they are able to apply this understanding effectively to their professional and personal lives.

In this textbook, you will learn to think critically by reading essays written by intelligent, interesting authors and by writing your own essays on a variety of topics. The next several pages offer guidelines for approaching the thinking, reading, and writing assignments in this book. These suggestions should also be useful to you in your other courses.

Thinking Critically

Recent psychological studies have shown that "thinking" and "feeling" are complementary operations. All of us have feelings that are automatic and instinctive. To feel pride after winning first place at a track meet, for example, or to feel anger at a spiteful friend is not behaviour we have to study and master; such emotions come naturally to human beings. Thinking, on the other hand, is much less spontaneous than feeling; research suggests that study and practice are required for sustained mental development.

Thinking critically involves grappling with the ideas, issues, and problems that surround you in your immediate environment and in the world at large. It does not necessarily entail finding fault, which you might naturally associate with the word *critical*, but rather suggests continually questioning and analyzing the world around you. Thinking critically is the highest form of mental activity that human beings engage in; it is the source of success at school and in our professional and personal lives. Fortunately, all of us can learn how to think more critically.

Critical thinking means taking apart an issue, idea, or problem; examining its various parts; and reassembling the topic with a fuller understanding of its intricacies. Implied in this explanation is the ability to see the topic from one or more new perspectives. Using your mind in this way will help you find solutions to difficult problems, design creative plans of action, and ultimately live a life consistent with your opinions on important issues that we all must confront daily.

Since critical or analytical thinking is one of the highest forms of mental activity, it requires a great deal of concentration and practice. Once you have actually felt how your mind works and processes information at this level, however, you will find that recreating the experience is somewhat like riding a bicycle: you will be able to do it naturally, easily, and skillfully whenever you want to.

Our initial goal, then, is to help you think critically when you are required to do so in school, on the job, or in any other area of your life. If this form of thinking becomes a part of your daily routine, you will quite naturally be able to call upon it whenever you need it.

Working with the rhetorical modes is an effective way to achieve this goal. With some guidance, each rhetorical pattern can provide you with a mental workout to prepare you for writing and critical thinking in the same way that physical exercises warm you up for various sports. Just as in the rest of the body, the more exercise the brain gets, the more flexible it becomes and the higher the levels of thought it can attain. Through these various guided thinking exercises, you can systematically strengthen your ability to think analytically.

As you move through the following chapters, we will ask you to isolate each rhetorical mode—much like isolating your abs, quads, and biceps in a weight-training workout—so that you can concentrate on these thinking patterns one at a time. Each rhetorical pattern we study will suggest slightly different ways of seeing the world, processing information, and solving problems. Each offers important ways of thinking and making sense of our immediate environment and the larger world around us. Looking closely at rhetorical modes or specific patterns of thought helps us discover how our minds work. In the same fashion, becoming more intimately aware of our thought patterns lets us improve our basic thinking skills as well as our reading and writing abilities. Thinking critically helps us discover fresh insights into old ideas, generate new thoughts, and see connections between related issues. It is an energizing mental activity that puts us in control of our lives and our environment rather than leaving us at the mercy of our surroundings.

Each chapter introduction provides three exercises specifically designed to help you focus in isolation on a particular pattern of thought. While you are attempting to learn what each pattern feels like in your head, use your imagination to play with these exercises on as many different levels as possible.

When you practise each of the rhetorical patterns of thought, you should be aware of building on your previous thinking skills. As the book progresses, the rhetorical modes become more complex and require a higher degree of concentration and effort. Throughout the book, therefore, you should keep in mind that ultimately you want to let these skills accumulate into a well-developed ability to process the world around you—including reading, writing, seeing, and feeling—on the most advanced analytical level you can master.

Reading Critically

Reading critically begins with developing a natural curiosity about an essay and nurturing that curiosity throughout the reading process. To learn as much as you can from an essay, you should first study any preliminary material you can find, then read the essay to get a general overview of its main ideas, and finally read the selection again to achieve a deeper understanding of its content. The three phases of the reading process explained below—preparing to read, reading, and rereading—will help you develop this "natural curiosity" so you can approach any reading assignment with an active, inquiring mind.

Preparing to Read

Focusing your attention is an important first stage in both the reading and the writing processes. In fact, learning as much as you can about an essay and its "context" (the circumstances surrounding its development) before you begin reading can help you move through the essay with an energetic, active mind and then reach some degree of analysis before writing on the assigned topics. In particular, knowing where an essay was first published, studying the writer's background, and doing some preliminary thinking on the subject of a reading selection will help you understand the writer's ideas and form some valid opinions of your own.

As you approach any essay, you should concentrate on four specific areas that will begin to give you an overview of the material you are about to read. We use an essay by Lewis Thomas to demonstrate these techniques.

1. *Title.* A close look at the title will usually provide important clues about the author's attitude toward the topic, the author's stand on an issue, or the mood of an essay. It can also furnish you with a sense of audience and purpose.

To Err Is Human

From this title, for example, we might infer that the author will discuss errors, human nature, and the extent to which mistakes influence human behaviour. The title is half of a well-known proverbial quotation (Alexander Pope's "To err is human, to forgive, divine"), so we might speculate further that the author has written an essay intended for a well-read audience interested in the relationship between errors and humanity. After reading only four words of the essay—its title—we already have a good deal of information about the subject, its audience, and the author's attitude toward both.

2. *Synopsis.* The Rhetorical Table of Contents in this text contains a synopsis of each essay, very much like the following, so that you can find out more specific details about its contents before you begin reading.

> Physician Lewis Thomas explains how we can profit from our mistakes—especially if we trust human nature. Perhaps someday, he says, we can apply this same principle to the computer and magnify the advantages of these errors.

From this synopsis, we learn that Thomas's essay will be an analysis of human errors and of the way we can benefit from those errors. The synopsis also tells us the computer has the potential to magnify the value of our errors.

3. *Biography.* Learning as much as you can about the author of an essay will generally stimulate your interest in the material and help you achieve a deeper understanding of the issues to be discussed. From the biographies in this book, you can learn, for example, whether a writer is young or old, conservative or liberal, open- or closed-minded. You might also discover if the essay was written at the beginning, middle, or end of the author's career or how well versed the writer is on the topic. Such information will invariably provide a deeper, more thorough understanding of a selection's ideas, audience, and logical structure.

LEWIS THOMAS

Lewis Thomas was a physician who, until his death in 1998, was president emeritus of the Sloan-Kettering Cancer Center and scholar-in-residence at the Cornell University Medical Center in New York City. A graduate of Princeton University and Harvard Medical School, he was formerly head of pathology and dean of the New York University-Bellevue Medical Center and dean of the Yale Medical School. In addition to having written over 200 scientific papers on virology and immunology, he authored many popular scientific essays, some of which have been collected in *Lives of a Cell* (1974), *The Medusa and the Snail* (1979), *Late Night Thoughts on Listening to Mahler's Ninth Symphony* (1983), *Etcetera, Etcetera* (1990), and *The Fragile Species* (1992). The memoirs of his distinguished career have been published in *The Youngest Science: Notes of a Medicine Watcher* (1983). Thomas liked to refer to his essays as "experiments in thought": "Although I usually think I know what I'm going to be writing about, what I'm going to say, most of the time it doesn't happen that way at all. At some point I get misled down a garden path. I get surprised by an idea that I hadn't anticipated getting, which is a little bit like being in a laboratory."

As this information indicates, Thomas was a prominent physician who published widely on scientific topics. We know that he considered his essays "experiments in thought," which makes us expect a relaxed, spontaneous treatment of his subjects. From this biography, we can also infer that he was a leader in the medical world and that, because of the positions he held, he was well respected in his professional life. Last, we can speculate that he had a clear sense of his audience because he was able to present difficult concepts in clear, everyday language.

4. *Preparing to read.* One other type of preliminary material will broaden your overview of the topic and enable you to approach the essay with an active, thoughtful mind. The "Preparing to Read" sections following the biographies are intended to focus your attention and stimulate your curiosity before you begin the essay. They will also get you ready to form your own opinions on the essay and its topic as you read. Keeping a journal to respond to the questions in this section is an excellent idea, because you will then have a record of your thoughts on various topics related to the reading selection that follows.

Discovering where, why, and how an essay was first written will provide you with a context for the material you are about to read: Why did the author write this essay? Where was it first published? Who was the author's original audience? This type of information enables you to understand the circumstances surrounding the development of the selection and to identify any topical or historical references the author makes. All the selections in this textbook were published elsewhere first—in another book, a journal, a website, or a magazine. Some are excerpts from longer works. The author's original audience, therefore, consisted of the readers of that particular publication.

Preparing to Read

The following essay, which originally appeared in the *New England Journal of Medicine* (January 1976), illustrates the clarity and ease with which Thomas explains complex scientific topics. As you prepare to read this essay, take a few moments to think about the role mistakes play in our lives: What are some memorable mistakes you have made in your life? Did you learn anything important from any of these errors? Do you make more or fewer mistakes than other people you know? Do you see any advantages to making mistakes? Any disadvantages?

From the sample "Preparing to Read" material, we learn that Thomas's essay "To Err Is Human" was originally published in the *New England Journal of Medicine*, a prestigious periodical read principally by members of the scientific community. Written early in 1976, the article plays upon its audience's growing fascination with computers and with the limits of artificial intelligence—subjects just as timely today as they were in the mid-1970s.

The questions here prompt you to consider your own ideas, opinions, or experiences in order to help you generate thoughts on the topic of errors in our lives. These questions are, ideally, the last step in preparing yourself for the active role you should play as a reader.

Reading

People read essays in books, newspapers, magazines, and journals for a great variety of reasons. One reader may want to be stimulated intellectually, whereas another seeks relaxation; one person reads to keep up with the latest developments in his or her profession, whereas the next wants to learn why a certain event happened or how something can be done; some people read in order to be challenged by new ideas, whereas others find comfort principally in printed material that supports their own moral, social, or political opinions. The selections in this textbook variously fulfill all these expectations. They have been chosen, however, not only for these reasons, but for an additional, broader purpose: Reading them can help make you a better writer.

Every time you read an essay in this book, you will also be preparing to write your own essay, concentrating on the same rhetorical pattern. For this reason, as you read each selection you should pay careful attention to both the content (subject matter) and the form (language, sentence structure, organization, and development of ideas) of each essay. You will also see how effectively experienced writers use particular rhetorical modes (or patterns of thought) to organize and communicate their ideas. Each essay in this collection features one dominant pattern that is generally supported by several others. In fact, the more aware you are of each author's writing techniques, the more rapidly your own writing process will mature and improve.

The questions before and after each essay teach you a way of reading that can help you discover the relationship of a writer's ideas to one another as well as to your own ideas. These questions can also help clarify for you the connection between the writer's topic, his or her style or manner of expression, and your own composing process. The questions are designed to help you understand and generate ideas, discover various choices the writers make in composing their essays, and finally realize the freedom you have to make related choices in your own writing. Such an approach to the process of reading takes some of the mystery out of reading and writing and makes them manageable tasks at which anyone can become proficient.

Three general guidelines, each of which is explained below in detail, will help you develop your own system for reading and responding to what you have read:

1. *Read the selection to get an overall sense of it.*

2. *Summarize the reading.*

3. *Read the questions and assignments that follow the selection.*

Guideline 1. *First, read the selection to get an overall sense of it in relation to its title, purpose, audience, author, and publication information.* Write (in the margins, on a separate piece of paper, or in a journal) your initial reactions, comments, and personal associations.

To illustrate, on the following pages is the Thomas essay with a student's comments in the margins, showing how the student reacted to the essay upon reading it for the first time.

LEWIS THOMAS

To Err Is Human

Boy is <u>this</u> true! Everyone must have had at least one personal experience with a computer error by this time. Bank balances are suddenly reported to have jumped from \$379 into the millions, appeals for charitable contributions are mailed over and over to people with crazy sounding names at your address, <u>department stores send the wrong bills</u>, utility companies write that they're turning everything off, that sort of thing. If you manage to get in touch with someone and complain, you then get instantaneously typed, guilty letters from the *exactly* same computer, saying, "Our computer was in error, and an adjustment is being made in your account." 1

Last spring this happened to me.

These are supposed to be the sheerest, blindest accidents. Mistakes are not believed to be part of the normal behavior of a *How can it* good machine. If things go wrong, it must be a personal, human *be?* error, the result of fingering, tampering, a button getting stuck, someone hitting the wrong key. The computer, at its normal best, is infallible. 2

I wonder whether this can be true. After all, the whole point of computers is that they represent an extension of the human brain, *In what way?* vastly improved upon but nonetheless human, <u>superhuman</u> maybe. A good computer can think clearly and quickly enough to beat you at chess, and some of them have even been programmed to write *Can this be* obscure verse. They can do anything we can do, and more besides. *proven?* 3

It is not yet known whether a computer has its own consciousness, and it would be hard to find out about this. When you *I expected this* walk into one of those great halls now built for the huge machines, *essay to be so* and stand listening, it is easy to imagine that the faint, distant noises *much more* are the sound of thinking, and the turning of the spools gives them *stuffy than it* *In what* the look of wild creatures rolling their eyes in the effort to concen- *is. I can even* *way?* trate, choking with information. <u>But real thinking, and dreaming, are</u> *understand it.* <u>other matters</u>. 4

On the other hand, the evidences of something like an unconscious, equivalent to ours, are all around, in every mail. As *good, clear* extensions of the human brain, they have been constructed with *comparison for* the same property of error, spontaneous, uncontrolled, and rich in *the general* possibilities. *reader* 5

so true <u>Mistakes are at the very base of human thought</u>, embedded *great image!* there, feeding the structure like <u>root nodules</u>. If we were not pro- *I don't* vided with the knack of being wrong, we could never get anything *understand* useful done. We think our way along by choosing between right *this* 6

I agree!
This is how
we learn
and wrong alternatives, and the wrong choices have to be made as frequently as the right ones. We get along in life this way. We are built to make mistakes, coded for error.

We learn, as we say, <u>by "trial and error."</u> Why do we always say that? Why not "trial and rightness" or "trial and triumph"? The old phrase puts it that way because that is, in real life, the way it is done.   7

Another
effective
comparison
for the
general
reader
A good laboratory, like a good bank or a corporation or government, has to run like a computer. Almost everything is done flawlessly, by the book, and all the numbers add up to the predicted sums. The days go by. And then, if it is a <u>lucky</u> day, and a lucky laboratory, somebody makes a <u>mistake</u>: the wrong buffer, something in one of the blanks, a decimal misplaced in reading counts, the warm room off by a degree and a half, a mouse out of his box, or just a misreading of the day's protocol. Whatever, when the results come in, something is obviously screwed up, and <u>then the action can begin</u>.   8

Isn't this
a contra—
diction?

What?

The misreading is not the important error; <u>it opens the way</u>. The next step is the crucial one. If the investigator can bring himself to say, "But even so, look at that!" then the new finding, whatever it is, is ready for snatching. What is needed, for progress to be made, is <u>the move based on error</u>.   9

aha!

Whenever new kinds of thinking are about to be accomplished, or new varieties of music, there has to be an argument beforehand. With two sides debating in the same mind, haranguing, there is an amiable understanding that one is right and the other wrong. Sooner or later the thing is settled, but there can be no action at all if there are not the two sides, and the argument. <u>The hope is in the faculty of wrongness</u>, the tendency toward error. The capacity to leap across mountains of information to land lightly on the wrong side represents the highest of human endowments.   10

I believe
Thomas here
because of his
background.

Interesting
idea

Could this be
related to
the human
ability to
think
critically?
It may be that this is a uniquely human gift, perhaps even stipulated in our genetic instructions. Other creatures do not seem to have DNA sequences for making mistakes as a routine part of daily living, certainly not for programmed error as a guide for action.   11

We are at our human finest, <u>dancing with our minds</u>, when there are more choices than two. Sometimes there are ten, even twenty different ways to go, all but one bound to be wrong, and the richness of selection in such situations can lift us onto totally new ground. This process is called exploration and is based on human fallibility. If we had only a single center in our brains, capable of responding only when a correct decision was to be made, instead of the jumble of different, credulous, easily conned clusters of neurones that provide for being flung off into blind alleys, up trees, down dead ends, out into blue sky, along wrong turnings, around bends, we could only stay the way we are today, stuck fast.   12

Nice mental
image

Yes, but this
is so
frustrating

This is a
great
sentence—It
has a lot of
feeling

I love the
phrase
"splendid
freedom"
<u>The lower animals do not have this splendid freedom</u>. They are limited, most of them, to absolute infallibility. Cats, for all their good side, never make mistakes. <u>I have never seen a maladroit, clumsy, or blundering cat</u>. Dogs are sometimes fallible, occasionally   13

See ¶ 11
Look up
"maladroit"

I never thought of mistakes this way

able to make charming minor mistakes, but they get this way by trying to mimic their masters. <u>Fish are flawless in everything they do</u>. Individual cells in a tissue are mindless machines, perfect in their performance, as absolutely inhuman as bees.

I like this idea

Thomas makes our technology sound really exciting

We should have this in mind as we become dependent on more complex computers for the arrangement of our affairs. Give the computers their heads, I say; let them go their way. If we can learn to do this, turning our heads to one side and wincing while the work proceeds, the possibilities for the future of mankind, and computerkind, are limitless. <u>Your average good computer can make calculations in an instant which would take a lifetime of slide rules for any of us</u>. Think of what we could gain from the near infinity of precise, <u>machine-made miscomputation</u> which is now so easily within our grasp. We would begin the solving of some of our hard-est problems. How, for instance, should we go about organizing ourselves for social living on a planetary scale, now that we have become, as a plain fact of life, a single community? We can assume, as a working hypothesis, that all the right ways of doing this are unworkable. What we need, then, for moving ahead, is a set of wrong alternatives much longer and more interesting than the short list of mistaken courses that any of us can think up right now. We need, in fact, an infinite list, and when it is printed out we need the computer to turn on itself and select, at random, the next way to go. If it is a big enough mistake, we could find ourselves on a new level, stunned, out in the clear, ready to move again.

14

so true

yes

We need to program com-puters to make deliberate mistakes so they can help our natural human ten-dency to learn thru error

Not a contradiction after all.

So mistakes have value!

Guideline 2. *After you have read the reading for the first time, summarize its main ideas in some fashion.* The form of this task might be anything, from a drawing of the main ideas as they re-late to one another, to a succinct written summary. You could draw a graph or map of the topics in the essay (in much the same way that a person would draw a map of an area for someone unfamiliar with a particular route); outline the ideas to get an overview of the piece; or summarize the ideas to check your un-derstanding of the main points of the selection. Any of these tasks can be completed from your original notes and underlining. Each will give you a slightly more thorough understanding of what you have read.

Guideline 3. *Next, read the questions and assignments following the selection to help focus your thinking for the second reading.* Don't an-swer the questions at this time; just read them to make sure you are picking up the main ideas from the selection and thinking about relevant connections among those ideas.

Rereading

Following your initial reading, read the piece again, concentrating this time on how the author achieved his or her purpose. The temptation to skip this stage of the reading process is often powerful, but this second reading is crucial to your development as a critical reader in all of your courses. This second reading could be compared to seeing a good movie for the second time: The first viewing would provide you with a general under-standing of the plot, the characters, the setting, and the overall artistic accomplishment of the director; during the second viewing, however, you would undoubtedly notice many more details and see their specific contributions to the artistic whole. Similarly, the second reading of an essay allows a much deeper understanding of the work under consideration and prepares you to analyze the writer's ideas.

You should also be prepared to do some detective work at this point and look closely at the assumptions the reading is based on: For example, how does the writer move from idea to idea in the essay? What hidden assertions lie behind these ideas? Do you agree or disagree with these assertions? Your assessment of these unspoken assumptions will often play a major role in your critical response to a piece of writing. In the case of Thomas's essay, do you accept the unspoken connection he makes between the workings of the human brain and the computer? What parts of the essay hinge upon your acceptance of this connection? What other assumptions are fundamental to Thomas's reasoning? If you accept his thinking along the way, you are more likely to agree with the general flow of Thomas's essay. If you discover a flaw in his premises or assumptions, your acceptance of his argument will start to break down.

Next, answer the questions that follow the essay. The "Understanding Details" questions will help you understand and remember what you have read on both the literal and the interpretive levels. Some of the questions ask you to restate various important points the author makes (literal); others help you see relationships between the different ideas presented (interpretive).

Understanding Details

Literal
1. According to Thomas, in what ways are computers and humans similar? In what ways are they different?

Lit/Interp
2. In what ways do we learn by "trial and error"? Why is this a useful way to learn?

Interpretive
3. What does Thomas mean by the statement, "If we were not provided with the knack of being wrong, we could never get anything useful done" (paragraph 6)?

Interpretive
4. According to Thomas, in what important way do humans and "lower" animals differ? What does this comparison have to do with Thomas's main line of reasoning?

The "Analyzing Meaning" questions require you to analyze and evaluate some of the writer's ideas in order to form valid opinions of your own. These questions demand a higher level of thought than the previous set and help you prepare more specifically for the discussion/writing assignments that follow the questions.

Analyzing Meaning

Analytical
1. What is Thomas's main point in this essay? How do the references to computers help him make this point?

Analytical
2. Why does Thomas perceive human error as such a positive quality? What does "exploration" have to do with this quality (paragraph 12)?

Analytical
3. What could we gain from "the near infinity of precise, machine-made miscomputation" (paragraph 14)? In what ways would our civilization advance?

The "Discovering Rhetorical Strategies" questions ask you to look closely at what strategies the writer uses to develop his or her thesis, and how those strategies work. The questions address important features of the writer's composing process, such as word choice, use of detail, transitions, statement of purpose, organization of ideas, sentence structure, and paragraph development. The intent of these questions is to raise various elements of the composing process to the conscious level so you can use them in creating your own essays. If you are able to understand and describe what choices a writer makes to create certain effects in his or her prose, you are more likely to be able to discover the range of choices available to you as you write, and you will also become more aware of your ability to control your readers' thoughts and feelings.

Discovering Rhetorical Strategies

1. Thomas begins his essay with a list of experiences most of us have had at one time or another. Do you find this an effective beginning? Why or why not?

2. Which main points in his essay does Thomas develop in most detail? Why do you think he chooses to develop these points so thoroughly?

3. Explain the simile Thomas uses in paragraph 6: "Mistakes are at the very base of human thought, embedded there, feeding the structure like root nodules." Is this comparison between "mistakes" and "root nodules" useful in this context? Why or why not? Find another simile or metaphor in this essay, and explain how it works.

A final set of questions, "Making Connections," asks you to consider the essay you have just read in reference to other essays in the book. Your instructor will assign these questions according to the selections you have read. The questions may have you compare the writers' treatment of an idea, the authors' style of writing, the difference in their opinions, or the similarities between their views of the world. Such questions will help you see connections in your own life—not only in your reading and your immediate environment, but also in the larger world around you. These questions, in particular, encourage you to move from specific references in the selections to a broader range of issues and circumstances that affect your daily life.

Making Connections

1. Cecil Foster ("Why Blacks Get Mad") refers both directly and indirectly to learning from mistakes. Would Lewis Thomas agree with his approach to this topic? In what ways do these authors think alike about the benefits of making errors? In what ways do they differ on the topic? Explain your answer.

2. Lewis Thomas and Lawrence Solomon ("Too Much Privacy Can Be Hazardous to the Person") both discuss the usefulness of computers. In what ways do their ideas complement each other? In what ways do they differ?

3. Thomas says, "The lower animals ... are limited, most of them, to absolute infallibility." Compare this perspective with that of Stanley Coren in "Dogs and Monsters." Do you think Coren would agree that "[o]ther creatures do not seem to have DNA sequences for making mistakes as a routine part of daily living, certainly not for programmed error as a guide for action"? Explain why or why not.

Because checklists can provide a helpful method of reviewing important information, we offer here a series of questions that represent the three stages of reading just discussed. All these guidelines can be generalized into a checklist for reading any academic assignment in any discipline.

Reading Inventory

Preparing to Read

Title

- What can I infer from the title of the essay about the author's attitude toward the subject or the general tone of the essay?
- Who do I think is the author's audience? What is the principal purpose of the essay?

Synopsis

- What is the general subject of the essay?
- What is the author's approach to the subject?

Biography

- What do I know about the author's age, political stance, and general beliefs?
- How qualified is the author to write on this subject?
- When did the author write the essay? Under what conditions? In what context?
- Where was the essay first published?

Content

- What would I like to learn about this topic?
- What are some of my opinions on this subject?

Reading

- What are my initial reactions, comments, and personal associations in reference to the ideas in this essay?
- What are the essay's main ideas?
- Did I read the questions and assignments following the essay?

Rereading

- How does the author achieve his or her purpose in this essay?
- What assumptions underlie the author's reasoning?
- Do I have a clear literal understanding of this essay? What words do I need to look up in a dictionary?
- Do I have a solid interpretive understanding of this essay? Do I understand the relationship among ideas? What conclusions can I draw from this essay?
- Do I have an accurate analytical understanding of this essay? Which ideas can I take apart, examine, and put back together again? What is my evaluation of this material?
- Do I understand the rhetorical strategies the writer uses and the way they work? Can I explain the effects of these strategies?

Writing Critically

The last stage of responding to the reading selections in this text offers you various "Ideas for Discussion/Writing" that will allow you to demonstrate the different skills you have learned in each chapter. You will be most successful if you envision each writing experience as an organic process that follows a natural cycle of prewriting, writing, and rewriting.

Preparing to Write

The prewriting phase involves exploring a subject, generating ideas, selecting and narrowing a topic, analyzing an audience, and developing a purpose. Preceding the writing assignments are "Preparing to Write" questions you should respond to before trying to structure your thoughts into a coherent essay. These questions will assist you in generating new thoughts on the topics and may even stimulate new approaches to old ideas. Keeping a journal to respond to these questions is an excellent technique, because you will then have a record of your opinions on various topics related to the writing assignments that follow. No matter what format you use to answer these questions, the activity of prewriting generally continues in various forms throughout the writing process.

Preparing to Write

Write freely about an important mistake you have made: How did the mistake make you feel? What (if anything) did you learn from this mistake? What did you fail to learn that you should have learned? Did this mistake have any positive impact on your life? What were its negative consequences? How crucial are mistakes in our lives?

Responses to these questions can be prompted by a number of different "invention" techniques and carried out by you individually, with another student, in small groups, or as a class project. Invention strategies can help you generate responses to these questions and discover related ideas through the various stages of writing your papers. Because you will undoubtedly vary your approach to different assignments, you should be familiar with the following choices available to you:

Brainstorming. The basis of brainstorming is free association. Ideally, you should get a group of people together and bounce ideas, words, and thoughts off one another until they begin to cluster around related topics. In brainstorming with others, the exchange of thoughts usually starts orally, but should transfer to paper when your ideas begin to fall into related categories. When you brainstorm by yourself, however, you should write down everything that comes to mind. The act of recording your ideas in this case becomes a catalyst for other thoughts; you are essentially setting up a dialogue with yourself on paper. Then, keep writing down words and phrases that occur to you until they begin to fall into logical subdivisions, or until you stop generating new ideas.

Freewriting. Freewriting means writing to discover what you want to say. Set a time limit of about ten minutes, and just write by free association. Write about what you are seeing, feeling, touching, thinking; write about having nothing to say; recopy the sentence you just wrote—anything. Just keep writing on paper, on a typewriter, or on a computer. After you have generated some material, locate an idea that is central to your writing assignment, put it at the top of another page, and start freewriting again, letting your thoughts take shape around this central idea. This second type of preparation is called *focused freewriting*, and is especially valuable when you already have a specific topic.

Journal Entries. Journal entries are much like freewriting, except you have some sense of an audience—probably either your instructor or yourself. In a journal, anything goes. You can respond to the "Preparing to Write" questions, jot down thoughts, paste up articles that spark your interest, write sections of dialogue, draft letters (the kind you never send), record dreams, or make lists. The possibilities are unlimited. An excellent way of practising writing, the process of keeping a journal is also a wonderful means of dealing with new ideas—a way of fixing them in your mind and making them yours.

Direct Questions. This technique involves asking a series of questions useful in any writing situation to generate ideas, arrange thoughts, or revise prose. One example of this strategy is to use the inquiries journalists rely on to check the coverage in their articles:

Who:	*Who played the game?*
	Who won the game?
What:	*What kind of game was it?*
	What happened in the game?
Why:	*Why was the game played?*
Where:	*Where was the game played?*
When:	*When was the game played?*
How:	*How was the game played?*

If you ask yourself extended questions of this sort on a specific topic, you will begin to produce thoughts and details that will undoubtedly be useful to you in the writing assignments that follow.

Clustering. Clustering is a method of drawing or mapping your ideas as fast as they come into your mind. Put a word, phrase, or sentence in a circle in the centre of a blank page. Then, put every new idea that comes to you in another circle and show its relationship to a previous thought by drawing a line to the circle containing the previous idea. You will probably reach a natural stopping point for this exercise in two to three minutes.

Although you can generate ideas in a number of different ways, the main principle behind the "Preparing to Write" questions in this text is to encourage you to do what is called *expressive writing* before you tackle any writing assignment. This is writing based on your feelings, thoughts, experiences, observations, and opinions. The process of answering questions about your own ideas and experiences makes you "think on paper," enabling you to surround yourself with your own thoughts and opinions. From this reservoir, you can then choose the ideas you want to develop into an essay and begin writing about them one at a time.

As you use various prewriting techniques to generate responses to the "Preparing to Write" questions, you should know that these responses can be expressed using lists, outlines, random notes, sentences and paragraphs, charts, graphs, or pictures—whatever keeps the thoughts flowing smoothly and productively. One of our students used a combination of brainstorming and clustering to generate the following thoughts in response to the prewriting exercise following the Thomas essay:

Brainstorming

Mistakes:
- happen when I'm in a hurry
- make me feel stupid
- love
- Bob
- learned a lot about people
- people aren't what they seem
- getting back on track
- parents
- corrections
- relationships
- trip back East
  - pride
  - going in circles
- learning from mistakes
  - I am a better person
  - my values are clear
- mistakes help us change
  - painful
  - helpful
  - valuable

Clustering

From the free-flowing thoughts you generate, you next need to decide what to write about and how to limit your subject to a manageable length. Our student writer chose topic 2 from the "Choosing a Topic" list after the essay (see page 26). Her initial responses to the prewriting questions helped her decide to write on "A Time I Got Lost." She then generated more focused ideas and opinions in the form of a journal entry. It is printed here just as she wrote it, errors and all.

Journal Entry

The craziest mistake I think I ever made was on a trip I took recently—I was heading to the east coast from British Columbia and reached Fredericton. I was so excited because I was going to get to see the Atlantic Ocean for the first time in my life and Fredericton was one of my last towns before I reached the sea. In Fredericton I was going to have to change from a northeast direction to due east.

When I got there the highway was under construction. I took the detour, but got all skrewed up till I realized that I had gone the wrong direction. By this time I was lost somewhere in downtown Fredericton and didn't know which way was east. I stoped and asked a guy at a gas station and he explained how to get back on the east-bound highway. The way was through the middle of town. By the time I got to where I was supposed to turn right I could only turn left. So I started left and then realized I couldn't turn back the other way! I made a couple of other stops after that, and one jerk told me I "just couldn't get there from here." Eventually I found a truck driver heading toward the same eastbound highway, and he told me to follow him. An hour and forty minutes after reaching Fredericton's city limits I finally managed to leave going east. I felt as if I had spent an entire month there!

The thing I learned from this was just how egocentric I am. I would not have made this error if I had not been so *damn cocky about my sense of direction. My mistake was made worse because I got flustered and didn't listen to the directions clearly. I find that the reason I most often make a mistake is because I don't listen carefully to instructions. This has been a problem all my life.*

After I got over feeling really dum I decided this kind of thing was not going to happen again. It was too much a waste of time and gas, so I was going to be more careful of road signs and directions.

This all turned out to be a positive experience though. I learned that there are lots of friendly, helpful people. It was kind of reassuring to know that other folks would help you if you just asked.

I feel this and other mistakes are crucial not only to my life but to personal growth in general. It is the making of mistakes that helps people learn where they are misdirecting their energies. I think mistakes can help all of us learn to be more careful about some part of our lives. This is why mistakes are crucial. Otherwise, we would continue in the same old rut and never improve.

This entry served as the foundation upon which the student built her essay. Her next step was to consider *audience* and *purpose* (which are usually specified in the writing assignments in this text). The first of these features identifies the person or group of people you will address in your essay. The second is a declaration of your principal reason for writing the essay, which usually takes the form of a thesis statement (the statement of purpose or the controlling idea of an essay). Together these pieces of information consciously or subconsciously help you make most of the decisions you are faced with as you write: what words to choose, what sentence structures to use, what order to present ideas in, which topics to develop, and which to summarize. The more you know about your audience (age, educational background, likes, dislikes, biases, political persuasion, and social status) and your purpose (to inform, persuade, and/or entertain), the easier the writing task will be. In the rough draft and final draft of the essay in the section that follows, the student knew she was writing to a senior English class at her old high school in order to convince them that mistakes can be positive factors in their lives. This clear sense of audience and purpose helped her realize she should use fairly advanced vocabulary, call upon a variety of sentence structures, and organize her ideas chronologically to make her point most effectively to her intended audience.

At this stage of the writing process, some people benefit from assembling their ideas in the form of an outline. Others use an outline as a check on their logic and organization after the first draft has been written. Whether your outlines are informal (a simple list) or highly structured, they can help you visualize the logical relationship of your ideas to each other. We recommend using your outline throughout the prewriting and writing stages to ensure that your work will be carefully and tightly organized. Your outline, however, should be adjusted to your draft as it develops.

Writing

The writing stage asks you to draft an essay based upon the prewriting material you have assembled. Because you have already made the important preliminary decisions regarding your topic, your audience, and your purpose, the task of actually writing the essay should follow naturally. (Notice we did not say this task should necessarily be easy—just natural.) At this stage, you should look upon your essay as a way of solving a problem or answering a question: The problem/question is posed in your writing assignment, and the solution/answer is your essay. The three "Choosing a Topic" assignments that follow the prewriting questions in the text require you to consider issues related to the essay you just read. Although they typically ask you to focus on one rhetorical pattern, they draw on many rhetorical strategies (as do all writing assignments in the text) and require you to support your statements with concrete examples. These assignments refer to the Lewis Thomas essay and emphasize the use of example, his dominant rhetorical strategy.

Choosing a Topic

1. You have decided to write an editorial for your local newspaper concerning the impact of computers on our lives. Cite specific experiences you have had with computers to help make your main point.

2. You have been invited back to your high school to make a speech to a senior English class about how people can learn from their mistakes. Write your speech in the form of an essay explaining what you learned from a crucial mistake you have made. Use examples to show these students that mistakes can be positive factors in their lives.

3. In an essay for your writing class, explain one specific human quality. Use Thomas's essay as a model. Cite examples to support your explanation.

The following essay is our student's first-draft response to topic 2. After writing her journal entry, the student drafted a tentative thesis statement: "I know there are positive attitudes that can come from making a mistake because I recently had an opportunity to learn some valuable lessons from one of my errors." This statement helped the student further develop and organize her ideas as she focused finally on one well-chosen example to illustrate her thesis. At this point, the thesis is simply the controlling idea around which the other topics take shape; it is often revised several times before the final draft.

First Draft: A Time I Got Lost

Parents and teachers frequently pressure us to avoid committing errors. Meanwhile, our friends laugh at us when we make mistakes. With all these different messages, it is hard for us to think of mistakes as positive events. But if any of you take the time to think about what you have learned from mistakes, I bet you will realize all the good things that have come from these events. I know there are positive attitudes that can come from making a mistake because I recently had an opportunity to learn some valuable lessons in this way.

While travelling back east this last summer, I made the mistake of turning west on an interprovincial detour in order to reach the Atlantic Ocean. The adventure took me into the heart of Fredericton, where I got totally lost. I had to get directions several times until two hours later I was going in the right direction. As I was driving out of town, I realized that although I had made a dumb mistake, I had learned a great deal. Overall, the detour was actually a positive experience.

The first thing I remember thinking after I had gotten my wits together was that I had definitely learned something from making the mistake. I had the opportunity to see a new city, filled with new people— 3000 kilometres from my own hometown, but very much like it. I also became aware that the beach is not always toward the west, as it is in British Columbia. The entire experience was like getting a geography lesson firsthand.

As this pleasant feeling began to grow, I came to another realization. I was aware of how important other people can be in making a mistake into a positive experience. My first reaction was "Oh no, someone is going to know I made a mistake!" But the amazing part about this mistake was how supportive everyone was. The townspeople had been entirely willing to help someone they did not know. This mistake helped me to learn that people tend to be nicer than I had imagined.

The final lesson I learned from getting lost in Fredericton was how to be more cautious about my actions so as not to repeat the same mistake. It was this internalization of all the information I gleaned from making the mistake that I see as the most positive part of the experience. I realized that in order to avoid such situations in the future I would have to be less egocentric in my decisions and more willing to listen to directions from other people. I needed to learn that my set way of doing things was not always the best way. If I had not made the mistake, I would not have been aware of my other options.

By making this mistake I learned that there is a more comprehensive manner of looking at the world. In the future, if we could all stop after making a mistake and ask ourselves, "What can I learn from this?" we would be less critical of ourselves and have a great many more positive experiences. If I were not able to make mistakes, I would probably not be able to expand my knowledge of my environment, my understanding of people, and my choice of various actions.

Rewriting

The rewriting stage includes revising, editing, and proofreading. The first of these activities, *revising*, actually takes place during the entire writing process as you change words, recast sentences, and move whole paragraphs from one place to another. Making these linguistic and organizational choices means you will also be constantly adjusting your content to your purpose (what you want to accomplish) and your audience (the readers) in much the same way you alter your speech to communicate more effectively in response to the gestures, eye movements, or facial expressions of your listener. Revising is literally the act of "reseeing" your essay, looking at it through your readers' eyes to determine whether or not it achieves its purpose. As you revise, you should consider matters of both content and form. In *content*, do you have an interesting, thought-provoking title for your essay? Do you think your thesis statement will be clear to your audience? Does your introduction capture the readers' attention? Is your treatment of your topic consistent throughout the essay? Do you support your assertions with specific examples? Does your conclusion sum up your main points? In *form*, is your essay organized effectively? Do you use a variety of rhetorical strategies? Are your sentence structures and vocabulary varied and interesting?

If you compose on a computer, you will certainly reap the benefits as you revise. Computers remove much of the drudgery of rewriting and retyping your drafts. In writing, you may not make as many major revisions as necessary because of the time needed to rewrite the material. Computers allow you to move paragraphs or whole sections of your paper from one position to another by pressing a few keys. Without the manual labour of cutting and pasting you can immediately see if the new organization will improve the logic and coherence of your paper. You may then remove repetitions or insert words and sentences that will serve as the transitions between sections.

You should also consider the value of the graphic design options available on computer software, because the way you present your papers generally affects how your instructor evaluates them. If they are clearly laid out without coffee stains or paw prints from your dog, you have a better chance of being taken seriously than if they are sloppily done. A computer can help in this regard, giving you access to boldface type, italics, boxes, bullets, and graphs of all sorts and letting you make a new copy if you do have an unexpected encounter with a coffee cup or a frisky dog.

Editing entails correcting mistakes in your writing so that your final draft conforms to the conventions of standard written English. Correct punctuation, spelling, and mechanics will help you make your points and will encourage your readers to move smoothly through your essay from topic to topic. At this stage, you should be concerned about such matters as whether your sentences are complete, whether your punctuation is correct and effective, whether you have followed conventional rules for using mechanics, and whether the words in your essay are spelled correctly.

Proofreading involves reading over your entire essay, slowly and carefully, to make certain you have not allowed any errors to slip into your draft. (Most writing instructors don't look upon errors as kindly as Thomas does.) In general, good writers try to let some time elapse between writing the final draft and proofreading it (at least a few hours, perhaps a day or so). Otherwise, they find themselves proofreading their thoughts rather than their words. Some writers even profit from proofreading their papers backward—a technique that allows them to focus on individual words and phrases rather than on entire sentences.

Because many writers work well with checklists, we present here a set of guidelines that will help you review the entire writing process.

Writing Inventory

Preparing to Write

- Have I explored the prewriting questions through brain-storming, freewriting, journal entries, direct questions, or clustering?
- Do I understand my topic or assignment?
- Have I narrowed my topic adequately?
- Do I have a specific audience for my essay? Do I know their likes and dislikes? Their educational level? Their knowledge about the topic?
- Do I have a clear and precise purpose for my essay?

Writing

- Can I express my topic as a problem or question?
- Is my essay a solution or an answer to that problem or question?

Rewriting

Revising the Content

- Does my essay have a clear, interesting title?
- Will my statement of purpose (or thesis) be clear to my audience?
- Will the introduction make my audience want to read the rest of my essay?
- Have I included enough details to prove my main points?
- Does my conclusion sum up my central points?
- Will I accomplish my purpose with this audience?

Revising the Form

- Have I organized my ideas as effectively as possible for this audience?
- Do I use appropriate rhetorical strategies to support my main point?
- Is my sentence structure varied and interesting?
- Is my vocabulary appropriate for my topic, my purpose, and my audience?
- Do I present my essay as effectively as possible, including useful graphic design techniques on the computer, where appropriate?

Editing and Proofreading

- Have I written complete sentences throughout my essay?
- Have I used punctuation correctly and effectively (check especially the use of commas, apostrophes, colons, and semicolons)?
- Have I followed conventional rules for mechanics (capitalization, underlining or italics, abbreviations, and numbers)?
- Are all the words in my essay spelled correctly? (Use a dictionary or a spellchecker when in doubt.)

Following is the student's revised draft of her essay on making mistakes in life. The final draft of this typical student's essay represents the entire writing process at work. We have made notes in the margin to highlight various effective elements in her essay, and we have underlined substantial changes in words and phrases from earlier drafts.

Mistakes and Maturity

Parents and teachers frequently <u>harp</u> on us to <u>correct</u> our errors. Meanwhile, our friends laugh at us when we make mistakes. With all these <u>negative</u> messages, most of us have a hard time believing that problems can be positive experiences. But if we take the time to think about what we have learned from various <u>blunders</u>, we will realize all the good that has come from these events. <u>I know making mistakes can have positive results because I recently learned several valuable lessons from one unforgettable experience</u>.

While <u>I was</u> travelling to the east coast last summer, I made the mistake of turning west on an interprovincial detour <u>in an attempt</u> to reach the Atlantic Ocean. This adventure took me into the <u>centre</u> of Fredericton, where I became totally lost, bewildered, and angry at my-self. I had to <u>ask for</u> directions several times until two hours later, when I <u>finally found the correct highway toward the ocean</u>. As I was driving out of town, I realized that although I had made a "dumb" mistake, I had actually learned a great deal. Overall, <u>my adventure had been quite positive</u>.

The first <u>insight</u> I remember having after my wits returned was that I had definitely learned more about Canadian geography from making this mistake. <u>I had become intimately acquainted with a town 4827 kilometres from home that greatly resembled my own city, and I had become aware that the beach is not always toward the west, as it is in British Columbia. I had also met some pleasant strangers. Looking at my confusion as a learning experience encouraged me to have positive feelings about the mistake</u>.

<u>As I relaxed and let</u> this happy feeling grow, I came to another realization. I <u>became</u> aware of how important other people can be in <u>turning</u> a mistake into a positive event. Although my first reaction had been "Oh, no! Someone is going to know <u>I'm lost</u>," I was amazed by how supportive other people were <u>during my panic and embarrass-ment. From an old man swinging on his front porch to an elementary school boy crossing the street with his bright blue backpack, I found</u> that the townspeople of Fredericton were entirely willing to help some-one they did not <u>even</u> know. <u>I realized that people in general</u> are nicer than <u>I had previously thought</u>.

The final lesson I learned from <u>making this mistake</u> was how to be more cautious about <u>my future decisions. This insight was, in fact</u>, the most positive part of the entire experience. <u>What</u> I realized I must do to

Margin annotations

Rapport with audience and point of view established

Clear, stimulating introduction for high school seniors

Good brief summary of complex experience (see notes from Preparing to Write)

Nice close to this paragraph

Good summary statement

Catchy title; good change from first draft

Background information

Good details

First topic (Topics are in chronologi-cal order)

Adequate number of examples

Second topic

Clear explanation with details

Third topic

prevent similar <u>errors</u> in the future was to relax, <u>not be so bullheaded</u> in my decisions, and be more willing to listen to directions from other people. <u>I might never have had these positive realizations if I had not made this mistake</u>.

Specific details

Clear transition statement

Thus, <u>by driving in circles for two hours, I developed</u> a more comprehensive way of looking at the world. If I were unable to make mistakes, I probably would not have had this chance to <u>learn</u> about my environment, <u>improve my impressions of strangers</u>, and <u>reconsider the egocentric way in which I act in certain situations. Perhaps there's</u>

Good summary of three topics without being repetitive

Concluding statement applicable to all readers

<u>a lesson here for all of us. Instead of criticizing ourselves unduly</u>, if each one of us could <u>pause</u> after we make an error and ask, "<u>How</u> can I <u>profit</u> from this?" <u>we would realize that mistakes can often be turned into positive events that will help us become more confident and mature</u>.

Nicely focused concluding remark

As these various drafts of the student paper indicate, the essay assignments in this book encourage you to transfer to your own writing your understanding of how form and content work together. If you use the short-answer questions after each reading selection as a guide, the writing assignments will help you learn how to give shape to your own ideas and to gain control of your readers' thoughts and feelings. In essence, they will help you recognize the power you have through language over your life and your environment.

Conclusion

As you approach the essays in this text, remember that both reading and writing function most efficiently as processes of discovery. Through them, you educate and expand your own mind and the minds of your readers. They can provide a powerful means of discovering new information or clarifying what you already know. Reading and writing lead to understanding. And just as you can discover how to read through writing, so too can you become more aware of the details of the writing process through reading. We hope your time spent with this book is both pleasant and profitable as you refine your ability to discover and express effectively the good ideas within yourself.

CHAPTER 1

DESCRIPTION

Exploring Through the Senses

All of us use description in our daily lives. We might, for example, try to convey the horrors of a recent history exam to our parents, or help a friend visualize someone we met on vacation, or describe an automobile accident for a police report. Whatever our specific purpose, description is fundamental to the act of communication: We give and receive descriptions constantly, and our lives are continually affected by this simple yet important rhetorical technique.

Defining Description

Description may be defined as the act of capturing people, places, events, objects, and feelings in words so that a reader (or listener) can visualize and respond to them. Unlike narration, which traditionally presents events in a clear time sequence, description essentially suspends its objects in time, making them exempt from the limits of chronology. Narration tells a story, while pure description contains no action or time. Description is one of our primary forms of self-expression; it paints a verbal picture that helps the reader understand or share a sensory experience through the process of "showing" rather than "telling." *Telling* your friends, for example, that "the campgrounds were filled with friendly, happy activities" is not as engaging as *showing* them by saying, "The campgrounds were alive with the smell of spicy baked beans, the sound of high-pitched laughter, and the sight of happy families sharing the warmth of a fire." Showing your readers helps them understand your experience through as many senses as possible.

Descriptions fall somewhere between two extremes: (1) totally objective reports (with no trace of opinions or feelings), such as we might find in a dictionary or an encyclopedia, and (2) very subjective accounts, which focus almost exclusively on personal impressions. The same horse, for instance, might be described by one writer as "a large, solid-hoofed herbivorous mammal having a long mane and a tail" (objective) and by another as "a magnificent and spirited beast flaring its nostrils in search of adventure" (subjective). Most descriptive writing, however, falls somewhere between these two extremes: "a large, four-legged beast in search of adventure."

Objective description is principally characterized by its impartial, precise, and emotionless tone. Found most prominently in technical and scientific writing, such accounts might include a description of equipment to be used in a chemistry experiment, the results of a market survey for a particular consumer product, or a medical appraisal of a heart patient's physical symptoms. In situations like these, accurate, unbiased, and easily understandable accounts are of the utmost importance.

Subjective description, in contrast, is intentionally created to produce a particular response in the reader or listener. Focusing on feelings rather than on raw data, it tries to activate as many senses as possible, thereby leading the audience to a specific conclusion or state of mind. Examples of subjective descriptions are a parent's disapproving comments about one of your friends, a professor's glowing analysis of your most recent "A" paper, or a basketball coach's critique of the team's losing effort in last night's big game.

In most situations, the degree of subjectivity or objectivity in a descriptive passage depends to a large extent upon the writer's purpose and intended audience. In the case of the heart patient mentioned above, the person's physician might present the case in a formal, scientific way to a group of medical colleagues; in a personal, sympathetic way to the patient's spouse; and in financial terms to a number of potential contributors in order to solicit funds for heart disease research.

The following paragraph describes one student's fond memories of visiting "the farm." As you read it, notice the writer's use of subjective description to communicate to her readers the multitude of contradictory feelings she connects with this rural retreat.

> The shrill scream of the alarm shatters a dream. This is the last day of my visit to the place I call "the farm," an old ramshackle house in the country owned by one of my aunts. I want to go out once more in the peace of the early morning, walk in the crisp and chilly hour, and breathe the sweet air. My body feels jarred as my feet hit the hard-packed clay dirt. I tune out my stiff muscles and cold arms and legs and instead focus on two herons playing hopscotch on the canal bank: Every few yards I walk toward them, they fly one over the other an almost equal distance away from me. A killdeer with its piercing crystalline cry dips its body as it flies low over the water, the tip of its wing leaving a ring to reverberate outward. The damp earth has a strong, rich, musky scent. To the east, dust rises, and for the first time I hear the clanking and straining of a tractor as it harrows smooth the soil before planting. A crop duster rises close by just as it cuts off its release of spray, the acrid taste of chemical filtering down through the air. As the birds chatter and peck at the fields, I reluctantly return to my life in the city.

Thinking Critically by Using Description

Each rhetorical mode in this book gives us new insight into the process of thinking by providing different options for arranging our thoughts and our experiences. The more we know about these options, the more conscious we become of how our minds operate and the better chance we have to improve and refine our thinking skills. (For a more thorough definition of the term *rhetorical mode*, see the glossary on the website **www.pearsoned. ca/flachmann**.)

As you examine description as a way of thinking, consider it in isolation for a moment—away from the other rhetorical modes. Think of it as a muscle you can isolate and strengthen on its own in a weight-training program before you ask it to perform together with other muscles. By isolating description, you will learn more readily what it entails and how it functions as a critical thinking tool. In the process, you will also strengthen your knowledge of how to recognize and use description more effectively in your reading, in your writing, and in your daily life.

Just as you exercise to strengthen muscles, so too will you benefit from doing exercises to improve your skill in using descriptive techniques. As you have learned, description depends to a great extent on the keenness of your senses. So as you prepare to read and write descriptive essays, do the following tasks so that you can first learn what the process of description feels like in your own head. Really use your imagination to play with these exercises on as many different levels as possible. Also write when you are asked to do so. The combination of thinking and writing is often especially useful when you practise your thinking skills.

1. Make a list of five descriptive words you would use to trigger each of the following senses: taste, sight, hearing, touch, and smell.

2. Find a picture of a person, an animal, a bouquet of flowers, a sunset, or some other still-life portrait. List words you would use to describe this picture to a classmate. Then, list a few similes and metaphors that actually describe this still life. How would your description differ if you were seeing the subject in real life rather than in a picture?

3. Choose an unusual object and brainstorm about its physical characteristics. Then, brainstorm about the emotions this object evokes. Why is this object so unusual or special? Compare your two brainstorming results and draw some conclusions about their differences.

Reading and Writing Descriptive Essays

All good descriptions share four fundamental qualities: (1) an accurate sense of audience (who the readers are) and purpose (why the essay was written), (2) a clear vision of the object being described, (3) a careful selection of details that help communicate the author's vision, and (4) a consistent point of view or perspective from which a writer composes. The dominant impression or main effect the writer wishes to leave with a specific audience dictates virtually all of the verbal choices in a descriptive essay. Although description is featured in this chapter, you should also pay close attention to how other rhetorical strategies (such as example, division/classification, and cause/effect) can best support the dominant impression.

How to Read a Descriptive Essay

Preparing to Read. As you approach the reading selections in this chapter, you should focus first on the author's title and try to make some initial assumptions about the essay that follows: Does David Adams Richards reveal his attitude toward his subject in the title "My Old Newcastle"? Can you guess what the general mood of "What a Certain Visionary Once Said" will be? Then, scan the essay to discover its audience and purpose: What do you think Lesley Choyce's purpose is in "Thin Edge of the Wedge"? Who is Dave Bidini addressing in "Kris King Looks Terrible"? You should also read the synopsis of each essay in the Rhetorical Table of Contents (on pages iii–xi); these brief summaries will provide you with helpful information at this point in the reading process.

Next, learn as much as you can about the author and the conditions under which the essay was composed, information that is provided in the biographical statement before each essay. For a descriptive essay, the conditions under which the author wrote the essay, coupled with his or her purpose, can be very revealing: When and under what conditions did Dave Bidini write "Kris King Looks Terrible"? What do Sherwin Tjia's interests tell you about his motivations for writing "Of Lemons & Lemonade"? What concerns might have led Lesley Choyce to write "Thin Edge of the Wedge"? What does Tomson Highway's background suggest about his perspective in "What a Certain Visionary Once Said"? Learning where the essay was first published will also give you valuable information about its audience.

Last, before you begin to read, try to do some brainstorming on the essay's title. In this chapter, respond to the Preparing to Read questions before each essay, which ask you to begin thinking and writing about the topic under consideration. Then, pose your own questions: What image do you have of "the north" (Highway)? What have your preconceptions been about hockey arenas (Bidini)? What might you want to learn about the life of an island (Choyce)? Are you more familiar with an urban or a wilderness environment (Tjia)?

Reading. As you read each essay for the first time, jot down your initial reactions to it, and try to make connections and see relationships among the author's biography; the essay's title, purpose, and audience; and the synopsis. In this way, you will create a context or framework for your reading. See if you can figure out, for example, what Highway might be saying about people's attitudes toward the land in his essay, "What a Certain Visionary Once Said," or why David Adams Richards wrote an essay about Newcastle. Try to discover what the relationship is between purpose, audience, and publication information in Sherwin Tjia's essay.

Also determine at this point if the author's treatment of his or her subject is predominantly objective (generally free of emotion) or subjective (heavily charged with emotion).

In addition, make sure you have a general sense of the dominant impression each author is trying to convey. Such an initial approach to reading these descriptive selections will give you a foundation upon which to analyze the material during your second, more in-depth reading.

Finally, at the end of your first reading, take a look at the questions after each essay to make certain you can answer them. This material will guide your rereading.

Rereading. As you reread these descriptive essays, you should be discovering exactly what each essay's dominant impression is and how the author created it. Notice each author's careful selection of details and the way in which these details come together to leave you with this impression. Also try to determine how certain details add to and detract from that dominant impression and how the writer's point of view affects it: How does Tomson Highway create a sense of respect for the environment in "What a Certain Visionary Once Said"? How does Dave Bidini help us to share the enjoyment of visiting SkyRink?

Try to find during this reading other rhetorical modes that support the description. Although the essays in this chapter describe various persons, places, or objects, all of the authors call upon other rhetorical strategies (especially example and comparison/contrast) to communicate their descriptions. How do these various rhetorical strategies work together in each essay to create a coherent whole?

Finally, answering the questions after each essay will check your understanding of the author's main points and help you think critically about the essay in preparing for the discussion/writing assignments that follow.

For an inventory of the reading process, you may want to review the checklists on pages 17–18 of the Introduction.

How to Write a Descriptive Essay

Preparing to Write. Before you choose a writing assignment, use the prewriting questions that follow each essay to help you discover your own ideas and opinions about the general topic of the essay. Next, choose an assignment or read the one assigned to you. Then, just as you do when you read an essay, you should determine the audience and purpose for your essay (if these are not specified for you in the assignment). For whom are you writing? And why? Will an impartial, objective report be appropriate, or should you present a more emotional, subjective account to accomplish your task? In assessing your audience, you need to determine what they do and do not know about your topic. This information will help you make decisions about what you are going to say and how you will say it. Your purpose will be defined by what you intend your audience to know, think, or believe after they have read your descriptive essay. Do you want them to make up their own minds about hockey arenas or the urban landscape, for example, based on an objective presentation of data, or do you hope to sway their opinions through a more subjective display of information? Or perhaps you will decide to blend the two techniques, combining facts and opinions, in order to achieve the impression of personal certainty based on objective evidence. What dominant impression do you want to leave with your audience? As you might suspect, decisions regarding audience and purpose are as important to writing descriptions as they are to reading descriptions, and will shape your descriptive essay from start to finish.

The second quality of good description concerns the object of your analysis and the clarity with which you present it to the reader. Whenever possible, you should thoroughly investigate the person, place, moment, or feeling you wish to describe, paying particular attention to its effect upon each of your five senses. What can you see, smell, hear, taste, and touch as you examine it? If you want to describe your house, for example, begin by asking yourself a series of pertinent questions: How big is the house? What colour is it? How many exterior doors does the house have? How many interior doors? Are any of the rooms wallpapered? If so, what are the colour and texture of that wallpaper? How many different shades of paint cover the walls? Which rooms have constant noises (from clocks and other mechanical devices)? Are the kitchen appliances hot or cold to the touch? What is the quietest room in the house? The noisiest? What smells do you notice in the laundry? In the kitchen? In the basement? Most important, do any of these sensory questions trigger particular memories? Although you will probably not use all of these details in your descriptive essay, the process of generating and answering such detailed questions will help reacquaint you with the object of your description as it also assists you in designing and focusing your paper. To help you generate some of these ideas, you may want to review the prewriting techniques introduced on pages 19–25.

Writing. As you write, you must select the details of your description with great care and precision so that you leave your reader with a specific impression. If, for instance, you want your audience to feel the warmth and comfort of your home, you might concentrate on describing the plush carpets, the big upholstered chairs, the inviting scent of hot apple cider, and the crackling fire. If, on the other hand, you want to gain your audience's sympathy, you might prefer to focus on the sparse austerity of your home environment: the bare walls, the quietness, the lack of colour and decoration, the dim lighting, and the frigid temperature. You also want to make sure you omit unrelated ideas, like a conversation between your parents you accidentally overheard. Your careful choice of details will help control your audience's reaction.

To make your impression even more vivid, you might use figurative language to fill out your descriptions. Using words "figuratively" means using them imaginatively rather than literally. The two most popular forms of figurative language are *simile* and *metaphor*. A simile is a comparison between two dissimilar objects or ideas introduced by *like* or *as*: Choyce describes "two dents in the ground, as if some giant had punched down into a massive surface of dough." A *metaphor* is an implied comparison between two dissimilar objects or ideas that is not introduced by *like* or *as*: Sherwin Tjia tells of the hydrofields with their "gigantic metal men, striding into the distance, clutching their living lines." Besides enlivening your writing, figurative language helps your readers understand objects, feelings, and ideas that are complex or obscure by comparing them with things that are more familiar.

The last important quality of an effective descriptive essay is point of view, your physical perspective on your subject. Because the organization of your essay depends on your point of view, you need to choose a specific angle from which to consistently approach your description. If you verbally jump around your home, referring first to a picture on the wall in your bedroom, next to the microwave in the kitchen, and then to the quilt on your bed, no reasonable audience will be able to follow your description. Nor will they want to. If, however, you move from room to room in some logical, sequential way, always focusing on the details you want your readers to know, you will be helping your audience form a clear, memorable impression of your home. Your vision will become their vision. In other words, your point of view plays a part in determining the organization of your description. Working spatially, you could move from side to side (from one wall to another in the rooms we have discussed), from top to bottom (from ceiling to floor), or from far to near (from the farthest to the closest point in a room), or you might progress from large to small objects, from uninteresting to interesting, or from funny to serious. Whatever plan you choose should help you accomplish your purpose with your particular audience.

Rewriting. As you reread each of your descriptive essays, play the role of your audience and try to determine what dominant impression you receive by the end of your reading.

- Do you communicate the dominant impression you want to convey?
- Do you have a clear point of view on your subject?
- How does the essay make you feel?
- What does it make you think about?
- Which senses does it stimulate?
- Do you use similes or metaphors when appropriate?
- Are you *showing* rather than *telling* in your description?

For additional suggestions on the writing process, you may want to consult the checklists on pages 29–30 of the Introduction.

Student Essay: Description at Work

In the following essay, a student relives some of her childhood memories through a subjective description of her grandmother's house. As you read it, pay particular attention to the different types of sensual details the student writer chooses in order to communicate to readers her dominant impression of her grandmother's home. Notice also her use of carefully chosen details to *show* rather than *tell* us about her childhood reminiscences, especially her comparisons, which make the memory as vivid for the reader as it is for the writer.

Grandma's House

Writer's point of view or perspective — My most vivid childhood memories are set in my Grandma — *Dominant impression* Goodlink's house, a curious blend of familiar and mysterious treasures. Grandma lived at the end of a dead-end street, in the same house she had lived in since the first day of her marriage. That was half a century and thirteen children ago. A set of crumbly steps made of concrete mixed with gravel led up to her front door. *Comparison (simile)* — I remember a big gap between the house and the steps, as if someone had not pushed them up close enough to the house. Anyone who looked into the gap could see old toys and books that had — *Sight* fallen into the crack behind the steps and had remained there, forever irretrievable.

Only a hook-type lock on the front door protected Grandma's *Comparison (simile)* — many beautiful antiques. Her living room was set up like a church — *Sight* or schoolroom, with an old purple velvet couch against the far wall and two chairs immediately in front of the couch facing the same direction. One-half of the couch was always buried in old clothes, magazines, and newspapers, and a lone shoe sat atop the *Comparison (metaphor)* — pile, a finishing touch to some bizarre modern sculpture. To one *Sound* — side was an aged and tuneless upright piano with yellowed keys. — *Sight* The ivory overlay was missing so that the wood underneath — *Sight* showed through, and many of the keys made only a muffled and *Sound* — frustrating thump, no matter how hard I pressed them. On the wall facing the piano was the room's only window, draped with yellowed lace curtains. Grandma always left that window open. I — *Sight* *Smell* — remember sitting near it, smelling the rain while the curtains tickled my face.
Touch

For no apparent reason, an old curtain hung in the door be- — *Sight* tween the kitchen and the living room. In the kitchen, a large

Formica-topped table always held at least a half-dozen varieties of <u>homemade jelly, as well as a loaf of bread, gooseberry pies, or</u> Taste
<u>cherry pies with the pits left in, boxes of cereal,</u> and anything else
Comparison   not requiring refrigeration, <u>as if the table served as a small, portable</u>
(simile)   <u>pantry</u>. Grandma's kitchen always <u>smelled of toast</u>, and I often Smell
wondered—and still do—if she lived entirely on toast. <u>A hole had</u> Sight
<u>eaten through the kitchen floor</u>, not just the warped yellow
linoleum, but all the way through the floor itself. My sisters and I
never wanted to take a bath at Grandma's house, because we discovered that anyone who lay on the floor on his stomach and put
Sight   one eye to the hole <u>could see the bathtub</u>, which was kept in the
<u>musty</u> basement because the upstairs bathroom was too small.   Smell
    The back bedroom was near the kitchen and adjacent to the
basement stairs. I once heard one of my aunts call that room a
firetrap, and indeed it was. The room was <u>wallpapered with the old</u> Sight
<u>newspapers</u> Grandma liked to collect, and the bed was stacked
Sight   high with <u>my mother's and aunts' old clothes</u>. There was no space
between the furniture in that room, only a narrow path against
one wall leading to the bed. A sideboard was shoved against the ⎫
opposite wall; a sewing table was pushed up against the side- ⎪
board; a short chest of drawers lay against the sewing table; and so ⎬ Sight
on. But no one could identify these pieces of forgotten furniture ⎪
without digging through the sewing patterns, half-made dresses, ⎭
dishes, and books. Any outsider would just think this was a part
of the room where the floor had been raised to about waist-level,
so thoroughly was the mass of furniture hidden.
Comprison   Stepping off Grandma's sloping back porch was <u>like stepping</u>
(simile)   <u>into an enchanted forest</u>. The grass and weeds were hip-level,
Comparison   with a tiny dirt path leading to nowhere, <u>as if it had lost its way in</u>
(simile)   <u>the jungle</u>. A <u>fancy white fence</u>, courtesy of the neighbours, bordered Sight
the yard in back and vainly attempted to hold in the <u>gooseberries,</u>
Sight   <u>raspberries, and blackberries</u> that grew wildly along the side of
Sight   Grandma's yard. <u>Huge crabapple, cherry, and walnut trees</u> shaded
the house and hid the sky. I used to stand under them and look up,
pretending to be deep in a magic forest. The ground was <u>cool and</u> Touch
<u>damp</u> under my bare feet, even in the middle of the day, and my
head would fill with the <u>sweet fragrance of mixed spring flowers</u> Smell
Sound   <u>and the throaty cooing of doves</u> I could never find but could always hear. But, before long, the wind would shift, and the <u>musty</u>
Smell   <u>aroma of petroleum</u> from a nearby refinery would jerk me back
to reality.

Grandma's house is indeed a place for memories. Just as her decaying concrete steps store the treasures of many lost child-

Dominant impression rephrased hoods, <u>her house still stands, guarding the memories of generations of children and grandchildren.</u>

Some Final Thoughts on Description

Because description is one of the most basic forms of verbal communication, you will find descriptive passages in most of the reading selections throughout this textbook. Description provides us with the means to capture our audience's attention and clarify certain points in all of our writing. The examples chosen for the following section, however, are predominantly descriptive—the main purpose in each being to involve the readers' senses as vividly as possible. As you read through each of these essays, try to determine its intended audience and purpose, the object of the description, the extent to which details are included or excluded, and the author's point of view. Equipped with these four areas of reference, you can become an increasingly sophisticated reader and writer of descriptive prose.

Description in Review

Reading Descriptive Essays

Preparing to Read

- What assumptions can you make from the essay's title?
- Can you guess what the general mood of the essay is?
- What is the essay's purpose and audience?
- What does the synopsis in the Table of Contents tell you about the essay?
- What can you learn from the author's biography?
- Can you guess what the author's point of view toward the subject is?
- What are your responses to the Preparing to Read questions?

Reading

- Is the essay predominantly objective or subjective?
- What dominant impression is the author trying to convey?
- Did you preview the questions that follow the essay?

Rereading

- How does the author create the essay's dominant impression?
- What other rhetorical modes does the author use to support the essay's purpose?
- What are your responses to the questions after the essay?

Writing Descriptive Essays

Preparing to Write

- What are your responses to the Preparing to Write questions?
- What is your purpose? Will you be primarily objective or subjective?
- Who is your audience?
- What is the dominant impression you want to convey?
- Do you know the object of your description well?

Writing

- Do the details you are choosing support your dominant impression?
- Do you use words literally and figuratively?
- What is your point of view toward your subject?
- Do you *show* rather than *tell* your dominant impression?

Rewriting

- Do you communicate the dominant impression you want to convey?
- Do you have a clear point of view on your subject?
- How does the essay make you feel?
- What does it make you think about?
- Which senses does it stimulate?
- Do you use similes or metaphors when appropriate?
- Are you *showing* rather than *telling* your description?

DAVID ADAMS RICHARDS

My Old Newcastle

Newcastle, New Brunswick, in the Miramichi valley, is often the subject and setting of choice, and formerly the home of novelist and poet David Adams Richards (1950–). After leaving St. Thomas University in Fredericton to try a career as a writer, he published a book of poems, *Small Heroics* (1972), at the age of 22. Much of the author's writing, including these early poems, shows his ability to transmute the sombre, even grim, quality of his perceptions of place into a source of beauty and interest. While he sets most of his fiction in his native area, Richards has stated that the great Russian novelists were his strongest literary influences. Indeed, the U.S.S.R. bought the publishing rights to his first novel, *The Coming of Winter* (1974), in 1980. His subsequent novels include *Lives of Short Duration* (1981); *Road to the Stilt House* (1985); *Hope in the Desperate Hour* (1996); and *The Bay of Love and Sorrows* (1998) as well as the Miramichi trilogy: *Nights Below Station Street* (1987), *Evening Snow Will Bring Such Peace* (1991), and *For Those Who Hunt the Wounded Down* (1993). Richards' novels show his compassion for, and continuing concern with, social and economic suffering, as well as deep feeling for his home environment. His love of the outdoors and keen eye for fine detail and local speech patterns make him a distinctly Canadian writer of the realist school. Richards' work has become familiar to a much wider audience in the last few years through the adaptation of several of his works for television.

Richards' recent works include *Lines on the Water: A Fisherman's Life on the Miramichi* (1998) in which he has captured his fly-fishing adventures on the Miramichi, and *Mercy Among the Children* (2001). In recognition of the quality of his writing, Richards has won the Governor General's Award twice (for fiction in 1988 and non-fiction a decade later in 1998) as well as the Canadian Authors Association Award (1991), the Canada-Australia Prize (1993), a Gemini Award in 1996 for his screenplay for *Small Gifts*, the Giller Prize (2001), the Canadian Booksellers Libris Awards for Fiction Book of the Year and Author of the Year (2001), and the Norma Epstein Award. Richards has held the position of writer-in-residence at six post-secondary institutions in Canada and the U.S. and currently lives in Toronto, Ontario.

Preparing to Read

In "My Old Newcastle," David Adams Richards gives us a portrait of a year in the life of his childhood locale, drawn from the standpoint of the author in 1992. He focuses his memory on the sights, sounds, smells, and seasons of his youth. Although an industrial town in New Brunswick may not strike the reader as the setting of much that is beautiful, Richards shows us otherwise. Indoor and outdoor life, business, and the progression of natural life, all had a rhythm and a sense of their own place for the author growing up beside the Miramichi River.

Where did you grow up? In one place or several? In a small town, in a rural setting, or in a city? What do you remember best about the people and places of your childhood? Your adolescence? Have you gone back to places where you grew up? What changes did you find?

In Newcastle, N.B., which I call home, we all played on the ice   1
floes in the spring, spearing tommy-cod with stolen forks tied to sticks. More than one of us almost met our end slipping off the ice.

All night the trains rumbled or shunted their loads off to   2
Halifax or Montreal, and men moved and worked. To this day I find the sound of trains more comforting than lonesome. It was somehow thrilling to know of people up and about in those hours, and wondrous events taking place. Always somehow with the faint, worn smell of gas and steel.

The Miramichi is a great working river.   3

There was always the presence of working men and women,   4
from the mines or mills or woods; the more than constant sound of machinery; and the ore covered in tarps at the side of the wharf.

But as children, sitting in our snowsuits and hats and heavy   5
boots on Saturday afternoons, we all saw movies that had almost nothing to do with us. That never mentioned us as a country or a place. That never seemed to know what our fathers and mothers did—that we went to wars or had a flag or even a great passion for life.

As far as the movies were concerned, we were in a lost, dark   6
country, it seemed. And perhaps this is one reason I write. Leaving the theatre on a January afternoon, the smell of worn seats and heat and chip bags gave way to a muted cold and scent of snow no movie ever showed us. And night came against the tin roofs of the sheds behind our white houses, as the long spires of our churches rose over the town.

Our river was frozen so blue then that trucks could travel   7
from one town to the other across the ice, and bonfires were lit by

kids skating; sparks rose upon the shore under the stars as mothers called children home at 9 o'clock.

All winter long the sky was tinted blue on the horizon, the 8
schools we sat in too warm; privileged boys and girls sat beside those who lived in hunger and constant worry. One went on to be a Rhodes scholar, another was a derelict at 17 and dead at 20. To this day I could not tell you which held more promise.

Spring came with the smell of mud and grass burning in the 9
fields above us. Road hockey gave way to cricket and then baseball. The sun warmed, the ice shifted and the river was free. Salmon and sea trout moved up a dozen of our tributaries to spawn.

In the summer the ships came in, from all ports to ours, to 10
carry ore and paper away. Sailors smoked black tobacco cigarettes, staring down at us from their decks; blackflies spoiled in the fields beyond town, and the sky was large all evening. Cars filled with children too excited to sleep passed along our great avenues lined with overhanging trees. All down to the store to get ice cream in the dark.

Adolescent blueberry crops and sunken barns dotted the 11
fields near the bay, where the air had the taste of salt and tar, and small spruce trees seemed constantly filled with wind; where, by August, the water shimmered and even the small white lobster boats smelled of autumn, as did the ripples that moved them.

In the autumn the leaves were red, of course, and the earth, 12
by Thanksgiving, became hard as a dull turnip. Ice formed in the ditches and shallow streams. The fields became yellow and stiff. The sounds of rifle shots from men hunting deer echoed faintly away, while women walked in kerchiefs and coats to 7 o'clock mass, and the air felt heavy and leaden. Winter coming on again.

Now the town is three times as large, and fast-food franchises 13
and malls dot the roadside where there were once fields and lumberyards. There is a new process at the mill, and much of the wood is clear-cut so that huge acres lie empty and desolate, a redundancy of broken and muted earth. The river is opened all winter by an ice-breaker, so no trucks travel across the ice, and the trains, of course, are gone. For the most part the station is empty, the tracks fiercely alone in the winter sun.

The theatre is gone now, too. And those thousands of movies 14
showing us, as children filled with happy laughter someplace in Canada, what we were not, are gone as well. They have given

way to videos and satellite dishes and a community that is growing slowly farther and farther away from its centre. Neither bad nor good, I suppose—but away from what it was.

UNDERSTANDING DETAILS

1. Why does Richards call the Miramichi "a great working river"?
2. Where are the points of difference between what the author saw in movies as a youth and what he knew in his own life? Why might this variance in perception have been a motivation to write?
3. How does Newcastle today differ from the town of Richards' youth?

ANALYZING MEANING

1. Life in small towns is never the simplistic picture that the media seem to show. What points in Richards' essay indicate that the texture of life in his boyhood may have been no less complex and interesting than it might have been in a city?
2. What descriptive details indicate that there was a real and vital quality to both the industrial and nature-based lives of the town of Newcastle? Does the author give a sense of a sort of reasonable coexistence of the two lives?
3. Do you agree with Richards' final statement about the Newcastle of today, that the changes which have come are "neither bad nor good" (paragraph 14)? Do you think that he is so neutral in his feelings? What specifically in this essay prompts your response?

DISCOVERING RHETORICAL STRATEGIES

1. "My Old Newcastle" as a descriptive essay demonstrates the use of a chronological method of structuring its episodes. Describe the framework of the author's pattern of organization. How does this pattern draw the reader through time? What elements in the final paragraph link back to the body of the essay?
2. Details strongly tied to our senses are frequently the most effective in communicating strong impressions. Richards uses vital visual, tactile, and olfactory descriptions, as well as direct and earthy figures of speech. Why might such strong and basic

writing be suitable to his subject? Which details and similes stand out most strongly to you and why?

3. What is the effect on you as a reader of the author's alternation of short and longer sentences? How do the author's sentences, and his choice of words, change in the final two paragraphs? Why?

MAKING CONNECTIONS

1. Richards writes with a passion about the land where he grew up and lived for many years. How does his attitude toward his subject matter compare to that of Lesley Choyce ("Thin Edge of the Wedge"), Tomson Highway ("What a Certain Visionary Once Said"), or Monte Hummel ("A Passion for the Environment: Two Accounts")?

2. David Adams Richards, in writing about Newcastle, is reflecting on his childhood memories much as Matt Cohen does in "Zada's Hanukkah Legacy." Whose childhood seems more appealing to you? Why?

3. Newcastle has changed significantly since Richards' childhood. How does the present-day Newcastle that Richards describes compare to the place portrayed by Will Ferguson ("The Sudbury Syndrome")? What do you think Ferguson would say about Newcastle?

IDEAS FOR DISCUSSION/WRITING

Preparing to Write

Try a freewriting exercise with a specific location where you grew up as subject. Write at the top of the page the name of a place where you spent at least several years of your childhood or your teenage years. Now, allowing yourself to play with your ideas and strongest memories, try "free associating" and simply write uninterruptedly anything that comes to mind for ten minutes. If you hit a blank, skip to the next idea that comes along or write something like "I don't know what to say," but don't stop writing.

Next, look at what you've written, and list words or thoughts that seem to form a pattern. What memories returned to you the most strongly? Why? Do you remember people or places or activities, or a mixture of all three? How do you feel about what you remember at this stage in your life?

Choosing a Topic

1. Write a descriptive essay in the form of a letter to a friend or a relative who shared a part and a place in your earlier life. Neither of you lives there any longer, but you have just returned from a visit. Describe your reactions to any changes you see, and to things and people that will interest both you and your reader. Be sure to give your essay a clear pattern of organization.

2. Using both memory and imagination, take a journey back to a particular moment or event in your past. Write an essay in which you describe in the clearest and strongest possible detail what you felt, saw, smelled, tasted, and touched at that time. What exactly were you doing? How did you feel? Who was with you? What is the strongest thing about this event that you are trying to convey?

3. What were your favourite games or activities as a child? Why? At what times of the year did you do these things? Describe these to your classmates so that you recapture for them some of the attraction, some of the reasons why you found these things such a pleasure. The order in which you place these in your essay depends on whether you wish to offer "the best first," or save it for the end.

WEBSITES

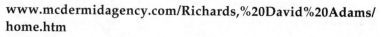

www.januarymagazine.com/profiles/darichards.html
Read the *January Magazine* interview with David Adams Richards.

www.nlc-bnc.ca/3/8/t8-6012-e.html
David Adams Richards won the Governor General's Award for non-fiction in 1998.

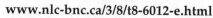

www.mcdermidagency.com/Richards,%20David%20Adams/ home.htm
At Richards' agent's site you will find a profile as well as information about Richards' books.

www.miramichi.org
The City of Miramichi website.

LESLEY CHOYCE

Thin Edge of the Wedge

Lesley Choyce is a Renaissance man with a multitude of jobs: Choyce teaches English at Dalhousie University, he hosts a television show called *Choyce Words*, he runs a literary publishing house called Pottersfield Press, he is a musician with a band called the Surf Poets, but he is best known as a writer. Since having his first book published by Fiddlehead Press in 1980, he has written more than 40 books representing a range of genres including poetry, young-adult fiction, and science fiction and appealing to a variety of audiences. In addition, Choyce is an accomplished surfer as evidenced by his winning of the Men's Open Canadian National Surfing Championship in 1995.

Choyce was born in New Jersey in 1951 and immigrated to Nova Scotia in 1979. His stories are often set around Lawrencetown, where he now lives, and they tell of people, most often young adults, who share his passions.

Preparing to Read

Environmentalists tell us that we are not separate from nature, that we are part of a greater biological pattern. Our lives affect and are affected by the total health and energy of the world around us. Lesley Choyce's essay "Thin Edge of the Wedge," first published in the spring of 1997 in *Canadian Geographic*, describes the dynamic life of an island in Nova Scotia. Interspersed between geological descriptions of the changes being wrought on this small piece of land is the portrayal of the human experience of this territory. The vivid passages show Choyce's intense fascination with his subject. As you read "Thin Edge of the Wedge," think about an island, a park, a beach, or some natural environment you know well. How has time changed this place? Does it have a rhythm, a life of its own? What patterns in your place's life belong to the cycles of nature, and what changes have people made?

Wedge Island is barely discernible on a road map of Nova   1
Scotia because there are no roads leading there. Although it is not truly an island, its tether to the eastern shore is so tenuous that it remains remote and seemingly adrift. Eroded by the forces of the North Atlantic, it is a mere fragment of what was once a

formidable headland. Within a lifetime, it will most likely be reduced to a rubble of stone, an insignificant reef at high tide. But for now, the Wedge exists, a reminder that nothing is permanent on this shore. Geologists define it as a "drowned coast" because the sea is gradually engulfing it. It has been for a long time.

Something like a dinosaur's bony spine of boulders leads a   2
wary hiker from the salt-bleached fish shacks on the mainland to the Wedge. If it's a fine July day—blue sky, big and bold above—the hiker might slide his hand along the silky beards of sea oats as he leaves solid land, then dance from rock to rock. Low tide is the best bet to make it there in one piece. Still, waves will spank the rocks from both sides, slap cold saltwater on his shoes and spit clean, frothy Atlantic into his face.

Wedge Island is a defeated drumlin, a dagger-shaped   3
remnant of land stretching a good kilometre out to sea. Smashed lobster traps, shreds of polypropylene rope as well as bones of birds and beasts litter the rocks near the shore. Thirty metres up the red dirt cliff sits a parliament of herring gulls peering down at a rare visitor with some suspicion. If the visitor scurries up the side of crumbling dirt, the gulls will complain loudly at his intrusion, then take to the sky and let him pass.

At the top is a grassy peninsula a mere 60 centimetres wide   4
where both sides have been sculpted away by rains and pounding seas. It's a place of vertigo and lost history. The land widens as it extends seaward onto this near-island of bull thistles, raspberry bushes and grass that seems cropped short as a putting green.

Farther out, at the very tip of the island, bare ribs of bedrock   5
protrude into the sea. This is the same rock you'd find if you could make one giant leap from here across the Atlantic and step ashore on the edge of the Sahara. It is the very rock that was once part of the super-continent that drifted north to crash into this coast, then drag itself away to form Africa.

This island is a forgotten domain on the edge of the continent.   6
It is easy to imagine that no man has ever been here before. But on the way back to the mainland, the truth reveals itself on the western shore. Not three metres from the edge of a cliff eight storeys high is a circle of lichen-covered rocks in the grass. A man-made well. The water is deep and long-legged insects skim along its obsidian surface. The well is full, nearly to the brim—it seems impossible given its elevation on this narrow wedge of land.

Nearby are two dents in the ground, as if some giant had   7
punched down into a massive surface of dough. Those two dents
were once the foundations of a farmhouse and barn. Nearby
fields sprouted cabbage and turnips. A family lived on vegetables
from the stony soil, cod and mackerel from the sea. There were
no roads, no cars, nothing but boats for commerce with Halifax.
A way of life long gone.

The rains and seas will continue to conspire to undo the   8
ribbon of land left between the well's fresh water and the sky.
The well's stone walls will collapse. The drumlin's cliff will be
pried by ice, and pocked by pelting rain. The sea will slip out
stones from beneath the hill, the turf up above will tumble, and
eventually the water of the farmer's well will gush out of the
heart of the headland and race down to meet the sea.

UNDERSTANDING DETAILS

1. What does Choyce predict will happen to Wedge Island? When?
2. How do geologists define Wedge Island? Why?
3. What is Wedge Island? What evidence is there of human habitation of the island?

ANALYZING MEANING

1. How does Choyce feel about his subject? How do you know this?
2. What is Choyce's thesis, and how does the description of the disappearance of Wedge Island develop his thesis?
3. What is the "truth [that] reveals itself on the western shore" in paragraph 6?

DISCOVERING RHETORICAL STRATEGIES

1. Choyce's essay contains several relatively unusual verbs that make his description particularly vivid. Find five examples of such verbs and explain why they are effective choices.
2. There are several striking similes and metaphors in Choyce's descriptive passages. The waves "spank the rocks," "slap cold saltwater on his shoes and spit clean, frothy Atlantic into his face" (paragraph 2), and the grass "seems cropped short as a putting green" (paragraph 4). What does Choyce's use of these figures of speech show the reader about the author's view of

his subject? How does it contrast with Choyce's use of scientific details?

3. Choyce frequently uses alliteration in "Thin Edge of the Wedge." Identify five examples of alliteration and explain how this figure of speech enhances Choyce's description.

MAKING CONNECTIONS

1. Like Tomson Highway ("What a Certain Visionary Once Said") and Sherwin Tjia ("Of Lemons & Lemonade"), Lesley Choyce is describing an environment he knows well. Compare and contrast the attitudes of these three writers to their subjects.

2. Lesley Choyce employs sentence fragments and several short, simple sentences in this essay. How is his style similar to, or different from, that of Joe Fiorito ("Breakfast in Bed") or Gwynne Dyer ("Flagging Attention")?

IDEAS FOR DISCUSSION/WRITING

Preparing to Write

Write freely about a place in the natural environment that you have known for some time. Why is it special to you? How long have you been familiar with this place? How often do its natural features change, and what causes these changes? What details stand out most clearly in your mind, and why? Do you see echoes of, or similarities to, your experience of life's patterns in any aspects of your special place?

Choosing a Topic

1. Basing your essay on specific sense details, describe your special place to a friend who has never been there. Decide on the main reason why your place is so meaningful to you, and try to communicate this dominant impression of your place as clearly as possible.

2. Are cities or towns as alive as a beach or a forest? Why? Using a logical order for arranging your arguments, describe exactly to someone whose point of view is not known which aspects of city or natural life make either or both living entities.

3. Using your imagination, travel backward in time to view and describe your special place as it might have been 500 years ago. What would be different from the way it looks today? Write

an essay that describes the differences and similarities in the two visions. Compare what your imagination's eye sees to what you see today, and decide on your point of view in the comparison.

WEBSITES

www.library.utoronto.ca/canpoetry/choyce
Offers a brief biography of Lesley Choyce along with several of his poems as well as his writing philosophy.

www.pottersfieldpress.com/authors/choyce1.html
Here you will find a list of Choyce's publications as well as a link to the publishing company he helps run.

www.writersunion.ca/c/choyce.htm
This site gives the Writers' Union of Canada biography of Choyce along with a list of selected publications.

TOMSON HIGHWAY

What a Certain Visionary Once Said

In the following essay, Tomson Highway (1951–) presents a loving and vibrant description of the region of Canada where he comes from. The eleventh of twelve children, Highway was born and raised on the Brochet Reserve in northern Manitoba, where his first language was Cree. Highway didn't begin learning English until he was six years old, when he was sent away to a Catholic boarding school. He graduated from the University of Western Ontario with a B.A. in music and English, and he began writing at about age 30. Now a resident of Toronto, Highway is the founder and was the first director of the Native Earth Performing Arts Theatre, and has received wide acclaim for the plays that he has written and produced, including the Dora Mavor Moore Award, the Toronto Arts Award (1990), and the Chalmers Canadian Play Award in 1986 for *The Rez Sisters* and again in 1990 for *Dry Lips Oughta Move to Kapuskasing*.

In an article in the *Toronto Sun*, John Coulbourn described Highway's "gentle, quiet humour, his great but unassuming pride, his passion and the dignity and strength of his spirit. ..." These qualities were undoubtedly taken into account when Highway was made a Member of the Order of Canada in 1994, and when he was chosen by *Maclean's* magazine as one of the 100 most important Canadians in history.

In 1997 Highway published his first novel, *Kiss of the Fur Queen*, a largely autobiographical story about two Cree brothers. *Rose*, a full-length musical sequel to *The Rez Sisters* and *Dry Lips*, was first produced in 2000. Most recently Highway has published *Caribou Song*, the first in a series of three illustrated books for children.

This essay first appeared as an insert in *The Bank of Montreal Annual Report* (1992).

Preparing to Read

The following essay is a vivid description of a part of the country Tomson Highway respects and admires. Before reading, think about the Canadian North. In your mind, travel north from the 49th parallel. How does the weather change as you progress? What do you notice about the landscape and the terrain? What happens to the population? What observations do you make about the vegetation? What about the wildlife? Are there any assumptions that you make about the seasons? Does your mode of transportation change as you travel north? What colours stand out to you?

Are there any distinctive smells? What sounds do you hear? What sounds do you not hear?

As you travel north from Winnipeg, the flatness of the prairie 1
begins to give way. And the northern forests begin to take
over, forests of spruce and pine and poplar and birch. The northern rivers and northern rapids, the waterfalls, the eskers, the
northern lakes—thousands of them—with their innumerable islands encircled by golden-sand beaches and flat limestone surfaces that slide gracefully into water. As you travel farther north,
the trees themselves begin to diminish in height and size. And get
smaller, until, finally, you reach the barren lands. It is from these
reaches that herds of caribou in the thousands come thundering
down each winter. It is here that you find trout and pickerel and
pike and whitefish in profusion. If you're here in August, your
eyes will be glutted with a sudden explosion of colour seldom
seen in any southern Canadian landscape: fields of wild raspber-
ries, cloudberries, blueberries, cranberries, stands of wild flowers
you never believed such remote northern terrain was capable of
nurturing. And the water is still so clean you can dip your hand
over the side of your canoe and you can drink it. In winter, you can
eat the snow, without fear. In both winter and summer, you can
breathe, this is your land, your home.

Here, you can begin to remember that you are a human 2
being. And if you take the time to listen—really listen—you can
begin to hear the earth breathe. And whisper things simple men,
who never suspected they were mad, can hear. Madmen who
speak Cree, for one, can in fact understand the language this
land speaks, in certain circles. Which would make madmen who
speak Cree a privileged lot.

Then you seat yourself down on a carpet of reindeer moss 3
and you watch the movements of the sky, filled with stars and
galaxies of stars by night, streaked by endlessly shifting cloud
formations by day. You watch the movements of the lake which,
within one hour, can change from a surface of glass to one of
waves so massive in their fury they can—and have—killed many
a man. And you begin to understand that men and women can,
within maybe not one hour but one day, change from a mood

of reflective serenity and self-control to one of depression and despair so deep they can—and have—killed many a man.

You begin to understand that this earth we live on—once   4
thought insensate, inanimate, dead by scientists, theologians and such—has an emotional, psychological and spiritual life every bit as complex as that of the most complex, sensitive and intelligent of individuals.

And it's ours. Or is it?   5

A certain ancient aboriginal visionary of this country once 6
said: "We have not inherited this land, we have merely borrowed it from our children."

If that's the case, what a loan!   7

Eh?   8

UNDERSTANDING DETAILS

1. For Highway, what is the essential appeal of the North?
2. In contrast to the view of traditional scientists and theologians, how does Highway characterize the earth? In your own words, characterize Highway's attitude toward the earth.
3. How many senses does Highway invoke in this description? Give one example of each from this essay.

ANALYZING MEANING

1. What is Highway's purpose in writing this description? Whom is he writing it for?
2. In paragraph 2, Highway refers to madmen. Who are these madmen and why does Highway label them this way? Does he really believe that they are mad?
3. Explain Highway's conclusion. Why does he end on a questioning note?

DISCOVERING RHETORICAL STRATEGIES

1. Is this description objective or subjective? Explain. How might a land surveyor's description of this area differ from Highway's?
2. How many times does the writer use the words *north* or *northern* in this essay? What effect does this have on the reader? How would more specific place names change the impression?

3. Does "What a Certain Visionary Once Said" contain the four fundamental qualities of descriptive essays that are outlined at the beginning of this chapter? Support your answer with specific details.

MAKING CONNECTIONS

1. Anita Rau Badami ("My Canada") describes travelling through the untamed parts of Canada, first in her search for orcas and then in exploring her adopted country. Does the land have the same effect on Badami that it has on Highway? Explain why or why not.
2. In "Pretty Like a White Boy," Drew Hayden Taylor writes about the attitude of white people toward Native Canadians. How does this attitude compare to Highway's comments about perceptions of people who can "understand the language this land speaks"?
3. Tomson Highway refers several times to the place he has journeyed to as "home." What does he value in his home? How do these things compare to the things that Allen Abel values in his "A Home at the End of the Journey"?

IDEAS FOR DISCUSSION/WRITING

Preparing to Write

Write freely about weather. How would you describe the climate of Canada generally? How would you describe the region where you live? What accommodations have you made in your life for the weather you experience? What kind of weather do you most enjoy? How does the weather influence your mood? Why is the weather such a common topic of conversation?

Choosing a Topic

1. In an essay for newcomers to your region of the country, describe your favourite season. Focus on the natural physical aspects of that season, as well as the effects they have on you and your community.
2. Think of a television program or movie that is set in the north of Canada (e.g., *North of 60, Atanarjuat*) and write an essay in which you discuss how its depiction of a northern community has either confirmed or changed your impressions.

3. Highway obviously feels very strongly about the place he describes. Write a short essay in which you describe a place that you very strongly dislike. Provide enough detail so that your audience will be sure to avoid this spot.

WEBSITES

www.playwrightsworkshop.org/tomsonbio.html
Here you will find biographical information about Tomson Highway, including a list of his publications and awards, and a link to an interview with the author.

tv.cbc.ca/lifeandtimes/bio1996/highway.htm
This biography of Tomson Highway comes from the CBC program *Life and Times*.

www.imperialoil.com/thisis/publications/review/mycanada.htm
This site contains an essay by Tomson Highway entitled "My Canada."

DAVE BIDINI

Kris King Looks Terrible

According to *Quill & Quire* magazine, in his first book, *On a Cold Road: Tales of Adventure in Canadian Rock*, "Bidini manages to layer and link themes and variations on our country's musical community, history, and players—famous and obscure—with equal measures of intricate (but unobtrusive) craft and gut-honest openness, creating a book rich and ripe with voices that bear repeated listening." *On a Cold Road* is Bidini's memoir of the adventures of the Rheostatics, the band for which he is the rhythm guitarist, and the tales of many other Canadian musicians. The same qualities of humour, honesty, and strong, vivid portraits come through when Bidini turns his focus to the world of hockey in *Tropic of Hockey*, the tales of his search for hockey in unlikely places. Bidini (1962–), a Toronto-based musician and writer, has also been a regular columnist for the *Toronto Star* and a book reviewer for *The Globe and Mail*, as well as a frequent contributor to the radio program *Definitely Not the Opera*. He is also a contributor to *The Original Six: True Stories from Hockey's Classic Era*, a collection edited by Paul Quarrington.

Preparing to Read

In 1999, Dave Bidini, along with his wife, Janet, set out for China as the first destination in Bidini's quest to find hockey in unlikely places. The selection here comes from Bidini's second book, *Tropic of Hockey*, the collection of tales that emerged from this quest. With what countries do you associate hockey? Within those countries, where is hockey played? What is characteristic of an outdoor hockey rink? What are hockey arenas typically like? What are some places where you would consider it unlikely to find hockey?

A fter a full day's rest, we headed into town to find SkyRink, the home of the tournament. 1

The thought crossed my mind that SkyRink might not be 2 anything close to what its name suggested. I almost expected to be disappointed since, these days, arena names make little sense. For instance, not only does the National Car Rental Center, home of the Florida Panthers, promise little in the way of aesthetics, you can't even rent a car there. Same with the horseless

Saddledome in Calgary. And despite the nation's affection for the old Maple Leaf Gardens, there's probably more foliage growing on the Hoover Dam. These erroneous names aren't reserved only for the pro ranks, either. In Toronto, new hockey complexes are being called Ice Gardens, Ice Land, and Ice Palace, names better suited to the American south, where the word "ice" is required so that people don't show up in shorts clutching frozen cappuccinos. But in Canada, what does one expect to find in an arena? Beach volleyball? The Antiques Roadshow? A name like Ice Land is proof of how insidious the American lexicon is in Canada's game. I prefer rinks to be named after dead people— Ted Reeve, Jimmy Simpson, Max Bell. The names suggest a persona, a link to the past, the warmth of someone's den.

Judging by the nature of other arenas with Sky in their name,   3 SkyRink did not hold much promise. SkyDome, the home of the Toronto Blue Jays, is fine if you enjoy the perils of sitting in a place where slabs of concrete have been known to come crashing down. In Edmonton, the Skyreach Centre is now the home of the Edmonton Oilers. The building used to be called Northlands Coliseum—a name that evokes hoarfrost and mulled wine and poplar trees—but the name was changed to Skyreach—which evokes nothing—when the local telephone company tossed a few million at the club, aping a trend that has besmirched more than a few stadia. The acquisition of naming rights is one of the scourges of modern sport. Candlestick Park in San Francisco was renamed 3Com Park after a software company, Jack Murphy Stadium in San Diego became QUALCOMM Stadium (software again), and Joe Robbie Stadium in Miami became Pro Player Stadium (you guessed it: men's underwear). Perhaps the most extreme example is the STAPLES Center, the home of the LA Kings. Until I heard the name, I hadn't realized how much hockey reminded me of the fast-paced world of office supplies.

The road out of the Bay was trimmed with long-armed trees   4 cupping orange and pink blossoms like altar boys holding candles. The flowers hung in bunches over the road and whipped against the flank of the bus, which rushed along the winding road gripping the edge of the cliff. The bus tilted and tipped as it fought corners and, with each turn, small vistas of the city were revealed: knots of blue and white high-rises; the shimmering green track of the Happy Valley raceway; a whitewashed mansion with guard dogs and gold gates; a regatta of iron ships floating in the bay; the stone shelves of an old terraced graveyard rising over the city; and, at the bottom of a street of Victorian homes, a procession of checker-skirted schoolgirls.

We drove under one overpass, then another, and suddenly   5
the city was very loud. The first few moments entering a strange city are always stage-directed by your senses. They're so inflamed by the newness of the environment that you find yourself thinking things like, "My God! That exhaust smells so wonderful and strange!" or "That garbage over there is just so darned colourful!" even as the locals are making choking sounds. While abroad, the senses refuse to be burdened by the mundane. They're wearing sombreros and drinking umbrella drinks and carrying on.

The bus let us off on Cheung Sha Wan Road in Kowloon   6
market, renowned throughout the world as the hub of the pirated electronics underground. The market rattled at full pelt. Stereo salesmen had dragged their tallest sound systems to the edge of the sidewalk and were blasting Canto-Pop at ear-splitting volumes. There was junk everywhere. An electronics boneyard littered the sidewalk with hacked-apart eight-tracks and CB radios—not to mention the obligatory box of used LPs with the same unloved Seals and Crofts albums you'd find at home—laid out on old newspapers and blankets. Fruit vendors came at me bearing weird-looking apples. In narrow alleyways, goat carcasses and pig heads and groupers the size of cricket bats hung under vinyl canopies. A corner apothecary offered boxes of Leung Chi See Dog Pills, Ping On Ointment, Essence of Deer, and Atomic Enema in its window; next door a young man sat, legs crossed behind a row of typewriters with flowers stemmed through their print bars; wholesale clothing depots flooded three city blocks— Fancy Fashion, Funny Fashion, Top and Top Fashion, Bukky Fashion and, of course, Fukky Fashion; shops tented in the middle of the street and lit by bare bulbs were festooned with cables, speaker wires, baskets of fuses, watches, and belt buckles; and a small pastry shop sold crates of sea prune, liquorice prune, and dried sour-cream prune, which young girls pressed into their mouths by the handful. The high clucking pitch of restaurant crowds filled the air.

I was in Parkdale no longer.   7

We stood in front of Dragon Centre mall, a huge building   8
that loomed arms-crossed over the market. The entrance was filled with a circus of laughing children being scooped up by an escalator. We rode with them, upwards into the building behind

a floor-to-ceiling glass façade. The ride was spectacular. We stared out at Kowloon across acres of high-rises pressed shoulder to shoulder, their sides thistled with television antennae. Laundry waved in a parade of coloured flags. Beyond that: smokestacks, the sea, the red horizon.

We floated higher.   9

Finally, on the eighth floor of the mall, I heard hockey—the 10 honking of the score-clock, the bang of the puck against the boards, the referee's whistle, skates chopping snow. I smelled the chemicals of the ice and the Zamboni diesel, and then I saw it: a rink small enough to fit in your palm, a sprite's pond, a place for Tom Thumb, Gabby Boudreau. To best describe it I have to use a word not often associated with the greatest sporting stadia of our time: cute.

It was a play rink.   11

It was one-fifth the size of an NHL oval—18 metres by 12 42 metres, to be exact. Perhaps a homesick architect from Trois-Rivières had been left with a narrow concrete channel and decided to fill it with ice. It was maybe the width of three bowling lanes. I suspected that bigger puddles had been left by the monsoon. Every element of SkyRink was odd. Since it was eight storeys up inside a glass tower, you could look out and forecast the weather from the way the clouds rolled in off the South China Sea. There was a mezzanine with an arcade—pinball machines, toy cars, and robotic clowns—that cantilevered over the rink and filled the air with the sound of bells and horns and children crying out to each other. Between the mezzanine and the rink was a yellow roller coaster that was close enough to the ice that you could reach up with a hockey stick and tap it. It was a flame-tongued, turquoise dragon that hurtled over the ice at high speeds, a frightful spectacle for even the most steel-nerved goaltender. It seemed that SkyRink had been designed with the idea of marrying amusement-park folly to hockey, and while hockey has experimented with this theme before—San Jose's shark blimp and Anaheim's daredevil duck come to mind, as do the barrel jumping and dogsled races that were part of intermissions in the 1920s—at least those novelties were kept at a safe distance from the action. But at SkyRink, there was no barrier or railing to prevent someone in the arcade from pelting the players with eggs or worse, and it did nothing to allay my fears of being killed by a large metal lizard.

At both ends of the ice, loose white netting was strung up   13
behind the goals. It reminded me of the mesh in those old Soviet
rinks, which Team Canada used to complain about. The SkyRink
netting served two purposes: to catch pucks and to act as a curtain
for the dressing area, which lay just behind the end boards. It
did neither job well. It whipped pucks back to the ice, and, like
Cheryl Tiegs' macramé tank top, if you looked closely enough,
you could see everything. Behind the netting, players freely
changed in and out of their clothes. The scene was like something
out of a rogue health club: fellows in towels strode to and from
the bathrooms, the odd player revealing his bare ass and hairy
stomach (or bare, hairy ass). This abundance of flesh did little
to ease my fear of being naked before strangers, and while not
every player flashed skin—some used a series of towels like
semaphore flags to guard their parts—many treated the area like
a Roman bath. Exhibitionists would dig SkyRink. I thought of
that brazen Canadian couple who were caught love-making in the
windows of the SkyDome Hotel. Here, you could press ham
before eight million people.

SkyRink had a Zamboni. It was old and dented and looked   14
as if it had stood in the way of a Matthew Barnaby shitfit. It had
South China Ice Hockey League written in Chinese and English
on the side and was driven by a young Chinese man in yellow
sweats who was far too slender to bring any credibility to
his job.

SkyRink had other credibility problems. Frankly, it didn't   15
smell bad enough. Let's face it: hockey stinks. It's a bloated,
heavy odour that you can poke with your finger. The first time I
set foot in a rink after years away from the game, I rushed a
hockey sock to my face to guard myself from the stench. Of
course, after a few weeks in my equipment bag, the sock was
well stewed and I was forced to wrap something else around
my mouth. When I ran out of socks, I had to embrace the game's
feral miasma.

But SkyRink smelled like jasmine (I should have been   16
grateful, I know). The source of this fragrance was Kathy K's Pro
Shop, which was stocked with a surprising complement of top-
of-the-line hockey gear. Unlike many skate-sharpening depots—
which tend to smell of plugged plumbing and are operated by
large, unshaven men—Kathy K's carried the scent of blossoms,
and if that wasn't strange enough, Kathy thanked you for your
business and offered a bowl of candies by the cash register,

allowing you to take to the ice chewing a gumball and spitting rainbow trails of purple, blue, and red.

There was also the food problem. And again, it wasn't so   17 much a problem as, well, a treat. There was no snack bar at SkyRink, unless you counted the Jack in the Box, which I only ever saw used by ex-pats teary-eyed for the taste of grease. Instead, there was a food court opposite the rink, where women with faces carved by time spooned sea snails the size of silver dollars and braised aubergine and double-cooked pork onto plastic plates, the aroma of garlic and soya and sesame oil scenting the air. There were kiosks selling blackened grouper, lemon chicken, bean curd seared in garlic and peppers, sushi, and hot soup with prawns—not your typical hockey cuisine.

The crowd at SkyRink was also its own. It was mostly seniors   18 who had wandered over from the food court (proving that, no matter where you go in the world, you'll find the same people hanging out in malls). It was a rare treat to skate along the boards and exchange glances with a group of old men who could have been extras in *The Last Emperor*. After a few days, I discovered that they appreciated pratfalls and gaffes rather than athletic grace and beauty. If someone scored an end-to-end goal, they'd get little reaction, but if they tripped over the net or were slew-footed or got slashed in the eye, the old men would laugh and pantomime their fall. The less able you were on your skates the more you were liked by the gallery; before the tournament ended, there was a real chance that I'd be a star.

UNDERSTANDING DETAILS

1. To Bidini, "these days, arena names make little sense." Why? How does Bidini believe they should be named? Explain his rationale.
2. What is it about SkyRink that leads Bidini to call it "cute"?
3. Who comes to SkyRink? Why, typically, do they come there?

ANALYZING MEANING

1. Does Bidini like SkyRink? Why or why not?
2. Bidini claims that SkyRink has "credibility problems" (paragraph 15). What are the credibility problems? What does Bidini mean by this term?

3. Paragraph 7 is a single sentence: "I was in Parkdale no longer." Explain what Bidini means by this sentence.

DISCOVERING RHETORICAL STRATEGIES

1. Bidini's writing includes details that appeal to each of the five senses. Find at least one example of each and then decide which you find most effective.
2. In addition to description, Bidini is using the rhetorical technique of comparison and contrast in this piece of writing. What is he comparing and contrasting? Why? What effect does this have on his intended audience?
3. Bidini fills his writing with specific examples, such as the names of fashion stores, the list of products available at the apothecary, and the names of different sports facilities. Explain the effect of these specific examples on Bidini's description.

MAKING CONNECTIONS

1. Dave Bidini and Anita Rau Badami ("My Canada") both write about travelling to an unfamiliar destination. How are their experiences similar? How do they differ?
2. Hockey is the subject of Bidini's essay as well as that of Michael McKinley ("Opera Night in Canada"). How do the two authors feel about the topic of hockey? How is the attitude of each conveyed?
3. Bidini and Paul Quarrington ("Home Brew") have collaborated on a book about hockey entitled *The Original Six*. What aspects of their writing styles are similar? Are there stylistic points on which you think they might have disagreed?

IDEAS FOR DISCUSSION/WRITING

Preparing to Write

Brainstorm or make a list of the trips you've taken in your life. What places stand out particularly vividly in your mind? What details make those places especially memorable? Are there any places that have disappointed you? If so, how did reality compare to your expectations? How do you choose what places you will visit? Are you more likely to revisit familiar places or to select new destinations? How much research do you do before travelling somewhere? How do you know what to expect when you visit a new place?

Choosing a Topic

1. Recall a time when you faced a significant new experience. Write a narrative essay in which you recreate the events and your feelings about them for your audience.
2. Think of a sport that you find particularly appealing (as a participant or a spectator). Write a descriptive essay with the goal of winning new fans or participants to your chosen sport.
3. Imagine that a new stadium is being built where you live. Write a 500-word essay explaining what it should be named and why.

WEBSITES

 www.bidini.ca
Dave Bidini's website.

 www.drog.com/rheostatics/start.html
The Rheostatics is Bidini's band.

 www.drog.com/rheostatics/stories/bidini/bid.html
Dave Bidini's writings from the Rheostatics website.

 www.savvytraveler.com/show/features/2001/20010525/feature3.shtml
Judith Ritter provides another description of SkyRink on the Savvy Traveller website.

SHERWIN SULLY TJIA

Of Lemons & Lemonade

Born in Toronto in 1975 and now based in Montreal, Sherwin Tjia is an artist, a comix creator, a writer of fiction and poetry, and a freelance journalist. Tjia graduated from Queen's University (B.F.A.) and Concordia (M.F.A.) and has shown his paintings in several group and solo shows. In addition, Tjia's writing has been published in a range of periodicals including *Quarry*, *Blood & Aphorisms*, *Sub-Terrain*, and *Adbusters*, the original source of the essay reprinted here.

Preparing to Read

Do you know what cornflowers are? In "Of Lemons & Lemonade" Sherwin Tjia gives a vivid description of the city landscape of suburban Toronto where he grew up. In contrast to the unfamiliar natural environment depicted in books like Margaret Laurence's *The Diviners*, Tjia is intimately acquainted with the landscape of suburban streets, shopping malls, playgrounds, and housing developments. Before reading Tjia's essay, think about the kind of environment in which you grew up. What are your impressions of the city suburbs? Of natural areas like provincial parks? Where would you rather be? Why?

When I came across the word "cornflowers" in Margaret Laurence's 1
The Diviners, I didn't know what it meant. I couldn't tell you whether cornflowers were proud and glowing, or taciturn and sweet; I just didn't know. The same thing occurred when I stumbled over "couchgrass" and "peonies." I had heard of them before, the names were familiar, yet, I couldn't put the names to a face, to a fragrance, or a touch.

I can, however, tell you about concrete, steel, tar and glass, 2
and go on endlessly about the myriad uses of bricks. Of these, the structures and lines remain rigid in my visual vocabulary; these I can envision with clarity. Though disgracefully ignorant about the natural world, this is my world, this world of malls and lawns and faceless houses, generic streets and measured sidewalks and parks where one can see the other side by standing at one end. And while sometimes one grows strangely nostalgic

for a world one's never really seen, except through a movie lens or the inscribed word, for what experience would I leave my familiar gridiron of Scarborough, Ontario? Would I leave it for a world of limitless lands, unscarred sunsets and fields? In a second. What kind of fields? I don't care; fields of wheat, grain, weeping willow leaves—fields of anything but shorn green grass and playgrounds. But I've never been to those places, so let me tell you about what I can see.

I can tell you about skinning bare knees on the coarse   3
schoolyard lot, and getting up bleeding and crying with pebbles still embedded like shrapnel around one's wicked-looking wound. I can tell you about the tremendous impetus the fixed playground was for our imaginations. When every recess game had to be new, the jungle gym becomes an island, a base, a prison, a fortress. The angular teeter-totters become skyward-gazing missile silos; the swings jet planes, or catapults; the sand pit the Middle East, the baseball cage an enemy wall to be climbed— everything was something. The playground was a proving ground.

When I do come across flora in the books, though, I can't just   4
dismiss it. To keep the illusion of the story intact I have to pull them in somehow; they must still exist somewhere. In such cases, I contrive a scattershot barrage of green, like in a Seurat painting, and let that pass. Or maybe I see pretty pink and red and yellow flowers and dot them among the green, but all to the purpose of setting the atmosphere that I want to feel as I'm sinking into the narrative. A flower's a flower, I tell myself, so it doesn't feel as if I'm missing much.

Suburban nights are quiet, if you're in among the houses   5
deep. I can tell you about the reflected glow of lamplight in rain- wet streets, dark like soil, but solid like glass, and how each car that passes glares with eyes of opulence and self-proclaimed righteousness. I can tell you about the perversion of grass that we cultivate; not long and billowy, but short and flat and uniform. Conform, they seem to say, even as I mow them angrily down and fret at the uselessness of the task. But we all do this because there is a law against not doing it, passed by those who can afford to pay others to do it for them. And so we conform, and grow affectionate for our lawns rather than standing up for what we believe. I can tell you about dull, repetitive genetic housing, as if they're all spawned from the same master plan—a monotonous mother brick. There's the fear of getting lost in one's own

neighbourhood, or even on one's own street if we're just not good with numbers. When all the streets for blocks all look the same at night, and when all the people stay safe with the face of the same expression, and we allow ourselves to grow detached, and we look warily at our neighbours for lack of knowing—this would make me leave. This is the essence of freshly mowed grass.

Once I went up north to Algonquin Park, and though I didn't 6 *know the name of anything, I picked up a water flower, fragrant and wet, and I knew that that was what I would see first the next time I thought about canoeing on a lake. It was a water lily I later learned, and I smiled because it should have been obvious.*

Let me tell you about the beauty of hydrofields, the great 7 open spaces of our land, with their gigantic metal men, striding into the distance, clutching their living lines. Sometimes these lines hum and join the crickets in a chorus in the blazing summer's heat. Sometimes they are downed in storms and children are electrocuted, and these children's dogs, and then scavengers which come to feed—like a morbid golden goose which holds you for a time. In the late summer, when the grass is yellow in the sunset, I like to pretend that it's Africa, on the Serengeti Plain. The animals are there, if only in my mind. Though sometimes the hazing of the heat causes them to appear in earnest and I wonder if it's sunstroke or an altered state of consciousness. Most often there are lone figures like me with their dogs before them, and once when I was very young, a couple making love. I remember his shadow on her upturned face as a very intense blue.

Sometimes I wish I had that natural vocabulary, and that I had 8 *grown up close to water, and that some old woman had taken me by the hand, and showed me the woods and pointed with gnarled stick at nature's ornaments, revealing their nature and their name.*

Let me tell you about the curious relationship between a 9 sidewalk's crack and your mother's back.

Sometimes I wish I could take my experiences in the wilderness 10 *for granted, like those who have had cabins up north all their lives. For while I would lose the aching awe of the wild world that I carry today, a childhood growing up among such wonders might have shaped me into a different person; possibly one more comfortable in situations requiring relinquishing thought and reason in favour of intuition and instinct. I don't know, maybe I would be less constrained, repressed. It is this possibility I regret, even if I had no choice at the time.*

Let me tell you about the brilliance of the clouds at night   11
over the car dealerships on the next street. Let me tell you about
the ubiquitous red stop signs, complementing green grass and
vivid against a blue sky. Let me tell you about the stream of cars
that flows continuously under formidable bridges that span
neighbourhood to neighbourhood, district to district. Let me tell
you about the crescents and the lanes, the circles and circuits,
groves and gates, courts and squares, all connected like a
madman's maze, in some secular sequence. And even in the
rurality of Suburbia, the churches are not the tallest structures
as they once used to be. Today it's the apartment buildings. Are
we losing or finding ourselves? Or do we have to do both?

The next time I think about entering the gates of heaven, what I'll   12
remember is coasting in a canoe across glassy water at night, shining
a flashlight though the rising mists off the lake; the paddles not making
a sound.

Let me tell you about the all-night donut shops, immaculate,   13
unchanging and overcharging; the perpetual light even at night;
the charisma and cheap intensity of malls; the lack of open-ended
gathering places; the solace of libraries; the elephantine
dumpsters; daily roadkill to greet school kids walking home; the
reined imagination in knowing what's over the next horizon—
more of the same; and parking lot wastelands and furtive
gropings.

Sometimes I am glad of the mystery of nature. That I cannot name   14
with a glance every plant or leaf that comes into view, is important.
That I can look at a landscape and wonder at its being, instead of
understanding it by clarifying it, defining it, is a freedom. Despite this,
when I first swam in an Algonquin lake at sunset, when the colours
imbued the waters, my first thought was that of swimming in a postcard.

Let me tell you a tale of lemons and lemonade. A boy and a   15
girl are selling lemonade by the side of the road. From a card
table with a plastic tablecloth hangs a sign alerting passersby
that a cup of their brew costs only 50 cents. I buy a cup and when
I ask them if it's made out of real lemons, they tell me no, it's
from a can of concentrate, the same can wherein they have
deposited my two quarters with a self-satisfied clink. "But why
didn't you use real lemons?" I ask, finishing my cup. "Because
this is all we had," the girl said. The cups are styrofoam, and I
drop mine into their plastic garbage bag.

UNDERSTANDING DETAILS

1. Where did Sherwin Tjia grow up? Does he prefer this environment or the natural world of places like Algonquin Park?
2. Describe Tjia's reaction to encountering unfamiliar flora and environments, both in literature and directly.
3. Why does Tjia choose to describe the landscape he does?

ANALYZING MEANING

1. Describe Tjia's attitude toward his subject. How is that attitude conveyed? Is the tone of this essay predominantly objective or subjective?
2. Explain the concluding story of the children selling lemonade.
3. Who is Tjia's intended audience. How do you know?

DISCOVERING RHETORICAL STRATEGIES

1. Tjia makes use of figurative language in several places in his essay. Find at least four examples of his use of figurative language and discuss the effect it has on the reader.
2. In addition to being a writer, Tjia is also a painter. Identify the details in "Of Lemons & Lemonade" that appeal particularly to the sense of sight.
3. Tjia is a poet as well as a journalist. What aspects of his writing have a particularly poetic quality to them? How is this quality achieved?

MAKING CONNECTIONS

1. In "Of Lemons & Lemonade," Tjia refers to the writer Margaret Laurence and the artist Seurat; in "Opera Night in Canada," Michael McKinley mentions three different operas; in "The Myth: The Prairies Are Flat," Sharon Butala evokes W.O. Mitchell's novel *Who Has Seen the Wind*. What function do these cultural references play in their respective essays?
2. In "Of Lemons & Lemonade" Tjia describes a place he knew well as a child. Compare and contrast his description of this place with the depictions of the childhood places of Monte Hummel ("A Passion for the Environment: Two Accounts") and David Adams Richards ("My Old Newcastle").

IDEAS FOR DISCUSSION/WRITING

Preparing to Write

Write freely about cities. Do you prefer to be in a city or in the country? Explain why. What is the appeal of cities? What don't you like about cities? What makes a city attractive?

Choosing a Topic

1. Write a descriptive essay in which you depict a familiar cityscape. Make sure your attitude toward this city is clearly conveyed in your essay.
2. Think of a particular place where you played as a child. Write a descriptive essay that conveys a sense of nostalgia for a place remembered.
3. Find a painting that particularly appeals to you and write a short descriptive essay that allows your readers to visualize it. Don't limit yourself solely to details that appeal to the sense of sight.

WEBSITES

www.pedigreegirls.com
See Tjia's Pedigree Girls website.

www.previewmysite.com/mcgilldaily.com/archives/ november152001/culture01.html
Read a profile of Sherwin Tjia.

www.exclaim.ca/common/display.php3?articleid=749
At this site you will find an article about Tjia and his Pedigree Girls website.

CHAPTER 2

NARRATION

Telling a Story

A good story is a powerful method of getting someone's attention. The excitement that accompanies a suspenseful ghost story, a lively anecdote, or a vivid joke easily attests to this effect. In fact, narration is one of the earliest verbal skills we all learn as children, providing us with a convenient, logical, and easily understood means of sharing our thoughts with other people. Storytelling is powerful because it offers us a way of dramatizing our ideas so that others can identify with them.

Defining Narration

Narration involves telling a story that is often based on personal experience. Stories can be oral or written, real or imaginary, short or long. A good story, however, always has a point or purpose. It can be the dominant mode (as in a novel or short story), supported by other rhetorical strategies, or it can serve the purpose of another rhetorical mode (as in a persuasive essay, a historical survey, or a scientific report).

In its subordinate role, narration can provide examples or explain ideas. If asked why you are attending college or university, for instance, you might turn to narration to make your answer clear, beginning with a story about your family's hardships in the past. The purpose of telling such a story would be to help your listeners appreciate your need for higher education by encouraging them to understand and identify with your family history.

Unlike description, which generally portrays people, places, and objects in *space*, narration asks the reader to follow a series of actions through a particular *time* sequence. Description often complements the movement of narration, though. People must be depicted, for instance, along with their relationships to one another, before their actions can have any real meaning for us; similarly, places must be described so that we can picture the setting and understand the activities in a specific scene. The organization of the action and the time spent on each episode in a story should be based principally on a writer's analysis of the interests and needs of his or her audience.

To be most effective, narration should prolong the exciting parts of a story and shorten the routine facts that simply move the reader from one episode to another. If you were robbed on your way to work, for example, a good narrative describing the incident would concentrate on the traumatic event itself rather than on such mundane and boring details as what you had for breakfast and what clothes you had put on prior to the attack. Finally, just like description, narration *shows* rather than *tells* its purpose to the audience. The factual statement "I was robbed this morning" could be made much more vivid and dramatic through the addition of some simple narration: "As I was walking to work at 7:30 a.m., a huge and angry-looking man ran up to me, thrust a gun into the middle of my stomach, and took my money, my new wristwatch, all my credit cards, and my pants—leaving me penniless and embarrassed."

The following paragraph written by a student recounts a recent parachuting experience. As you read this narrative, notice especially the writer's use of vivid detail to *show* rather than *tell* her message to the readers.

> I have always needed occasional "fixes" of excitement in my life, so when I realized one spring day that I was more than ordinarily bored, I made up my mind to take more than ordinary steps to relieve that boredom. I decided to go parachuting. The next thing I knew, I was stuffed into a claustrophobically small plane with five other terrified people, rolling down a bumpy, rural runway, droning my way to 3500 feet and an exhilarating experience. Once over the jump area, I waited my turn, stepped onto the strut, held my breath, and then kicked off into the cold, rushing air as my heart pounded heavily. All I could think was, "I hope this damn parachute opens!" The sensation of falling backward through space was unfamiliar and

disconcerting till my chute opened with a loud "pop," momentarily pulling me upward toward the distant sky. After several minutes of floating downward, I landed rudely on the hard ground. Life, I remembered happily, could be awfully exciting. And a month later, when my tailbone had stopped throbbing, I still felt that way.

Thinking Critically by Using Narration

Rhetorical modes offer us different ways of perceiving reality. Narration is an especially useful tool for sequencing or putting details and information into some kind of logical order, usually chronological. Working with narration helps us see clear sequences separate from all other mental functions.

Practising exercises in narrative techniques can help you see clear patterns in topics you are writing about. Although narration is usually used in conjunction with other rhetorical modes, we are going to isolate it here so that you can appreciate its specific mechanics separately from other mental activities. If you feel the process of narration in your head, you are more likely to understand exactly what it entails and thus to use it more effectively in reading other essays and in organizing and writing your own essays.

For the best results, we will once again single out narration and do some warm-up exercises to make your sequencing perceptions as accurate and successful as possible. In this way, you will actually learn to feel how your mind works in this particular mode and then be more aware of the thinking strategies available to you in your own reading and writing. As you become more conscious of the mechanics of the individual rhetorical modes, you will naturally become more adept at combining them to accomplish the specific purpose and the related effect you want to create.

The following exercises, which require a combination of thinking and writing skills, will help you practise this particular strategy in isolation. Just as in a physical workout, we will warm up your mental capabilities one by one as if they were muscles that can be developed individually before being used together in harmony.

1. Make a chronological list of the different activities you did yesterday, from waking in the morning to sleeping at night. Randomly pick two events from your day, and treat them as the

highlights of your day. Now, write freely for five minutes, explaining the story of your day and emphasizing the importance of these two highlights.

2. Recall an important event that happened to you between the ages of five and ten. Brainstorm about how this event made you feel at the time it happened. Then, brainstorm about how this event makes you feel now. What changes have you discovered in your view of this event?

3. Create a myth or story that illustrates a belief or idea that you think is important. You might begin with a moral that you believe in and then compose a story that "teaches" or demonstrates that moral.

Reading and Writing Narrative Essays

To read a narrative essay most effectively, you should spend your time concentrating on the writer's main story line and use of details. To create an effective story, you have some important decisions to make before you write and certain variables to control as you actually draft your narrative.

During the prewriting stage, you need to generate ideas and choose a point of view through which your story will be presented. Then, as you write, the preliminary decisions you have made regarding the selection and arrangement of your details (especially important in a narrative) will allow your story to flow more easily. Carefully controlled organization, along with appropriate timing and pacing, can influence your audience's reactions in very powerful ways.

How to Read a Narrative Essay

Preparing to Read. As you prepare to read the narratives in this chapter, try to guess what each title tells you about that essay's topic and about the author's attitude toward that topic. Can you tell, for example, what Matt Cohen's attitude toward his subject is from his title, "Zada's Hanukkah Legacy," or how Allen Abel feels about Canadian citizenship in "A Home at the End of the Journey"? Also, scan the essay and read its synopsis in the Rhetorical Table of Contents to help you anticipate as much as you can about the author's purpose and audience.

The more you learn from the biography of the author and the circumstances surrounding the composition of a particular essay, the better prepared you will be to read the essay. For a narrative essay, the writer's point of view or perspective toward the story and its characters is especially significant. From the biographies, can you determine something about Karen Connelly's view of Thailand in "Touch the Dragon," or Alison Wearing's reason for writing her essay, "Last Snowstorm"? What do you learn about Steven Heighton's views about war in "Elegy in Stone"? Last, before you begin to read, answer the Preparing to Read questions and then try to generate some of your own inquiries on the general subject of the essay: What do you want to know about the celebration of Hanukkah (Cohen)? What are your thoughts about Canadian citizenship (Abel)? What do you think about Thailand (Connelly)?

Reading. As you read a narrative essay for the first time, simply follow the story line and try to get a general sense of the narrative and of the author's general purpose. Is Connelly's purpose to make us feel sympathetic to her situation or amused by it? Is Steven Heighton trying to encourage us to visit the monument at Vimy Ridge, or is he simply trying to show us more about the nature of Canada? Record your initial reactions to each essay as they occur to you.

Based on the biographical information preceding the essay and on the essay's tone, purpose, and audience, try to create a context for the narrative as you read. How do such details help you understand your reading material more thoroughly? A first reading of this sort, along with a survey of the questions that follow the essay, will help prepare you for a critical understanding of the material when you read it for the second time.

Rereading. As you reread these narrative essays, notice the author's selection and arrangement of details. Why does Abel organize his essay one way and Connelly another? What effect does their organization create? Also pay attention to the timing and the pacing of the story line. What do the detailed descriptions of her son's outfit add to Wearing's narrative? What does the quick pace of Abel's "A Home at the End of the Journey" communicate?

In addition, consider at this point what other rhetorical strategies the authors use to support their narratives. Which

writers use examples to supplement their stories? Which use
definitions? Which use comparisons? Why do they use these
strategies?

Finally, when you answer the questions after each essay, you
can check your understanding of the material on different levels
before you tackle the discussion/writing topics that follow. For
a general checklist of reading guidelines, please see pages 17–18
of the Introduction.

How to Write a Narrative Essay

Preparing to Write. First, you should answer the prewriting
questions to help you generate thoughts on the subject at hand.
Next, as in all writing, you should explore your subject matter
and discover as many specific details as possible. (See pages
19–25 of the Introduction for a discussion of prewriting
techniques.) Some writers rely on the familiar journalistic checklist of Who, What, When, Where, Why, and How to make sure
they cover all aspects of their narrative. If you were using the
story of a basketball game at your college or university to demonstrate the team spirit of your school, for example, you might
want to consider telling your readers *who* played in the game
and/or *who* attended; *what* happened before, during, and after the
game; *when* and *where* it took place; *why* it was being played (or
why these particular teams were playing each other or *why* the
game was especially important); and *how* the winning basket
was shot. Freewriting, or a combination of freewriting and the
journalistic questions, is another effective way of getting ideas
and story details on paper for use in a first draft.

Once you have generated these ideas, you should always let
your purpose and audience ultimately guide your selection of
details, but the process of gathering such journalistic information
gives you some material from which to choose. You will also
need to decide whether to include dialogue in your narrative.
Again, the difference here is between *showing* and *telling*: Will
your audience benefit from reading what was actually said, word
for word, during a discussion, or will a brief description of the
conversation be sufficiently effective? In fact, all the choices you
make at this stage of the composing process will give you material
with which to create emphasis, suspense, conflict, and interest
in your subject.

Next, you must decide upon the point of view that will most readily help you achieve your purpose with your specific audience. Point of view includes the (1) person, (2) vantage point, and (3) attitude of your narrator. *Person* refers to who will tell the story: an uninvolved observer, a character in the narrative, or an omniscient (all-knowing) narrator. This initial decision will guide your thoughts on *vantage point*, which is the frame of reference of the narrator: close to the action, far from the action, looking back on the past, or reporting on the present. Finally, your narrator will naturally have an *attitude*, or *personal feeling*, about the subject: accepting, hostile, sarcastic, indifferent, angry, pleased, or any of a number of similar emotions. Once you adopt a certain perspective in a story, you must follow it for the duration of the narrative. This consistency will bring focus and coherence to the story.

Writing. After you have explored your topic and adopted a particular point of view, you need to write a thesis statement and to select and arrange the details of your story coherently so that the narrative has a clear beginning, middle, and end. The most natural way to organize the events of a narrative, of course, is chronologically. In your story about the school basketball game, you would probably narrate the relevant details in the order in which they occurred (i.e., sequentially, from the beginning of the game to its conclusion). More experienced writers may elect to use flashbacks: An athlete might recall a significant event that happened during the game, or a coach might recollect the contest's turning point. Your most important consideration is that the elements of a story follow some sort of time sequence, aided by the use of clear and logical transitions (e.g., "then," "next," "at this point," "suddenly") that help the reader move smoothly from one event to the next.

Rewriting. As you reread the narrative you have written, pretend you are a reader and make sure you have told the story from the most effective point of view, considering both your purpose and your audience:

- Is your purpose (or thesis) clearly stated?
- Who is your audience?
- To what extent does this narrator help you achieve your purpose?

Further, as you reread, make certain you can follow the events of the story as they are related:

- Does one event lead naturally to the next?
- Are all the events relevant to your purpose?
- Do you *show* rather than *tell* your message?

For more advice on writing and editing, see pages 29–30.

Student Essay: Narration at Work

The following essay characterizes the writer's mother by telling a story about an unusual family vacation. As you read it, notice that the student writer states her purpose clearly and succinctly in the first paragraph. She then becomes an integral part of her story as she carefully selects examples and details that help convey her thesis.

A Vacation With My Mother

First-person narrator I had an interesting childhood—not because of where I grew up and not because I ever did anything particularly adventuresome or thrilling. In fact, I don't think my life seemed especially interesting to me at the time. But now, telling friends about my supposedly ordinary childhood, I notice an array of responses ranging Specific subject from astonishment to hilarity. The source of their surprise and amusement is my mother—gracious, charming, sweet, and totally out of synchronization with the rest of the world. One strange family trip we took when I was eleven captures the essence of her zaniness.

General subject

Thesis statement

My two sets of grandparents lived in Calgary and Regina, respectively, and my parents decided we would spend a few weeks driving to those cities and seeing all the sights along the relaxed and rambling way. My eight-year-old brother, David, and I had Narrator's attitude some serious reservations. If Dad had ever had Mom drive him to school, we reasoned, he'd never even consider letting her help drive us anywhere out of town, let alone out of Vancouver. If we weren't paying attention, we were as likely to end up at her office or the golf course as we were to arrive at school. Sometimes she'd Examples drop us off at a friend's house to play and then forget where she'd left us. The notion of going on a long trip with her was really unnerving.

Transition   <u>How can I explain my mother to a stranger?</u> Have you ever watched reruns of the old *I Love Lucy* with Lucille Ball? I did as a child, and I thought Lucy Ricardo was normal. I lived with somebody a lot like her. Now, Mom wasn't a redhead (not usually,

Narrator's anyway), and Dad wasn't a Cuban nightclub owner, but <u>at home</u>
vantage <u>we had the same situation of a loving but bemused husband try-</u>
point <u>ing to deal with the off-the-wall logic and enthusiasm of a fre-</u>
<u>quently exasperating wife. We all adored her, but we had to admit</u>
<u>it: Mom was a flaky, absent-minded, genuine eccentric.</u>

Transition   <u>As the first day of our trip approached</u>, David and I reluctantly said good-bye to all of our friends. Who knew if we'd ever see any of them again? Finally, the moment of our departure arrived,   Careful
and we loaded suitcases, books, games, some camping gear, and   selection of
a tent into the car and bravely drove off. We bravely drove off   details
again two hours later after we'd returned home to get the purse and traveller's cheques that Mom had forgotten.

David and I were always a little nervous when using gas station
Use of bathrooms if Mom was driving while Dad napped: "You stand out-
dialogue side the door and play lookout while I go, and I'll stand outside the door and play lookout while you go." I had terrible visions: "Honey, where are the kids?" "What?! Oh, gosh ... I thought they were being   Examples
awfully quiet. Uh ... Lethbridge?" We were never actually abandoned in a strange city, but we weren't about to take any chances.

Transition   <u>On the fourth or fifth night of the trip</u>, we had trouble finding   Passage of
a motel with a vacancy. After driving futilely for an hour, Mom   time
suddenly had a great idea: Why didn't we find a house with a likely-looking back yard and ask if we could pitch our tent there?   Example
To her, the scheme was eminently reasonable. Vowing quietly to each other to hide in the back seat if she did it, David and I groaned in anticipated mortification. To our profound relief, Dad vetoed the idea. Mom never could understand our objections. If a strange family showed up on her front doorstep, Mom would have been delighted. She thinks everyone in the world is as nice as she is. We finally found a vacancy in the next town. David and I were thrilled—the place featured bungalows in the shape of teepees.

Transition   <u>The Native motif must have reminded my parents that we had</u>
<u>not yet used the brand-new tent, Coleman stove, portable mat-</u>
<u>tress, and other camping gear we had brought</u>. We headed to a national park the next day and found a campsite by a lake. It took
Chronologi- hours to figure out how to get the tent up: It was one of those   Careful
cal order deluxe models with mosquito-net windows, canvas floors, and   selection of
details

enough room for three large families to sleep in. It was after dark before we finally got it erected, and the night had turned quite cold. We fixed a hurried campfire dinner (chicken burned on the outside and raw in the middle) and prepared to go to sleep. That was when we realized that Mom had forgotten to bring along some important pieces of equipment—our sleeping bags. The four of us huddled together on our thin mattresses under the carpet from the station-wagon floor. That ended our camping days. Give me a stucco teepee any time.

We drove through three provinces and saw lots of interesting sights along the way: a working mine, a logging camp, caves, mountains, waterfalls, even a haunted house. David and I were excited and amazed at all the wonders we found, and Mom was just as enthralled as we were. Her constant pleasure and sense of the world as a beautiful, magical place was infectious. I never realized until I grew up how really childlike—in the best sense of the word—my mother actually is. She is innocent, optimistic, and always ready to be entertained.

Examples (spatial order)

Transition   Looking back on that long-past family vacation, I now realize that my childhood was more special because I grew up with a mother who wasn't afraid to try anything and who taught me to look at the world as a series of marvellous opportunities to be explored. What did it matter that she thought England was bordered by Germany? We were never going to try to drive there. So what if she was always leaving her car keys in the refrigerator or some other equally inexplicable place? In the end, we always got where we were going—and we generally had a grand time along the way.

Narrator's attitude

Examples

Concluding remark

Some Final Thoughts on Narration

Just as with other modes of writing, all decisions regarding narration should be made with a specific purpose and an intended audience constantly in mind. As you will see, each narrative in this section is directed at a clearly defined audience. Notice, as you read, how each writer manipulates the various features of narration so that the readers are simultaneously caught up in the plot and deeply moved to feel, act, think, and believe the writer's personal opinions.

Narration in Review

Reading Narrative Essays

Preparing to Read

- What assumptions can you make from the essay's title?
- Can you guess what the author's mood is?
- What is the essay's purpose and audience?
- What does the synopsis in the Rhetorical Table of Contents tell you about the essay?
- What can you learn from the author's biography?
- Can you guess what the author's point of view toward the subject is?
- What are your responses to the Preparing to Read questions?

Reading

- What is the essay's general story line?
- What is the author's purpose?
- Did you preview the questions that follow the essay?

Rereading

- What details did the author choose and how are they arranged?
- How does the author control the pace of the story?
- What other rhetorical modes does the author use to support the essay's purpose?
- What are your responses to the questions after the essay?

Writing Narrative Essays

Preparing to Write

- What are your responses to the Preparing to Write questions?
- What is your purpose?
- Who is your audience?
- What is your narrator's point of view—including person, vantage point, and attitude toward the subject?

Writing

- What is your thesis?
- What details will best support this thesis?
- How can you arrange these details most effectively?
- Do you show rather than tell your story?
- Does your narrative essay follow a time sequence?

Rewriting

- Is your purpose (or thesis) clearly stated?
- Who is your audience?
- To what extent does your narrator help you achieve your purpose?
- Does one event lead naturally to the next?
- Are all the events relevant to your purpose?
- Do you show rather than tell your message?

ALLEN ABEL

A Home at the End of the Journey

Born in Brooklyn, New York, in 1950, Allen Abel grew up to be a sports writer in his early years as a newspaper journalist. Now a resident of Arizona, he is a writer and broadcaster of wide-ranging interests and talents. After receiving a Bachelor of Science degree in 1971 from Rensselaer Polytechnic in New York State, Abel's focus of activities took an abrupt turn into a career as a sports journalist, where he won a number of journalism awards. He moved to Toronto in the late 1970s, and became a well-known sports columnist for *The Globe and Mail* from 1977 until 1983. Abel has also worked as a sports commentator for CFRB and wrote a documentary about the Canadian women's Olympic hockey team going to the Nagano Olympics. Abel's *Globe* columns always revealed an intelligent and ironic style, and often some more "serious" interests, which may have resulted in an extraordinary career shift for the author: *The Globe* made him its Peking correspondent in 1983 and in 1986 he became a reporter and producer of CBC-TV's *The Journal* for eight years. His career as a political observer has also led him into the production of documentary films of international interest, including *The Price of Freedom* (about East Germany) and *The Fires of Kuwait*. Allen Abel is the author of four books: *But I Loved It Plenty Well* (1983), *Scaring Myself to Death: Adventures of a Foreign Correspondent* (1992), *Flatbush Odyssey: A Journey to the Heart of Brooklyn* (1995), and *Abel's Outback: Explorations and Misadventures on Six Continents, 1990–2000* (2001), and he has also served as a columnist for the *National Post*.

Preparing to Read

"A Home at the End of the Journey" first appeared in *Maclean's* magazine in January of 1995. In this narrative essay Abel relates the experience of becoming a Canadian citizen, and particularly the citizenship ceremony in which he participated. Before you read about Abel's experience, think about the concept of citizenship. What does it mean to be a citizen of a country? What rights and responsibilities accompany citizenship? How do these obligations and opportunities vary from one country to another? What difference is there between being a citizen of a country by birth and being a citizen of that country through choice? What do people need to do to become citizens of Canada?

O n an early winter evening in the bottomlands of Toronto's   1
untamed River Don, 70 would-be Canadians file into a blind-
ing bright conference room and take their seats in the alphabetical
order of their mutually incomprehensible names. Outside, a first
frosting has rendered this quadrant of the city even more pic-
turesque than usual. The coatracks are crammed like Tokyo
commuters; overshoes slump limply on the floor.

The 70 are to take the Oath of Citizenship, pledging allegiance   2
to the woman in England—and her lovelorn son and *his* son and
so forth forever—who still embodies the vast, infant Canadian
state. In front of the oath-takers, a speaker's podium has been
set up, and there is a small desk on which are piled the certifying
documents, emblazoned with Lion and Unicorn, that each new
citizen will receive. I'm a little nervous, my throat a bit dry. I am
one of the 70.

Now the clerk of the court comes out, a tall, energetic woman   3
in billowing robes, dashing around like a refugee claimant from
the cast of *Sister Act 2*. The ceremony will begin soon, she
announces. When the oath has been sworn, she instructs, we
new Canadians are to proceed from our seats in a seamless
serpentine to shake the hand of the presiding judge and then,
doing a single axel in front of the podium, we are to return
immediately to our assigned chairs. All of this is to be accomplished swiftly, to leave more time for speeches.

Photography is permitted, the clerk says, but not during the   4
swearing of the oath itself. This act, it seems, is as sacred as the
fox dance of the British Columbia Musqueam, and snapshots
would defile the affair. But Beta cameramen from local television
stations are here, and they will roll right over the taboo, and no
one will complain or try to halt them.

It is International Human Rights Week, so the ceremony is to   5
include more ceremony than usual. Decorated dignitaries from
various ethnic communities of Metro Toronto have been invited
to witness the swearing-in and then—it is a lovely touch—they
are to reaffirm their own loyalty to Crown and Canada by taking
the oath themselves. A red-coat Mountie stands at crisp attention,
and officers of the Canadian Jewish Congress warmly greet each
immigrant family. It is they who are hosting this group
naturalization, here at their modern headquarters in this
snowbound suburban vale.

I study my fellow foreigners as they arrive, and I try to guess   6
which ones are war orphans and day laborers and entrepreneurs,

and which ones are gangsters and welfare cheats. Tonight's new Canadians, we are informed, have come from 27 countries, borne by the strange and sweeping currents of life to reunite, for this brief instant, in the saying of 43 words. Then, we will scatter into the infinite city, to meet again in fear or fellowship only at bus shelters, and some other less Toronto-centric place. But around me now, as the presiding judge arrives and the crowded room falls to a hush, I see the faces I have faced as a foreign correspondent in the refugee camps of Kurdistan, the back alleys of Havana, the cages of Hong Kong that hold escaped Vietnamese. It is a swirling sensation—that I have been sent from this city to their worlds and now their worlds have joined with mine.

(An hour earlier, I had thought: this is the night I finally 7 leave Brooklyn, my home town, behind me. But then, my wife and I had jumped into a taxi to make the ceremony on time and it had been outfitted with a bullet-proof partition between driver and passenger, an emblem of the new urban Canada. No one spoke; I stared glumly at the snow. Brooklyn had followed me north.)

The presiding judge greets us. An immigrant herself from 8 some European duchy, I cannot locate her accent—Latvia? Luxembourg?—she has performed this procedure manifold times but her voice still swells with proud anticipation. We are gaining a new country, she tells us. The gifts of this land will be limited only by the capacity of our hearts.

We stand at the clerk's command and begin the affirmation, 9 some of us mumbling, some nearly shouting, others utterly lost in the antiquated Anglophile creed ("I will be faithful and bear true allegiance ..."). The cameras are on us. We will observe the laws of Canada, we utter. We will fulfil our duties. We will remain standing and do it all over again, says the presiding judge—in French.

The slow parade to the podium begins. I clasp the judge's 10 hand, receive my Commemoration of Canadian Citizenship. Now, the Canadians who have been citizens for longer than six minutes are invited to restate their vows. In the peanut gallery to my right, I see my Canadian wife with her right hand raised, serenely chanting along. But I am already contemplating the fruits of my neonate heritage: seats on royal commissions; diplomatic postings to warm, benign republics; poets' allowances; jury duty. Shaking me from this reverie, *O Canada* begins, sung by two young stars of *Miss Saigon*.

The ceremony is over. We take our coats and re-enter the 11
intemperate night. Shivering, our teeth playing marimba
melodies, we give up on the bus after a couple of minutes and
hail another cab. I slide in, expecting more anticrime plastic,
more mistrust, more silence.

Instead there is a slim, blushing Arab in the driver's seat and 12
a giggling Chinese woman right beside him. They both are in
their 20s, lost in laughter. Turning east on Sheppard, skating
sideways on the pond, the pilot turns around to shake my hand
and to introduce his companion.

"Don't be afraid," the driver says. "This is my girlfriend." 13

"Congratulations!" I tell him. I'm thinking: Maybe this place 14
can work.

UNDERSTANDING DETAILS

1. Abel is relating an event in which there are many participants.
   What is his relationship to the participants of this citizenship
   ceremony?
2. What does Abel mean when he says "Brooklyn had followed me
   north"?
3. Explain the significance of the ceremony that Abel is depicting
   in this essay. How might the importance of this ceremony vary
   for the range of participants that Abel describes?

ANALYZING MEANING

1. What is Abel's thesis in this essay? What specific examples does
   he include that develop this central idea?
2. How many different nationalities or cultures does Abel refer
   to in "A Home at the End of the Journey"? Why does he
   include such a variety of references?
3. Characterize Abel's tone in this essay. What does the tone
   convey about the author's attitude toward his subject?

DISCOVERING RHETORICAL STRATEGIES

1. Abel uses many stylistic devices to make his writing interesting
   and effective. Find examples of similes, metaphors, personification, and alliteration in this essay.

2. How is Abel's past experience as a foreign correspondent and a sports writer reflected in the details and images he chooses to include in this essay?
3. How does Abel give his narrative a sense of completion? How does the conclusion of his essay link back to the introduction?

MAKING CONNECTIONS

1. The citizenship ceremony described in "A Home at the End of the Journey" has made Abel a Canadian. How does Abel's view of what is a Canadian compare to Anita Rau Badami's view ("My Canada")?
2. Steven Heighton ("Elegy in Stone") conveys a sense of pride in Canada for the understatement, quiet dignity, and reluctance to glorify war that he finds reflected in the park at Vimy Ridge. How do you think Allen Abel would react to this little piece of Canada in France?

IDEAS FOR DISCUSSION/WRITING

Preparing to Write

Before you begin writing, think of a ceremony in which you have participated that stands out in your mind. It might have been a graduation or a wedding or a coming-of-age ceremony such as a Bar or Bat Mitzvah, or it might have been a citizenship ceremony such as Abel's. What do you remember about the event? Who attended? What rituals were involved? How did you feel about the ceremony beforehand? Did you feel differently during the event? After it was over, what emotions do you recall experiencing? Did your participation in that ceremony give you any particular understanding about the world or the people in it?

Choosing a Topic

1. Abel uses his narrative to make a point about the multicultural nature of Canada. Choose a particular incident or event in which you have participated or that you have witnessed that illustrates your view about this aspect of Canada. Write a narrative essay in which you recreate that incident or event and link it clearly to your view about multiculturalism in Canada.

2. Choose an incident or event from your life that has given you particular insight into human nature. Relate the event in a narrative essay with a clear thesis.

3. Ceremonies often change to adapt to a progressive world. Write a narrative essay in which you describe one ceremony you have attended or participated in that in some way did not follow tradition or convention. Use your essay to show how our world is changing. Make it clear through your choice of details and language whether you consider this change positive or negative.

WEBSITES

www.cic.gc.ca/english/citizen/look/look-20e.html
This site features the questions that appear on the citizenship test.

www.macleans.ca
Abel's article first appeared in *Maclean's* magazine.

STEVEN HEIGHTON

Elegy in Stone

"If being a poet is possessing a heightened sense of perception, then in his latest collection of essays, *The Admen Move on Lhasa: Writing and Culture in a Virtual World*, Steven Heighton is every inch a poet. Here he is sometimes chatty, even wistful; at other times, wholly serious, even lamenting; and at others still, lyrical, poetic. But whatever voice he assumes, he is sure to hold your attention."

So opens L. Brent Robillard's review in the *Backwater Review* of Heighton's collection of essays from which the selection here is taken. *The Admen Move on Lhasa* (1997) followed the publication of three collections of poetry: *Stalin's Carnival* (1989), *Foreign Ghosts* (1989), and *The Ecstasy of Skeptics* (1994); and two books of fiction: *Flight Paths of the Emperor* (1992) and *On Earth As It Is* (1995). Steven Heighton has consistently been recognized for his writing with awards including the Canadian Authors Association Air Canada Award for most promising young writer in 1989, the Gerald Lampert Memorial Award (1990), and a National Magazine Awards gold medal for fiction in 1992. In addition, Heighton's *Flight Paths of the Emperor* was a Trillium Book Award finalist in 1993 and *On Earth As It Is* was nominated for the Governor General's Award for poetry in 1995. In 2000, Heighton's novel *The Shadow Boxer* was published.

Steven Heighton was born in Toronto in 1961 and grew up there and in Red Lake in Northern Ontario. After graduating from Queen's University with a B.A. and an M.A. in English, he spent time teaching in Japan and then returned to Kingston where he became editor of *Quarry* magazine. He has also lived in Alberta and British Columbia, and now lives with his family in Kingston, Ontario, where he works as a writer.

Preparing to Read

"Elegy in Stone" is taken from a collection of essays entitled *The Admen Move on Lhasa* (1997). In this essay Steven Heighton relates his visit to the national park and monument at Vimy Ridge in France. Before reading Heighton's essay, think about war and the attitudes toward war. What images are evoked by the terms *honour, valour,* and *bravery*? How have attitudes toward war changed with new technologies that change the way wars are fought? How has increased understanding about the psychological effects of war on survivors (e.g., post-traumatic stress syndrome) changed our attitudes about war?

Vimy Ridge, April 1992

The park's entrance—a border crossing, really—was modest   1
enough: a small sign you could easily miss if you were
driving past. But we were on foot. And though it turned out to
be a much longer walk than we'd expected, it was a good place
to walk, the fields along the road billowing with mustard, wheat,
and poppies, the oaks and maples fragrant with new growth. We
could be in Canada, I thought—then remembered that, for official purposes, we were.

The wind as we neared the ridge grew chilly, the sky grey.   2

Before long the road passed through a forest of natural   3
growth and entered an old plantation of white pines, thick and
towering, a spacious colonnade receding in the gloom. Fences
appeared along the road, then signs warning us not to walk
among the trees where sheep foraged above grassed-in trenches,
shell holes, unexploded mines. In the blue-green, stained-glass
light of the forest, the near-silence was eerie, solemn, as in the
cathedral at Arras.

Finally we heard voices, saw a file of parked cars ahead   4
through the trees and came out at the main exhibit site of the
park, some distance below the monument that crowns Vimy
Ridge. Here, in 1917, from a line of trenches now preserved in
concrete and filled daily with French tourists, the Canadian troops
had launched their attack. Preserved likewise is the first obstacle
they had met: the front-line German trench, barely a grenade's
throw away. This whites-of-their-eyes proximity surprised us
and made stories of verbal fraternization between the lines—of
back and forth banter in broken English and German—all the
more plausible, and poignant.

A few years after the end of the First World War the   5
government of France gave Canada a sizeable chunk of the
cratered, barren terrain around Vimy Ridge, where 20,000
Canadians fell before the ridge was finally taken on 12 April
1917. Today many Canadian visitors to France pass the memorial
park en route to Arras or Lille without realizing the site is
officially a small piece of Canada. Though "plot" might be a
better word, for although the trenches where Canadian and Allied
soldiers lived and died during their siege have healed over, the
fields are scarred with cemeteries and the woodlots filled with
unmarked graves.

We'd arrived the night before in nearby Arras, finding a   6
hotel and visiting the town's medieval cathedral. The hotel
manager had elaborately regretted that we hadn't come two
weeks earlier, on Easter Monday, when French President François
Mitterrand and Prime Minister Brian Mulroney and a handful
of Vimy veterans had arrived for the seventy-fifth anniversary of
the ridge's fall. I told the manager that I'd read about the
ceremony back home, but felt the park was probably best
experienced without the crowds and fanfare of an official visit. I
could have said more but didn't trust my French enough to try
explaining how disturbed I'd been by photographs of those heads
of state and their aides beaming glibly among the hunched
veterans, whose nation-building sacrifice was clearly far from
the politicians' minds.

Nation-building sacrifice sounds far too much like the kind of   7
pious, pushy rhetoric I've learned to mistrust and fear, yet for
years the bloody achievement of the Canadians on Vimy Ridge
did stand, like the ridge itself, as a landmark, a high point around
which the idea of a distinct Canadian identity could form.

"*C'est magnifique*," the manager told us when we explained   8
we wanted to go. "*Magnifique*."

At the park's main exhibit site we went into a small,   9
undistinguished brick building to see about a tour of the tunnel
system under the trenches. The young guides, in Parks Canada
uniforms, explained that we'd just missed the tour and
unfortunately would have to wait for the next. But as we turned
and went outside to confer, they must have noticed the small
Canadian flag sewn onto my backpack, because one of them
came out after us and beckoned us toward the tunnels. "You
should have told us you're Canadian," he said with a soft
Manitoba-French accent. "We don't get all that many."

The low-ceilinged, labyrinthine "subways"—where men ate   10
and slept before the attack and couriers ran with their messages
and sappers set charges under the German lines—have been
carefully restored, but more or less unembellished. The
impression, as above in the trenches, was sobering. I was relieved
that this sad, clammy underworld had not been brightened up
into some gaudy monument to Our Glorious Past; I was relieved
that it still looked, and felt, like a tomb. It reminded me of the
tunnels of the besieged Huguenots under the cathedral in Arras.

It was good to get back up into the daylight. We agreed to   11
meet Mario and the other guides for a beer that night in town.

We followed the road up the last part of the ridge to the   12
monument, wind blowing over the bare fields in a steady barrage.
Seventy-five years before, the Canadians had advanced at dawn
through driving sleet and snow, and now, nearing the exposed
crown of the ridge, we could see how weather of that intensity
must be quite common. The monument stands atop Hill 145, the
Canadians' final objective and the highest point for miles
around—but on the morning of the attack it must have been
invisible through the snow and the timed barrage behind which
the men were advancing.

Before the hilltop and the monument came in sight I'd felt   13
uneasy, recalling the many monuments I had seen that stylized
or made over the true face of war so as to safeguard an ideology,
to comply with aesthetic conventions, or to make life easier for the
recruiters of future wars. But as we neared the monument—two
enormous white limestone pillars that meet at the base to form a
kind of elongated U—I was impressed. And, as before, relieved.
I'd first become anxious when the hotel keeper had told us to
expect something "*magnifique*," but now I saw that in a sense he
was right, for here was something magnificent in its simplicity,
its solemnity, its understatement. And brilliant in its implication,
because the pillars did not quite form a triumphant V, as you
might expect, but a shape uncannily resembling the sights
mounted on machine guns of the First World War—the kind that
claimed tens of thousands of Canadian lives in the war and
several thousand on the morning of the attack.

I don't believe such resemblances can be assigned to chance.   14
An artist's hand is always guided in large part by the
subconscious. I don't know whether the architect of the Vimy
monument was ever asked about his intentions, conscious or
subconscious, but in a sense they're no longer the point; unlike so
many other old monuments, Walter Seymour Allward's is
strikingly modern because of the way it surpasses, or second-
guesses, all conventional intent.

We drew closer. Our feeling that this monolith was more a   15
cenotaph, a vast elegy in stone instead of petrified hot air, grew
stronger. And with it a feeling of pride. But a kind of pride very
different, I think, from the tribal, intolerant swagger so many
monuments have been built to inspire. A shy pride in our
country's awkwardness at blowing its own horn—because sooner
or later every country that does blow its own horn, with
flamboyance, starts looking for somebody else to outblow. A

pride in our reluctance—our seeming inability—to canonize brave, scared, betrayed adolescents as bearded heroes of mythic dimension, larger than life. Unreal.

And the monument is a cenotaph: we find its base inscribed 16 with the names of the 11,285 Canadians whose final resting place is unknown. Blown to pieces. Lost in the mud, or buried anonymously in the graveyards below the ridge. The parade of names marches on and on, a kind of elegy whose heartbreaking syllables are English- and French-Canadian, Ojibway, Ukrainian, Dutch, German, Italian, Japanese ...

Many are the names of our own distant relations. 17

The figures carved on and around the monument, though 18 dated in style, are not blowing trumpets or beating breasts or drums. They seem instead to grieve. We round the monument and the Douai Plain fans out below us: another figure, much larger, cloaked, stands apart at the edge of the monument overlooking the plain. Behind her a sparely worded inscription, in English and French, tells of the ridge's fall.

The figure, we will learn later that night, is Canada, 19 "mourning her lost sons."

Tonight in Arras we'll learn other things as well from the 20 Canadian guides we meet for a beer. That the whole park is planted with shrubs and trees from Canada. That 11,285 pines were planted after the war for every lost man whose name appears on the monument. That the prime minister's Easter visit was indeed a grand and lavish affair—everything the monument itself is not—but that the old soldiers on display carried themselves with dignity and a quiet, inconspicuous pride. And it's that feeling we end up coming back to towards the end of the night when the drinks have made us a bit more open and, I suppose, sentimental. Because we learn that these young expatriates have all felt just as we have about the austerity of the Vimy monument—and, by implication, the Canadian tendency to downplay the "heroism" of our achievements, to refuse to idealize, poeticize, and thus censor an obscene, man-made reality.

Or am I wrong to offer Canada these drunken toasts on a 21 virtue that's largely a matter of historical and political necessity? Perhaps what I'm trying to say is that Canadians are lucky to have been spared, so far, that sense of collective power combined with intense tribal identity that makes every imperial nation so arrogant, competitive, and brutal. And as our friends guide us back to our hotel, I wonder if Canadians will ever stop berating themselves for not believing—as too many other nations have believed, and keep on believing—that they're better than others, that they're the chosen, the elect, the Greatest Nation on Earth, with God on their side.

"Make sure to let people back home know about the 22 memorial," Mario calls out as we enter our hotel. And I reflect that a visit to the monument and the many battlefields around it might help convince some Canadians that there are worse things than uncertainty and understatement.

And if the monument doesn't convince them, or the 23 battlefields, then surely the graveyards will. In the park or within walking distance lie thirty cemeteries where the remains of over 7,000 Canadians are buried. They are peaceful places, conscientiously tended. Flowers bloom over every grave. Many are poppies. The paint on the crosses is fresh, a dazzling white in the April sun. Here, no doubt, many of the boys whose names appear on the monument are actually buried, beneath long files of anonymous crosses, or stones ranked like chairs in a vast, deserted cathedral. Another endless parade, this time of the nameless—though here and there we do find stones inscribed with a name, an age. David Mahon, 1901–1917. IN MEMORY OF OUR DEAR AND ONLY CHILD.

We recite the words aloud, but this time the feeling they 24 inspire has little to do with pride. The huge limestone gunsight looms above us on the ridge as we enter yet another aisle, and read, yet again:

A SOLDIER OF THE GREAT WAR
A Canadian Regiment
Known Unto God

UNDERSTANDING DETAILS

1. What is the significance of Vimy Ridge? Explain why there is a park situated here.
2. What does the monument Heighton finds in the park look like? Draw a picture of the monument incorporating as many details as possible. When was it built? By whom?
3. What is the role of Mario in Heighton's essay?

ANALYZING MEANING

1. According to Heighton, what aspects of Canada do the monument and park at Vimy Ridge reflect? Does Heighton see these aspects as positive or negative?
2. Why is Heighton glad he missed the prime minister's visit?
3. Describe Heighton's reaction to all that he finds at Vimy Ridge. Why is he "relieved that this sad, clammy underworld had not been brightened up into some gaudy monument to Our Glorious Past [and] ... relieved that it still looked, and felt, like a tomb" (paragraph 10)?

DISCOVERING RHETORICAL STRATEGIES

1. What is the dominant tone of Heighton's essay? How does this tone suit the purpose of the essay?
2. Heighton incorporates many figures of speech into this essay. Find examples of alliteration, metaphor, simile, and personification. What is the effect of each of these on Heighton's essay?
3. While narration is the primary rhetorical strategy used in Heighton's essay, he also writes very descriptively. Find examples in "Elegy in Stone" of particularly vivid descriptive images or passages. How do these enhance Heighton's narration?

MAKING CONNECTIONS

1. Heighton's essay is largely about war and the ways that citizens of different countries view war. Barbara Ehrenreich ("The Ecstasy of War") summarizes different theories about the way wars are waged. What do you think Heighton's "theory of war" would be?
2. Both Steven Heighton and Anita Rau Badami ("My Canada") are writing about the national character of Canada and Canadians. Whose view do you agree with more strongly? Why?
3. In his description of visiting Vimy Ridge, Heighton mentions several symbolic elements (the monument, the crosses, the trees and shrubs), but the only flag seems to be the one sewn on his backpack. What do you think military historian Gwynne Dyer ("Flagging Attention") would think about the apparent unimportance of flags?

IDEAS FOR DISCUSSION/WRITING

Preparing to Write

Write freely about monuments constructed to remember people or events. What purpose do monuments serve? Who builds them? Who maintains them? What kinds of monuments are public? Which are personal? What monuments are you familiar with? What kinds of emotions do they evoke?

Choosing a Topic

1. Write an essay in which you describe a place that is a good representation of Canada's identity or reflection of values. Link the aspects of the place clearly with the qualities you believe they represent.
2. Write a narrative essay about a visit you have made to some site of historical significance. Why did you go there? What was your predominant impression of this place?
3. Monuments are sometimes built in recognition of people who have been killed in some tragic way. Choose a situation such as a specific natural disaster, and then outline, in a descriptive essay, what kind of monument you would design to recognize and remember this person or people.

WEBSITES

www.randomhouse.ca/newface/heighton.php
Random House Canada's profile of Steven Heighton.

www.mcdermidagency.com/heighton.htm
Read a profile of Heighton from his agent.

www.vac-acc.gc.ca/general/sub.cfm?source=memorials/ ww1mem/vimy
Veterans Affairs Canada site with information and pictures of Vimy Ridge.

MATT COHEN

Zada's Hanukkah Legacy

Acknowledgement of Matt Cohen's contribution to the literary world of
Canada has taken many forms. Friends, family, colleagues, and readers
recognize his talents as a writer of over forty books, including novels,
short stories, poetry, and books for children (under the pseudonym Teddy
Jam), and he earned great respect for his work as an advocate for writers.
At the corner of Bloor Street and Spadina Avenue in Toronto there is a
park named in honour of Matt Cohen, featuring plaques with a biography
of Cohen along with excerpts from a selection of his novels. The 2002
publication *Uncommon Ground*, a collection of original essays, archival
photographs, and author interviews, is another vehicle for celebrating
Matt Cohen's life and legacy as a writer. It includes an excerpt from
Dennis Lee's eulogy for Cohen:

> I knew Matt first as a creature of contradictions. He was a lone wolf
> with a marvellous gift for friendship. He was also a city guy who
> came into his own when he connected with the land. A spiky
> intellectual in love with the physical world; a brain with a killer
> jump shot. And a workaholic who just hung out. For the first ten
> years I knew Matt, I tried to find a key that would resolve the con-
> tradictions. And for the next twenty, I realized I'd been missing
> the point. There was nothing to resolve: Matt simply was a denizen
> of opposites, and it was that multiplicity that made him himself.

Born in Kingston, Ontario, in 1942, and raised in Ottawa, Cohen
earned his bachelor's and master's degrees from the University of Toronto
and began his career teaching political philosophy at McMaster University.
Cohen went on to become a full-time writer whose work was recognized
with the Toronto Arts Award (1998), two National Magazine Awards for
short fiction, the John Glassco Translation Prize (1990), and the Governor
General's Award for fiction (1999) for *Elizabeth and After*.

One of the founding members of the Writers' Union of Canada, Matt
Cohen also served as writer-in-residence at several Canadian universities and was visiting professor at the University of Bologna in Italy in
1985. Matt Cohen died of cancer in December of 1999.

Preparing to Read

In "Zada's Hanukkah Legacy," first published in *Canadian Geographic*
magazine in 1995, Matt Cohen reflects on his childhood celebration of
Hanukkah with his family. Before reading the essay, think about

Hanukkah. Do you celebrate Hanukkah? If so, in what way? If not, what traditions do you associate with Hanukkah? What is the general tone of the holiday of Hanukkah? Why is Hanukkah celebrated?

O̤ne winter, when I was a child, we travelled from Ottawa to   1
Toronto to be with my father's parents for Hanukkah. As we drove slowly through the wintry twilight, the snow crunched and squeaked beneath the tires of our old snout-nosed Dodge. When we arrived, it was almost dark.

My grandmother opened the door before we could knock.   2
As always, she was wearing a black dress that made her look even thinner than she was, and square-heeled shoes that emphasized the fragility of her legs and ankles. Although my grandmother lived into her 90s, she had been on the verge of death since she was 35. We children went in first, apparently out of politeness but in fact because my parents were even more terrified of my grandparents than we were.

The table was set. The silver gleamed and the ritual   3
candelabra—the *menorah*—was in place along with the patterned white dinner service—big plates with wide soup bowls on top. From the kitchen came the familiar smells of chicken soup, *kasha* (buckwheat), and roast beef that had probably been in the oven since the Pleistocene Epoch.

We had been delayed on the road and sunset, which marked   4
the beginning of the holiday, was upon us. As soon as our coats were off, *Zada* (grandfather) led me to the menorah and asked me if I knew the blessing for the Hanukkah candles. He lowered his head so his face was almost level with mine. He wore his invariable dark suit pants, black belt, black shoes, white shirt with expansion bracelets on the arms, suspenders, a tie held in place by a golden tiepin, and of course his *yarmulkah* (skull cap). He had lost his hair following a bout of scarlet fever, but his moustache and beard, trimmed to a squarish spade a few inches below his chin, gave him—to my eyes—a wild and hairy look that was emphasized by the contrasting pinkness of his lips and tongue. Bearded, candid, utterly foreign, his face was an outburst from a past I couldn't begin to imagine. A devout believer, his passionate Jewishness made it completely natural to talk about

biblical figures as though they were neighbours we had just met on the street.

Soon I was holding the match and reciting, in Hebrew, the   5 blessing I'd learned in the car. My grandfather, knowing full well this was a surface acquisition, nodded and hummed along.

Zada Cohen was a short and stocky man, renowned for feats   6 of strength we grandchildren never saw but were told about—the most amazing being that during a fire he had carried two pigs, one under each arm, from a neighbour's barn. This was notable not only because carrying two pigs would be so difficult, but because my grandfather had demonstrated an unsuspected ecumenical streak. When the fire happened, I have no doubt he was wearing his usual costume, down to the tiepin, the suspenders and the yarmulkah.

The first time I remember meeting him was when I was six   7 years old. He took me by the hand and walked me to an empty synagogue. We stood in the middle of what was—to me—a cavernous dusty room filled with the smell of old books and rotting cloth. My grandfather pointed out the ark where the Torah was kept, the gallery reserved for women, and the Bimah where the rabbi delivered his sermon and the cantor sang the sacred texts. Then he crouched down so his eyes were directly opposite mine.

"*You* will be a rabbi," my grandfather announced to me.   8 Fortunately, even at the time, we both knew this was extremely unlikely.

Over the years, he maintained this special way of fixing his   9 eyes on mine. At such moments I knew that as the eldest (although religiously unworthy) grandson, I was being singled out to receive, absorb, and somehow shoulder the responsibility for some piece of Jewish lore he felt it essential for me to know.

"Mordecai," he always called me by my Hebrew name, "do   10 you know—"

Of course, I never did.   11

Hanukkah, the Feast of Lights, is celebrated each year for eight   12 days beginning on the 25th day of the Hebrew month Kislev. Since the Jewish calendar is based on the lunar month, Hanukkah's date in the modern calendar varies from late November to late December. For Jews, the year's most important holidays are Yom Kippur and Rosh Hashanah. Although these holidays often allow Jewish children to miss school during the

World Series, they feature fasting, repentance and promises to be good.

Hanukkah, a relatively minor holiday in the Jewish religious   13
pantheon, has not only presents, but a terrific story. "Do you know," Zada would ask me, "that we celebrate Hanukkah because a certain man with a name like yours, a Mattathias, had the courage to say no?" Or: "Do you know that to join his army, a young man had to be strong enough to rip a tree from the ground with his bare hands while galloping past on horseback? At full speed?" At first I viewed the story merely as about wild battles won by out-numbered Jewish soldiers. But the real story of Hanukkah is broader, because it is also the story of the Jewish rejection—after a period of great temptation—of the Greek Empire and Greek culture.

In the 5th century BC, the Jewish people, after a brief exile in   14
Babylon, returned to Judea and restored the Temple in Jerusalem. Then began a period of consolidation in which the scribes and the written word gained a predominant influence. Meanwhile, in the Greek city of Athens, another intellectual revolution was taking place. This was the era of Socrates, Plato and Aristotle.

In 334 BC, Alexander of Macedon began his conquests, which   15
included Palestine. The Greeks allowed the Jews a prominent role in the founding of Alexandria, and it was in conjunction with the Greek Empire that the Jews began to establish themselves as a mercantile force in the Mediterranean basin. The Jews found themselves tremendously attracted to—and seduced by—Hellenic culture, customs and language. The translation of the Hebrew scriptures into Greek became a major event in Jewish intellectual life. During this period, the Jews, although Hellenized in many respects, were still free to follow their own religious practices.

But in 175 BC, Antiochus, an Athens-born Greek warrior,   16
ascended the throne. He soon established domination over Judea and in the process, Jerusalem was converted into a Greek city. A proclamation was issued that forced all citizens to follow the Greek religion. Even the Temple in Jerusalem would be used for pagan religious rituals, including the slaughter of pigs on its altar.

At this time, through the influence of the scribes, Judaism   17
favoured piety and tolerance over fighting. As a result, thousands of religious Jews martyred themselves. Even the less devout

refused to fight on the Sabbath, and opposing armies soon learned that was the day on which the Jews were most easily attacked.

In 168 BC, in the marketplace of a small town called Modein 18 to the northwest of Jerusalem, the Syrian soldiers erected an altar. The men of Modein were assembled there and the soldiers' captain ordered Mattathias, a Jewish priest and elder, to sacrifice a pig to Jupiter in honour of Antiochus. Mattathias did not budge. Another stepped forward, offering to perform the sacrifice. The plan was that those Jews who refused to eat the meat of the pig would be executed. Suddenly, the aged Mattathias snatched the sword from the captain, killed the traitor who had offered to perform the sacrifice, then killed the captain. Mattathias's sons then surrounded him, and they and their followers fled to the hills.

So began the Maccabee uprising. The rebels—not the first 19 Jewish guerilla group in history—had made the singular decision to temporarily suspend the ordinance against fighting on the Sabbath, giving them a tremendous military advantage over their unsuspecting enemies. In a matter of four years, the Maccabees' victories brought them to Jerusalem itself, where their first task was to clean and reconsecrate the Temple. Removing the stones that had been used for pagan sacrifices, they built a new altar.

On the 25th day of Kislev, 165 BC, they lit the sacred lamp— 20 only to discover there was enough oil for just one day. Horsemen were sent in every direction to find more oil. Eight days later, someone finally returned—but remarkably, the lamp had continued to burn. Hanukkah commemorates the reconsecration of the temple and the miracle of the lasting oil.

Because my wife is not Jewish, Hanukkah in our family doesn't 21 compete with Christmas or replace it. It has its own special status and everyone enjoys it for what we have made it. Hanukkah is also familiar to my children from their classrooms and day-care. For them, this holiday is a normal part of their public and private lives.

The situation was entirely different in the late 1940s when I 22 grew up. Then, Jews were still trying to come to terms with the enormity of their losses during World War II. If the word "holocaust" existed then, I never heard it. There was no single word to describe what had happened. Nor was Hanukkah celebrated and discussed in school on an equal footing with Christmas. Such a possibility was unthinkable because Judaism and Hanukkah had no public place.

On the contrary, being Jewish was something best kept to   23
oneself: when I was in Grade 5, my refusal to say the Lord's
Prayer led to my spending each morning in the corridor while the
teacher, a Sunday School organist in his spare time, led the rest
of the class through their religious exercises. For me, Jewish
holidays were not only religious events, but also another way
of being singled out, set aside, sent to the corridor until secular
life resumed and I was returned to the main room.

Hanukkah's gift-giving aspects are constantly growing, but   24
when I was a child it seemed a weak and almost pitiful
counterpoint to the public splendour that made Christmas the
emotional and commercial centrepiece of winter. For this
extravaganza, people put up trees in their houses and store
windows, chains of lights festooned downtown and residential
areas, Santa Claus and his reindeer dashed through skies and
shopping centres. On the day itself, I knew, Christian children
would receive armloads of presents, then, after a huge lunch,
settle down to watching television specials that celebrated the
triumph of their virtues and their happiness.

For whatever reasons, the Jews of Ottawa did not compete by   25
putting electric Stars of David on their roofs or erecting Hanukkah
bushes in their living rooms. It's true that Jewish children got
presents, but they weren't the sort of thing you'd brag about at
school if you wanted to survive recess. Nonetheless, though it
took a long time, I came to value Hanukkah for its own virtues
and—mostly because of my grandfather—to realize how complex
and full of contemporary resonance its story was.

Now that I am an adult and a parent, I look forward to   26
Hanukkah as a warm family celebration that over the years has
become a mid-winter opportunity to explore with my children a
little of the meaning and history of Judaism. It is also an occasion
for gift-giving and family visiting which—aside from the potato
pancakes and the candles—are the main attraction for the
children.

When potato pancakes—*latkas*—were served at that long-ago   27
Hanukkah at my grandparents' house, Zada explained the
traditional holiday food had originated during the battles of the
Maccabees: passing through a village one time, the Jewish
guerillas were served the pancakes because that was the only
food there was time to make.

After tea, presents were distributed. As they did every single   28
Hanukkah for decades, my grandparents gave my brother and
me white shirts. These were always "Eatonia" shirts, with
starched collars and holes for cufflinks, and they were for wearing
to synagogue—a place we didn't go very often. Then my
grandfather recounted the battle when the Jews defeated the
Syrians, who rode powerful elephants instead of horses. He asked
us if we thought we would be strong enough to tear trees out of
the ground. Of course we would.

When the evening was finished—not before we'd all had   29
several desserts and numerous helpings of chocolates and
cookies—we went out to the car. Despite the cold, my
grandparents stood in the open door, framed by the yellow light,
and watched us drive off. They were, I suddenly realized, like
survivors on some magical ark that had arrived from thousands
of years ago. To them, Hanukkah had nothing to do with
Christmas or being sent to the hallway or television specials—it
was a magic ritual mysteriously connected to their mysterious
past. One I could participate in and grow into until I, too,
appeared to my children or grandchildren as a friendly but
bizarre relic out of a past they will never otherwise touch.

UNDERSTANDING DETAILS

1. Explain why Matt Cohen's family travelled to Toronto each
   winter. Who is the "Zada" of the title?
2. Summarize the historical events that led to the Maccabee
   uprising.
3. How is Hanukkah celebrated? How does Hanukkah compare
   to Christmas?

ANALYZING MEANING

1. As an adult, how does Cohen view Hanukkah? How does this
   compare to his childhood experience of this Jewish holiday?
2. What is the purpose of Cohen's essay? Has he successfully
   achieved this purpose? Explain why or why not.
3. Explain the title of Cohen's essay.

DISCOVERING RHETORICAL STRATEGIES

1. In addition to narration, Cohen has employed several other rhetorical modes in this essay. Identify at least two other rhetorical modes and discuss their contribution to the essay.
2. What is Cohen's thesis? Where in the essay is it located?
3. In addition to his personal narrative, Cohen gives a chronological account of historical events. Explain how he has combined these two elements in a single essay. Is this an effective organizational strategy? Why or why not?

MAKING CONNECTIONS

1. In this essay Cohen contrasts his childhood view of Hanukkah with his adult view. Compare and contrast this dual perspective with those of Barbara Kingsolver ("Life Without Go-Go Boots") and Monte Hummel ("A Passion for the Environment: Two Accounts"). Describe the tone of each of the adult perspectives as they reflect on their childhood experiences.
2. Matt Cohen and Steven Heighton ("Elegy in Stone") have both incorporated descriptions of historical events into their essays. Discuss the effectiveness of their portrayals of history.
3. Cohen's essay is largely about the significance of a religious holiday he has observed in some way through his entire life. How do you think Neil Bissoondath ("Religious Faith Versus Spirituality") would react to Cohen's essay? Do you think that Bissoondath would share Cohen's sense of this holiday being "a magic ritual mysteriously connected to their mysterious past"?

IDEAS FOR DISCUSSION/WRITING

Preparing to Write

Write freely about religious traditions. Do you observe any religious holidays? Why or why not? If so, which ones? How are they observed? Have your practices changed over time? What religious traditions do other people in your community practise? What is your reaction to these observances? Do you understand their practices?

Choosing a Topic

1. Write a narrative essay in which you relate the story of a child-hood celebration of a particular holiday (religious or non-religious).
2. Write an essay in which you compare and contrast the observances of holidays from two different cultures or religions. For example, you might compare Tet (Vietnamese) with Rosh Hashanah (Jewish) or Nowrooz (Zoroastrian), or Ramadan (Muslim) with Lent (Christian).
3. Think of a grandparent (or other adult in your life) who made a particularly strong impression on you. Choose a story that highlights the key characteristics of your subject, and write a narrative essay in which you convey the impact of this person on your life.

WEBSITES

www.nlc-bnc.ca/3/8/t8-7006-e.html
Matt Cohen won the Governor General's Award for fiction in 1999.

www.web.net/owtoad/cohen.html
Margaret Atwood's appreciation of Matt Cohen was published in *The Globe and Mail* in December 1999.

KAREN CONNELLY

Touch the Dragon

In 1993, at the age of 24, Karen Connelly (1969–) won the Governor General's Award for non-fiction for *Touch the Dragon: A Thai Journal,* an account of a year she spent in Thailand as an exchange student. This book spent several months on the bestseller lists and has been reprinted many times. Connelly has also published four books of poetry: *The Small Words in My Body* (1990), for which she won the Pat Lowther Memorial Award, *This Brighter Prison: A Book of Journeys* (1993), *The Disorder of Love* (1997), and *The Border Surrounds Us* (2000). Connelly's work *One Room in a Castle: Letters from Spain, France & Greece* (1995) again recounts her travels, this time in the Mediterranean, and she has recently completed a book of essays and stories about gypsies and travellers. She has also served as writer-in-residence at Okanagan University College, the University of New Brunswick, and the University of British Columbia's Green College. Karen Connelly now lives in Greece and is working on a novel about Burma.

Preparing to Read

Karen Connelly wrote *Touch the Dragon* as an account of her year in Thailand as a Rotary Club exchange student when she was 17. The excerpt here comes from the beginning of her book and describes her arrival in Thailand and her initial impressions of the land, the people, and the culture. Connelly describes it as "a record of living in a place that awakened every possibility of growth in me." Before reading this selection think about what you know of Thailand. What images come to mind? What associations do you have with this part of the world? Have you ever had the experience of travelling to a culture much different from your own? What parts of that experience stand out in your memory?

August 21, 1986

Leaving Canada. A view of the body of mountains: deep sock-   1
ets of aquamarine, blue veins slipping over cliff-sides, stone
edges splintering from the earth like cracked bones.

When I think of the span of countries, when I run my fingers 2
over the skin of a map, I get dizzy. I am too high up now—I
should have glided into this journey on a boat. As the country
pulls out from under me, I overturn like a glass on a yanked
table-cloth, I spill. Land steadies people, holds them, even if they
imagine they control it. Land owns and defines us. Without it, we
become something else.

After refuelling in Kyoto, we are moving again, rising into 3
another time zone, another time. These are the first pages of a
new country. There's almost nothing to write yet because I know
so little. I can't even imagine where I'm going. I am utterly alone,
a small bit of dust blown into Asia's deep green eye. I lean against
the glass and gaze down at an emerald flood, knowing I'll never
be able to soak up such radiance. It's a colour I never knew I'd
see, the astonishing canvas of a dream, undreamed.

At the airport in Bangkok, a bald foreigner lugs three gallons 4
of water on his shoulder. He explains to suspicious customs
officials that he has brought water from home because the water
here is unsafe. There is laughter, a waving of dark arms and pale
palms. I stumble through customs, crippled by luggage and jet
lag. One English word rings out: taxi. The world is a wet braid of
heat and flesh, glimpses of gold-studded teeth, shirts open to
shining bellies, purple tattoos, wreaths of jasmine. Above the
horde of cab drivers looms a hand-painted sign warning all
tourists to beware of thieves, illicit business deals, drugs and
fake gems. The air slides over me thick as honey. I have never
felt such tropical warmth before.

Then I see a cardboard sign with my name on it bobbing up 5
in the crowd. Someone has come to get me. Someone has come to
take me (farther) away.

August 22

We are driving northwards under black clouds, through 6
darkness broken by lightning. I could believe now that the earth
is flat, and its far edges are sparking flame. Rice fields, tree groves,
gleaming oval ponds flash out of the night. Mr. Prasit Piyachinda
and Mr. Prasert Jeenanukulwong have both suggested I call them
paw for the sake of simplicity. Paw Prasit speaks English. "We
will treat you like a daughter, and you will treat us like father."
The Rotary Club of Denchai has almost twenty members. I can't
pronounce any of their names. "You must learn to speak Thai
very quickly," Paw Prasit explains. "It will not be difficult. No one

in your family speaks English. You have no choice." He turns around to smile at me. He talks about spicy food, a famous Buddhist monk who is also a great fortune-teller, the school I will go to, the people who are anxious to meet me. When I ask why these people want to meet me, he giggles. "Why, because you are a falang." A foreigner. It is my first Thai word.

Sudden light spears the heavy rain. I squint out the streaming windows. The men laugh at my fascination with the countryside. "Are you afraid of the ... the ..."   7

"The lightning," I finish for Paw Prasit.   8

"Ah, yes, yes, are you afraid of it? My daughter, yes, is. She will not look at fields at night, fields of rain." He points towards a distant clump of trees and taps at the window. "Dragons. She says they are dragons." He laughs, turns to Prasert, translates, they laugh again, then hoot more at some other joke. I peer through the glass; his daughter is right. There they are, tree-dragons, moulded by wind and shadow, heavy-skulled dinosaurs gathered under lightning at the edges of ponds. They lean down to the water, their scaled flanks gleaming with rain.   9

I fall asleep, sliding down onto the seat, listening to Paw Prasit say, "And people will call you falang in the street because at first they will not know your name." I will be the only white person in the town. "You will be popular. Also there is a green fruit in Thailand called falang and when you eat it, everyone will laugh and say 'Falang eat falang. Hahaha. Ha ha.'" Again he translates for Paw Prasert (why are their names so similar?) and both men slap their knees at this hilarious play on words. I keep missing the jokes in everything, possibly because I'm so tired. What time is it here? What time is it in Canada? Canada? The word sounds funny. I slump down farther on the seat and listen to wheels humming and my guardians speaking Thai. It is indecipherable birdsong. They talk on, their voices climbing and sliding down the banisters of five tones and strange letters. This is not comparable to high school French.   10

Suddenly, inexplicably, they are standing outside the car and calling me. "Kalen, Kalen, to bathroom now. We are in Phitsanulok. For pee-pee." The door is opened for me. I receive a handful of toilet paper and a gentle push in the right direction. I am disoriented, eyes salted with sleep. The young men hanging about the gas pumps stare and stare.   11

Once I am in the dark little washroom, reality swarms; the pungent odour of urine burns the dreamy quality out of   12 everything. I lose my footing on the wet edges of the Thai toilet and laugh, imagining the embarrassment of breaking my ankle in a toilet the very first day. This is Thailand, the land of smiles, the Venice of the Orient, the pearl of Asia. The travel-agency phrases run off my tongue as mosquitoes settle on my thighs, arms, neck. Are they malarial or harmless? A few dark stains move up and down the walls, and my skin shivers, waiting for invasions.

Walking back across the lot, I notice small reddish lights   13 glowing behind a cage with thin bars. I walk towards them, curious, moving closer, closer, stretching out my hand ... Paw Prasit yells, "No, no!" but it's too late. All I do is touch the bars and half a dozen gibbons leap shrieking towards my hand.

I scream at their screams, the gas-station attendants come   14 loping across the lot and my Thai fathers rush forward to pull me away. I apologize to everyone. The gibbons are the ones making the fuss. Their furious bodies spring and bounce inside the cage. "You must learn to be careful, Kalen." Paw Prasit takes my arm, his glasses steamed with worry. "There are snakes, too. You know?" He stares at me for a moment, then laughs and says something in Thai, which makes Paw Prasert laugh, too. Even the gas-pumpers giggle and kick a few pebbles, looking up at me even though their heads are lowered. I open the car door and crawl in. When we drive away, the boys wave us off. I stare back at the neon lights of the station for a long time, the savage human faces of the monkeys still vivid in my mind.

We reach Denchai in the dark, so I see little, other than dogs   15 running through the beams of the headlights, barely making it. We finally stop at the last building on the street. "Liquor store," Paw Prasit says. "This is the liquor store of Paw Prasert. This is where you'll live." Prasert is already out of the car and up on a bench, stretching to press a door buzzer. As soon as his finger flexes, I hear barking and the rattling slap of a chain. The dog inside the building hurls itself against the metal door. We wait until the dog begins to whimper, then hear an old man's grunt and sniffle. There's a clatter of keys and a frightening roar of phlegm from the recesses of a throat; finally the door scrapes open along the cement floor. A balding old man beams at us. His skin is the colour and texture of a walnut, he is toothless and he wears nothing but a baggy pair of black satin trousers. Prasit says to me, "Old father is much blind." After awkward introductions, the three of them begin to speak in Thai. I smile and smile. Before coming in with us, the old man shuffles to the road and vigorously spits a small chunk of his lung into the gutter.

Inside the shop, the German shepherd once again begins to   16
bark and strain against her chain. Her lips are pulled back over yellow teeth. Paw Prasert grins proudly, pulls up some long-forgotten vestige of English and yells over the barking, "My dog!" I smile back, nod. Paw Prasit adds, "But no worry, it not hurt you." She leaps toward us again, only to be choked back by the chain. After the old man hits her on the nose, she whimpers and slumps to the ground, chin between her paws. We walk deeper into the liquor store, past piles of dusty crates, a display of Thai whisky, a television, an old desk piled with newspapers and small bags of rice. Each of the men has one of my suitcases and is breathing audibly under its weight, insisting how light it is. We come to a small fridge. Paw Prasert opens it and whispers to Paw Prasit, who turns to me. "He say you take anything you want, you are like a daughter to him. You know?"

Thanking them, I glance into the fridge. It's full of water   17
bottles and a few pots of murky sauces or oil paints.

Up one staircase: bathroom, sister's room, children's room.   18
Paw Prasert's room. The top of another staircase brings us to an uninhabited floor. The one bedroom is for me. "You have room all to self." I am smiling, smiling my thanks. Now the men turn to leave. Yes, yes, see you tomorrow, to begin learning Thai, to begin learning, tomorrow, yes.

And the door closes. I look around: a low bed of cushions, a   19
child's desk, a small mirror, a woven straw chair. Green curtains, green bedspread. A stark naked Thai girl with an erotic smile stares down from a picture on the wall. This smile—she must be kidding—does the trick. I sit on the edge of the bed, hug my elbows and sob for everything that isn't here. I think of the hundreds of days, the thousands of hours I have to stay here. Everything I understand, everything I own is buried in my skull, intangible. I am not feeling particularly brave. I'm sniffling, alone but for a Thai porn queen and three beaten-up suitcases. This does not feel exotic. Around me, the pool of night trembles with crickets and frogs, breaks with the distant bark of dogs, and slowly, slowly, closes over my head.

UNDERSTANDING DETAILS

1. To what country has Connelly come to live? What part of this country will she be staying in? How did she get there from Canada?
2. What language does Connelly need to learn in her new home? What is the first word that she learns?
3. Animals and insects figure largely in Connelly's initial impressions of Thailand. List the various creatures she sees in her first two days and explain how she reacts to them.

ANALYZING MEANING

1. What are Karen Connelly's feelings about the place where she has come to live? Do they change from August 21 to August 22? In what ways?
2. Explain why Connelly says the word *Canada*, in paragraph 10, sounds funny.
3. How does Connelly react to the climate and the land in Thailand? Give specific examples of the details that recreate her experience of each so vividly.

DISCOVERING RHETORICAL STRATEGIES

1. The use of figurative language is one of the qualities that makes Connelly's narrative distinctive and memorable. Find specific examples of similes and metaphors that contribute to her vivid description.
2. Connelly frequently mentions the colours in this new land she has come to. What colour predominates? Cite the specific places where she mentions it. What other colours contribute to her image of Thailand?
3. Connelly's description of her Thai adventure originated as a collection of letters and journal entries that were later edited for her book *Touch the Dragon*. The dedication at the front of the book says, "This book is for the people of Thailand. ..." Who is her intended audience?

MAKING CONNECTIONS

1. Karen Connelly and Dave Bidini ("Kris King Looks Terrible") both write about travelling to an Asian country. How are their

experiences similar? Have your travel experiences been more like Bidini's or more like Connelly's?

2. Seven rules for writing are outlined in Natalie Goldberg's essay ("The Rules of Writing Practice"). Which of these rules has Connelly followed? Given that this selection comes from an edited, published work, is it possible to evaluate it against all of Goldberg's rules? Which ones work and which ones don't?

IDEAS FOR DISCUSSION/WRITING

Preparing to Write

Brainstorm or make a list of the trips you've taken in your life. What are the first words and thoughts and feelings that come to mind about each? Are there connections between any of these patterns of words? What ideas or sensations appear frequently in your prewriting exercise? Would you try to experience any of these things on future travels? Do you enjoy travelling? How much do you enjoy new and different experiences? What sorts of things do we learn from travelling?

Choosing a Topic

1. Recall a time when you faced a significant new experience. Write a narrative essay in which you recreate the events and your feelings about them for your audience.

2. Choose a trip, real or imagined, and write a promotional article for your college newspaper about it. What might make readers want to visit your location(s), and why? How can you best make your ideal holiday appealing to this audience?

3. Connelly's book began as a series of journal entries and letters detailing her day-to-day experiences. Write an essay in which you discuss why people keep journals. What kind of information goes into journal entries? How does journal writing differ from letter writing or essay writing?

WEBSITES

www.poets.ca/linktext/direct/connelly.htm
Connelly is a member of the League of Canadian Poets.

www.lonelyplanet.com.au/dest/sea/thai.htm
Learn more about Thailand at the Lonely Planet site.

shanmonster.lilsproutz.com/interview/001.html
Read an interview with Karen Connelly.

ALISON WEARING

Last Snowstorm

Alison Wearing (1968–) is the winner of the National Magazine Awards Gold Medal for Travel Writing, the recipient of the Western Magazine Award for Travel Writing, and a runner-up for the Journey Prize for fiction. This reflects her writing ability in both fiction and non-fiction genres. Wearing, who lives near Peterborough, Ontario, is probably most widely known for her book *Honeymoon in Purdah*, her story of travelling for a year through Iran. In addition to this book, however, Wearing has had travel stories published in a range of national newspapers and journals, and her work has been broadcast on CBC Radio.

Preparing to Read

Before reading Wearing's poignant narrative about a visit she makes to Montreal, think about growing old. When does someone become old? What distinguishes an old person from a middle-aged person? Why do people often resist growing old? How do they resist aging?

The airport limo arrives. My eight-month-old baby is bundled up in a fleecy suit with ears that make him look like a little bear. I don't normally go in for this kind of cutesy stuff, but the outfit was a gift and, despite myself, I quite like it. In addition to Noah, I am carrying only one small backpack containing three essential items: my wallet, the airline tickets, a diaper. All other bags are in the car, which J (Noah's father) is driving to the same destination to which Noah and I are about to fly. The reasons for these travel arrangements are too tedious to get into right now. Main thing is: the bags are in the car. J leaves about twenty minutes before I do and jokes that he'll probably get to Montreal first.

Then the limo arrives. As I was saying.

Now, I'm not sure who coined the phrase "airport limo," but whoever it was didn't live in Toronto. What we climb into is just a regular old, beat-up cab that happens to go to the airport, this one with such a foul smell that I begin to wonder if the cabbie has a wet dog riding up front with him. I even lean forward and peek down at the floor—don't see anything. We get to the airport. I hoist Noah onto my hip (where he spends most of his life), fling my ultralight pack onto my shoulder, and go to check in. Then I look around quizzically, because that cabbie's wet dog seems to have followed us into the airport. Or ... no.

I lift Noah's butt up to my nose. Head for the nearest   4 washroom. I realize I'm in trouble the moment I sit him on the counter between the sinks. The mess has soaked right through his cute little bear suit.

Wads and wads of paper towel later, I have most of it off his   5 body, though he has so many little rolls and creases in his thighs that it's difficult to be sure. Also, since my left hand is busy keeping him from sliding into the sink or onto the floor, and my right hand is trying to work the water and reach for more paper towels, I'm incapable of doing a thorough job. The worst part is the little jumpsuit, which has the stuff oozing out of the back, the front, the legs, even—inexplicably—up near the neck. I can't wet it, as it's freezing outside and this is the only thing the sweet babe has to wear. I decide just to wipe it out with dry paper towel and live with the results. Somewhere in the middle of this exercise a woman comes out of one of the stalls and says, as she is washing her hands, "You should always travel with an extra set of little clothes." Then, with emphasis, "... for *Exactly This Reason*."

Only because I am otherwise occupied do I refrain from   6 saying, "I'm So Glad you're not my mother."

With the reeking outfit back on again, and a layer of paper   7 towels between us, I hoist a smiling Noah onto my hip and we catch our plane. We land in Montreal just after six. Noah and I have dinner plans for seven. We take a cab first to the hotel, in the distant hope that J will have arrived before us and will be able to provide for a change of wardrobe. No such luck. I do a bit more cursory wiping of the shitsuit and hail another cab. Step out in front of that exquisite house and ring the bell.

"Hi Alison, come in, come in."   8

He has aged so much in a single year. He now radiates the   9 lightness that comes with age, when the eyes have stopped focusing on dailiness and detail; when, even as they are looking at you, they are looking into distance. There is a sadness in this light, but also a serenity. He knows I notice. Looks apologetic. Or slightly embarrassed.

I take this moment to introduce Noah, who shows off his   10 two bottom teeth and clings to me, giggling. "I'm going to have to ask you to hold him while I take off my coat," I start, "but be careful because he's had a bit of an accident." I hand the little poo-bear over and watch how easily he is taken into this old man's arms. "Don't worry about accidents," he says, "they're part of life." We move to the kitchen and sit on stools at the counter. Noah cranes his head to see who is holding him, then reaches up and sticks his finger in the man's nose.

We laugh together, all of us.   11

He moves so slowly, it is painful to watch. A minute to cross   12
the kitchen. Several frustrating, fruitless minutes to open a package: the frozen dinners we're eating tonight. He is full of apologies. Hopes I don't mind. "It's not caviar," he says, putting the plastic trays in the microwave, "but they're not bad."

We pick at each other's lasagna and Chinese food—both   13
think the other's tastes better—and talk of Mexican villages, the startling irrelevance of book reviews, canoe routes in Temagami, babies, the reason his hands are shaking.

"I should probably tell you, I have Parkinson's ... You don't   14
die from it, but it makes you look like an old man, even if you don't feel like one."

He takes another trembling bite.   15

"I don't care what you look like, you're not an old man to   16
me."

He stops, puts his fork down, we look into each other's sad   17
eyes, and smile.

Noah paws at my shirt.   18

"If you don't mind," I say, "I'm just going to nurse him right   19
here."

"I don't mind, as long as you don't mind if I watch."   20

"Not at all," I laugh and cradle Noah in my lap. When I look   21
up, across the table, the old man is staring so tenderly, as though he were witnessing a miracle. Eyes full of tears.

After dinner, we move into the living room—the room with   22
thirty-foot ceilings and an emptiness that is impossible to fill. There is a portrait of his youngest son resting against the wall, waiting to be hung. My eyes are drawn to it, again and again. It is haunting, the way the young man's spirit swims in these slicks of coloured oils. We don't say a word about it, or him, though we stand at the window and watch the snowstorm together, and it amounts to the same thing.

When it is time to leave, Noah cries while I put my coat on.   23

"He wants his mother," the man says, shifting the baby   24
around in his arms. "He's got good taste."

We wait for the taxi by the front door and talk about the   25
Schubert Lieder I once sang at the (out of tune) piano here. Words
that, when sung, rise to the heavens:

Ruhn in Frieden, alle Seelen	Rest in peace, all souls
Die vollbracht ein banges Quälen,	Who have had done with anxious torment,
Die vollendet süssen Traum,	Who have had done with sweet dreams,
Lebenssatt, geboren kaum,	Who, sated with life and hardly born,
Aus der Welt hinüberschieden	Have departed from this world:
All Seelen ruhn in Frieden.	All souls, rest in peace.

Smiles. A touch of hands. A long, deep hug. We say nothing   26
of "next time" or "soon." We say nothing.

Outside, a few steps from the road, Noah folded up under my   27
coat, I turn to wave. I stand, instead, in the falling snow, and
watch his door, gently, close.

UNDERSTANDING DETAILS

1. Where is Wearing travelling and how? Why does she question
   the term "airport limo"?
2. What is the source of the "wet dog" smell in the cab?
3. Describe Wearing's reaction to the man she goes to visit.

ANALYZING MEANING

1. Who is the old man Wearing visits in Montreal? Why has she
   gone to visit him?
2. Reread the final paragraph of the essay. Instead of waving, why
   does Wearing "stand, instead, in the falling snow and watch
   his door, gently, close"?
3. Much of the communication between Wearing and the old man
   is non-verbal. What unspoken messages are being conveyed?
   How are those messages transmitted?

DISCOVERING RHETORICAL STRATEGIES

1. Although she is writing a narrative piece, Wearing incorporates many descriptive details into her story. Find at least four

examples of particularly vivid descriptive phrases that help
Wearing's narrative come to life.
2. How would you describe the pacing of Wearing's narrative?
How has she achieved this effect?
3. Narrative is made effective through the careful selection of
detail. Why has Wearing incorporated the detail about the music
she sang in the past?

MAKING CONNECTIONS

1. Much of the communication in Wearing's narrative is non-
verbal. What role does non-verbal communication play in
stories such as that of Steven Heighton's visit to Vimy Ridge
("Elegy in Stone")?
2. Wearing is best known as a travel writer. Dave Bidini ("Kris
King Looks Terrible") writes about his trip to Hong Kong, Karen
Connelly ("Touch the Dragon") relates her experience arriving
in Thailand, and Anita Rau Badami ("My Canada") writes about
her trip from India to Canada. Are there similarities in the writing styles of these four authors as they relate the stories of their
visits to their respective destinations?

IDEAS FOR DISCUSSION/WRITING

Preparing to Write

Write freely about non-verbal communication. How do people
communicate without using words? What techniques do
people have for conveying ideas without using words? Why
do people often use looks or touch to communicate emotions
rather than voicing those feelings? What percentage of a message
is typically communicated through non-verbal rather than verbal
means?

Choosing a Topic

1. Write an essay in which you convey the potential confusion
created by non-verbal communication by relating a specific personal story of a misunderstanding. Make sure that you select
and organize your details effectively to serve your purpose
clearly.
2. Recall a time when you faced a significant new experience.
Write a narrative essay in which you recreate the events and

your feelings about them for your audience. Be sure to *show* your audience the events and feelings rather than telling about them.

3. Write a narrative essay in which you relate an interaction between two people in which no words were exchanged. Show your readers clearly what message or messages were conveyed and how.

WEBSITES

www.globebooks.com/interviews/alisonwearing.html
A *Globe and Mail* interview with Alison Wearing.

www.colage.org/kids/newsletter.html#tales
"Tales from a Multifunctional Family" by Alison Wearing.

CHAPTER 3

EXAMPLE

Illustrating Ideas

Citing an example to help make a point is one of the most instinctive techniques we use in communication. If, for instance, you state that being an internationally ranked tennis player requires constant practice, a friend might challenge that assertion and ask what you mean by "constant practice." When you respond "about three hours a day," your friend might ask for more specific proof. At this stage in the discussion, you could offer the following illustrations to support your statement: When not on tour, Venus Williams practises three hours per day; Pete Sampras, four hours; and Martina Hingis, five hours. Your friend's doubt will have been answered through your use of examples.

Defining Examples

Well-chosen examples and illustrations are an essay's building blocks. They are drawn from your experience, your observations, and your reading. They help you show rather than tell what you mean, usually by supplying concrete details (references to what we can see, smell, taste, hear, or touch) to support abstract ideas (such as faith, hope, understanding, and love), by providing specifics ("I like chocolate") to explain generalizations ("I like sweets"), and by giving definite references ("Turn left at the second stoplight") to clarify vague statements ("Turn in a few blocks"). Though illustrations take many forms, writers often find themselves indebted to description or narration (or some combination of the two) in order to supply enough relevant examples to achieve their rhetorical intent.

As you might suspect, examples are important ingredients in producing exciting, vivid prose. Just as crucial is the fact that carefully chosen examples often encourage your readers to feel one way or another about an issue being discussed. If you tell your parents, for instance, that living in a college residence is not conducive to academic success, they may doubt your word, perhaps thinking that you are simply attempting to coerce money out of them for an apartment. You can help dispel this notion, however, by giving them specific examples of the chaotic nature of residence life: the party down the hall that broke up at 2 a.m. when you had a chemistry exam that same morning at 8 o'clock; the stereo next door that seems to be stuck on its highest decibel level at all hours of the day and night; and the new "friend" you recently acquired who thinks you are the best listener in the world—especially when everyone else has the good sense to be asleep. After such a detailed and well-documented explanation, your parents could hardly deny the strain of this difficult environment on your studies. Examples can be very persuasive.

The following paragraphs, written by a student, use examples to explain how he reacts to boredom in his life. As you read this excerpt, notice how the writer shows rather than tells the readers how he copes with boredom by providing exciting details that are concrete, specific, and definite:

> We all deal with boredom in our own ways. Unfortunately, most of us have to deal with it far too often. Some people actually seek boredom. Being bored means that they are not required to do anything; being boring means that no one wants anything from them. In short, these people equate boredom with peace and relaxation. But for the rest of us, boredom is not peaceful. It produces anxiety.
>
> Most people deal with boredom by trying to distract themselves from boring circumstances. Myself, I'm a reader. At the breakfast table over a boring bowl of cereal, I read the cereal box, the milk carton, the wrapper on the bread. (Have you ever noticed how many of those ingredients are unpronounceable?) Waiting in a doctor's office, I will gladly read weekly news magazines of three years ago, a book for five-year-olds, advertisements for drugs, and even the physician's odd-looking diplomas on the walls. Have you ever been so bored you were reduced to reading through all the business cards

Example   127

in your wallet? Searching for names similar to yours in the phone book? Browsing through the *National Enquirer* while waiting in the grocery line? At any rate, that's my recipe for beating boredom. What's yours?

Thinking Critically by Using Examples

Working with examples gives you yet another powerful way of processing your immediate environment and the larger world around you. It involves a manner of thinking that is completely different from description and narration. Using examples to think critically means seeing a definite order in a series of specific, concrete illustrations that are related in some way that may or may not be immediately obvious to your readers.

Isolating this rhetorical mode involves playing with related details in such a way that they create various patterns that relay different messages to the reader. Often, the simple act of arranging examples helps both the reader and the writer make sense of an experience or idea. In fact, ordering examples and illustrations in a certain way may give one distinct impression, while ordering them in another way may send a completely different message. Each pattern creates a different meaning and, as a result, an entirely new effect.

With examples, more than with description and narration, patterns need to be discovered in the context of the topic, the writer's purpose, and the writer's ultimate message. Writers and readers of example essays must make a shift from chronological to logical thinking. A writer discussing variations in faces, for example, would be working with assorted memories of people, incidents, and age differences. All of these details will eventually take shape in some sort of statement about faces, but these observations would probably not follow a strictly chronological sequence.

The exercises here will help you experience the mental differences among these rhetorical modes and will also prepare you to make sense of details and examples through careful arrangement and rearrangement of them in your essay. These exercises will continue to give you more information about your mind's abilities and range.

1. For each sentence below, provide two to three examples that would illustrate the generalization:

   a. I really liked (disliked) some of the movies released this year.

   b. Many career opportunities await a college graduate.

   c. Some companies make large sums of money by selling products with the names of professional sports teams on them.

2. Give an example (as specific as possible) of each item listed here: car, pizza, song, musician, event, friend, emotion, vacation, plant.

3. Jot down five examples of a single problem at your school that bothers you. First, arrange these examples in an order that would convince the president of your school that making some changes in this area would create a more positive learning environment. Second, organize your five examples in such a way that they would convince your parents that the learning environment at your current school cannot be salvaged and you should immediately transfer to another school.

Reading and Writing Essays That Use Examples

A common criticism of college- and university-level writers is that they often base their essays on unsupported generalizations, such as "All sports cars are unreliable." The guidelines discussed in this introduction will help you avoid this problem and use examples effectively to support your ideas.

As you read the essays in this chapter, take time to notice the degree of specificity the writers use to make various points. To a certain extent, the more examples you use in your essays, the clearer your ideas will be and the more your readers will understand and be interested in what you are saying.

Notice also that these writers know when to stop—when "more" becomes too much and boredom sets in for the reader. Most students err by using too few examples, however, so we suggest that, when in doubt about whether or not to include another illustration, you should go ahead and add one.

Example   129

How to Read an Essay That Uses Examples

Preparing to Read. Before you begin reading the essays in this chapter, take some time to think about each author's title: What can you infer about Anita Rau Badami's attitude toward her subject from her title "My Canada"? What do you think is Cecil Foster's view of blacks in Canadian society? In addition, try to discover the writer's audience and purpose at this point in the reading process. Scanning the essay and surveying its synopsis in the Rhetorical Table of Contents will provide you with useful information for this task.

Also important as you prepare to read is information about the author and about how a particular essay was written. Most of this material is furnished for you in the biography preceding each essay. From it, you might learn why Barbara Kingsolver is qualified to write about fashion or why Sharon Butala wrote "The Myth: The Prairies Are Flat."

Finally, before you begin to read, take time to answer the Preparing to Read questions and to make some associations with the general subject of the essay: What are some of your opinions on racism in Canada (Foster)? How familiar are you with the Canadian Prairies (Butala)?

Reading. As you first read these essays, record any thoughts that come to mind. Make associations freely with the content of each essay, its purpose, its audience, and the facts about its publication. For example, try to determine why Cecil Foster writes about black discontent in Canadian society or why Barbara Kingsolver titles her essay "Life Without Go-Go Boots." At this point, you will probably be able to make some pretty accurate guesses about the audience each author is addressing. Creating a context for your reading—including the writer's qualifications; the essay's tone, purpose, and audience; and the publication information—is an important first step toward being able to analyze your reading material in any mode.

Finally, after you have read an essay in this section once, preview the questions after the selection before you read it again. Let these questions focus your attention for your second reading.

Rereading. As you read the essays in this chapter for a second time, focus on the examples each writer uses to make his or her point: How relevant are these examples to the thesis and purpose of each essay? How many examples do the writers use? Do they vary the length of these examples to achieve different goals? Do the authors use examples their readers can easily identify with and understand? How are these examples organized in each case? Does this arrangement support each writer's purpose? For example, how relevant are Anita Rau Badami's examples of people she met in Canada to her central idea? How many examples does Barbara Kingsolver use to make each point? Does Cecil Foster vary the length of each of his examples to accomplish different purposes? How does Sharon Butala organize her examples? Does this arrangement help her accomplish her purpose? In what way? Does Cecil Foster use examples that blacks, as well as people of other races, can identify with? How effective are his examples? How effective are Butala's examples?

As you read, consider also how other rhetorical modes help each writer accomplish his or her purpose. What are these modes? How do they work along with examples to help create a coherent essay?

Last, answering the questions after each essay will help you check your grasp of its main points and will lead you from the literal to the analytical level in preparation for the discussion/ writing assignments that follow.

For a thorough summary of reading tasks, you might want to consult the checklists on pages 17–18 of the Introduction.

How to Write an Essay That Uses Examples

Preparing to Write. Before you can use examples in an essay, you must first think of some. One good way to generate ideas is to use some of the prewriting techniques explained in the Introduction (pages 19–25) as you respond to the Preparing to Write questions that appear before the writing assignments for each essay. You should then consider these thoughts in conjunction with the purpose and the audience specified in your chosen writing assignments. Out of these questions should come a number of good examples for your essay.

Writing. In an example essay, a thesis statement or controlling idea will help you begin to organize your paper. (See pages 24–25 for more information on thesis statements.) Examples become the primary method of organizing an essay when they guide the readers from point to point in reference to the writer's

Example 131

thesis statement. The examples you use should always be relevant to the thesis and purpose of your essay. If, for instance, the person talking about tennis players cited the practice schedules of only unknown players, her friend certainly would not be convinced of the truth of her statement about how hard internationally ranked athletes work at their game. To develop a topic principally with examples, you can use one extended example or several shorter examples, depending on the nature and purpose of your assertion. If you are attempting to prove that Canadians are more health conscious now than they were 20 years ago, citing a few examples from your own neighbourhood will not provide enough evidence to be convincing. If, however, you are simply commenting on a neighbourhood health trend, you can legitimately refer to these local cases. Furthermore, always try to find examples with which your audience can identify so that they can follow your line of reasoning. If you want your parents to help finance an apartment, citing instances from the lives of current rock stars will probably not prove your point, because your parents may not sympathize with these particular role models.

The examples you choose must also be arranged as effectively as possible to encourage audience interest and identification. If you are using examples to explain the imaginative quality of Canada's Wonderland, for instance, the most logical approach would probably be to organize your essay by degrees (i.e., from least to most imaginative or most to least original). But if your essay uses examples to help readers visualize your bedroom, a spatial arrangement of the details (moving from one item to the next) might be easiest for your readers to follow. If the subject is a series of important events, like graduation weekend, the illustrations might most effectively be organized chronologically. As you will learn from reading the selections that follow, the careful organization of examples leads quite easily to unity and coherence in your essays. *Unity* is a sense of wholeness and interrelatedness that writers achieve by making sure all their sentences are related to the essay's main idea; *coherence* refers to logical development in an essay, with special attention to how well ideas grow out of one another as the essay develops. Unity and coherence produce good writing—and that, of course, helps foster confidence and accomplishment in school and in your professional life.

Rewriting. As you reread your example essays, look closely at the choice and arrangement of details in relation to your purpose and audience:

- Have you included enough examples to develop each of your topics adequately?
- Are the examples you have chosen relevant to your thesis?
- Have you selected examples that your readers can easily understand?
- Have you arranged these examples in a logical manner that your audience can follow?

For more detailed information on writing, see the checklists on pages 29–30 of the Introduction.

Student Essay: Examples at Work

In the following essay, a student uses examples to explain and analyze her parents' behaviour as they prepare for and enjoy their grandchildren during the Christmas holidays. As you read it, study the various examples the student writer uses to convince us that her parents truly undergo a transformation each winter.

Mom and Dad's Holiday Disappearing Act

General topic — Often during the winter holidays, people find surprises: Children discover the secret contents of brightly wrapped packages that have teased them for weeks; cooks are astonished by the wealth of smells and memories their busy kitchens can bring about; workaholics stumble upon the true joy of a few days' rest. — Details to capture holiday spirit

Background information — My surprise over the past few winters has been the personality transformation my parents go through around mid-December as they change from Dad and Mom into Poppa and Granny. Yes, they become grandparents and are completely different from the people I know the other eleven and a half months of the year. — Thesis statement

The first sign of my parents' metamorphosis is the delight they take in visiting toy and children's clothing stores. — First point

Examples relevant to thesis — These two people, who usually despise anything having to do with shopping malls, become crazed consumers. While they tell me to budget my money and shop wisely, they are buying every doll, dump truck, and velvet outfit in sight. And this is only the beginning of the holidays!

Example   133

Transition   When my brother's children arrive, Poppa and Granny come into full form. First they throw out all ideas about a balanced diet for the grandkids. While we were raised in a house where every-   Second point
one had to take two bites of broccoli, beets, or liver (foods that appeared quite often on our table despite constant groaning), the grandchildren never have to eat anything that does not appeal to them. Granny carries marshmallows in her pockets to bribe the   Humorous examples (organized from most to least healthy)
littlest ones into following her around the house, while Poppa offers "surprises" of candy and cake to them all day long. Boxes of chocolate-covered cherries disappear while the bran muffins get hard and stale. The kids love all the sweets, and when the sugar revs up their energy levels, Granny and Poppa can always decide to leave and do a bit more shopping or go to bed while my brother and sister-in-law try to deal with their supercharged, hyperactive kids.

Transition   Once the grandchildren have arrived, Granny and Poppa also seem to forget all of the responsibility lectures I so often hear in my   Third point
daily life. If little Tommy throws a fit at a friend's house, he is "overwhelmed by the number of adults"; if Mickey screams at his sister during dinner, he is "developing his own personality"; if Nancy breaks Granny's vanity mirror (after being told twice to   Examples in the form of comparisons
put it down), she is "just a curious child." But, if I track mud into the house while helping to unload groceries, I become "careless"; if I scold one of the grandkids for tearing pages out of my calculus book, I am "impatient." If a grandchild talks back to her mother, Granny and Poppa chuckle at her spirit. If I mumble one word about all of this doting, Mom and Dad reappear to have a talk with me about petty jealousies.

When my nieces and nephews first started appearing at our   Transition to conclusion
home for the holidays a few years ago, I probably was jealous, and I complained a lot. But now I spend more time simply sitting back and watching Mom and Dad change into what we call the
Writer's   "Incredible Huggers." They enjoy their time with these grand-
attitude   children so much that I easily forgive them their Granny and Poppa faults.

I believe their personality change is due to the lack of respon-   Writer's
sibility they feel for the grandkids: In their role as grandparents,   analysis of situation
they don't have to worry about sugar causing cavities or temporary failures of self-discipline turning into lifetime faults. Those problems are up to my brother and sister-in-law. All Granny and Poppa have to do is enjoy and love their grandchildren. They have all

the fun of being parents without any of the attendant obligations.

Concluding remark And you know what? <u>I think they've earned the right to make</u> <u>this transformation—at least once a year.</u> Specific reference to introduction

Some Final Thoughts on Examples

Although examples are often used to supplement and support other methods of development—such as cause/effect, comparison/contrast, and process analysis—the essays in this section are focused principally on examples. A main idea is expressed in the introduction of each, and the rest of the essay provides examples to bolster that contention. As you read these essays, pay close attention to each author's choice and arrangement of examples; then, try to determine which organizational techniques are most persuasive for each specific audience.

Example in Review

Reading Example Essays

Preparing to Read

- What assumptions can you make from the essay's title?
- Can you guess what the general mood of the essay is?
- What is the essay's purpose and audience?
- What does the synopsis in the Rhetorical Table of Contents tell you about the essay?
- What can you learn from the author's biography?
- Can you guess what the author's point of view toward the subject is?
- What are your responses to the Preparing to Read questions?

Reading

- What general message is the author trying to convey?
- Did you preview the questions that follow the essay?

Example 135

Rereading

- What examples help the author communicate the essay's general message?
- How are these examples organized?
- What other rhetorical modes does the author use to support the essay's purpose?
- What are your responses to the questions after the essay?

Writing Example Essays

Preparing to Write

- What are your responses to the Preparing to Write questions?
- What is your purpose?
- Who is your audience?
- What is the message you want to convey?

Writing

- What is your thesis or controlling idea?
- Do the examples you are choosing support this thesis?
- Are these examples arranged as effectively as possible?
- What is your point of view toward your subject?
- How do you achieve unity and coherence in your example essay?

Rewriting

- Have you included enough examples to develop each of your topics adequately?
- Are the examples you have chosen relevant to your thesis?
- Have you arranged these examples in a logical manner that your audience can follow?

ANITA RAU BADAMI

My Canada

Born in eastern India, Anita Rau Badami (1961–) was raised and educated in India, where she began her writing career as a journalist. After
coming to Canada with her husband and son in 1991, Badami registered
for a creative writing course at the University of Calgary and, subse-
quently, a master's degree in English literature. From this base, Badami has
became a successful fiction writer in Canada with the publication of several short stories and two novels: *Tamarind Mem* (1996) and *The Hero's
Walk* (2000), which won the 2001 Regional Commonwealth Best Book
Prize. Badami is now a resident of Montreal. Her forthcoming novel, *Can
You Hear the Nightbird Call?*, is scheduled for publication in 2003.

Preparing to Read

In this essay, originally published in the *Imperial Oil Review*, Badami reflects
on her attempts to define Canada and the process of coming to view
Canada as her home. Think about the idea of home. Where do you consider "home"? Has your home changed at any point in your life? Do you
expect that the place that is home for you now will always be home?
What distinguishes a place where one lives from a place that one calls
home?

Early one morning in June last year, my family and I travelled   1
from Vancouver to Tofino, a small town on the western coast
of Vancouver Island. We had come in search of whales, particularly
the magnificent orca. If we were lucky, we might even get to see a
whole pod of them.

When I was growing up in India, nothing had seemed more   2
remote and exotic to me than these great mammals. I had seen
pictures of them in geography texts and wildlife magazines, but
the depictions were extremely unsatisfactory. The creatures were
generally obscured by water or captured as a dim submarine
shape by an underwater camera—sometimes there was merely a
spout of water shooting upwards from a brief arc of grey that
might well have been the shoulder of a wave. By the time I left
India for Canada, the orca had assumed mythical proportions,

and a huge desire had ballooned in me to see this whale in its natural habitat.

The trip to Tofino had been inspired by an advertisement 3 for whale-watching tours in a Vancouver paper. "Let's go this weekend," I had said to my husband and son. After several telephone calls to book a room in a hotel, we were on our way.

It was a grey morning when we left to catch the ferry to 4 Victoria. But nothing could keep my hopes down; we were going to see those whales no matter what. The intensity of my longing, I was convinced, would keep the rain away from Tofino. The crossing to Victoria was rough and cold, and by the time we had driven across the island and reached the small coastal town, we could barely see the way through the rain to our hotel. I had encountered rain like this only in India during the monsoons and had come to expect nothing more in this country than the gentle drizzle that was so characteristic of Vancouver. This wild downpour, accompanied by the roar of thunder and the crackle of lightning, was a glimpse of a Canada that I had never seen before—the country had been doing a slow dance for me over the nine years that I had lived here, showing me tantalizing little bits of itself every now and then.

That first day, we were trapped inside our hotel room with 5 nothing to do but gaze at the Pacific Ocean, which was hurling itself furiously at the beach. But the next morning, to our delight, was bright and sunny, and we rushed down to the jetty where the whale-watching tours began. "Too rough to go out in the open sea," said the tour operator regretfully. "I can take you on calmer waters between islands." A lone orca had been spotted grazing in those channels, and if we were lucky, we might catch a glimpse of it. We drifted in and out of dark green fingers of water whose otherwise still surface was now pocked by the rain that had started again. We saw a black bear at the edge of a stand of pines on a tiny island, an eagle gliding on currents of air against the grey sky, otters and stellar seals, but not a single whale. We started our journey home disappointed but determined to come back the next year.

And then it happened. On the ferry from Victoria, a cry went 6 up from the crowd of people strolling the decks. There, cleaving the steely, restless ocean, was a large pod of orca whales—bulls, cows, calves—rolling and diving, sending up plumes of water. I had hoped to see *one* of these creatures, and here I was being treated to a whole family when I least expected it.

Looking for the Canada that has gently seeped into my   7
bloodstream is like looking for those whales. I find her at
unexpected moments: in the sudden kindness of a stranger's
smile; in the graceful flight of a hundred snow geese; or in the
cascading, iridescent shimmer of the aurora borealis lighting up
the midnight sky. Several years ago, a friend asked me what I
thought of this land of vast, empty spaces, of mountains and
trees and snow and water, where almost every person claims
ancestry in another culture, another land, and where a hundred
different histories mingle to create a new set of memories. I had
said that Canada reminded me of a beautiful, enigmatic woman
who looks down demurely most of the time, but then surprises
the watcher with a sudden glance from a pair of mischievous
eyes. A shy coquette, I said, pleased at having found the words
to describe a country with which I was just beginning a
relationship.

In those early stages, I tried to define Canada in terms of   8
other places, as a series of negatives: not as colourful and noisy
as India, not as old as China, not as brash and individualistic as
the United States. I would read all the Canadian newspapers
and magazines and watch all the Canadian television shows I
could (including curling tournaments, even though I am not a
sports enthusiast and couldn't see the point of a game that
involved a teapotlike object and a broom). I travelled as much
as possible into the mountains; breathed the moist air of ancient
forests that held secrets of an unknowable past; wandered over
the weird, moonlike surface of the Badlands at Drumheller, Alta.,
marvelling at the skeletal remains of dinosaurs that had roamed
there aeons ago; tried skiing and ice-skating and rock climbing,
ending up with little more than sore muscles. The more I looked,
the less I seemed to see Canada. Until that afternoon on the deck
of the ferry, when, as I watched the whales floating in the ocean,
it came to me: there was no point in trying to find one fixed
image of this land. It would always be an accumulation of events
and experiences, smells, sights and sounds. I was, after all, seeing
it through so many different lenses: a writer's, a woman's, an
immigrant's, a lover's, a mother's. It was at that moment that I
began to think of Canada without reference to any other country,
to love it on its own terms for what it was, rather than what it
wasn't.

We came to Canada from India a little more than nine years ago.   9
My husband had woken up one morning and decided that he
wanted to reinvent himself. He was tired of his engineering
degree and his job in a vast, faceless corporation. Our relatives
were alarmed by this sudden decision. They couldn't understand
why we wanted to leave good jobs (I was a newspaper journalist)
and comfortable lives for an uncertain future. And why Canada
of all places, they wanted to know. Wasn't that somewhere near
the North Pole? Horribly cold? With bears and wild animals that
mauled people to death?

By September 1990, my husband had arrived in Canada and   10
was taking a master's degree in environmental studies at the
University of Calgary. By March of the next year, I had cleaned
out our flat in the bustling metropolitan city of Bangalore, sold all
our furniture and packed most of our other belongings in boxes
and trunks to store in my parents-in-law's home. No point taking
everything with us—we would be back in a few years, I told
myself and everybody else, resenting this move and quite certain
that I would never want to live in a country that I knew basically
as a vague band of land between the United States of America
and the North Pole. At school we had learned a huge amount
about Britain and Europe, and at university, American literature
was one of the areas I had opted to study in addition to the
standard menu of Shakespeare, the Renaissance poets, Victorian
fiction and Indo-Anglian writing (works written in English by
Indians). But I had studied almost nothing about Canada and
had certainly never heard of Canlit.

I had once seen a picture in a geography book of a vast, flat   11
prairie with a grain elevator rising from its heart. Another time,
in an ancient issue of *Reader's Digest*, I had read about a forest
fire in the Rockies. The article was accompanied by a lurid picture
of dark stands of pines licked by flames against a red, yellow
and orange sky. These, and the photographs of the aurora borealis
and of a grizzly bear, were the sum of my experience of Canada,
a country that had hitherto existed only in the outer edges of my
imagination—until I found myself in the Calgary airport in March
1991, dressed in nothing warmer than a mohair sweater and a
pair of canvas sneakers. My husband, who had already lived in
the city for six months and had survived an extremely frigid
winter, had buoyantly assured me that spring had come to
Calgary. It was deliciously warm, there was joy in the air, all the
trees were in bud, and I would love it. My four-year-old son and

I emerged from the nearly empty airport to be hit by a blast of freezing air. I could see nothing for a few moments as my eyes and nose had started to water with the cold. My lungs had panicked and seized up. I was wheezing like an old pair of bellows. It was –15 Celsius, and we had just arrived from a city where the temperature had been hovering at 47 Celsius in the shade. In the week that followed, the desire to go back from whence I'd come became ever stronger. I missed the noise, the bustle of people, the smells and the circuslike atmosphere of Indian streets. What was I doing in this barren city where the sky covered everything like blue glass, where I could hear my own footsteps echoing on an empty street, and where I was frequently the only passenger on a bus? I wanted to go home.

Two months later, the lilacs were in bloom, filling the air   12
with their scent. There were daffodils thrusting up from the earth, followed by tulips and irises and hundreds of other flowers. The trees had burst into bloom, and I was looking at a different world. I had spent all my life in a country where the seasons merge into one another. This drama of death and regeneration was something I had never witnessed. I was instantly captivated. I would stay another year, I told myself, if for nothing other than to see the seasons change. Four years slipped by, and I was still in Canada. By now I had worked in a variety of places, including a china store, a book shop and a library. A few months after I'd arrived, I had signed up for a creative writing course at the University of Calgary and then began a master's degree in English literature. I'd had several stories published, and I'd begun to love the crisp winter mornings, the sudden excitement of a chinook, which seems to melt the snow in minutes and peel veils of cloud away from the distant snowcapped mountains. Now, every time I stepped out of my house, I bumped into a friend or someone I knew. It was a wonderful feeling to know so many people in the city. All my fears about leaving my writing career in India, about forgetting how to write, seemed ridiculous. I had also found my métier in fiction writing and had finished the first draft of a novel.

In 1995, my first novel was accepted for publication, and we   13
moved to Vancouver. Once again I was filled with that wretched feeling of being torn from all that was familiar and beloved, of leaving home, except this time, home was Calgary, and what I yearned for was long silent streets and canola fields shimmering yellow under an endless blue sky.

In the years since I arrived here I have travelled the length and   14
breadth of this land and collected many different images of it.
Now if somebody asks me what I think or feel about Canada, I tell
of all the people and places, sights and events that have woven
a pattern in my heart. I tell stories about Shinya and Mayo, who
had come here from Japan and shared with us a passion for spicy
eggplant curry and Charlie Chaplin. And Carole, who arrived
like a Santa in the middle of our first spring with a bag full of
toys for our son, just, she explained cheerfully, to make him feel
at home. I talk about Serena and Mike, our neighbours, with
whom we watched dozens of late-night movies after shared
dinners and delicious fruit flans created by Mike. Or about Grant,
who took us on a trip to Waterton Lakes National Park in
southwestern Alberta, rowed us out to the middle of one of the
many lakes and handed the paddles to my husband and me. "If
you want to be Canadian," he declared, grinning, "you will have
to learn to row a boat." And who, after watching us quarrel for
20 minutes, during which time we managed to describe tighter
and tighter circles in the centre of the lake, decided that there
were safer ways of becoming Canadian.

There were all those evenings with Suni and Ravi and   15
Mayura and Ratna, celebrating Indian festivals just as winter
was beginning to take hold, nudging away those last warm fall
days, and the many times that they took care of me while I tried
to juggle work and school and home.

My Canada, I tell anyone who asks, is the driver who made   16
sure that I was on the last bus out of Calgary's North Hill Centre
when I was working the late shift there, even if it meant delaying
the bus an extra 10 minutes. And the members of my creative
writing group, who gave me their undiluted comments and
prepared me for a career as a novelist. "When your first book is
out there being trashed by the reviewers," they told me, "you'll
thank us for your thick skin." My Canada includes all those
people who made me feel like I belonged.

To my album of memories I will add an enchanted night   17
spent lying on a sloping field in Calgary with a group of friends
to watch a meteor shower streaking silver lines across the
midnight sky. I will tell all who ask about the time I stood on
Alberta's Athabasca Glacier surrounded by mountains eternally
capped by snow, and drank crystalline water from a deep spring
so ancient that time itself had no measure for it; of the moon full
and golden, floating up over the mountains surrounding Lake

Louise, and a lynx's eyes flaring green at us before the creature
snarled and vanished into the darkness; of the flood of people
on Main Street, Vancouver, celebrating the Sikh festival Baisakhi;
of Chinatown, where a beautiful woman in a small, dark shop
sold me exquisite paper and a stamp with a character that, she
told me, meant "good luck"; of writers' festivals all over the
country, where a medley of voices from many cultures was heard;
and of a café in a remote Yukon town where I met a man who
believed that he was the reincarnation of Elvis Presley.

I visited India recently, the second time that I had gone back   18
since 1991. When it was time to leave, I realized with a small jolt
that I felt none of the regret that I had experienced on the
previous trip. The needle of my emotional compass had swung
around and set itself in a different direction. While I still cherished
the brilliant colours of India, I was also beginning to recognize
and appreciate the subtle tints and textures of the Canadian
fabric. And I knew that even though a part of me would always
look with love towards the land of my birth, and deep inside I
would for ever straddle two continents, two realities (the East
and the West), my home was now here, in Canada.

UNDERSTANDING DETAILS

1. Where did Badami grow up? When and why did she come to
   Canada?
2. Why do Badami and her family travel to Tofino? Are their
   expectations met?
3. Where is Badami's home?

ANALYZING MEANING

1. Chart the shift in Badami's attitude toward Canada over time.
   What are the significant turning points in her perspective?
2. Badami tells the reader about her expectations in coming to
   Canada and then about the reality of what she found here. How
   does the reality compare to Badami's expectations?
3. What is the main point Badami is making in her essay? What
   examples serve to illustrate this thesis particularly effectively?

DISCOVERING RHETORICAL STRATEGIES

1. Although the author's dominant rhetorical method is the use of example, what other strategies has Badami used to organize her information? Give examples of these strategies.
2. Where in this essay do you find Badami's purpose most clearly stated? How does the organization of the major examples in this essay demonstrate the author's thesis statement?
3. Badami uses figurative language frequently in "My Canada." Identify at least three examples of her use of figurative language. What specific techniques has she used (e.g., metaphor, personification, simile) and what is the effect of these language choices on the reader?

MAKING CONNECTIONS

1. Anita Rau Badami and Allen Abel ("A Home at the End of the Journey") both adopted Canada as their home. How are their attitudes toward Canada similar? Imagine a conversation between the two writers; on what points do you think their views of Canada would be similar? Do you expect there would be any major points of disagreement?
2. Badami uses many personal examples to illustrate the points she makes in "My Canada." How does this compare to the use of examples by Cecil Foster ("Why Blacks Get Mad") and Barbara Kingsolver ("Life Without Go-Go Boots")?

IDEAS FOR DISCUSSION/WRITING

Preparing to Write

Write freely about Canada. How long have you lived in Canada? What are your dominant impressions of Canada? How would you describe Canada to someone in another country? What qualities or characteristics make Canada unique? Has Canada changed over the time that you have lived here? If so, in what ways? For better or for worse?

Choosing a Topic

1. Following Badami's lead, write an essay entitled "My Canada" in which you use specific examples to illustrate what Canada is

to you. Make sure that your attitude toward your subject is clearly conveyed in your essay.

2. The reality of Canada that greeted Badami when she first arrived did not meet her expectations. Write an essay about a situation in which the reality you encountered was quite different from what you had expected. Use specific details to make your essay clear and effective.

3. Write about a place that you know well, using specific examples to create a clear, strong image of this place for your reader. Make sure that you define your place on its own terms rather than in comparison to another place.

WEBSITES

www.januarymagazine.com/profiles/raubadami.html
Read the *January Magazine* interview with Anita Rau Badami.

www.emory.edu/ENGLISH/Bahri/Badami.html
A biography of Badami along with an essay about her novel *Tamarind Mem*.

www.bookbrowse.com/dyn_/author/authorID/779.htm
At BookBrowse you will find a biography of Badami along with an interview and an excerpt from *Tamarind Mem*.

www.imperialoil.ca/thisis/publications/review
Badami's essay originally appeared in the *Imperial Oil Review*.

SHARON BUTALA

The Myth: The Prairies Are Flat

Sharon Butala's name is familiar to many Canadians, as it has appeared on both the fiction and non-fiction bestseller lists during her writing career. Butala (1940–) is an award-winning author who writes, as in this selection, about life on and around the Saskatchewan ranch where she has lived for over two decades.

After teaching at the University of Saskatchewan, Butala began her career as a writer when she was 38 years old. Since then she has published novels, short stories, plays, magazine and newspaper essays and articles, and works of non-fiction, including *Perfection of the Morning* (1994), which was nominated for the Governor General's Award for non-fiction, and *Wild Stone Heart* (2000).

Preparing to Read

In this essay, first published in *enRoute*, Air Canada's in-flight magazine, Sharon Butala presents an effective argument against a common perception about the region of the country in which she resides. Before you read "The Myth: The Prairies Are Flat," think about the Prairies. What provinces fall within the Prairies? What image do you have of the Prairies? Where does that image come from? Have you seen the Prairies? If so, how would you describe the terrain? Geographically, is it consistent or varied? Is the prairie landscape appealing? Why or why not?

Yesterday I relaxed as I set the car on cruise and leaned back to   1
enjoy the scenery along the 145-kilometre stretch between Rosetown and Swift Current, my favourite part of the trip from Saskatoon to my home in southwest Saskatchewan. I like the way the land rolls, rising and falling and rising again, spreading out around me for miles until it meets the far-off horizon.

There is a pleasant scarcity of people as I travel between   2
small, half-deserted villages through an expansive landscape uncluttered by forests, rushing streams, waterfalls or mountains. There's no denying that wide-openness takes getting used to, as the first settlers often reported to their less adventurous relatives

back in Europe. But contrary to popular belief, that soul-stirring spaciousness is far from being a boring stretch of flatness.

In school I learned that the word *prairie* refers to a plain—a   3
flat area—while *Prairies* is an abbreviation for the Prairie provinces, Alberta, Saskatchewan and Manitoba, which are flat. I was baffled by this because I was born and spent my earliest years among the trees, lakes and rivers in the immense northern bush country of east-central Saskatchewan, none of which is flat. And, like most everyone, I learned at school that Alberta is defined by its Rocky Mountains. I was 20 before I saw the Regina Plains, a glacial lake bed that is as flat as flat ever gets. My understandably astonished reaction was, "Oh, so this is what the teachers meant when they said the Prairies are flat."

When I met a rancher from Saskatchewan's south-west, who   4
I later married, I'd never been south of the Trans-Canada Highway other than around Regina. Since the Trans-Canada runs through the flattest land in western Canada, I remember asking my husband-to-be a little nervously before my first visit to his ranch, "Is it flat?"

Not at all. I was amazed to discover a vast, wide-open   5
country of grassy, high, rolling hills. On unbearably hot Sundays in July, we would go with most of our neighbours up to the Cypress Hills to revel in the coolness of the 1,400-metre altitude. "Didn't you know," my husband asked in surprise, "that the Cypress Hills is the highest point in Canada between the Rockies and Labrador?"

On other occasions, we went to the Great Sand Hills, an area   6
of sand dunes covering 3,400 square kilometres. But you won't find these either, unless you leave the Trans-Canada Highway. No wonder many Canadians believe that the vast area from Ontario to the Rockies, from the 49th parallel to the Arctic, is as flat as a billiard table.

Both my parents were raised on Prairie farms and since   7
agricultural equipment couldn't negotiate steep hills or fill in and level low, boggy areas back then, they spent their first 20 years on flat land. This included the horrendous Dust Bowl of the 1930s when the rest of the country was inundated with images of massive dust clouds sweeping across expanses of the flattest land where farms once flourished. And because these places were the worst afflicted, they got all the press. The fact is that forests grow over half of Manitoba and Alberta and a third of Saskatchewan, and lakes cover one-fifth of Manitoba.

Literature is also to blame. W.O. Mitchell's *Who Has Seen the* 8
Wind, published in 1947 and one of Canada's great novels, remains the most widely read book to come out of Saskatchewan. And it's set—guess where—on the Regina Plains. That story continues to perpetuate the myth of flatness for thousands who've never seen the Prairies.

Since the Dust Bowl era and the publication of *Who Has Seen* 9
the Wind, there have been countless more books about the Prairies, with full-colour cover photos of the flattest land possible and a sky that fills three-quarters of the page—as if the Prairie provinces offer no other landscapes. No graphic artist would think of putting Nistowiak Falls on the cover of a book called *Saskatchewan*, nor a picture of Lake Winnipeg to identify Manitoba.

Yesterday, as I sped across the wide landscape toward the 10
distant, mirage-ridden horizon, watching the clouds through my windshield as they shifted and changed and sent shadows chasing each other across the sweep of hills and fields, I felt fully free. And I pitied all those "flat and boring" philosophers who fail to see, whether level as a tabletop or not, the exquisite and singular beauty of the Prairies.

UNDERSTANDING DETAILS

1. What is the difference between "prairie" and "the Prairies"? Why is Butala confused about the definition of "the Prairies"?
2. What or who has perpetrated the myth that the Prairies are flat?
3. According to Butala, what is the truth about the Prairies?

ANALYZING MEANING

1. Butala uses the term "soul-stirring spaciousness" to describe the terrain in her region of the country. What does she mean by this phrase?
2. What is Butala's purpose in writing this essay? Given the original source of publication, who do you think is her intended audience?
3. Why do myths get created and perpetuated? What role do they play in helping people deal with the world in which they live?

DISCOVERING RHETORICAL STRATEGIES

1. Butala has used multiple examples to make her point about the myth that the Prairies are flat. How has she selected these examples? Which do you find most effective? Why?
2. The language Butala uses is particularly descriptive and incorporates metaphors and similes. Identify at least four examples of figures of speech in Butala's essay.
3. Consider Butala's perspective on this subject. What biographical details give her argument credibility?

MAKING CONNECTIONS

1. Butala writes with a passion about the land where she lives. How does her attitude toward her subject compare to that of Lesley Choyce ("Thin Edge of the Wedge") or Tomson Highway ("What a Certain Visionary Once Said")?
2. Malcolm Gladwell ("Is the Belgian Coca-Cola Hysteria the Real Thing?") explains one way in which ideas become contagious and spread, even though they may have no basis in fact. In what way is the mass hysteria that Gladwell describes similar to the way in which the myth of the flat Prairies has been spread?
3. Sharon Butala writes to counter a myth about a landscape. In what ways is her purpose similar to that of Drew Hayden Taylor ("Pretty Like a White Boy") or Cecil Foster ("Why Blacks Get Mad")?

IDEAS FOR DISCUSSION/WRITING

Preparing to Write

What is a myth? Write freely about myths and the role that they play in a community or society. How are myths created? What is the appeal of myth? What sustains myths? How are myths debunked? Can myths do harm if they are misrepresenting something? How are contemporary myths different from traditional myths? What do they have in common?

Choosing a Topic

1. Think of a popular myth about the area of the country where you live. Write an essay for the readers of *enRoute* magazine in

which you debunk that myth, supporting your point with specific illustrative examples.

2. Create a myth about a place with which you are familiar. Select specific examples to support your claim and to make it credible.

3. Urban myths and legends are frequently transmitted over the internet. Write an essay in which you explain the reason for the prevalence of urban myths and legends in an online environment. Use specific examples to illustrate your points.

WEBSITES

www.writersunion.ca/b/butala.htm
Read a biography and bibliography of Sharon Butala.

www.shared-vision.com/old_site/y00m06/storya01.html
This site contains an interview with Sharon Butala from *Shared Vision* magazine.

CECIL FOSTER

Why Blacks Get Mad

Cecil Foster (1954–) is an assistant professor in the Department of Sociology and Anthropology at the University of Guelph. He is also an award-winning author of several works of fiction and non-fiction and is a respected social commentator. Foster immigrated to Canada in 1979 from Barbados. He has worked in a variety of journalistic positions in Barbados and in Canada. The former editor of *Contrast*, a Toronto black community newspaper, Foster has also worked as senior editor at the *Financial Post*, as a reporter at *The Globe and Mail Report on Business* and the *Toronto Star*, as host of a talk show on CFRB radio, as a teacher of journalism at Ryerson University and Humber College, and as a policy advisor to the Ontario Minister of Citizenship and Culture. Foster's first novel, *No Man in the House*, was published in 1991 and was written for his children to help them better understand the immigration experience. It was followed in 1995 by *Sleep On, Beloved*, the award-winning *A Place Called Heaven: The Meaning of Being Black in Canada* (1996), *Caribana: The Greatest Celebration (1997)*, *Slammin' Tar* (1998), *Island Wings: A Memoir* (1998), and *Dry Bone Memories* (2001).

Preparing to Read

In this article from *Chatelaine* magazine, Foster examines the problem of racism in Canada. Before reading Foster's views, think about racism. What is racism? What distinguishes racism from other forms of discrimination? Have you ever been subjected to racism? Do you consider yourself racist? What examples of racism have you observed in Canada? What causes racism? How can racism be overcome or eliminated?

I felt totally helpless the night of May 4, as I sat in front of my television set watching Toronto's Yonge Street reduced to skirmishes between the police and angry, alienated young people—many of them black. 1

Only a few nights earlier, my wife, Glenys, and I had been glued to the set while youths across the United States torched sections of Los Angeles, Atlanta and New York. The Rodney King verdict, which exonerated L.A.'s finest in a monstrous 2 beating of a black man, had triggered the worst outbreak of violence since the Watts riots of 1965.

Now, it was Toronto's turn, and those of us in the black 3 community who had predicted such an eruption for years could only agonize about what we were witnessing. Glenys and I thought about our two sons, Munyonzwe, 10, and Michello, 9, sleeping upstairs. Would they feel compelled to take to the streets in another six or seven years?

This clash between black and white was particularly poignant 4 for middle-class blacks like Glenys and me. In our late 30s, with a fairly comfortable home and jobs—I am a senior editor at *The Financial Post* and a novelist, Glenys owns a Pizza Pizza franchise in Toronto—we may be said to have achieved many of the dreams we brought with us from Barbados in the '70s. But when the rampage started, we understood its roots as no white viewer could, because we too know the bitterness and frustration blacks experience every day in white society.

We didn't expect it to be this way. When I was growing up 5 in Barbados, I believed that, if I got myself an education, I would achieve success as a writer. Later on, I believed that, if I immigrated to Canada and did well, I would find acceptance in a multicultural society.

As it turned out, I did work hard, did achieve success, but 6 acceptance is another matter. The worst thing about racism in Canada is that it is not open but subtle. I can't remember anybody ever calling me nigger and yet I feel the pain of racism in the way people talk to me, handle me or just simply assume I am up to no good. It's what blacks call white stereotypical expectations.

I first encountered this stereotyping when I visited Canada in 7 1976, the year of the Montreal Olympics. I was still living in the West Indies and preparing to study mass communications at the Jamaican campus of the University of the West Indies on a scholarship later that year. I had saved every penny for almost two years to get to Montreal, see the Olympics and spend three weeks with my girlfriend, Glenys, also from Barbados.

I arrived at Mirabel airport with all my papers in order but, 8 while white passengers were processed quickly, I was held back for questioning. Would I be looking for a job? Would I take a job—even part-time—if offered?

I had been warned to expect this by Barbadians who had   9
visited Canada earlier. The immigration officer, they told me,
would automatically assume I planned to be an illegal immigrant.

Three years later, in 1979, aged 24, I did immigrate—legally—   10
and joined Glenys, whom I had known since high school. She
had taken the gamble in 1975 of coming to Montreal to study
secretarial science at the then Sir George Williams University.
We were planning to marry and we chose Toronto as our future
home, lured by the promise of economic improvement and of
raising our kids in an environment that would allow them to
develop to the best of their ability.

Finding a job was a problem at first. I remember being at a   11
Friday night dominoes session at a friend's house when the
question of a job came up. I said my only skill was reporting.
"Reporting!" a friend echoed. "Look at that television and tell
me what you see." There was a Stanley Cup game on the screen.
"That is Canada there. All white. If you see a black face, it must
be a Buffalo station."

I was living in my brother Errol's apartment at this time. To   12
cover my living expenses, I became a bad telephone salesman
for Grolier at night, hawking encyclopedias, and by day editing
Contrast, the now-defunct black newspaper. I also started
university courses at York, eventually completing two B.A.
degrees in administrative studies and economics.

One day, as I was walking to a West Indian store to buy some   13
week-old Barbadian newspapers, a young white policeman
pulled up on a motorcycle. An interrogation began: Who was I?
Did I have any identification? Was I a legal immigrant in the
country? I was frightened. My voice broke when I answered.
No, I didn't have any I.D. I had neglected my brother's advice—
never go out without a passport. And I became very conscious of
the gun on this policeman's hip. In Barbados, policemen don't
carry guns.

Finally, he said I could go; he was on the lookout for someone   14
just like me. My friends laughed at this when I told them. "He
didn't mistake you. He just wanted to stop you."

During those early days, I left applications and résumés at   15
every Toronto media house. My hopes rose when I learned there
was an opening at The Canadian Press news agency. Believing
my experience at Reuters and the Caribbean News Agency would
be an asset, I asked for the editor concerned. The man said he
would be delighted to chat with me. He told me his desk was

right across from the elevator, so he would see me when I got off. I should bring my clippings.

The conversation sounded so promising, but when I got off 16 the elevator, the man at the nearest desk checked his watch and frowned. I waited. Eventually, he said, "Are you Mr. Foster?" He apologized for promising me an interview. He should have known it was going to be a busy day and he wouldn't have time for a longish chat. In any case, the opening he had in mind was filled, but he'd keep me in mind. He never looked at my clippings.

But I did get a job in late 1979 at *The Toronto Star*. I now had 17 a regular paycheque, but this did not save me from stereotyping. One day, I went to interview the head of a volunteer group for some charity. She had told me to come to the back of her affluent home in North Toronto, as she was having renovations made to the front. As I walked around piles of gravel and sand, I heard a woman shout angrily from the doorway, "So now you decide to show up? Do you know how long I've been waiting for you?"

"Didn't we agree on 10 o'clock?" 18

"Who are you?" 19

"The reporter from *The Star*." 20

"Oh, my God," she said. In spite of my jacket and briefcase, 21 one glance had been enough for her to classify me as a construction worker. It was not the only time someone has assumed that a reporter with an anglicized name at a major newspaper must be white. This is one reason we gave our sons African first names.

In 1980, Glenys and I were married and went to live in the St. 22 James Town apartment complex in downtown Toronto. It was our first home together. I was working steadily and attending college at night, she was working as a secretarial clerk in a freight-forwarding company. Life was looking better, and we started to plan for our own family. The next year, Glenys became pregnant with our first son.

But however positive we felt about our new life, the racist 23 undercurrent remained. By this time, I was working for *The Globe and Mail's Report on Business*. I was assigned to interview the executive director of some business association. As I waited in his outer office, I could see the executive through the glass. He was on the phone, and his assistant put a note on his desk, informing him of my arrival. The man got off the phone, took up some papers, looked at his watch and did some more work. Then, he made more phone calls. One of them, I learned later, was to my office, asking why I had not arrived. Finally, I asked the assistant to find out when he would see me.

The executive came out, very apologetic. He had not read   24 the note, he said, had assumed I was someone seeing his assistant. Now, it was too late for the interview.

Blacks put up with such incidents in the name of our   25 paycheques, but they frustrate and anger us.

In 1983, our second son, Michello, was born, and over the   26 next several years, Glenys and I worked hard to build the kind of life we'd dreamed about in Barbados. As well as working as a reporter by day and studying by night, I started writing fiction, as a means of escape. *No Man in the House*, my first novel, was published in Canada in 1991 and was well received. This fall, it is being released in the U.S.

In 1989, we were able to take out a mortgage on a small house   27 in the suburbs. At about that time, Glenys realized a dream she had had from the time when she used to help her brother with his grocery store in Barbados. She had always wanted to run her own business and, when the chance came to buy into a Pizza Pizza franchise, she took the plunge.

She enjoys the work, but stereotyping is routine. White   28 customers often bypass her to speak to white employees. Once, two yuppies saw her sweeping up and offered her a job cleaning their homes.

"I don't try to explain anymore," Glenys says. "Being black   29 and a woman, they just don't expect me to be the owner."

Because Glenys and I are adults, we can laugh about these   30 incidents, but they are not funny when they affect our kids. Four years ago, our son Michello, then 5, faced his first racist incident.

We knew something was up when he ran home from school   31 and burrowed under his brother's bedcover. A classmate had not invited him to her birthday party. Her parents didn't like blacks, she told him. My son believed that, if he slept in his brother's bed under his cover, he would become like him—fairer-skinned—and get the invitation.

We were devastated. What could we tell him? That it   32 wouldn't happen again? We knew it would. But why should a kid so young be robbed of his innocence?

He's older now, and racist taunts in the schoolyard are   33 common. He tries to give as good as he gets, but "How many times can I call them 'vanilla'?" he asks us. "They have so many names for me: 'brown cow,' 'peanut butter,' 'chocolate cookie.'"

We encourage him to be tolerant but as peer pressure grows,   34
he may try his own solutions. In fact, at about the time of the Yonge Street incidents, the principal sent home a note saying my son had hit someone in the mouth.

Anger, like racism, starts young. And it builds up, fueled by   35
successive slights. "You go into work on Monday morning and you hear everybody in the office talking about the party, the picnic over the weekend or the invitations to the cottage, and you say to yourself, why wasn't I invited?" says my friend Lloyd, a midmanagement worker at a trust company. It should surprise no one when rage erupts, as it did recently in Toronto, Montreal and Halifax. Blacks have felt for too long that they are not invited to the party.

The riots last May told us just how desperate young blacks   36
feel about their prospects. But if the violence jolted the whites, there was also a shock in store for middle-class blacks. We discovered that these youths believe that middle-class blacks are as big a problem as white supremacists.

Pioneer blacks who have become doctors, chartered   37
accountants, journalists, bank managers, even elected politicians are perceived not as role models but as sellouts, Uncle Toms, house niggers, Oreos (black outside, white within). We are accused of failing to confront racism, of swallowing our anger and being too careful not to rock the boat.

Blacks have a term for this: white burnout. It comes when   38
you give up trying to fight the system. Austin Clarke, an outstanding novelist, also from Barbados, who used to speak out vehemently, now says, "I had two daughters at The Bishop Strachan School [an expensive private school]. I found it easier to pay the fees working inside the system than outside."

There is also the fear that, if we do fight the system, we   39
endanger our jobs.

As middle-class blacks watch violence erupt, a kind of   40
paralysis sets in. We know we must support the kids on the streets and help them build a secure future—but we also know that because of the deep resentment they feel toward us we aren't any damn use at this point.

So, whites who expect "role model" blacks to act as   41
intermediaries between them and militant youths should look

elsewhere. Role model blacks are too busy patching things up with their fellow blacks.

As Austin Clarke told me the day after the riots, "I remember, 42 back in the '60s, saying the next generation of blacks is not going to stand for this shit. The next generation has now grown up."

And what the new generation sees is discouraging. Look at 43 Toronto blacks: our unemployment rate is high, and 87 percent make less than $25,000 annually. Single parent homes are three times more common among black families, and 25 percent of these families rely on government for all income.

The result is hopelessness, and the result of that has now 44 become clear to everyone: I haven't met any black community leader who doesn't anticipate more violence. If our kids' frustrated rage is to be replaced by a new sense of hope, we will need to reform the place where most of their problems have their roots—the educational system. At present, 60 percent of black youths in Toronto do not finish high school. But kids must remain in school if they are to get the tools to prepare themselves for better jobs and escape the poverty cycle. A college degree will go a long way toward instilling confidence in young people, even when facing the most bigoted employer. An educated kid knows about antidiscrimination laws and regulations and will use them to battle overt racism. More than that, he or she will have choices in employment.

Meanwhile, governments must act fast to open up institutions 45 to blacks. This means continuing to put pressure on government agencies such as the police and the judicial system who deal daily with blacks. Professions such as law and medicine must reexamine their entry criteria to rid them of racial biases.

But perhaps the best thing the wider society can do is simply 46 to let blacks feel that we belong, that there's a place for us in the schools, in politics, the arts and, most importantly, in the work force. Simply put, that we are Canadians and equal. Society has brought pressure to bear on smoking, drunk driving and sexism in the workplace. Now, it must make people equally uncomfortable about stereotyping blacks.

At the same time, there is a lot of work to be done by the 47 black community. Not only must we create the peer pressure to make our kids want to stay in school, but more adults must be willing to sacrifice time, effort and even money to guide them. We have to teach them how to live in a racist society and, hard as it is, we cannot afford to appear to be losing hope. We must encourage youths to dream, to believe they can bring about changes.

And it must be done fast. Already, too many blacks believe 48 they will always be on the outside looking in. Too many blacks feel betrayed by Canadian schools, churches, human-rights commissions, law courts and police. And too many blacks already believe this society isn't worth maintaining and are willing to try to destroy it.

The prospects are that bleak.   49

UNDERSTANDING DETAILS

1. In what aspects of his life has Foster experienced racism?
2. Why did Foster and his wife, Glenys, give their sons African names?
3. What does Foster believe governments should do to overcome racism? What about professions? Wider society? The black community?

ANALYZING MEANING

1. Why did Foster immigrate to Canada? Have his expectations been fulfilled? Explain.
2. "Anger, like racism, starts young" (paragraph 34). Explain this statement with specific examples you have experienced or observed.
3. Define the following terms and give specific examples to help differentiate between them: *discrimination, racism, stereotyping*.

DISCOVERING RHETORICAL STRATEGIES

1. How has Foster organized his examples? Is this pattern effective? Why or why not?
2. Describe the tone that Foster creates in this article. How does he establish this tone? Is this tone appropriate for his intended audience?
3. Foster's examples come from his own experience. What effect does this have on the readers?

MAKING CONNECTIONS

1. Allen Abel finishes his essay ("A Home at the End of the Journey") with the comment, "I'm thinking: Maybe this place *can* work." How do you think Foster would respond to Abel's story of his citizenship ceremony and his concluding comment about Canada?

2. Drew Hayden Taylor ("Pretty Like a White Boy") and Cecil Foster both write about the difficulties of being judged on their appearance and "not looking the part," but their essays have very different tones. While Taylor uses humour, Foster is very serious. Which approach do you find more effective? Explain why.

3. Foster uses personal experience to make his point about discrimination. Compare and contrast this strategy to that chosen by Judy Rebick in "The Culture of Overwork."

IDEAS FOR DISCUSSION/WRITING

Preparing to Write

Write freely about expectations. What expectations do you have for your life? What things do you hope to achieve? What goals have you set? To what degree are your expectations shaped by others in your family, your peer group, or your community? How is your behaviour influenced by the expectations of those around you?

Choosing a Topic

1. "Overall, Canada is a good country in which to live." Write an essay in which you support this statement with plenty of specific examples.

2. Foster discusses the problem of feeling caught in the middle that many middle-class blacks face in Canada. Write an essay in which you describe an experience of feeling "caught in the middle." Use specific, detailed examples to convey your position clearly.

3. Write an essay for a college- or university-educated audience in which you claim that your school or your community is either more racist or less racist than it used to be. Specific examples will help you to build a convincing argument.

WEBSITES

www.canoe.ca/JamBooksReviewsS/sleepon_foster.html
This site gives a book review of Foster's novel *Sleep On, Beloved*.

www.magenta.nl/crosspoint/cnd.html
This site gives a number of links to anti-racist websites throughout Canada.

www.naacp.org
Visit the official website for the National Association for the Advancement of Colored People.

BARBARA KINGSOLVER

Life Without Go-Go Boots

In the FAQ section of her website (**www.kingsolver.com**) Barbara Kingsolver offers the following advice to those who want to be writers: "If you want to be a writer, don't picture yourself writing. DO writing. It's really that simple." Kingsolver has done much writing in the form of novels, short stories, essays, scientific articles, poems, and non-fiction books.

Kingsolver was born in Kentucky in 1955 and eventually left for Indiana to earn a degree in biology at DePauw University. Kingsolver pursued her studies further with a Master of Science degree at the University of Arizona and now makes her home with her family in Tucson, Arizona. While studying biology and ecology, Kingsolver worked at various points as an archaeologist, copy editor, X-ray technician, house-cleaner, biology researcher, and translator of medical documents, but she eventually came to focus on a career as a writer. While her initial focus was on technical and scientific writing, after suffering from insomnia during her first pregnancy, she turned to writing fiction and her first novel, *The Bean Trees*, was published in 1988. Her most recent books include the novels *The Poisonwood Bible* (1998), *Prodigal Summer* (2000), and a collection of essays titled *Small Wonder* (2002).

Preparing to Read

"Life Without Go-Go Boots" was originally published in the catalogue of Lands' End, an American clothing company. Before reading the essay, think about the clothing that you wear. Where do you buy your clothes? How do you make your purchasing decisions? How would you describe the clothing sold by Lands' End? (If you are not familiar with Lands' End, see its website at **www.landsend.com**). Why do you think a clothing company would include an essay in its catalogue?

1 Fashion nearly wrecked my life. I grew up beyond its pale, convinced that this would stunt me in some irreparable way. I don't think it has, but for a long time it was touch and go.

2 We lived in the country, in the middle of an alfalfa field; we had no immediate access to Bobbie Brooks sweaters. I went to school in the hand-me-downs of a cousin three years older. She had excellent fashion sense, but during the three-year lag her

every sleek outfit turned to a pumpkin. In fifth grade, when girls were wearing straight shifts with buttons down the front, I wore pastel shirtwaists with cap sleeves and a multitude of built-in petticoats. My black lace-up oxfords, which my parents perceived to have orthopedic value, carried their own weight in the spectacle. I suspected people noticed, and I knew it for sure on the day Billy Stamps announced to the lunch line: "Make way for the Bride of Frankenstein."

I suffered quietly, casting an ever-hopeful eye on my eighth-grade cousin whose button-front shifts someday would be mine. But by the time I was an eighth grader, everyone with an iota of social position wore polka-dot shirts and miniskirts. For Christmas, I begged for go-go boots. The rest of my life would be endurable if I had a pair of those white, calf-high confections with the little black heels. My mother, though always inscrutable near Christmas, seemed sympathetic; there was hope. Never mind that those little black heels are like skate blades in inclement weather. I would walk on air.   3

On Christmas morning I received white rubber boots with treads like a pair of Michelins. My mother loved me, but had missed the point.   4

In high school I took matters into my own hands. I learned to sew. I contrived to make an apple-green polyester jumpsuit that was supremely fashionable for about two months. Since it took me forty days and forty nights to make the thing, my moment of glory was brief. I learned what my mother had been trying to tell me all along: high fashion has the shelf life of potato salad. And when past its prime, it is similarly deadly.   5

Once I left home and went to college I was on my own, fashion-wise, having bypassed my cousin in stature and capped the arrangement off by moving to another state. But I found I still had to reckon with life's limited choices. After classes I worked variously as a house cleaner, typesetter, and artists' model. I could spend my wages on trendy apparel (which would be useless to me in any of my jobs, particularly the latter), or on the lesser gratifications of food and textbooks. It was a tough call, but I opted for education. This was Indiana and it was cold; when it wasn't cold, it was rainy. I bought an army surplus overcoat, with zip-out lining, that reached my ankles, and I found in my parents' attic a green pith helmet. I became a known figure on campus. Fortunately, this was the era in which army boots were a fashion option for coeds. And besides, who knew? Maybe   6 under all that all-weather olive drab was a Bobbie Brooks sweater. My social life picked right up.

As an adult, I made two hugely fortuitous choices in the   7 women's-wear department: first, I moved out West, where the buffalo roam and hardly anyone is ever arrested for being unstylish. Second, I became a novelist. Artists (also mathematicians and geniuses) are greatly indulged by society when it comes to matters of grooming. If we happen to look like an unmade bed, it's presumed we're preoccupied with plot devices or unifying theories or things of that ilk.

Even so, when I was invited to attend an important author   8 event on the East Coast, a friend took me in hand.

"Writers are *supposed* to be eccentric," I wailed.   9

My friend, one of the people who loves me best in the world,   10 replied: "Barbara, you're not eccentric, you're an anachronism," and marched me down to an exclusive clothing shop.

It was a very small store; I nearly hyperventilated. "You   11 could liquidate the stock here and feed an African nation for a year," I whispered. But under pressure I bought a suit, and wore it to the important author function. For three hours of my life I was precisely in vogue.

Since then it has reigned over my closet from its dry-cleaner   12 bag, feeling unhappy and out of place, I am sure, a silk ambassador assigned to a flannel republic. Even if I go to a chichi restaurant, the suit stays home. I'm always afraid I'll spill something on it; I'd be too nervous to enjoy myself. It turns out I would rather converse than make a statement.

Now, there is fashion, and there is *style*. The latter, I've found,   13 will serve, and costs less. Style is mostly a matter of acting as if you know very well what you look like, thanks, and are just delighted about it. It also requires consistency. A friend of mine wears buckskin moccasins every day of her life. She has daytime and evening moccasins. This works fine in Arizona, but when my friend fell in love with a Tasmanian geologist and prepared to move to a rain forest, I worried. Moccasins instantaneously decompose in wet weather. But I should have known, my friend has sense. She bought clear plastic galoshes to button over her moccasins, and writes me that she's happy.

I favor cowboy boots. I don't do high heels, because you   14 never know when you might actually have to get somewhere, and most other entries in the ladies-shoes category look to me like Ol' Dixie and Ol' Dobbin trying to sneak into the Derby, trailing their plow. Cowboy boots aren't trying. They say, "I'm no pump, and furthermore, so what?" That characterizes my whole uniform, in fact: oversized flannel shirts, jeans or cotton leggings, and cowboy boots when weather permits. In summer I lean toward dresses that make contact with the body (if at all) only on the shiatsu acupressure points; maybe also a Panama hat; and sneakers. I am happy.

I'm also a parent, which of course calls into question every 15 decision one ever believes one has made for the last time. Can I raise my daughter as a raiment renegade? At present she couldn't care less. Maybe obsessions skip a generation. She was blessed with two older cousins whose sturdy hand-me-downs she has worn from birth, with relish. If she wasn't entirely a fashion plate, she also escaped being typecast. For her first two years she had no appreciable hair, to which parents can clamp those plastic barrettes that are gender dead giveaways. So when I took her to the park in cousin Ashley's dresses, strangers commented on her blue eyes and lovely complexion; when she wore Andrew's playsuits emblazoned with trucks and airplanes (why is it we only decorate our boys with modes of transportation?), people always commented on how strong and alert my child was—and what's his name?

This interests me. I also know it can't last. She's in school 16 now, and I'm very quickly remembering what school is about: two parts ABCs to fifty parts Where Do I Stand in the Great Pecking Order of Humankind? She still rejects stereotypes, with extraordinary good humor. She has a dress-up collection to die for, gleaned from Goodwill and her grandparents' world travels, and likely as not will show up to dinner wearing harem pants, bunny ears, a glitter-bra over her T-shirt, wooden shoes, and a fez. But underneath it all, she's only human. I have a feeling the day might come when my daughter will beg to be a slave of conventional fashion.

I'm inclined to resist, if it happens. To press on her the larger 17 truths I finally absorbed from my own wise parents: that she can find her own path. That she will be more valued for inward individuality than outward conformity. That a world plagued by poverty can ill afford the planned obsolescence of *haute couture*.

But a small corner of my heart still harbors the Bride of 18 Frankenstein, eleven years of age, haunting me in her brogues and petticoats. Always and forever, the ghosts of past anguish compel us to live through our children. If my daughter ever asks for the nineties equivalent of go-go boots, I'll cave in.

Maybe I'll also buy her some of those clear plastic galoshes   19 to button over them on inclement days.

UNDERSTANDING DETAILS

1. As a child, why does Kingsolver want go-go boots? Do her parents oblige her in this desire? Why or why not?
2. Kingsolver's friend tells her she is "an anachronism" rather than eccentric (paragraph 10). What is the difference between the two? Do you agree with the friend?
3. As an adult, how does Kingsolver dress? Why?

ANALYZING MEANING

1. What is Kingsolver's thesis? How is it revealed in the examples that she relates in her essay?
2. Characterize Kingsolver's attitude toward fashion as a child. How does this compare to her attitude toward fashion as an adult?
3. What is the difference between fashion and style? How do you think the original audience for this essay would classify Kingsolver's appearance?

DISCOVERING RHETORICAL STRATEGIES

1. Describe the tone of Kingsolver's essay. How is this tone achieved? Is it effective in making her point? Explain why or why not.
2. The use of examples to illustrate her point characterizes Kingsolver's essay. How many examples of fashion faux-pas does Kingsolver include? Which example do you find the most effective?
3. Kingsolver's essay originally appeared in the catalogue of a clothing retailer. Describe the intended audience and purpose. Do you think Kingsolver has written an effective essay for this situation? Explain.

MAKING CONNECTIONS

1. Barbara Kingsolver's sense of humour is apparent in "Life Without Go-Go Boots" although she is making some serious points. Compare Kingsolver's use of humour to that of Drew Hayden Taylor ("Pretty Like a White Boy") or Dave Bidini ("Kris King Looks Terrible").
2. Kingsolver's essay focuses largely on the importance of image. Compare her views with those of Laura Robinson ("Starving for the Gold") and Naheed Mustafa ("My Body Is My Own Business"). On what points do you think these women would agree? On which points might they disagree?
3. In "Life Without Go-Go Boots" Kingsolver reflects on her own childhood experiences and some of the reasons her parents may have made the choices they did. Compare the rationale for the choices made by Kingsolver's parents to the rationale for those made by Evelyn Lau's parents ("More and More").

IDEAS FOR DISCUSSION/WRITING

Preparing to Write

Write freely about fashion and the fashion industry. How would you describe your own sense of fashion? Is fashion important to you? Why or why not? Why is the fashion industry so big? How are fashion standards set? Why do people care about being "in fashion" when it comes to appearance?

Choosing a Topic

1. Kingsolver claims that artists (including writers), mathematicians, and geniuses are indulged by society in terms of their grooming. Are all writers a little eccentric? What makes anyone unique or special? Are we all a little odd? Are our odd qualities or apparent eccentricities sometimes assets? Using examples drawn from your own experience, write a character portrait of someone who seems eccentric to you.
2. Write an essay in which you use a series of specific examples to illustrate a particular lesson that you learned in growing up.
3. Kingsolver refers to the "planned obsolescence of *haute couture*." Write an essay in which you use specific examples to explain this phrase.

WEBSITES

www.kingsolver.com
Visit Barbara Kingsolver's official website.

www.salon.com/16dec1995/departments/litchat.html
Read an interview with Barbara Kingsolver from *Salon*.

www.commondreams.org/views01/0923-03.htm
"A Pure, High Note of Anguish" is an essay by Kingsolver published on Sunday, September 23, 2001, in the *Los Angeles Times*.

www.landsend.com
Kingsolver's essay originally appeared in the Lands' End catalogue.

CHAPTER 4

PROCESS ANALYSIS

Explaining Step by Step

Human nature is characterized by the perpetual desire to understand and analyze the process of living well. The bestseller list is always crowded with books on how to know yourself better, how to be assertive, how to become famous, how to avoid a natural disaster, or how to be rich and happy—all explained in three easy lessons. Open almost any popular magazine and you will find numerous articles on how to lose weight, how elections are run in this country, how to dress for success, how political rallies evolved, how to gain power, or how to hit a successful topspin backhand. People naturally gravitate toward material that tells them how something is done, how something happened, or how something works, especially if they think the information will help them improve their lives in a significant way.

Defining Process Analysis

A *process* is a procedure that follows a series of steps or stages; *analysis* involves taking a subject apart and explaining its components in order to better understand the whole. Process analysis, then, explains an action, a mechanism, or an event from beginning to end. It concentrates on either a mental or a physical operation: how to solve a chemistry problem, how to tune up your car, how the Canadian Senate is formed, how the internet works. In fact, the explanation of the writing process, beginning on page 19 of this book, is a good case in point: It divides writing into three interrelated verbal activities and explains how they work—separately and together.

A process analysis can take one of two main forms: (1) It can give directions, thereby explaining how to do something (directive), or (2) it can give information about how something happened (informative). The first type of analysis gives directions for a task the reader may wish to attempt in the future. Examples include how to make jelly, how to lose weight, how to drive to Saskatoon, how to assemble stereo equipment, how to make money, how to use a microscope, how to knit, how to resuscitate a dying relationship, how to win friends, how to discipline your child, and how to backpack.

The second type of analysis furnishes information about what actually occurred in specific situations or about how something works. Examples include how Hiroshima was bombed, how certain rock stars live, how the tax system works, how *Titanic* was filmed, how Mario Lemieux earned a place in the Hockey Hall of Fame, how gold was first discovered in the Yukon, how computers work, how a kibbutz functions, and how the Gulf War began. These subjects and others like them respond to a certain fascination we all have with mastering some processes and understanding the intricate details of others. They all provide us with opportunities to raise our own standard of living, either by helping us directly apply certain processes to our own lives, or by increasing our understanding of how our complex world functions.

The following student paragraph analyzes the process of constructing a garden compost pit. Written primarily for people who might wish to make such a pit, this piece is directive rather than informative. Notice in particular the amount of detail the student calls upon to explain each stage of the process and the clear transitions she uses to guide us through her analysis.

No garden is complete without a functioning compost pit. Here's a simple, inexpensive way to make your garbage work for you! To begin with, make a pen out of hog wire or chicken wire, four feet long by eight feet wide by four feet high, splitting it down the middle with another piece of wire so that you end up with a structure that looks like a capital "E" on its side. This is a compost duplex. In the first pen, place a layer of soda ash, just sprinkled on the surface of the dirt. Then, pile an inch or so of leaves, grass clippings, or sawdust on top of the soda ash. You're now ready for the exciting part. Start throwing in all the organic refuse from your kitchen (no meat, bones, or grease, please). After the food is a foot or so deep, throw in a shovelful of steer manure, and cover the entire mess with a thin layer of dirt. Then water it down. Continue this layering process until the pile is three to three-and-a-half feet high. Allow the pile to sit until it decomposes (from one month in warm climates to six months in colder weather). Next, take your pitchfork and start slinging the contents of pen one into pen two (which will land in reverse order, of course, with the top on the bottom and the bottom on the top). This ensures that everything will decompose evenly. Water this down and begin making a new pile in pen one. That's all there is to it! You now have a ready supply of fertilizer for your garden.

Thinking Critically by Using Process Analysis

Process analysis embodies clear, careful, step-by-step thinking that takes one of three different forms: chronological, simultaneous, or cyclical. The first follows a time sequence from "first this" to "then that." The second forces you to deal with activities or events that happen or happened at the same time, such as people quietly studying or just going to work when the September 11th terrorist attacks hit New York and Washington. And the third requires you to process information that is continuous, like the rising and setting of the sun. No other thinking pattern will force you to slow down as much as process analysis because the process you are explaining probably won't make any sense if you leave out even the slightest detail.

Good process analysis can truly help your reader see an event in a totally new light. An observer looks at a product already assembled or at an event already completed and has no way of knowing without the help of a good process analysis how it got to this final stage. Such an analysis gives the writer or speaker as well as the observer a completely new way of "seeing" the subject in question. Separating process analysis from the other rhetorical modes lets you practise this method of thinking so that you will have a better understanding of the various mental procedures going on in your head. Exercising this possibility in isolation will help you feel its range and its intricacies so that you can become more adept at using it, fully developed, in combination with other modes of thought.

1. List as many examples of each type of process (chronological, simultaneous, and cyclical) as you can think of. Share your list with the class.

2. Write out the process of tying a shoe, step by step. Have another person follow your steps exactly to test how well you have analyzed this process.

3. Write a paragraph telling how not to do something. Practise your use of humour as a technique for creating interest in the essay by emphasizing the "wrong" way, for example, to wash a car or feed a dog.

Reading and Writing Process Analysis Essays

Your approach to a process analysis essay should be fairly straightforward. As a reader, you should be sure you understand the author's statement of purpose and then try to visualize each step as you go along. As a writer, you need to adapt the mechanics of the way you normally write to the demands of a process analysis paper, beginning with an interesting topic and a number of clearly explained ideas or stages. As usual, the intended audience determines the choice of words and the degree of detail.

How to Read a Process Analysis Essay

Preparing to Read. Preparing to read a process analysis essay is as uncomplicated as the essay itself. The title of Paul Quarrington's essay in this chapter, "Home Brew," tells us exactly what we're going to learn about. Maureen Littlejohn's phrase "You Are a Contract Painkiller" describes clearly what her article will teach us about. Scanning each selection to assess the author's audience will give you an even better idea of what to expect in these essays, while the synopsis of each in the Rhetorical Table of Contents will help focus your attention on its subject.

Also important as you prepare to read these essays are the qualifications of each author to write on this subject: Has he or she performed the task, worked with the mechanism, or seen the event? Is the writer's experience firsthand? When Paul Quarrington tells us about making beer at home, is he actually writing from personal experience? Has Maureen Littlejohn actually experienced the effect of ASA on pain or fever? What is Stanley Coren's experience with dogs? How does he know about the genetic engineering of dogs? The biography preceding each essay will help you uncover this information and find out other publication details that will encourage you to focus on the material you are about to read.

Finally, before you begin reading, answer the prereading questions, and then do some brainstorming on the subject of the essay: What do you want to know about mass hysteria (Gladwell)? How much do any of us really know about how ASA works, and why might we want to know more?

Reading. When you read the essays in this chapter for the first time, record your initial reactions to them. Consider the preliminary information you have been studying in order to create a context for each author's composition: Why did Maureen Littlejohn write "You Are a Contract Painkiller"? What circumstances prompted Coren's "Dogs and Monsters"? Who do you think is Fiorito's target audience in "Breakfast in Bed"?

Also determine at this point whether the essay you are reading is *directive* (explaining how to do something) or *informative* (giving information about how something happened). This fundamental understanding of the author's intentions, along with a reading of the questions following the essay, will prepare you to approach the contents of each selection critically when you read it a second time.

Rereading. As you reread these process analysis essays, look for an overview of the process at the beginning of the essay so you know where each writer is headed. The body of each essay, then, is generally a discussion of the stages of the process.

This central portion of the essay is often organized *chronologically* (as in Quarrington's essay), with clear transitions so that readers can easily follow the writer's train of thought. Other methods of organization are *cyclical* (such as the process of genetic engineering described by Coren), describing a process that has no clear beginning or end, and *simultaneous* (such as the effects of ASA outlined in Littlejohn's essay), in which many activities occur at the same time with a clear beginning and end. Most of these essays discuss the process as a whole at some point. During this second reading, you will also benefit from discovering what rhetorical modes each writer uses to support his or her process analysis and why these rhetorical modes work effectively. Do the historic examples that Littlejohn uses add to our understanding of the process she is explaining? What do Paul Quarrington's step-by-step instructions, complete with scientific data and cause-and-effect explanations of results, add to his essay on beer-making? How do all the rhetorical modes in each essay help create a coherent whole? After reading each essay for a second time, answer the questions that follow the selection to see if you are understanding your reading material on the literal, interpretive, and analytical levels before you take on the discussion/writing assignments.

For an overview of the entire reading process, you might consult the checklists on pages 17–18 of the Introduction.

How to Write a Process Analysis Essay

Prewriting. As you begin a process analysis assignment, you first need to become as familiar as you can with the action, mechanism, or event you are going to describe. If possible, try to go through the process yourself at least once or twice. If you can't actually carry out the procedure, going through the process mentally and taking notes is a good alternative. Then, try to read something about the process. After all this preparation (and careful consideration of your audience and purpose), you should be ready to brainstorm, freewrite, cluster, or use your favourite prewriting technique (see pages 19-25 of the Introduction) in response to the prewriting questions before you start composing your paper.

Writing. The essay should begin with an overview of the process or event to be analyzed. This initial section should introduce the subject, divide it into a number of recognizable steps, and describe the result once the process is complete. Your thesis in a process essay is usually a purpose statement that clearly and briefly explains your approach to the procedure you will discuss: "Building model airplanes can be divided into four basic steps" or "The American courts follow three stages in prosecuting a criminal case."

Next, the directive or informative essay should proceed logically through the various stages of the process, from beginning to end. The parts of a process usually fall nicely into chronological order, supported by such transitions as "at first," "in the beginning," "next," "then," "after that," and "finally." Some processes, however, are either simultaneous, forcing the writer to choose a more complex logical order for the essay (such as classification), or cyclical, requiring the writer to choose a starting point and then explain the cycle stage by stage. Playing the guitar, for example, involves two separate and simultaneous components that must work together: holding the strings against the frets with the fingers of one hand and strumming with the other hand. In analyzing this procedure, you would probably want to describe both parts of the process and then explain how the hands work together to produce music. An example of a cyclical process would be the changing of the seasons. To explain this concept to a reader, you would need to pick a starting point, such as spring, and describe the entire cycle, stage by stage, from that point onward.

In a process paper, you need to be especially sensitive to your intended audience, or readers will not be able to follow your explanation. The amount of information, the number of examples and illustrations, and the terms to be defined all depend on the prior knowledge and background of your readers. A writer explaining to a group of amateur cooks how to prepare a soufflé would take an entirely different approach to the subject than he or she would if the audience were a group of bona fide chefs hoping to land jobs in elegant French restaurants. The professional chefs would need more sophisticated and precise explanations than their recreational counterparts, who would probably find such an approach tedious and complicated because of the extraneous details.

The last section of a process analysis paper should consider the process as a whole. If, for example, the writer is giving directions on how to build a model airplane, the essay might end with a good description or drawing of the plane. The informative essay on our legal system might offer a summary of the stages of judging and sentencing a criminal. And the essay on cooking a soufflé might finish with a photograph of the mouth-watering dish.

Rewriting. In order to revise a process analysis essay, first make sure your main purpose is apparent throughout your paper:

- Have you written a directive or an informative essay?
- Is your purpose statement clear?

Next, you need to determine if your paper is aimed at the proper audience:

- Have you given your readers an overview of the process you are going to discuss?
- Do you go through the process you are explaining step by step?
- At the end of the essay, do you help your readers see the process as a complete entity?

The checklists on pages 29–30 will give you further guidelines for writing, revising, and proofreading.

Student Essay: Process Analysis at Work

The student essay that follows analyzes the process of using a "home permanent" kit. Notice that, once the student gives an overview of the process, she discusses the steps one at a time, being careful to follow a logical order (in this case, chronological) and to use clear transitions. Then, see how the end of the essay shows the process as a whole.

Follow the Simple Directions

Although fickle hairstylists in Paris and Hollywood decide what is currently "in," many romanticists disregard fashion and yearn for a mane of delicate tendrils. <u>Sharing this urge but resenting the cost, I opted for a "home perm" kit</u>. Any literate person with normal dexterity could follow illustrated directions, I reasoned, and the eight easy steps would energize my limp locks in less than two hours. "Before" and "after" photos of flawless models showed the metamorphosis one might achieve. Confidently, I assembled towels, rollers, hair clips, waving lotion, neutralizer, end papers, and a plastic cap. <u>While shampooing</u>, I chortled about my ingenuity and economy.

<u>After towel-drying my hair, I applied the gooey, acidic waving lotion thoroughly. Then I wrapped an end paper around a parted section and rolled the first curl ("securely but not too tightly")</u>. Despite the reassuring click of the fastened rollers, as I sectioned each new curl the previous one developed its own volition and slowly unrolled itself. Resolutely, I reapplied waving lotion and rewound—and rewound—each curl. <u>Since my hair was already saturated, I regarded the next direction skeptically: "Apply</u>

Left margin annotations:

Purpose statement for informative process analysis

First step (chronological order)

Transition

Right margin annotations:

Overview

Second step

Third step

Fourth step

waving lotion to each curl." Faithfully, however, I complied with the instructions. Ignoring the fragile state of the fastened rollers, I then feigned assurance and enclosed my entire head in a plastic cap. In forty minutes, chemical magic would occur.

Transition

Fifth step

Restless with anticipation, I puttered about the house; while absorbed in small chores, I felt the first few drops of lotion escape from the plastic tent. Stuffing wads of cotton around the cap's edges did not help, and the small drops soon became rivulets that left red streaks on my neck and face and splattered on the floor. (Had I overdone the waving lotion?) Ammonia fumes so permeated each room that I was soon asked to leave. Retreating to the bathroom, I opened the window and dreamed of frivolous new hairstyles.

Finally, the waving time had elapsed; neutralizing was next. I removed my plastic cap, carefully heeding the caution: "Do not disturb curlers as you rinse waving lotion from hair." With their usual impudence, however, all the curlers soon bobbed in the sink; undaunted, I continued. "This next step is critical," warned the instructions. Thinking half-hearted curls were better than no curls at all, I poured the entire bottle of neutralizer on my hair. After a drippy ten-minute wait, I read the next step: "Carefully remove rollers." As this advice was superfluous, I moved anxiously to the finale: "Rinse all solution from your hair, and enjoy your curls."

Transition

Sixth step

Transition

Seventh step

Transition

Eighth step

Lifting my head from the sink and expecting visions of Aphrodite, I saw instead Medusa's image in the mirror. Limp question-mark spirals fell over my eyes, and each "curl" ended in an explosion of steel-wool frizz. Reflecting on my ineptitude, I knew why the direction page was illustrated only with drawings. After washing a large load of ammonia-scented towels, I took two aspirin and called my hairdresser. Some repair services are cheap at any price.

Final product

Concluding remark

Some Final Thoughts on Process Analysis

In this chapter, a single process dictates the development and organization of each of the essays. Both directional and informational methods are represented here. Notice in particular the clear purpose statements that set the focus of the essays in each case, as well as the other rhetorical modes (such as narration, comparison/contrast, and definition) that are used to help support the writers' explanations.

Process Analysis in Review

Reading Process Analysis Essays

Preparing to Read

- What assumptions can you make from the essay's title?
- Can you guess what the general mood of the essay is?
- What is the essay's purpose and audience?
- What does the synopsis in the Rhetorical Table of Contents tell you about the essay?
- What can you learn from the author's biography?
- Can you guess what the author's point of view toward the subject is?
- What are your responses to the Preparing to Read questions?

Reading

- Is the essay *directive* (explaining how to do something) or *informative* (giving information about how something happened)?
- What general message is the author trying to convey?
- Did you preview the questions that follow the essay?

Rereading

- Does the author furnish an overview of the process?
- How is the essay organized—*chronologically, cyclically,* or *simultaneously*?
- What other rhetorical modes does the author use to support the essay's purpose?
- What are your responses to the questions after the essay?

Writing Process Analysis Essays

Preparing to Write

- What are your responses to the Preparing to Write questions?
- What is your purpose?
- Who is your audience?

- Are you as familiar as possible with the action, mechanism, or event you are going to explain?

Writing

- Do you provide an overview of the process at the beginning of the essay?
- Does your first paragraph introduce your subject, divide it into recognizable steps, describe the result once the process is complete, and include a purpose statement?
- Is your process analysis essay either *directive* or *informative*?
- Do you proceed logically through the various steps of the process?
- Are the essay's details organized *chronologically, simultaneously*, or *cyclically*?
- What is your audience's background?
- Does your essay end considering the process as a whole?

Rewriting

- Have you written a *directive* or an *informative* essay?
- Is your purpose statement clear?
- Have you given your readers an overview of the process you are going to discuss?
- Do you go through the process you are explaining step by step?
- At the end of the essay, do you help your readers see the process as a complete entity?

PAUL QUARRINGTON

Home Brew

Fly fisherman, beermeister, rock musician, and acclaimed young Canadian novelist: meet Paul Quarrington (1953–). Quarrington, whose brother and fellow brewer is a musician with the Toronto Symphony, grew up in suburban Toronto. Following a brief stint in academia at the University of Toronto, this prolific and lively writer-to-be published his first novel, *The Service* (1978), at twenty-five. If beer is one of Quarrington's consuming interests, as he suggests, then rock music—beer's inevitable companion—has been another amusing sideline in his career. He has played bass and co-produced LPs performed with yet another Quarrington brother as part of the group Joe Hall and the Continental Drift, during the heyday of Toronto's Queen Street night culture. Quarrington's interest in rock gave him the subject of another of his bestselling novels, *Whale Music* (1989), which concerns itself with a fictionalized version of the reclusive Brian Wilson of the Beach Boys. This novel won Quarrington the Governor General's Award for fiction in 1990. His ability to make stories out of his interests produced three novels about sports: *Home Game* (1983), *King Leary* (1987), and *Hometown Heroes* (1988); a collection of stories edited by Quarrington entitled *Original Six: True Stories from Hockey's Classic Era* (1996); and a work of non-fiction, *Fishing with My Old Guy* (1995). In addition, Quarrington has written screenplays for popular television shows *Due South, Once a Thief*, and *Power Play*. Quarrington lives in Toronto and his latest books include *The Boy on the Back of the Turtle* (1997), a non-fiction book about travelling through the Galapagos Islands with his seven-year-old daughter and his seventy-three-year-old father, and *The Spirit Cabinet* (1999).

Preparing to Read

Paul Quarrington's lively tribute to "home brew," which first appeared in *Harrowsmith* magazine in the spring of 1992, presents this writer's adventures with the pleasures and problems of making Canada's favourite beverage at home. The contents of the ubiquitous brown and green bottles have been brewed by humans since the beginning of civilization. But does this mean that making beer is an easy process? As you prepare to try "Home Brew," think of what might motivate you to try to make "homemade anything": Would it be your fondness for that product? Would it be the chance to save money? Would it be the challenge of trying to better a commercial product? Or would you be driven by curiosity about the process of making something yourself? Could you then teach someone else to follow your procedure successfully?

The first thing I must explain is that my brother helped me with this project. We share certain traits my brother and I, and chief among them is a fondness, nay an *over*-fondness for beer. We have even developed a Trivial Pursuit–type game featuring questions about beer. Indeed, every question can be answered by bellowing, "Beer!" My brother and I take a foolish delight in ordering drinks in the same fashion, screaming out "Beer!" at helpful bartenders and waiters, deviating from this only to the extent of making it "More beer!" as the evening progresses. 1

At any rate, when asked by this fine journal if I would look into the making of beer—home brewing—my brother stepped into the breach (I could not stop him), and his presence shall make itself known. For example, at one point during the procedure, I took to ruminating aloud. "Making beer," I mused, "is as natural as childbirth." 2

"True," agreed my brother, "but the child could be a homicidal maniac." 3

By which my brother made oblique reference to the truly vile bogswill that people had forced upon us in days long gone by, bottles filled half with a dull, cloudy liquid, half with some other-worldly sludge. It used to be that no words filled me with as much dread as "homemade beer." But I have learned much— the aforementioned bogswill was likely the doing of "the wild yeasties"—and, while learning, have tasted many exceptional beers. My brother and I are very pleased with our own batch and have spent several lovely evenings in his living room, occasionally glancing up at each other and bellowing, "Beer!" 4

But let us get down to basics; let us make sure we all know exactly what is going on here. Beer is a beverage that is fermented from cereals and malt and flavoured with hops. From this simple statement, all else shall follow, so it is good to fix it in your mind, to repeat it inwardly a couple of times. (Or, put as a question in our game: What beverage is fermented from cereals and malt and flavoured with hops? Answer: Beer!) 5

The first significance arising from the statement is that beer is made with cereals rather than with fruit as is, say, wine. The process of fermentation occurs when a molecule of sugar splits, creating two molecules of carbon dioxide (CO_2) and two molecules of ethyl alcohol (C_2H_5OH). Starch, such as that found in those cereals, cannot be converted into alcohol. This would be extremely bad news for us beer lovers, except for a vegetable enzyme called amylase. You see, starch is, chemically speaking, 6 a long chain of molecules ($C_6H_{10}O_5$, et cetera, et cetera). Amylase breaks up the chain, pairs the molecules and adds a water molecule, thus creating $C_{12}H_{22}O_{11}$, which is a maltose sugar molecule that can thence undergo fermentation, praise the Lord. It is this process that is carried out at malting houses, which is why we begin our beermaking with a large can of malt extract (usually hopped malt extract) rather than with a bucketful of barley.

I will abandon the pseudoscientific tone now. It is bound to   7
go down in flames right around the time I try to throw in the scientific name for the yeast used to make lager beers, *Saccharomycescarlsbergensis*. That yeast, you see, was named for the place where it was discovered, and do not be embarrassed if you, too, failed to realize that there are all sorts of different yeasts with all sorts of fancy names—not to mention those unruly thugs and hooligans, the wild yeasties. Yeast is what does the actual work of fermentation. It is a plant organism, a living thing; and when it dies, it sinks to the bottom and forms sludge.

Malt and yeast are all you truly need to make beer, and   8
humankind has been making it for something like 8,000 years. (Q: What has humankind been making for 8,000 years? A: Beer!) Hops did not appear on the European scene until the 12th century, and even at that time, there was resistance in the form of laws forbidding their use. Hops are the flowers of the female hop vine (an aggressive spreader, it has earned the lovely nomenclature *Humulus lupulus* and is also known as the "wolf of the willows"), and their resins and oils impart flavour of a slightly bitter nature to the beer.

There are many different kinds of hops; they all have different   9
names (Cluster, Fuggles, Tetenang), and they come in either pellet or leaf form. It really is quite mind-boggling. That is why it is important to have a firm grip on the basics. (Q: Combine malt, hops, yeast and water, and in time, you will have what? A: Beer!) This is no more mysterious than, say, the baking of bread. Not coincidentally, the Old English *breowan* gives us both "brew" and "bread."

The first step in making beer at home is to leave it—your   10
home, that is—and hie down to a specialty shop. We chose a Wine-Art/Brewers-Art store (in Toronto) because it happened to be closest, but Wine-Art/Brewers-Art stores also have a reputation for helpfulness, and many of the home brewers I spoke with steered me in that direction. And indeed, we were

greeted by a friendly sort, Martin Jordan (manager), who spent a long time explaining things. The process detailed below is, in fact, Martin's Improved Method.

You need to acquire some basic equipment: a primary 11 fermenter, a secondary fermenter and a siphoning hose. This should run you somewhere between $30 and $40. Allow me a moment to deal with the financial advantages of home brewing. Clearly, home brew is a lot less expensive than buying beer at the beer store. This seems to me, however, to be one of the least noble reasons for undertaking the endeavour. You will encounter people who brew because it is cheap, and they usually give themselves away by saying something like, "And the beer is just as good as the stuff you buy."

These people are missing the point, I think. The great thing 12 about home brewing is that you can make some really wonderful beers, you can alter recipes to suit your individual taste and if it ends up being economical, that is a fact to be savoured rather than gloated over. Besides, it may not be all that economical: although the three items listed above are all you really need, they are not all you will end up carting out of the store.

You will want a hydrometer to measure specific gravity 13 (I will explain in a moment). You will want a vapour lock, and you will want a plastic J-tube which is crooked at the bottom so that you don't have to stand there holding the siphoning hose. You will want a hose clamp for when you are bottling, which reminds me—you need some bottles. And caps. And a capper. And you will want some potassium metabisulphite crystals to cleanse and disinfect all that stuff.

The primary fermenter is typically a large plastic pail— 14 preferably a food-grade pail, but nothing used for oils or vinegars—with a tight-fitting lid. The secondary fermenter is typically a large glass bottle (such as might contain a genie). These are called, for reasons that have not been explained to my satisfaction, carboys. They come in two sizes, 19 and 23 litres. Those are the two quantities you make beer in, 19 and 23 litres. We are going to be making 23 litres.

Now that you have your basic equipment, you need to 15 purchase the ingredients for the wort. The wort is the combination of malt, grains and hops whence flows your batch of beer. My brother and I chose to make an English-style bitter and purchased a can of hopped malt extract with the word BITTER printed on it. You could purchase Brown Ale, American

Light, Stout, Pale Ale, et cetera. Each can contains 1.5 kilograms of hopped malt extract, yeast and instructions, and costs around $15. One could make a batch of beer just by using the stuff in the can (actually, you need some corn sugar), but Martin Jordan suggested that we also purchase some roasted barley and bittering hops. This we did, because he said the resulting beer would taste like Smithwick's, a statement that had my brother and me leaping about the store like puppies.

So now you are all loaded up, and it cost approximately $75, 16 of which perhaps $55 was a one-time investment. Therefore, for about $20, you are going to get 23 litres of beer. (I find it hard not to get excited.)

The first step takes place in the kitchen, where you cook up 17 the wort in a huge pot. To begin, you bring four to six litres of water to a boil. You add the bittering hops. The hops look like rabbit pellets, which is a bit off-putting. Martin Jordan suggested that in the course of cooking the wort, you occasionally take a single hop and fling it with a certain élan into the mixture. I think this is sage advice. I doubt that a single hop affects the flavour much, but it does help the novice brewmaster to relax.

At any rate, you let the hops boil for 15 to 20 minutes, at 18 which point you add the sugar. Let that boil for another five minutes, then add the crushed malt grains. (Take a pinch and eat them; you'll be surprised how good they taste.) Let that simmer for five minutes, then add the malt extract, which you will discover is a thick, glutinous syrup with the consistency of molasses. Return the mixture to a low simmer.

While the wort is cooking (and whenever you are not flinging 19 hop pellets into it) is a good time to clean and disinfect your primary fermenter—or, in my case, a good time to discover that your brother has an obsessive-compulsive personality disorder. I counsel thoroughness rather than monomania. For instance, if, having disinfected your primary fermenter, you then pick it up to move it closer to the stove, it is not necessary—although my brother found it so—to redisinfect where the offending fingers were placed. It is a good idea to mark the 23-litre level on the inside of the container.

Now put some cold water in that primary fermenter. (A tip 20 from Mr. Jordan: You might draw the water the day before and let it sit overnight, which helps get rid of the chlorine taste.) You now strain the wort into it. You stir and then add more water until you reach the 23-litre mark. You pitch the yeast, which is less strenuous than it sounds, adding it when the mixture is between 70 and 80 degrees F. (Warning: If it is too hot, you will kill the yeast.)

Now, ahem, allow me to get a little scholarly here. The 21 specific gravity of water is 1.000. Liquids containing sugar have a higher specific gravity because they are denser. Alcohol is lighter than water. Therefore, during fermentation, the specific gravity of your brew will drop as more and more of the sugar is converted into alcohol. Some of the malt will not convert (which is what gives beer its taste), so although the final specific gravity will approach 1.000 again, it will never truly arrive.

A rule of thumb is that when the specific gravity stops 22 dropping, fermentation is complete. Got it? For this reason, we now take our hydrometer, which looks like a futuristic fishing float, and place it in our beer-to-be. It might read, say, 1.046. The higher the figure, the more potential alcohol, and some recipes will even say, "At this point, your starting s.g. should be 1.048," in which case you would add more malt and/or sugar until that level is attained.

All right now. Fermentation splits a molecule of sugar into 23 ethanol and carbon dioxide. The latter is gas, gas that is exuded with a series of very satisfying mulching galoomps. So we need to let the gas escape. But if we leave the container uncovered, guess what's going to get into it? The wild yeasties! For even though many yeasts are civilized and gentrified, there are unruly yeasts floating about in the air, little gangs of them just looking to mess up somebody's beer. To get into it and produce *off flavours*. That is Martin Jordan's way of saying the wild yeasties will make, you know, bogswill. You therefore cover your primary fermenter very securely, having purchased a lid for that purpose. You will notice that the lid has a largish hole dead centre, which seems foolish until you see that your fermentation lock's rubber stopper will plug it admirably. The fermentation lock is a twisted piece of tubing, half-filled with water, which will let out the CO_2, and vent the last gasps of expiring yeast without admitting the dreaded hordes.

You then move down to the basement, especially if you are 24 attempting to make a lager. Lager, derived from the German for "storage," cannot be properly made when the weather is too warm, so if you are doing this in the summer, you had best make an ale. Ale is fermented at higher temperatures, which causes most of the yeast to rise to the top. Ale is thus a top-fermenting

brew, lager a bottom-fermenting brew. And there, at last, we
know the difference between the two.

You can relax now for approximately five days. It should be   25
easy to determine whether fermentation is taking place (bubbles
in the vapour lock), although our brew appeared strangely
inactive. Martin Jordan suggested that the gas was probably
escaping from somewhere else, perhaps from around the lid
rather than through the vapour lock, and by taking a series of
readings with the carefully sterilized hydrometer, we were able
to determine that all was as it should be.

On day five, you siphon into the secondary fermenter. Your   26
primary fermenter will have developed a sludgy bottom layer
made up of yeast corpses, and although the siphoning tube has
a crook at the bottom, hopefully raising it above it all, great care
should be taken not to transfer the sludge. By the way, you realize
I am assuming that all of this stuff has been cleansed and
sterilized. Any slip-up on the sanitation front could result in *off
flavours,* so never let down your guard. (While we were making
our beer, a number of bad batches were reported to Martin Jordan
at his store, as if the wild germs and yeasties had gone on a
citywide rampage. Beware.)

On day 15, you add the "finings," commonly isinglass, which   27
is made from the scrapings of sturgeons' swim bladders. This
makes your beer less cloudy. Don't ask how, just do it.

On day 20, you bottle. Beer's effervescence is created from   28
extra fermentation at the end of the process, so you now add a
little more corn sugar or finishing malt. You could add about
half a teaspoon of sugar per bottle, although the sensible thing to
do is add 1-1/4 cups to the 23-litre carboy. Siphon off some beer,
dissolve the sugar in it, then reintroduce it to the brew. Don't
start stirring in your carboy, lest you disturb the sludge.

My brother and I bottled in plastic litre bottles with screw-on   29
plastic caps, which I realize is cheating, but I thought it worked
wonderfully. A potential downside is that you need to drink a
litre whenever you want a beer, but my brother and I conceived
of this as *no big problem.* You might choose to bottle the standard
341-millilitre size, which you would then cap in the traditional
manner. My big tip here is to purchase a clamp for the end of
your siphoning tube, a simple device that stops the flow
momentarily as you move from bottle to bottle.

If you are still in the basement at this point, it might be an   30
idea to move your lot upstairs where it is warmer to sort of kick-

start this last bit of fermentation. Five days later, you should return your beer to a cool place, and five days after that, you could drink one. Which is to say, it is the earliest you should drink one, but time will only improve your beer. Many claim it is best in three months.

Perhaps the diciest aspect of home brew comes with the   31 actual drinking. That final bit of fermentation produced bubbles, a little more alcohol and some dead yeast cells, which are now lying on the bottom of the bottle. When pouring the beer, it is best to hold the bottle in front of a light so that you can view the sludge's advent toward the neck. The trick is to avoid dead yeast without leaving behind half a bottle of beer. And once you have poured the beer, rinse out the bottle immediately, because as the remaining liquid evaporates, the sludge will adhere to the inside and render it useless as a beer receptacle.

So there you have it. The procedure is simple, virtually idiot-   32 proof—nothing can stop those yeasts from splitting up sugar molecules—and also educational.

Q: What beverage contains pelletized wolf of the willows   33 and sturgeon swim bladder scrapings?

A: You got it.   34

UNDERSTANDING DETAILS

1. What are the constituent parts of the recipe for beer? What role does each play in making the finished beverage?
2. What living ingredient plays a vital role in the fermentation of beer? How does it work? Why might it sometimes produce "vile bogswill," or a brewed offspring which is "a homicidal maniac"?
3. Describe the preparation of wort. What must be added to wort to produce beer? What is the function of each added ingredient?

ANALYZING MEANING

1. Has Quarrington convinced you that making your own beer is "simple" and "virtually idiot-proof"? Which of his instructions seems the easiest to follow, and which the most difficult? Why?
2. With which characteristics of the author do you identify? Where do you find evidence of such in the essay? Do these aspects of his personality make him more or less credible as someone writing a real set of instructions?

3. Quarrington's essay contains several sidetrips into what he calls "the pseudoscientific tone," passages that explain the chemical aspects of beer production. Are these passages clear and understandable to you? Explain why or why not.

DISCOVERING RHETORICAL STRATEGIES

1. Although "Home Brew" is very clearly both a directive and descriptive piece of process writing, other rhetorical strategies are used. Giving details from the essay to support your answer, explain which other rhetorical forms you discover.
2. Humour in writing often deflates the importance of the speaker, or discounts the seriousness of what is said. Is this true of Paul Quarrington's use of humour? What comic concept does he use as a unifying thematic link throughout the essay?
3. In spite of the writer and his brother being portrayed to some degree as "Garth and Wayne," there is clear evidence of Quarrington's fondness for using new and delightful words. Where do you find examples of interesting word use? How do these shifts in diction affect you as a reader? What do they add to your perception of the writer? How do they affect the overall tone of the essay?

MAKING CONNECTIONS

1. Paul Quarrington, like Joe Fiorito ("Breakfast in Bed"), is basing his essay on a recipe. Explain how each of these authors makes a recipe interesting and entertaining to read.
2. Quarrington, like Drew Hayden Taylor ("Pretty Like a White Boy") and Susan Swan ("Nine Ways of Looking at a Critic"), is noted for the humour that characterizes his writing. How do each of these writers achieve a humorous tone in their respective essays?
3. In this essay, Quarrington incorporates stories of his family members. Compare the effect of this personalization to Barbara Kingsolver's ("Life Without Go-Go Boots") or Evelyn Lau's ("More and More") use of family anecdotes in their essays.

IDEAS FOR DISCUSSION/WRITING

Preparing to Write

Write freely about one of your more memorable experiments with trying to make something on your own for the first time. What were you trying to make? Why? Had you been given any prior instructions? Were you trying your "recipe" alone, or with someone else? What were the results of your first "do-it-yourself" attempt? Were they humorous at the time? Were the results a success, or even usable? What happens when you try to show someone else how to do something you do well?

Choosing a Topic

1. Your school newspaper has just asked you to write the first column in a "Student Cooking" series. Write an article based on the process format in which you tell readers who have cooking skills similar to yours how to make a dish you've learned to cook. Include such information as why this dish is suitable to student cooking abilities, available equipment and facilities, how many it will serve, and what it would cost.

2. Using your own experience with a hobby or with making something that others might buy from a store, write a process essay that persuades the reader to try this "do it yourself" project. Explain your reasons for finding the activity and the end-product valuable and enjoyable as you give detailed instructions for making the same thing.

3. Beer, soft drinks, wine, mineral water, coffee: We all have favourite beverages. Explain in a process essay why your favourite drink holds such appeal to you. What do you know about this beverage that will interest your readers? Choose a tone and clear points of detailing that will be most interesting to your audience.

WEBSITES

 www.quarrington.org
This is an excellent site with extensive information about Quarrington.

 www.us.imdb.com/Name?Quarrington,+Paul
The Internet Movie Database Ltd. has a filmography and biography for Paul Quarrington.

 www.realbeer.com
This extensive beer site includes the following sections: brew tour, breweries, links, brew 'zines, burp me, notes, events, patrons, games, brew travels, authors, and retail.

MALCOLM GLADWELL

Is the Belgian Coca-Cola Hysteria
the Real Thing?

Since growing up in Elmira, Ontario, Malcolm Gladwell (1963–) has experienced impressive success in his writing career. After holding the positions of reporter and northeastern bureau chief of *The Washington Post*, Gladwell moved to writing a popular column in *The New Yorker* magazine and a book called *The Tipping Point*, in which he examines the idea of social epidemics and the ways in which change happens in a society.

Gladwell was born in England and lived there, as well as in the United States and Jamaica, before his family settled in rural Ontario in 1969. In 1984, he graduated from the University of Toronto with a history degree and got an internship at *The American Spectator* in Indiana. Less than a year later, he landed a job as a reporter at *The Washington Post* and, over time, moved from writing on topics with a business focus to those with a more general science bent. After complementing his work at the *Post* with freelance assignments for *The New Yorker*, Gladwell eventually won a contract as a staff writer with *The New Yorker* in 1996. Gladwell continues to write for *The New Yorker* and to do public speaking engagements based on *The Tipping Point*.

Preparing to Read

In the summer of 1999, Malcolm Gladwell wrote the following essay that appeared in *The New Yorker*. "Is the Belgian Coca-Cola Hysteria the Real Thing?" relates the story of an apparent food poisoning outbreak in Belgium and then speculates as to the real cause of the affliction that struck about 100 children. Before reading Gladwell's essay, think about food safety. What responsibility do food manufacturers have for food safety? How should a company respond to complaints that their products have caused illness? What role should government legislation play in upholding standards of food safety?

The wave of illness among Belgian children last month had the 1 look and feel—in the beginning, at least—of an utterly typical food poisoning outbreak. First, forty-two children in the Belgian town of Bornem became mysteriously ill after drinking Coca-Cola and had to be hospitalized. Two days later, eight more school children fell sick in Bruges, followed by thirteen in Harelbeke the next day and forty-two in Lochristi three days after that—and on and on in a widening spiral that, in the end, sent more than one hundred children to the hospital complaining of nausea, dizziness, and headaches, and forced Coca-Cola into the biggest product recall in its hundred-and-thirteen-year history. Upon investigation, an apparent culprit was found. In the Coca-Cola plant in Antwerp, contaminated carbon dioxide had been used to carbonate a batch of the soda's famous syrup. With analysts predicting that the scare would make a dent in Coca-Cola's quarterly earnings, the soft-drink giant apologized to the Belgian people, and the world received a sobering reminder of the fragility of food safety.

The case isn't as simple as it seems, though. A scientific study   2
ordered by Coca-Cola found that the contaminants in the carbon dioxide were sulfur compounds left over from the production process. In the tainted bottles of Coke, these residues were present at between five and seventeen parts per billion. These sulfides can cause illness, however, only at levels about a thousand times greater than that. At seventeen parts per billion, they simply leave a bad smell—like rotten eggs—which means that Belgium should have experienced nothing more than a minor epidemic of nose-wrinkling. More puzzling is the fact that, in four of the five schools where the bad Coke allegedly struck, half of the kids who got sick hadn't drunk any Coke that day. Whatever went on in Belgium, in other words, probably wasn't Coca-Cola poisoning. So what was it? Maybe nothing at all.

"You know, when this business started I bet two of my   3
friends a bottle of champagne each that I knew the cause," Simon Wessely, a psychiatrist who teaches at the King's College School of Medicine in London, said.

"It's quite simple. It's just mass hysteria. These things usually   4
are."

Wessely has been collecting reports of this kind of hysteria for   5
about ten years and now has hundreds of examples, dating back as far as 1787, when millworkers in Lancashire suddenly took ill after they became persuaded that they were being poisoned by tainted cotton. According to Wessely, almost all cases fit a pattern. Someone sees a neighbor fall ill and becomes convinced that he is being contaminated by some unseen evil—in the past it was demons and spirits; nowadays it tends to be toxins and gases—and his fear makes him anxious. His anxiety makes him dizzy

and nauseous. He begins to hyperventilate. He collapses. Other people hear the same allegation, see the "victim" faint, and they begin to get anxious themselves. They feel nauseous. They hyperventilate. They collapse, and before you know it everyone in the room is hyperventilating and collapsing. These symptoms, Wessely stresses, are perfectly genuine. It's just that they are manifestations of a threat that is wholly imagined. "This kind of thing is extremely common," he says, "and it's almost normal. It doesn't mean that you are mentally ill or crazy."

Mass hysteria comes in several forms. Mass motor hysteria, 6 for example, involves specific physical movements: shaking, tremors, and convulsions. According to the sociologist Robert Bartholomew, motor hysteria often occurs in environments of strict emotional repression; it was common in medieval nunneries and in nineteenth-century European schools, and it is seen today in some Islamic cultures. What happened in Belgium, he says, is a fairly typical example of a more standard form of contagious anxiety, possibly heightened by the recent Belgian scare over dioxin-contaminated animal feed. The students' alarm over the rotten-egg odor of their Cokes, for example, is straight out of the hysteria textbooks. "The vast majority of these events are triggered by some abnormal but benign smell," Wessely said. "Something strange, like a weird odor coming from the air conditioning."

The fact that the outbreaks occurred in schools is also typical 7 of hysteria cases. "The classic ones always involve school-children," Wessely continued. "There is a famous British case involving hundreds of schoolgirls who collapsed during a 1980 Nottinghamshire jazz festival. They blamed it on a local farmer spraying pesticides." Bartholomew has just published a paper on a hundred and fifteen documented hysteria cases in schools over the past three hundred years. As anyone who has ever been to a rock concert knows, large numbers of adolescents in confined spaces seem to be particularly susceptible to mass hysteria. Those intent on pointing the finger at Coca-Cola in this sorry business ought to remember that. "We let the people of Belgium down," Douglas Ivester, the company's chairman, said in the midst of the crisis. Or perhaps it was the other way around.

UNDERSTANDING DETAILS

1. What were the symptoms experienced by the Belgian children in Gladwell's essay? What caused these symptoms?
2. List the steps in the process of mass hysteria setting in.
3. What causes mass hysteria?

ANALYZING MEANING

1. How did Coca-Cola respond to the apparent poisoning of the people in Belgium? Was this response appropriate? Why or why not?
2. What is Gladwell's purpose in this essay? What is the main topic of Gladwell's essay?
3. Who is particularly susceptible to mass hysteria? Why?

DISCOVERING RHETORICAL STRATEGIES

1. A significant portion of Gladwell's essay is spent describing a series of events in Belgium. Explain why he spends so much time detailing these events.
2. Gladwell has quoted and cited other people in his essay. Why has he done this? What effect does this have?
3. What is Gladwell's purpose in this essay? Does he achieve this purpose?

MAKING CONNECTIONS

1. Gladwell is fascinated with the popularity of different social phenomena and the reasons people behave the way they do. Imagine a conversation between Gladwell and Judy Rebick ("The Culture of Overwork"). What do these two writers have in common? What topics of conversation do you imagine might engage them?
2. Barbara Kingsolver ("Life Without Go-Go Boots") and Judy Rebick ("The Culture of Overwork") both cite examples of people's behaviour being modelled on that of those around them. Are these examples of the mass hysteria that Gladwell outlines? Why or why not?
3. Like Gladwell, David Foot ("Boomers Dance to a New Beat") is interested in factors that influence the behaviour of groups of people. How do you think Foot would explain Gladwell's point about cases of mass hysteria typically involving schoolchildren?

IDEAS FOR DISCUSSION/WRITING

Preparing to Write

Write freely about contagious behaviour. What types of behaviour are "contagious"? What kinds of things do we do because we observe others around us doing them? Can yawning or blushing be caused by suggestion? If we observe others around us yawning, is it possible to keep ourselves from yawning as well?

Choosing a Topic

1. In a process essay directed to your classmates, explain how you believe a company should react in a case where their product seems to be contaminated. Decide on your tone and purpose before you begin.
2. Write an essay for a local newspaper or magazine in which you outline the process for ensuring that the foods you consume at home are safe.
3. Gladwell explains how mass hysteria takes hold and what factors create it. Write a narrative essay in which you relate a story illustrating the power of the "mob mentality." How did the actions of individuals get dictated by the group of which they were a part? Were the consequences of this behavioural influence positive or negative?

WEBSITES

www.gladwell.com
Gladwell's site contains details about his book *The Tipping Point*, an archive of his *New Yorker* articles, and biographical information.

www.bookbrowse.com/index.cfm?page=author&authorID=392&view=interview
An interesting interview with Gladwell.

www.theatlantic.com/unbound/interviews/ba2000-03-29.htm
Interview with Malcolm Gladwell in *The Atlantic*.

www.pbs.org/newshour/gergen/jan-june00/gladwell_5-22.html
PBS interview with Malcolm Gladwell.

STANLEY COREN

Dogs and Monsters

You can see Stanley Coren as a guest on numerous television shows as well as in the role of host on his weekly television show *Good Dog*; you can hear him on radio programs such as *Dan Rather, Ideas, Quirks and Quarks*, and *The Osgood Report*; and you can read his work in articles published in *USA Today, The Globe and Mail, The New York Times, The Chicago Tribune, Time, People, Maclean's, Cosmopolitan*, and *Entertainment Weekly*. Coren has also published several books about dogs, including *How to Speak Dog, Why We Love the Dogs We Do, The Intelligence of Dogs*, and *Sleep Thieves*. He has published a multitude of academic and scientific writings related to his research into various areas of psychology and his current role as a professor and director of the Human Neuropsychology and Perception Laboratory at the University of British Columbia. If you wanted to meet Coren, you could register for a psychology class he teaches at UBC, you could take a course with the Vancouver Dog Obedience Training Club, or you could attend one of the many fundraising events for the SPCA in which he participates.

Coren was born in Philadelphia in 1942 and educated at the University of Pennsylvania (undergraduate) and Stanford University (doctorate). This prolific writer and researcher now lives in Vancouver with his wife, two dogs, and a cat.

Preparing to Read

One recent cellular phone ad campaign highlights the similarities in appearance between people and the dogs they choose as pets. Do you have a dog? If so, what kind of dog do you have? What characteristics made you choose that type of dog? Generally, do you think dogs are good pets? Why or why not? How has the role of pets changed over the last century? In this essay, originally published in *Saturday Night* magazine in May 2000, Stanley Coren outlines the process of bioengineering dogs to adapt to the current technologies and needs of their human owners.

Today's headlines routinely raise fears about genetic engineer- 1
ing. The biggest concern is that "tampering with creation" to fashion new strains of plants and animals may result in the devastation of the world by upsetting the natural balance among

species. Even Prince Charles has joined the debate, claiming that genetic engineering "takes us into areas that should be left to God. We should not be meddling with the building blocks of life in this way." But the genetic manipulation of species is far from new. In fact, it began at least 14,000 years ago, when human beings created the first deliberately engineered organism—the dog.

The bioengineered canine was not created in a high-level 2 biocontainment lab; rather, its beginnings were accidental. Wolves and jackals (the domestic dog's predecessors) were attracted to human camps because primitive humans left bones, bits of skin, and other scraps of leftover food scattered near their dwellings. The wolves and jackals learned that by loitering around the settlement they could grab an occasional bite to eat without the exertion involved in hunting. These primitive dogs were initially tolerated by humans because they functioned as de facto garbage-disposal units.

The dogs near the campsite provided another key benefit: 3 security. They barked whenever wild beasts or strangers approached, removing the need for human guards to be posted at night, and thus affording the villagers more rest and increased safety. The bark was critical—the most effective guard dogs, obviously, were those with loud, persistent barks. And so a selective breeding program was begun: those dogs that barked loudly were kept and bred with other loud barkers, while those that did not bark were simply killed or chased off. In fact, one of the major distinctions between wild canines and domestic dogs today is that domestic dogs bark, while wild dogs seldom do. The persistent racket that irritates so many people is actually a human innovation.

It wasn't until the end of the fifteenth century, though, that 4 the dog as a genetic creation became truly unique—almost more an invention than a species. At this point people began cross-breeding dogs, not just to cater to their changing needs, but to suit advancing technology. Typically, humans had tailored machines to suit organisms. With dogs, they began modifying an organism to fit a machine. The machine was the gun, and the organism was the gun dog.

The earliest gun dogs were the pointers, which appeared in 5 Europe in the 1500s. The hunting weapon of choice at the time was the muzzle-loading musket, a primitive device that was notoriously laborious to use. On sighting his quarry, a hunter had to take out his powder horn, dump gunpowder down the barrel, followed by a lead ball wrapped with oiled paper or cloth, and tamp down the shot and powder with a tamping rod; then he had to fire the gun. The process took a minimum of thirty seconds, all in the service of a weapon with an effective range of twenty-five to fifty yards. To accommodate musket technology, the pointer was designed to be slow, silent, and patient. The pointer's job was to find a bird, then to hold its position while pointing at the bird's location for the agonizingly long time it took the hunter to load and shoot his weapon. If a lucky shot actually killed a bird the pointer was expected to go out and bring the game back as well. But the retrieval was window-dressing; the pointer's genetic value lay in its ability to stretch time out, to live in a slow-motion world.

As weapons technology improved, guns became easier to   6 load, with better range and accuracy. To match this new equipment, dog breeders in the late 1700s created a new kind of dog—the setter. Setters moved much more quickly than pointers, and indicated their proximity to the prey not by the stillness of their point but by the beat of their tails. The faster a setter wagged its tail, the closer it was to the game.

As more land was cultivated and cities and towns sprang up,   7 hunters were forced to turn to wilderness areas, particularly wetlands, where they hid behind blinds and waited for their quarry to come to them. These circumstances placed a premium on a dog that was not simply quiet, as the pointer had been, but that possessed an almost preternatural obedience and patience. Thus, the retriever became the bioengineered star of the next century. Retrievers were bred to wait—to do nothing: not to point, not to flush, not to run, not to bark—and retrieve. They were bred to be less, not more, which, given the physiognomy of the species, may have been the more remarkable biotechnological feat.

Canada is responsible for the newest and most intriguing   8 genetic invention in the retriever group: the Nova Scotia duck tolling retriever, a handsome, auburn-hued dog that stands about twenty inches high and weighs about forty-five pounds. The need for the toller arose when duck hunters found that they could better attract their quarry by having wooden "lures," or decoys, carved to look like ducks, floating in the nearby water. Ducks are also attracted to unusual movement and activities. This is where the toller comes in. Tolling simply means that the dog runs back and forth on the shore, spinning and making noise, or swims erratically near the shore to attract the birds. Curious ducks fly near to see what all the activity is about, and come within range of the hunter's gun. Tollers will do this for hours if needed. Of course, once the bird is shot the dog is then expected to swim out and bring it back to its lazy master.

Like any piece of technology—the 78 rpm record player, or 9 the pedal-driven sewing machine—a bioengineered dog can become outmoded and obsolete. One of the most common breeds of the eighteenth and nineteenth centuries, the Spanish pointer, was so popular in its day that it can be seen in scores of early paintings of hunts. These dogs were perfect for the era of the muzzle-loading musket—slow, quiet, and the most meticulous of the pointers. Today the breed is effectively extinct. Spanish pointers were simply too slow for impatient modern hunters, with their new, superior equipment—both guns and dogs.

Walk into homes today, and what you'll find are dogs 10 engineered for a wholly different piece of technology: the TV remote control. Perhaps our faith in biogenetic engineering would be improved if we recognized that for those of us who don't hunt, some dogs have also been designed specifically to be our companions—to fit the couch-potato mentality of our current, leisure-addicted era. It is a wonder to me that starting with the DNA of a wolf, we have spent 14,000 years of biotechnology and genetic manipulation in the creation of the little white beast who is right now gently snoring with his head resting against my foot.

UNDERSTANDING DETAILS

1. What is Coren's thesis? Where in the essay is it stated?
2. Outline the significant stages of development in the process of breeding dogs. What key characteristics identify each stage?
3. What has motivated humans to genetically engineer dogs over the last 14 000 years? What is the relationship between dogs and various forms of technology?

ANALYZING MEANING

1. Explain the title "Dogs and Monsters." Is it effective? Why or why not?
2. In the first paragraph of Coren's essay, he refers to the fear about genetic modification expressed in current headlines. How does Coren's discussion of the bioengineering of dogs relate

to foods that are now the focus of the genetic modification controversy?

3. What is Coren's purpose in writing this essay? What gives him credibility in his discussion of genetic modification and bio-engineering?

DISCOVERING RHETORICAL STRATEGIES

1. What strategies has Coren used to unify the introduction and conclusion of his essay?
2. In addition to chronologically outlining the history of the bio-engineering of dogs, Coren uses other rhetorical strategies in his essay. What other methods of organization has he employed?
3. Which of the three forms of process analysis does Coren's essay follow? Explain your answer.

MAKING CONNECTIONS

1. In what ways are the views of Juanita Polegi ("There's a Better Environmental Way to Farm") and Stanley Coren comple-mentary or contradictory in regard to human manipulation of processes such as growing crops and animal breeding?
2. Coren explains that dogs have been bred over time to adapt to the current technology available to people. Imagine that Coren is in conversation with Evan Solomon ("The Babar Factor") about adaptation to technology. In what ways have our forms of entertainment adapted over time to suit the technology avail-able? Do you think Coren and Solomon would agree on the beneficial value of this type of adaptation?
3. Stanley Coren adds interest to his essay with the personal detail about his own dog in his conclusion. Compare this strategy to that of Gwynne Dyer ("Flagging Attention"), Judy Rebick ("The Culture of Overwork"), or Neil Bissoondath ("Religious Faith Versus Spirituality").

IDEAS FOR WRITING/DISCUSSION

Preparing to Write

Coren opens his essay by pointing to recent fears about genetic modification. Write freely about genetic modification and the implications it has for our society. In what areas of our life are you aware of genetic modification happening? Do you see it as a good thing or a bad thing? Why does genetic modification frighten people? What are the benefits of genetic modification? Should the government prohibit the production of genetically modified organisms?

Choosing a Topic

1. Write an essay in which you argue for or against companies being allowed to bioengineer foods. Make sure you support your position with specific examples.
2. Humans are constantly inventing new tools to help them adapt to a changing environment. Think of one particular techno-logical advance of the last twenty years, and outline how and why that change happened.
3. Write an essay for the humane society newsletter in which you outline the process for adopting a pet. Be sure to explain clearly how people should select the pets they wish to adopt.

WEBSITES

www.stanleycoren.com
Stanley Coren's official website.

www.spca.bc.ca/animalsense/Spring2001/dogSenseSpring 2001. htm
Read an article by Stanley Coren in *Animal Sense Magazine*.

MAUREEN LITTLEJOHN

You Are a Contract Painkiller

For a writer, "it is important to listen and never assume" as well as to "ask a lot of questions," according to Maureen Littlejohn, a journalist who has specialized in pop culture for about fifteen years. Littlejohn began her journalistic career working on *Campus Digest* (now *Campus Canada*) after graduating with an honours B.A. (general arts) from the University of Toronto and completing the magazine journalism program at Ryerson Polytechnic Institute. She then moved on to roles including Entertainment/Lifestyles features writer at the *Winnipeg Free Press* and editor of the annual Juno Souvenir Program. While at U of T, Littlejohn, who always wanted to go into the field of communications, worked at the *Varsity* campus newspaper as a writer and typesetter. Later, Littlejohn further developed her writing skills through participating in the Banff Publishing Workshop. Littlejohn also worked as an on-air music critic for Global TV for three years and edited *Network* magazine for six years.

Littlejohn's articles have appeared in a variety of publications including the *Financial Post* magazine, *Flare* magazine, the Canadian Airlines in-flight magazine, *The Music Scene*, *CARAS News*, *Canadian Musician*, *Network*, and *Equinox*, where the piece included here was first published.

Preparing to Read

ASA, or aspirin, is a medication that is readily available and familiar to most of us. In this essay, Maureen Littlejohn outlines the process by which ASA works to relieve our pain and the process through which ASA was developed. Before reading this essay, think about familiar medications. What do you typically keep stocked in your medicine cabinet at home? Do you ever use aspirin? When? Why? What other nonprescription medications do you use? Do you favour medications available from pharmacies or more natural remedies? Why?

You are a contract painkiller, code name ASA, also known to your clients as aspirin. Pain is your gain—Canadians swallow almost one billion of your agents each year. You have achieved renown by destroying headaches but you are equally effective in countering sprains, burns, or blows. You stop swelling and reduce fever and research suggests you may even help prevent heart attack and stroke.

On your latest mission, your client has just had a fight with   2 her boss, and her head is pounding. Involuntary muscle contractions on her scalp and at the back of her neck, triggered by the argument, are now causing swelling and throbbing. In reaction, her body has produced an enzyme called prostaglandin, which is sensitizing the nerve endings in her scalp, especially around her temples and sending a message of pain to her brain.

Taken with a modest stream of water or ginger ale, your   3 chalky, round self begins the mission by moving through the host's esophagus, into the stomach, then the upper small intestine, where you are dissolved and passed into the bloodstream. There, you slop into a molecular chain of events and disable the enzyme that converts the acid in cell membranes into prostaglandins. The nerve endings are now desensitized, that pain message to the brain is stopped, and your host is smiling again.

You reduce fever in a similar way. If your host were suffering   4 from the flu, her white blood cells would be fighting the virus by producing prostaglandins that, in turn, cause the body's temperature to rise. You head off the prostaglandins and bring the fever down.

You are not the only pain-relieving agent at work. Ibuprofen   5 and other aspirinlike drugs known as nonsteroidal anti-inflammatory drugs (NSAIDs) do much the same thing. You all share possible side effects—in 2 to 6 percent of your clients, you cause stomach irritation and possibly bleeding and, in extreme cases, kidney failure. Prostaglandins help maintain the integrity of the stomach lining, and in their absence, the acidic NSAIDs give the host a queasy feeling.

As a tonic for hire, you have been around for a century, but   6 your family tree goes back much further. In ancient Greece, Hippocrates noted that chewing on willow leaves reduced fever. In the 1800s, two Italian chemists confirmed that willow bark contains one of your main ingredients, the antipyretic (fever-reducing) salicin. A Swiss pharmacist then found that meadowsweet, a shrub in the spirea family, has even more of the magic substance than willow bark. And while experimenting with salicin, a German chemist created salicylic acid (the SA of ASA). He called it *Spirsäure* after spirea, hence the "spirin" part of your name. The "a" was added for "acetyl," the substances— including a salt—that made the SA easier on the stomach. In

1893, Felix Hoffmann at the Bayer AG Chemical Works in Germany purified and stabilized you, and that's when you first claimed celebrity status as one of the world's most popular, inexpensive pain relievers. Today you are synthesized from coal tar or petroleum instead of plants.

Beyond garden-variety aches and pains, you are prescribed   7 as a remedy for arthritis because of your genius for blocking prostaglandins that trigger the pain and swelling of joints. Your most recent prostaglandin-fighting potential is to prevent heart attack and stroke. There is even talk that you may help ward off cancer and senility. Mission impossible? We'll see.

UNDERSTANDING DETAILS

1. What is ASA made from? What does *ASA* stand for?
2. When was ASA invented? By whom?
3. Explain how ASA works to relieve pain and reduce fever.

ANALYZING MEANING

1. Why has ASA become so popular over time? What do you anticipate its status will be in the future?
2. Describe Littlejohn's attitude toward her subject. What specific examples contribute to this impression?
3. Explain why ASA is now synthesized from coal tar or petroleum. Why have we moved beyond simply ingesting willow leaves and meadowsweet?

DISCOVERING RHETORICAL STRATEGIES

1. Littlejohn uses the second person to detail the history and the effect of ASA. What is the effect of casting the reader in the role of an ASA tablet? Why has she chosen this strategy? How effective is her choice to address the inanimate subject of her essay directly?
2. In this essay Littlejohn uses an extended metaphor. To what does she compare ASA? List five examples where she makes this connection.
3. Is this essay a directive or a descriptive process analysis? Why is this an appropriate strategy for this topic?

MAKING CONNECTIONS

1. Littlejohn uses an extended metaphor in this essay to make her subject more interesting and easier to understand. Explain how her use of figurative language compares to that of Lesley Choyce ("Thin Edge of the Wedge"), Dave Bidini ("Kris King Looks Terrible"), or Sherwin Tjia ("Of Lemons & Lemonade").
2. "You Are a Contract Painkiller" addresses the reader directly as "you" and, in fact, casts the reader as the subject of the essay. How is this approach similar to that of Joe Fiorito's "Breakfast in Bed"? How is the role of the reader different in these two essays?
3. Maureen Littlejohn is presenting scientific information in this essay and incorporating terminology that may initially be unfamiliar to her readers. What strategies has she used to make this subject accessible and interesting to her audience? How does her approach compare to that of Stanley Coren ("Dogs and Monsters")?

IDEAS FOR DISCUSSION/WRITING

Preparing to Write

Write freely about common pain medications with which you are familiar. What do you do if you burn yourself with an iron? How do you remedy a headache? What do you do for bee stings? What is the best way to relieve sunburn pain? How do you treat a sprain? How did you learn about these treatments? How do you gauge their effectiveness?

Choosing a Topic

1. Think of a practice that was once commonly accepted for treating some ailment. It might be the use of mustard plasters or cod liver oil to cure or prevent colds, electric shock therapy to treat psychological problems, amputation to prevent the spread of infection, or lobotomies to cure psychological disorders. In a short essay, explain how and why this practice fell out of favour.
2. There are many things that we may find disagreeable but that we do because we recognize the benefits that they offer. This might include getting our teeth cleaned at the dentist's, exercising, or cleaning the bathroom. Describe one such process, focusing on its positive aspects.

3. Taking medication is one response to relieving pain, but many people are resistant to taking medications such as ASA. Write an essay in which you present some alternative responses to treating a headache or other "garden-variety aches and pains."

WEBSITES

www.nursespdr.com/members/database/ndrhtml/ acetylsalicylicacid.html

This site contains information on ASA from the *PDR Nurse's Drug Handbook*.

JOE FIORITO

Breakfast in Bed

Originally from Thunder Bay, Ontario, Joe Fiorito (1948–) began his writing career in Montreal, Quebec, where he worked as a columnist for the Montreal *Gazette* and *Hour* magazine. Fiorito now lives in Toronto and contributes regular columns to Air Canada's *enRoute* magazine and the *National Post*. He has worked for CBC Radio, where he produced *The Food Show*, and he is also a published poet. His book *Comfort Me With Apples* (1994) is a collection of essays that originally were published as a weekly column in *Hour* magazine. While Fiorito has no formal journalism training, in 1996 he won a national newspaper award for his *Gazette* columns. A collection of these profiles, or "people pieces," has now been published in a book entitled *Tango on the Main*. Most recently, Fiorito has written a memoir, *The Closer We Are to Dying* (1999), about his family, and a novel entitled *The Song Beneath the Ice* (2002).

Preparing to Read

While "Breakfast in Bed" is taken from *Comfort Me With Apples*, it originally appeared in *Hour* magazine in 1993. In this short essay, Fiorito gives the reader a recipe and a reason for making popovers. Before you begin to read, think about the importance of smell in your life. What is the difference between a smell and a scent? What about an odour? What smells do you find appealing? What smells are repulsive or annoying? Do you have a favourite perfume or cologne? What is it? How would you describe its scent?

1 The Inuit greet face to face, but they don't rub noses, exactly, and you shouldn't call it kissing. It is a form of greeting every bit as intimate as a kiss, but it goes deeper than that; it's a way for friends to take in each other's smell. It's how friends fill the empty places caused by absence.

2 Smell is fundamental to happiness. I know a man who travels with a piece of his wife's clothing sealed in a plastic bag. When the separation is too much to bear, he opens the bag and breathes.

3 Traces of this signature mark our sheets and pillows; this is what makes crawling into bed on a cold night such a comfort.

Smell is one of the many nameless things you miss when   4
love goes wrong. That smell will linger, it will haunt you and
exhaust you long after your lover has gone.

Think I'm exaggerating? Wake early one Sunday and smell   5
the person sleeping next to you. Do it. Lean over. The side of the
neck will do, just below the ear. Take a deep breath. The
knowledge of this scent is lodged in the deepest part of your
brain. Breathe deeply, if only to remind yourself of why you are
where you are, doing what you're doing.

Now go to the kitchen. Throw two eggs into a bowl with a   6
cup of milk and a cup of flour. Add a quarter teaspoon of salt
and a tablespoon of melted butter. Mix until smooth, but don't
overdo it.

Pour the batter into buttered muffin tins, filling the cups no   7
more than half full. Put the tins in a cold oven. Turn on the heat
to 450°F. After fifteen minutes, turn the oven down to 350°F.
Wait fifteen minutes more.

This recipe comes from the *Fannie Farmer Baking Book* by   8
Marion Cunningham. It's an important book, with clear recipes
and much new thinking. For example, prior to Marion, popovers
were always started in a hot oven. This is a small thing, but one
which changed my life.

While you're changing yours, make some coffee and squeeze   9
a couple of oranges. Do what you want with a pear or a pine-
apple. Get a tray ready to take back to bed.

Now open the oven. It will make you smile. They don't call   10
these things popovers for nothing. They look like little domes,
golden brown and slightly crisp on the outside. The texture inside
is as soft as your partner's neck. The smell is just as warm and
every bit as earthy.

Take them out of the muffin tins and put them in a basket.   11
They'll steam as you break them open. Eat them with a little
butter and the best jam or honey in the cupboard. A soft
camembert isn't out of place if you have it.

Breakfast together is the second- or third-most intimate thing   12
you can share. If someone new is sleeping over and you want
to make an impression, make these. If you're worried about what
to talk about while you're eating, remember what Oscar Wilde
said. Only dull people are brilliant at breakfast.

If you haven't got a partner, make popovers anyway. It's   13
easy enough to cut this recipe in half. It's good practice. It's its

own reward. The butter melts into the jam and the sun pours onto your breakfast bed. And you have another way to fill the emptiness caused by absence.

UNDERSTANDING DETAILS

1. How does Fiorito suggest that one can fill the emptiness that results from loneliness?
2. What process is Fiorito explaining in this essay?
3. What are popovers? How did they get their name?

ANALYZING MEANING

1. Explain the relationship between smell and memory.
2. What does Fiorito mean when he says that smell is fundamental to happiness?
3. Explain why, in Fiorito's estimation, breakfast together is such an intimate experience.

DISCOVERING RHETORICAL STRATEGIES

1. In this essay, Fiorito is giving the readers a recipe. How does it differ from the way a popover recipe might be written in *The Joy of Cooking* or any other cookbook?
2. How does Fiorito link the beginning and the end of his essay? Does he have an effective introduction and conclusion?
3. Describe Fiorito's tone in this essay. Use specific examples to show how his style (use of language) creates this tone.

MAKING CONNECTIONS

1. Joe Fiorito's writing is distinguished by a conversational tone and an informal style. Compare his style to that of Laura Robinson ("Starving for the Gold") or Janice Gross Stein ("Developing a National Voice"). Whose style do you find more effective? Why?
2. Fiorito takes a subject that seems relatively simple and potentially boring and creates interest through the incorporation of specific detail. Explain how this approach makes his topic interesting and entertaining. How does this compare to the approach of Sharon Butala ("The Myth: The Prairies Are Flat") or Dave Bidini ("Kris King Looks Terrible")?

IDEAS FOR DISCUSSION/WRITING

Preparing to Write

Write freely about your favourite food. What do you know about its national origins or about the history of its preparation? Where and when do you eat this food? Do you associate it with any particular events or people in your life? Could you write a recipe for this food yourself? What ingredients does it contain? Is your favourite food healthy and nutritious, junk food, or a bit of both?

Choosing a Topic

1. Write an essay in which you include a recipe for one of your favourite foods that is fairly simple to prepare. Instead of writing it in "cookbook instruction style," present the information in a narrative like Fiorito does, in which you also provide a context and some subjective information about this dish. Make sure that you provide enough detail so that your reader will be able to follow your recipe.

2. In "Breakfast in Bed" Fiorito says that breakfast together is one of the most intimate experiences you can share. Think of some particular ritual that you share with others that involves food. This might be preparing or eating a family meal, preserving fruit or vegetables, making wine or beer, or going out for a drink after work. How often does this ritual happen? Who participates? Where does this ritual fall on the intimacy scale? Write an essay in which you describe this event in a descriptive process analysis.

3. In "Breakfast in Bed" Fiorito cites Oscar Wilde as saying, "Only dull people are brilliant at breakfast." Write an essay in which you explain to your audience how to appear brilliant at any meal you choose.

WEBSITES

www.signature-editions.com/xbjf.htm
Here you will find a brief biography of Fiorito along with links to excerpts from his books.

www.ryerson.ca/rrj/content/print/2001/summer/mcphee.html
Read an interview with Joe Fiorito.

cbc.ca/millennium/authors/fiorito.html
"That's Progress," an essay by Fiorito.

www.epicurious.com/run/fooddictionary/browse?entry_id=9702
Epicurious dictionary: popover.

CHAPTER 5

DIVISION/
CLASSIFICATION

Finding Categories

Both division and classification play important roles in our everyday lives: Bureau drawers separate one type of clothing from another; kitchen cabinets organize food, dishes, and utensils into proper groups; grocery stores shelve similar items together so shoppers can easily locate what they want to buy; school notebooks with tabs help students divide up their academic lives; newspapers classify local and national events in order to organize a great deal of daily information for the general public; and our own personal classification systems assist us in separating what we like from what we don't so that we can have access to our favourite foods, our favourite cars, our favourite entertainment, our favourite people. The two processes of division and classification are so natural to us, in fact, that we sometimes aren't even aware we are using them.

Defining Division/Classification

Division and classification are actually mirror images of each other. Division is the basic feature of process analysis, which we studied in the last chapter: It moves from a general concept to subdivisions of that concept or from a single category to multiple subcategories. Classification works in the opposite direction, moving from specifics to a group with common traits, or from multiple subgroups to a single, larger, and more inclusive category. These techniques work together in many ways: A college, for example, is *divided* into departments (single to multiple), whereas courses are *classified* by department (multiple to single); the medical field is *divided* into specialties, whereas doctors are *classified* by a single specialty; a cookbook is *divided* into chapters, whereas recipes are *classified* according to type; and athletics is *divided* into specific sports, whereas athletes are *classified* by the sport in which they participate. Division is the separation of an idea or an item into its basic parts, such as a home into rooms, a course into assignments, or a job into various duties or responsibilities; classification is the organization of items with similar features into a group or groups, such as identifying all green-eyed people in a large group, cutting out all carbohydrates from your diet, or watching only the track and field events during the Olympics.

Classification is an organizational system for presenting a large amount of material to a reader or listener. This process helps us make sense of the complex world we live in by letting us work with smaller, more understandable units of that world. Classification must be governed by some clear, logical purpose (such as focusing on all lower-level course requirements), which will then dictate the system of categories to be used. The plan of organization that results should be as flexible as possible, and it should illustrate the specific relationship to each of the other items in a group and of the groups themselves to one another.

As you already know, many different ways of classifying the same elements are possible. If you consider the examples at the outset of this chapter, you will realize that bureau drawers vary from house to house and even from person to person; that no one's kitchen is set up exactly the same way as someone else's; and that grocery stores have similar but not identical systems of food classification. (Think, for instance, of the many different schemes for organizing dairy products, meats, diet foods, etc.) In addition, your friends probably use a method different from yours to organize their school notebooks; different newspapers vary their presentation of the news; and two professors will probably teach the same course material in divergent ways. We all have distinct and uniquely logical methods of classifying the elements in our own lives.

The following student paragraph about friends illustrates both division and classification. As you read it, notice how the student writer moves back and forth smoothly from general to specific and from multiple to single:

> The word "friend" can refer to many different types of relationships. Close friends are "friends" at their very best: people for whom we feel respect, esteem, and, quite possibly, even love. We regard these people and their well-being with kindness, interest, and goodwill; we trust them and will go out of our way to help them. Needless to say, we could all use at least one close friend. Next come "casual friends," people with whom we share a particular interest or activity. The investment of a great amount of time and energy in developing this type of friendship is usually not required, though casual friends often become close friends with the passage of time. The last division of "friend" is most general and is composed of all those individuals whose acquaintance we have made and who feel no hostility toward us. When one is counting friends, this group should certainly be included, since such friendships often develop into "casual" or "close" relationships. Knowing people in all three groups is necessary, however, because all types of friends undoubtedly help us live healthier, happier lives.

Thinking Critically by Using Division/Classification

The thinking strategies of division and classification are the flip sides of each other: Your textbook is *divided* into chapters (one item divided into many), but chapters are *classified* (grouped) into sections or units. Your brain performs these mental acrobatics constantly, but to be as proficient at this method of thinking as possible, you need to be aware of the cognitive activities you go through. Focusing on these two companion patterns of thought will develop your skill in dealing with these complex schemes as it simultaneously increases your overall mental capabilities.

You might think of division/classification as a driving pattern that goes forward and then doubles back on itself in reverse. Division is a movement from a single concept to multiple categories, while classification involves gathering multiple concepts into a single group. Dividing and/or classifying helps us make sense of our subject by using categories to highlight similarities and differences. In the case of division, you are trying to find what differences break the items into separate groups, while, with classification, you let the similarities among the items help you put the material into meaningful categories. Processing your material in this way helps your readers see your particular subject in a new way and often brings renewed insights to both reader and writer.

Experimenting with division and classification is important to your growth as a critical thinker. It will help you process complex information so you can understand more fully your options for dealing with material in all subject areas. Practising division and classification separately from other rhetorical modes makes you concentrate on improving this particular pattern of thinking before adding it to your expanding arsenal of critical thinking skills.

1. Study the table of contents of a magazine that interests you. Into what sections is the magazine divided? What distinguishing features does each section have? Now study the various adver-tisements in the same magazine. What different categories would you use to classify these ads? List the ads in each category.

2. Make a chart classifying the English instructors at your school. Explain your classification system to the class.

3. List six to eight major concerns you have about Canadian society. Which of these are most important? Which are least important? Now classify these concerns into two or three distinct categories.

Reading and Writing Division/ Classification Essays

Writers of division/classification essays must first decide if they are going to break down a topic into many separate parts or group together similar items into one coherent category; a writer's purpose will, of course, guide him or her in this decision. Readers must likewise recognize and understand which of these two parallel operations an author is using to structure an essay. Another important identifying feature of division/classification essays is an explanation (explicit or implicit) of the significance of a particular system of organization.

How to Read a Division/Classification Essay

Preparing to Read. As you approach the selections in this chapter, you should study all the material that precedes each essay so you can prepare yourself for your reading. First of all, what hints does the title give you about what you are going to read? To what extent does Amy Willard Cross reveal in her title her attitude toward the pace of life? Who do you think Susan Swan's audience is in "Nine Ways of Looking at a Critic"? Does David Foot's title give us any indication about his point of view in "Boomers Dance to a New Beat"? Then, see what you can learn from scanning each essay and reading its synopsis in the Rhetorical Table of Contents.

Also important as you prepare to read the essays in this chapter is your knowledge about each author and the conditions under which each essay was written: What does the biographical material tell you about Gwynne Dyer's "Flagging Attention"? About Judith Wallerstein and Sandra Blakeslee's " Second Chances for Children of Divorce"? Knowing where these essays were first published will give you even more information about each author's purpose and audience.

Finally, before you begin to read, answer the Preparing to Read questions, and then think freely for a few minutes about the general topic: What do you want to know about the different types of book critics discussed by Susan Swan in "Nine Ways of Looking at a Critic"? What are some of your own stories about living in a time-conscious society (Cross)?

Reading. As you read each essay for the first time, write down your initial reactions to the topic itself, to the preliminary material, to the mood the writer sets, or to a specific incident in the essay. Make associations between the essay and your own experiences.

In addition, create a context for each essay by drawing on the preliminary material you just read about the essay: What is David Foot telling us about the baby boom generation, and why is this of interest? What is Swan saying about the role of the critic in the creative process? According to Dyer, why are the designs of our flags significant?

Also, in this first reading, notice whether the writers divided (split up) or classified (gathered together) their material to make their point. Finally, read the questions after each essay, and let them guide your second reading of the selection.

Rereading. When you read these division/classification essays a second time, notice how the authors carefully match their dominant rhetorical approach (in this case, division or classification) to their purpose in a clear thesis. What, for example, is Swan's dominant rhetorical approach to her subject? How does this approach further her purpose? What other rhetorical strategies support her thesis? Then, see how these writers logically present their division or classification systems to their readers, defining new categories as their essays progress. Finally, notice how each writer either implicitly or explicitly explains the significance or value of his or her division/classification system. How does Gwynne Dyer explain his system of organization? And how does Cross give her organizing principle significance? Now, answer the questions after each essay to check your understanding and to help you analyze your reading in preparation for the discussion/writing topics that follow.

For a more complete survey of reading guidelines, you may want to consult the checklist on pages 17–18 of the Introduction.

How to Write a Division/Classification Essay

Preparing to Write. You should approach a division/classification essay in the same way you have begun all your other writing assignments—with some kind of prewriting activity that will help you generate ideas, such as the Preparing to Write questions featured in this chapter. The prewriting techniques outlined in the Introduction on pages 19–25 can help you approach these questions imaginatively. Before you even consider the selection and arrangement of details, you need to explore your subject, choose a topic, and decide on a specific purpose and audience. The best way to explore your subject is to think about it, read about it, and then write about it. Look at it from all possible angles and see what patterns and relationships emerge. To choose a specific topic, you might begin by listing any groups, patterns, or combinations you discover within your subject matter. Your purpose should take shape as you form your thesis, and your audience is probably dictated by the assignment. Making these decisions before you write will make the rest of your task much easier.

Writing. As you begin to write, certain guidelines will help you structure your ideas for a division/classification essay:

1. First, declare an overall purpose for your classification.
2. Then, divide the item or concept you are dealing with into categories.
3. Arrange these categories into a logical sequence.
4. Define each category, explaining the difference between one category and another and showing that difference through specific examples.
5. Explain the significance of your classification system. (Why is it worth reading? What will your audience learn from it?)

All discussion in such an essay should reinforce the purpose stated at the beginning of the theme. Other rhetorical modes—such as narration, example, and comparison/contrast—will naturally be used to supplement your classification.

To make your classification as workable as possible, take special care that your categories do not overlap and that all topics fall into their proper places. If, for example, you were classifying all the jobs performed by students in your writing class, the categories of (1) indoor work and (2) outdoor work would probably be inadequate. Most delivery jobs, for example, fall into both categories. At a pizza parlour, a florist, or a gift shop, a delivery person's time would be split between indoor and outdoor work. So you would need to design a different classification system to avoid this problem. The categories of (1) indoor work, (2) outdoor work, and (3) a combination of indoor and outdoor work would be much more useful for this task. Making sure your categories don't overlap will help make your classification essays more readable and more accurate.

Rewriting. As you rewrite your division/classification essays, consider carefully the probable reactions of your readers to the form and content of your paper:

- Does your thesis communicate your purpose clearly?
- Have you divided your topic into separate and understandable categories?
- Are these categories arranged logically?
- Are the distinctions between your categories as clear as possible?

- Do you explain the significance of your particular classification system?

More guidelines for writing and rewriting are available on pages 29–30 of the Introduction.

Student Essay: Division/Classification at Work

The following student essay divides skiers into interesting categories based on their physical abilities. As you read it, notice how the student writer weaves the significance of his study into his opening statement of purpose. Also, pay particular attention to his logical method of organization and clear explanation of categories as he moves with ease from multiple to single and back to multiple again throughout the essay.

People on the Slopes

When I first learned to ski, I was amazed by the shapes who whizzed by me and slipped down trails marked only by a black diamond signifying "most difficult," while others careened awkwardly down the "bunny slopes." These skiers, I discovered, could be divided into distinct categories—for my own entertainment and for the purpose of finding appropriate skiing partners.

First are the poetic skiers. They glide down the mountainside silently with what seems like no effort at all. They float from side to side on the intermediate slopes, their knees bent perfectly above parallel skis, while their sharp skills allow them to bypass slower skiers with safely executed turns at remarkable speeds.

The crazy skiers also get down the mountain quickly, but with a lot more noise attending their descent. At every hill, they yell a loud "Yahoo!" and slam their skis into the snow. These go-for-broke athletes always whiz by faster than everyone else, and they especially seem to love the crowded runs where they can slide over the backs of other people's skis. I often find crazy skiers in mangled messes at the bottoms of steep hills, where they are yelling loudly, but not the famous "Yahoo!"

After being overwhelmed by the crazy skiers, I am always glad to find other skiers like myself: the average ones. We are polite on the slopes, concentrate on improving our technique with every

Margin annotations:

Thesis statement · Subject · Overall purpose

First category · Definition · Supporting details

Second category · Definition · Supporting details (with humour)

Third category · Transition

Definition run, and ski the beginner slopes only at the beginning of the day to warm up. We go over the moguls (small hills) much more cautiously than the crazy or poetic skiers, but we still seek adventure with a slight jump or two each day. We remain a silent majority on the mountain. *Supporting detail (comparative)*

Fourth category
Definition
Below us in talent, but much more evident on the mountainside, are what I call the eternal beginners. These skiers stick to the same beginner slope almost every run of every day during their vacation. Should they venture onto an intermediate slope, they quickly assume the snowplow position (a pigeon-toed stance) and never leave it. Eternal beginners weave from one side of the run to the other and hardly ever fall, because they proceed so slowly; however, they do yell quite a bit at the crazies who like to run over the backs of their skis. *Transition*

Supporting details

Transition
Having always enjoyed people-watching, I have fun each time I am on the slopes observing the myriad of skiers around me. I use these observations to pick out possible ski partners for myself and others. Since my mother is an eternal beginner, she has more fun skiing with someone who shares her interests than with my dad, who is a poetic skier with solitude on his mind. After taking care of Mom, I am free to find a partner I'll enjoy. My sister, the crazy skier of the family, just heads for the rowdiest group she can find! As the years go by and my talents grow, I am trusting my perceptions of skier types to help me find the right partner for life on and off the slopes. No doubt watching my fellow skiers will always remain an enjoyable pastime. *Significance of classification system*

Concluding remarks

Some Final Thoughts on Division/Classification

The essays collected in this chapter use division and/or classification as their primary organizing principle. All of these essays show both techniques at work to varying degrees. As you read these essays, you might also want to be aware of the other rhetorical modes that support these division/classification essays, such as description and definition. Finally, pay particular attention to how these authors bring significance to their systems of classification and, as a result, to their essays themselves.

Division/Classification in Review

Reading Division/Classification Essays

Preparing to Read

- What assumptions can you make from the essay's title?
- Can you guess what the general mood of the essay is?
- What is the essay's purpose and audience?
- What does the synopsis in the Rhetorical Table of Contents tell you about the essay?
- What can you learn from the author's biography?
- Can you guess what the author's point of view toward the subject is?
- What are your responses to the Preparing to Read questions?

Reading

- What do you think the "context" of the essay is?
- Did the author use division or classification most often?
- Did you preview the questions that follow the essay?

Rereading

- How does division or classification help the author accomplish his/her purpose?
- What other rhetorical strategies does the author use to support the essay's purpose?
- How does the writer explain the significance of his/her division/classification system?
- What are your responses to the questions after the essay?

Writing Division/Classification Essays

Preparing to Write

- What are your responses to the Preparing to Write questions?
- What is your purpose?
- Who is your audience?

Writing

- Do you declare an overall purpose for your essay?
- Do you divide the item or concept you are dealing with into categories?
- Do you arrange these categories into a logical sequence?
- Do you define each category, explaining the difference between one category and another and demonstrating that difference through examples?
- Do you explain the significance of your division/classification system?
- Are the categories in your essay distinct from one another so they don't overlap?
- What rhetorical strategies support your essay?

Rewriting

- Does your thesis communicate your purpose clearly?
- Have you divided your topic into separate and understandable categories?
- Are these categories arranged logically?
- Do you explain the significance of your particular classification system?

JUDITH WALLERSTEIN
SANDRA BLAKESLEE

Second Chances for Children of Divorce

Judith Wallerstein (1921–) grew up in New York City, earned her Ph.D. at Lund University in Sweden, and now lives and works in Marin County, California, where she serves as director of the Center for the Family in Transition. Since 1965, she has taught psychology at the University of California at Berkeley, where she specializes in divorce and its effect on family members. Her first book, *Surviving the Breakup* (coauthored by Joan Kelly, 1980), analyzes the impact of divorce on young children in the family. Her next, *Second Chances: Men, Women, and Children a Decade After Divorce* (1989), is a study of the long-term effects of divorce on teenagers and young adults. Her most recent book, *The Unexpected Legacy of Divorce* (2000), is a study of the effects of divorce on children twenty-five years after their parents' breakup. Now hard at work on a study of happy marriages, Wallerstein is very concerned about what is happening to the American family. "There's a lot of anger in relationships between men and women today," she explains. "It's always easier to express anger than love." An avid reader, she collects ideas the way "other people collect recipes." She advises college students to read as much as possible: "The first prerequisite a writer must have is a love of reading." Her coauthor on *Second Chances*, Sandra Blakeslee (1943–), was born in Flushing, New York, and earned her B.S. degree at Berkeley, where her specialty was neurobiology. She is currently the West Coast science and medicine correspondent for *The New York Times*. A former Peace Corps volunteer in Borneo, she advises students using *Reader's Choice* to travel as much as possible: "You need a wide range of experiences to be a good writer." Blakeslee goes mountain biking and runs in her spare time.

Preparing to Read

In the following essay from *Second Chances*, Wallerstein and Blakeslee classify the psychological tasks children who have suffered through the divorce of their parents must complete to free themselves from the past. As you prepare to read this essay, take a few minutes to think about the effects of divorce on yourself or someone you know: How close have you been to a divorce experience? How were people directly associated with the experience affected? What differences did you notice in the way adults and children responded to the same situation? What feelings were most common among the adults? Among the children? Why do you think the divorce rate has been so high during the last fifty years? Do you think this trend will continue, or will it taper off in the next few years?

A t each stage in the life cycle, children and adults face predictable and particular issues that represent the coming together of the demands of society and a biological and psychological timetable. Just as we physically learn to sit, crawl, walk, and run, we follow an equivalent progression in our psychological and social development. Each stage presents us with a sequence of tasks we must confront. We can succeed or fail in mastering them, to varying degrees, but everyone encounters the tasks. They begin at birth and end at death. 1

Children move upward along a common developmental ladder, although each goes it alone at his or her own pace. Gradually, as they pass through the various stages, children consolidate a sense of self. They develop coping skills, conscience, and the capacity to give and receive love. 2

Children take one step at a time, negotiating the rung they are on before they can move up to the next. They may—and often do—falter in this effort. The climb is not steady under the best of circumstances, and most children briefly stand still in their ascent. They may even at times move backward. Such regressions are not a cause for alarm; rather, they may represent an appropriate response to life's stresses. Children who fail one task are not stalled forever; they will go on to the next stage, although they may be weakened in their climb. Earlier failures will not necessarily imperil their capacity as adults to trust a relationship, make a commitment, hold an appropriate job, or be a parent—to make use of their second chances at each stage of development. 3

I propose that children who experience divorce face an additional set of tasks specific to divorce in addition to the normal developmental tasks of growing up. Growing up is inevitably harder for children of divorce because they must deal with psychological issues that children from well-functioning intact families do not have to face. 4

The psychological tasks of children begin as difficulties, escalate between the parents during the marriage, and continue through the separation and divorce and throughout the postdivorce years. 5

TASK: *Understanding the Divorce*

The first and most basic task at the time of separation is for the   6
children to understand realistically what the divorce means in
their family and what its concrete consequences will be. Children,
especially very young children, are thrown back on frightening
and vivid fantasies of being abandoned, being placed in foster
care, or never seeing a departed parent again, or macabre
fantasies such as a mother being destroyed in an earthquake or
a father being destroyed by a vengeful mother. All of these
fantasies and the feelings that accompany them can be undone
only as the children, with the parents' continuing help, begin to
understand the reality and begin to adjust to the actual changes
that the divorce brings.

The more mature task of understanding what led to the   7
marital failure awaits the perspective of the adolescent and young
adult. Early on, most children regard divorce as a serious error,
but by adolescence most feel that their parents never should have
married. The task of understanding occurs in two stages. The
first involves accurately perceiving the immediate changes that
divorce brings and differentiating fantasy fears from reality. The
second occurs later, when children are able at greater distance
and with more mature understanding to evaluate their parents'
actions and can draw useful lessons for their own lives.

TASK: *Strategic Withdrawal*

Children and adolescents need to get on with their own lives as   8
soon as possible after the divorce, to resume their normal
activities at school and at play, to get back physically and
emotionally to the normal tasks of growing up. Especially for
adolescents who may have been beginning to spread their wings,
the divorce pulls them back into the family orbit, where they
may become consumed with care for siblings or a troubled parent.
It also intrudes on their academic and social life, causing them to
spend class time preoccupied with worry and to pass up social
activities because of demands at home. This is not to say that
children should ignore the divorce. Their task is to acknowledge
their concern and to provide appropriate help to their parents
and siblings, but they should strive to remove the divorce from
the center of their own thoughts so that they can get back to their
own interests, pleasures, problems, and peer relationships. To

achieve this task, children need encouragement from their parents to remain children.

TASK: *Dealing with Loss*

In the years following divorce, children experience two profound   9
losses. One is the loss of the intact family together with the symbolic and real protection it has provided. The second is the loss of the presence of one parent, usually the father, from their daily lives.

In dealing with these losses, children fall back on many   10
fantasies to mask their unhappiness. As we have seen, they may idealize the father as representative of all that is lacking in their current lives, thinking that if only he were present, everything would be better.

The task of absorbing loss is perhaps the single most difficult   11
task imposed by divorce. At its core, the task requires children to overcome the profound sense of rejection, humiliation, unlovability, and powerlessness they feel with the departure of one parent. When the parent leaves, children of all ages blame themselves. They say, "He left me because I was not lovable. I was not worthy." They conclude that had they been more lovable, worthy, or different, the parent would have stayed. In this way, the loss of the parent and lowered self-esteem become intertwined.

To stave off these intensely painful feelings of rejection,   12
children continually try to undo the divorce scenario, to bring their parents back together, or to somehow win back the affection of the absent parent. The explanation "Had he loved me, he would not have left the family" turns into a new concern. "If he loved me, he would visit more often. He would spend more time with me." With this in mind, the children not only are pained at the outset but remain vulnerable, sometimes increasingly, over the years. Many reach out during adolescence to increase contact with the parent who left, again to undo the sad scenario and to rebuild their self-esteem as well.

This task is easier if parents and children have a good   13
relationship, within the framework of a good visiting or joint custody arrangement.

Some children are able to use a good, close relationship with   14
the visiting parent to promote their growth within the divorced family. Others are able to acknowledge and accept that the

visiting parent could never become the kind of parent they need,
and they are able to turn away from blaming themselves. Still
others are able to reject, on their own, a rejecting parent or to
reject a role model that they see as flawed. In so doing, these
youngsters are able to effectively master the loss and get on with
their lives.

TASK: Dealing with Anger

Divorce, unlike death, is always a voluntary decision for at least   15
one of the partners in a marriage. Everyone involved knows this.
The child understands that divorce is not a natural disaster like
an earthquake or tornado; it is caused by the decision of one or
both of the parents to separate. Its true cause lies in the parents'
failure to maintain the marriage, and someone is culpable.

Given this knowledge, children face a terrible dilemma. They   16
know that their unhappiness has been caused by the very people
charged with their protection and care—their parents are the
agents of their distress. Furthermore, the parents undertook this
role voluntarily. This realization puts children in a dreadful bind
because they know something that they dare not express—out
of fear, out of anxiety, out of a wish to protect their parents.

Children get angry at their parents, experiencing divorce as   17
indifference to their needs and perceiving parents sometimes
realistically as self-centered and uncaring, as preaching a corrupt
morality, and as weak and unable to deal with problems except
by running away.

At the same time, children are aware of their parents'   18
neediness, weaknesses, and anxiety about life's difficulties.
Although children have little understanding of divorce, except
when the fighting has been open and violent, they fully recognize
how unhappy and disorganized their parents become, and this
frightens them very much. Caught in a combination of anger
and love, the children are frightened and guilty about their anger
because they love their parents and perceive them as unhappy
people who are trying to improve their lives in the face of severe
obstacles. Their concern makes it difficult even to acknowledge
their anger.

A major task, then, for children is to work through this anger,   19
to recognize their parents as human beings capable of making
mistakes, and to respect them for their real efforts and their real
courage.

Cooling of anger and the task of forgiveness go hand in hand 20
with children's growing emotional maturity and capacity to
appreciate the various needs of the different family members.
As anger diminishes, young people are better able to put the
divorce behind them and experience relief. As children forgive
their parents, they forgive themselves for feeling anger and guilt
and for failing to restore the marriage. In this way, children can
free themselves from identification with the angry or violent
parent or with the victim.

TASK: Working Out Guilt

Young children often feel responsible for divorce, thinking that 21
their misbehavior may have caused one parent to leave. Or, in a
more complicated way, they may feel that their fantasy wish to
drive a wedge between their mother and father has been
magically granted. Many guilty feelings arise at the time of
divorce but dissipate naturally as children mature. Others persist,
usually with roots in a profound continuing sense of having
caused the unthinkable—getting rid of one parent so as to be
closer to the other.

Other feelings of guilt are rooted in children's realization 22
that they were indeed a cause of marital difficulty. Many divorces
occur after the birth of a child, and the child correctly compre-
hends that he or she really did drive a wedge between the adults.

We see another kind of guilt in girls who, in identifying with 23
their troubled mothers, become afraid to surpass their mothers.
These young women have trouble separating from their mothers,
whom they love and feel sorry for, and establishing their own
successful relationships with suitable young men. The children
of divorce need to separate from guilty ties that bind them too
closely to a troubled parent and to go on with their lives with
compassion and love.

TASK: Accepting the Permanence of the Divorce

At first, children feel a strong and understandable need to deny 24
the divorce. Such early denial may be a first step in the coping
process. Like a screen that is alternately lowered and raised, the
denial helps children confront the full reality of the divorce, bit
by bit. They cannot take it in all at once.

Nevertheless, we have learned that five and even ten years 25
after divorce, some children and adolescents refuse to accept the

divorce as a permanent state of affairs. They continue to hope, consciously or unconsciously, that the marriage will be restored, finding omens of reconciliation even in a harmless handshake or a simple friendly nod.

In accepting permanence, the children of divorce face a more   26
difficult task than children of bereavement. Death cannot be undone, but divorce happens between living people who can change their minds. A reconciliation fantasy taps deep into children's psyches. Children need to feel that their parents will still be happy together. They may not overcome this fantasy of reconciliation until they themselves finally separate from their parents and leave home.

TASK: Taking a Chance on Love

This is perhaps the most important task for growing children   27
and for society. Despite what life has dealt them, despite lingering fears and anxieties, the children of divorce must grow, become open to the possibility of success or failure, and take a chance on love. They must hold on to a realistic vision that they can both love and be loved.

This is the central task for youngsters during adolescence   28
and at entry into young adulthood. And as we have seen, it is the task on which so many children tragically flounder. Children who lose a parent through death must take a chance on loving with the knowledge that all people eventually die and that death can take away our loved ones at any time. Children who lose the intact family through divorce must also take a chance on love, knowing realistically that divorce is always possible but being willing nevertheless to remain open to love, commitment, marriage, and fidelity.

More than the ideology of hoping to fall in love and find   29
commitment, this task involves being able to turn away from the model of parents who could not stay committed to each other. While all the young people in our study were in search of romantic love, a large number of them lived with such a high degree of anxiety over fears of betrayal or of not finding love that they were entirely unable to take the kind of chances necessary for them to move emotionally into successful young adulthood.

This last task, taking a chance on love, involves being able to   30
venture, not just thinking about it, and not thinking one way

and behaving another. It involves accepting a morality that truly guides behavior. This is the task that occupies children of divorce throughout their adolescence. It is what makes adolescence such a critical and difficult time for them. The resolution of life's tasks is a relative process that never ends, but this last task, which is built on successfully negotiating all the others, leads to psychological freedom from the past. This is the essence of second chances for children of divorce.

UNDERSTANDING DETAILS

1. Name the seven categories into which Wallerstein and Blakeslee divide the psychological growth of the children of divorce. How long will it take most children to perform these tasks?
2. According to Wallerstein and Blakeslee, what is probably the most difficult task that results from divorce? Why do the authors believe this stage is so painful?
3. What did Wallerstein and Blakeslee find out about their subjects' ability to deal with love in their lives?

ANALYZING MEANING

1. In your opinion, which of the emotional tasks that Wallerstein and Blakeslee describe is likely to be most traumatic in a child's life after a divorce? On what do you base your conclusion?
2. What is the relationship suggested in this essay between the parents' divorce and a child's sense of rejection?
3. How might an understanding of the seven tasks discussed in this essay help people deal more effectively with children affected by divorce?

DISCOVERING RHETORICAL STRATEGIES

1. How do Wallerstein and Blakeslee organize their categories in this essay? Why do they place these tasks in this particular order?
2. What is the authors' general attitude toward divorce? What references in the essay reveal this point of view?
3. Describe the authors' intended audience. What makes you think they are directing their comments to this group?

MAKING CONNECTIONS

1. Wallerstein and Blakeslee outline the psychological tasks required of children of divorce. Are any of these tasks ones that might also be required of other children, who are not children of divorce? Do you think that Evelyn Lau ("More and More"), Drew Hayden Taylor ("Pretty Like a White Boy"), or Wayson Choy ("I'm a Banana and Proud of It") might have faced any of the tasks described in Wallerstein and Blakeslee's essay?

2. Compare and contrast the tone of Wallerstein and Blakeslee's essay with that adopted by Susan Swan ("Nine Ways of Looking at a Critic") or Amy Willard Cross ("Life in the Stopwatch Lane"). Why do you think each of these writers has made the choice she did about tone?

3. Wallerstein and Blakeslee divide their essay into seven "tasks" that must be accomplished by children of divorce. Find a division/classification essay in this section of *Reader's Choice* that has more subdivisions. Then find one that has fewer. How does the number of subdivisions in a division/classification essay affect your ability to understand the author's entire argument? Which of these essays is the easiest to follow? Which is the most difficult? Why?

IDEAS FOR DISCUSSION/WRITING

Preparing to Write

Write freely about your thoughts on divorce and the effects of divorce on others: Do you know anyone who has gone through a divorce? How did the experience affect the couple getting divorced? How did it affect their friends, their relatives, and their children? How do you think the high divorce rate is affecting North Americans in general? Why is North America's national divorce rate so high? What changes could we make to lower the divorce rate?

Choosing a Topic

1. Assume that you are an expert on the variety and scope of college relationships. In an essay written for your classmates, divide your observations on different types of relationships into categories that will show students the full range of these associations in a college setting.

2. Because you have been involved with divorce in some way, you have been asked to submit to your college newspaper an editorial classifying the various ways in which different types of people react to divorce (husbands, wives, children, friends, and so on). You have been told to pay particular attention to the reactions of college students whose parents are going through or have gone through a divorce.

3. In an essay written for the general public, speculate about the reasons for the high national divorce rate. Use your own experience, interview others, or consult sources in the library to investigate the reasons for this trend. Suggest how we could solve this problem in North America.

WEBSITES

www.divorcesoftware.com/advisors/Dr_Judith_Wallerstein.htm This Divorce Software site includes a biography of Judith Wallerstein and a bibliography of her books.

www.divorceinfo.com/judithwallerstein.htm
www.4children.org/news/198coon.htm
Two critiques of Wallerstein's research.

search.barnesandnoble.com/bookSearch/isbnInquiry.asp?userid =6WLRY27W87&isbn=0786863943&displayonly=excerpt Read an excerpt from Wallerstein and Blakeslee's latest book here.

DAVID FOOT

Boomers Dance to a New Beat

David Foot is a professor of Economics at the University of Toronto who
has become very well known for his work concerning the role of demographics in determining societal and economic trends. Foot's book *Boom,
Bust and Echo: Profiting from the Demographic Shift in the 21st Century*,
co-written with Daniel Stoffman, quickly became a bestseller and has
made Foot a popular speaker and authority on future Canadian trends.

Prior to the 1996 publication of *Boom, Bust and Echo*, Foot had published two other books: *Canada's Population Outlook: Demographic Futures
and Economic Challenges* (1982) and, with Blossom T. Wigdor, *The Over
Forty Society* (1988). Foot's other publications are listed on his website
(**www.footwork.com**).

David Foot was born in England in 1944, grew up in Australia where
he completed an undergraduate degree, and then continued his education
at Harvard University where he earned a doctorate in economics. While
his writing has attracted much attention, Dr. Foot has also been recognized for his teaching ability. He is a two-time recipient of the University
of Toronto undergraduate teaching award. As well, in 1992, he received
a 3M Award for Teaching Excellence from the Society for Teaching and
Learning in Higher Education, which recognizes outstanding Canadian
university educators.

Preparing to Read

Before you read this essay, think about different generations. To what
generation do you belong? What generation are your parents a part of?
What defines a generation? What is a "generation gap"? Which generation
has had the most significant impact on our society? Why?

Cocooning is dead, the trend-spotters have proclaimed. 1

In the eighties, North Americans hunkered down in their 2
house-fortresses with remote control to avoid an increasingly
unsafe world. Now, this cocooning trend, first labelled by guru
Faith Popcorn, is in reverse.

Canadians and Americans are watching less TV and going 3
out more to movies, museums, the performing arts and

restaurants. Crime rates have stopped rising and, in many jurisdictions, they are falling.

All forms of home entertainment are either stagnant or 4
declining in popularity. The Internet does not seem to be catching on as home entertainment or as a shopping vehicle. There has been a resurrection of city streets and a renewed concern for communities. According to a recent *Globe and Mail* article, we are rejecting the "bland fruits of wired isolation."

But is all this so surprising? A careful understanding of 5
demographic trends provides a logical and easily understood explanation. For managers and marketers, it also serves as a foundation for anticipating new trends.

In a person's teens and 20s, "action" is important. The 6
downtown cores of major cities provide this action. Being "grounded" by a tough parent is real punishment; moving out, usually into a city apartment, is a common goal.

Growing up into the late 20s and early 30s often means 7
partnering and family formation. For many parents, the city core doesn't seem like a great place to raise kids, so they buy houses in the suburbs. This means a mortgage and other loans to purchase furniture, appliances and the minivan.

So it was with the baby boomer generation, which has 8
dominated, if not determined, postwar economic and social trends in North America. The 10 million boomers in Canada, born between 1947 and 1966, comprise the biggest generation in the history of this country. Watching them can provide an understanding of these trends.

The first boomer became a teen-ager in 1960. So the sixties 9
and seventies were dominated by boomers moving through their teen-age years into their 20s. They rushed into cities, stimulating massive urbanization. They rented apartments, driving down vacancies and increasing rents. They went to movies and rock concerts and they ate lots of cheap food.

In 1977, a significant event went almost unnoticed—the first 10
boomer reached the dreaded age of 30. The early boomers started buying homes in the suburbs. By the mid-eighties, the new trend became an avalanche. Suburbanization took off.

Debt levels soared and the "echo generation" was spawned. 11
Minivan sales took off. Young children and lots of debt put a damper on going out. Technology and TV in particular, including video rentals, became the main entertainment media. Cocooning was established.

So Faith Popcorn was right, but it was not because of new   12
societal values. The biggest generation in history was leaving its
action years behind and moving into its family ones. Not
surprisingly, family values emerged as a new social trend. Rental
housing, movie theatres and take-out restaurants experienced
much slower growth and, in some cases, decline.

Spending growth was focused on family and home. Pet-food   13
sales were still brisk but convenience-store sales sagged. Boomers
started paying off their loans and mortgages, leaving no cash for
luxuries or savings.

With kids to raise and careers to manage, the boomers in   14
their 30s and 40s were running "99 Lives"—another Popcorn
trend. They were trying to be good parents to their kids and
good children to their aging parents. They were working overtime
and competing for promotion to ever-fewer mid-management
positions. Woe betide any organization that wasted their time.
The "vigilante consumer" had arrived in full force.

But last year, another watershed was reached—the first   15
boomers turned 50. This is mid-life crisis time. The kids are
beginning to leave home and those sprained ligaments are taking
longer to heal.

Running shoes have become walking shoes, and the treadmill   16
purchased to replace visits to the fitness centre now induces
guilt. Resting has become a pleasurable activity, especially at the
cottage. Anyone ignorant of the power of demographics might
think values are changing again.

With lower interest rates and evaporating loans, there is   17
more discretionary income, making it possible to afford a luxury
or a sport-utility vehicle, a restaurant meal, and a show.

The teen-age or twentysomething kids don't need babysitting   18
any more, so going out is possible again. But the show is less
likely to be a movie or a rock concert unless, of course, the Rolling
Stones are back in town. Increasingly, the lavish musical, the
symphony and maybe the opera hold more attraction.

So boomers are emerging from their cocoons. Surprise! They   19
are watching less TV—home entertainment is dropping in
popularity—they are shopping in their neighbourhoods and they
are not using the Internet. Their beloved pets are aging and the
vet is becoming as familiar as the doctor.

Their parents are also getting old and mortality has come   20
closer to home. Aging has entered a deeply psychological, almost

spiritual phase. Boomers are snapping up books on the topic, provided the print is large.

But the seven million "echo" kids are also having an impact. 21 Movie attendance is rising, mainly because of the increased numbers of teen-agers. Similarly, the growth in confectionary, pop and some fast-food sales has little to do with boomers trying to relive youth. Their echo kids born in the eighties are delivering these trends.

The marketplace of the future is becoming more complex. 22 While the leading boomers are killing cocooning, their kids are reigniting the trends of the sixties. Rock stars have a bright future, as does new technology. Of course, it should not be surprising to see a reversal of the downward trend in crime rates as the echo generation enters its prime crime-prone ages.

But will this drive the boomers back to cocoons? Hardly. 23 They are finding time to volunteer, to give to charity and to support their communities. They are increasingly worried about pensions, investing in the market and thinking about moving out of the urban rat race. These are the trends of the future.

The boomer generation is predictably shifting into the next 24 phase of life: They are beginning to move from parenthood to grandparenthood.

Managing this new trend is both a personal and a societal 25 challenge, with all the associated opportunities and tribulations. Demographic analysis can provide us with a window to understand these changes, to disentangle them and to predict them. What more could the successful manager ask for?

UNDERSTANDING DETAILS

1. List the stages of life that Foot identifies, including the defining events and interests.
2. Who are the two groups currently impacting trends? Explain why.
3. Who exactly are the baby boomers and why have they had such a big impact on major trends in our society?

ANALYZING MEANING

1. Why is demographic analysis important?
2. What trends are likely to emerge in the next decade as a result of demographics, given the influences that Foot outlines?

3. "Anyone ignorant of the power of demographics might think values are changing again" (paragraph 16). Explain this quotation from Foot's essay. What is the distinction between changing values and the power of demographics?

DISCOVERING RHETORICAL STRATEGIES

1. How does Foot organize his categories in this essay? Why does he place these categories in this particular order?
2. Describe the author's intended audience. What makes you think he is directing his comments to this group?
3. What other rhetorical modes does Foot use in this essay besides division and classification? How do these other modes support the author's division/classification system?

MAKING CONNECTIONS

1. David Foot outlines how the baby boomer generation has influenced economic and societal trends in postwar North America. How might Foot explain the phenomena of television in public places (Cowan, "TV Me Alone") and the increasing homogeneity/suburbanization of places like Sudbury (Ferguson, "The Sudbury Syndrome")?
2. Amy Willard Cross ("Life in the Stopwatch Lane") is part of the boomer generation. At what stage in the boomers' lives was her essay originally published? How do you think demographics may have contributed to the categories of time Cross has identified in her essay? If she were writing this essay today how might it be different?
3. Barbara Kingsolver ("Life Without Go-Go Boots") has written about fashion and some of the changes that it has undergone. Based on demographics, what would you predict for the future of fashion?

IDEAS FOR DISCUSSION/WRITING

Preparing to Write

Write freely about your thoughts on your generation. What things define your generation? What music? What attitudes and ideas? What leisure activities? What clothing? What values identify someone of your generation? Do you like the image of your generation? Why or why not? What would you like to change about your generation?

Choosing a Topic

1. As a young entrepreneur you want to start a small business in the next decade. Explain what kind of business you believe would be successful, based on the demographic trends that are outlined in Foot's essay.

2. You are a manager of a mid-size company and you want to hire and retain the best employees. Describe what kind of working environment you will aim to establish to appeal to the workforce of the early 2000s. Where will your employees be located? What kinds of benefits will you offer them? What hours will your employees be expected to work?

3. Imagine you are contributing to the next edition of *Reader's Choice* in 2006. Find one new essay that you think should be included. Write a letter to the editor of this text in which you justify your choice based on its merits, including its appeal to your audience.

WEBSITES

www.canspeak.com/speakers/footd.htm
Read Canspeak's biographical information of David Foot.

www.thelavinagency.com/canada/davidfoot.html
Read the Lavin Agency's biography of David Foot.

www.couch.ca/history/1992/Foot.html
Here you will find a summary of one of David Foot's lectures.

AMY WILLARD CROSS

Life in the Stopwatch Lane

Amy Willard Cross is a writer who manages to divide her time between the stopwatch pace of the city and the more relaxed tempo of her other home "in the woods." *The Summer House: A Tradition of Leisure* (1992) is Cross's first book. In it, she examines the North American practice of escaping to the more leisurely life of a cottage or summer house. Born in Washington, D.C., in 1960, Cross currently lives in Canada. Her articles can be found in *City and Country Home*, *The Globe and Mail*, and *Cottage Life*, and she is currently health editor at *Chatelaine*.

Preparing to Read

This article first appeared in *The Globe and Mail*'s "Facts & Arguments" column in 1990. In "Life in the Stopwatch Lane," Amy Willard Cross examines the trend toward dividing time into progressively smaller units and labelling different types of time. Before reading this essay, think about the concept of time and how it has changed. How is time viewed differently in different cultures? What value do you place on your time? How do you measure time and what labels do you use to identify different divisions of time?

If time is money, the rates have skyrocketed and you probably   1
can't afford it. North Americans are suffering a dramatic time shortage since demand greatly exceeds supply. In fact, a recent survey revealed that people lost about 10 hours of leisure per week between 1973 and 1987. Maybe you were too busy to notice.

Losing that leisure leaves a piddling 16.6 hours to do   2
whatever you want, free of work, dish-washing or car-pooling. In television time, that equals a season of 13 *thirtysomething* episodes, plus $3\frac{1}{2}$ reruns. Hardly enough time to write an autobiography or carry on an affair.

How has replacing free time with more billable hours affected   3
society? It has created a new demographic group: the Busy Class—who usurped the Leisure Class. Easy to recognize, members of the Busy Class constantly cry to anyone listening,

"I'm *soooooo* busy." So busy they can't call their mother or find change for a panhandler. Masters of doing two things at once, they eke the most out of time. They dictate while driving, talk while calculating, entertain guests while nursing, watch the news while pumping iron. Even business melts into socializing—people earn their daily bread while they break it.

In fact, the Busies must make lots of bread to maintain   4 themselves in the standard of busy-ness to which they've become accustomed. To do that, they need special, expensive stuff. Stuff like call waiting, which lets them talk to two people at once. Stuff like two-faced watches, so they can do business in two time zones at once. Neither frenzied executives nor hurried housewives dare leave the house without their "book"—leather-bound appointment calendars thick as bestsellers. Forget hi-fi's or racing cars, the new talismans of overachievers also work: coffee-makers that brew by alarm; remote-controlled ignitions; or car faxes. Yet, despite all these time-efficient devices, few people have time to spare.

That scarcity has changed how we measure time. Now it's   5 being scientifically dissected into smaller and smaller pieces. Thanks to digital clocks, we know when it's 5:30 (and calculate we'll be home in three hours, eight minutes). These days lawyers can reason in 1/10th of an hour increments; they bill every six minutes. This to-the-minute precision proves time's escalating value.

Time was, before the advent of car phones and digital clocks,   6 we scheduled two kinds of time: time off and work hours. Not any more. Just as the Inuit label the infinite varieties of snow, the Busy Class has identified myriad subtleties of free time and named them. Here are some textbook examples of the new faces of time:

Quality time. For those working against the clock, the quality   7 of time spent with loved ones supposedly compensates for quantity. This handy concept absolves guilt as quickly as rosary counting. So careerist couples dine à deux once a fortnight. Parents bond by reading kids a story after nanny fed and bathed them. When pressed for time, nobody wastes it by fighting about bad breath or unmade beds. People who spend quality time with each other view their relationships through rose-coloured glasses. And knowing they've created perfect personal lives lets the Busy Class work even harder—guilt-free.

Travel time. With an allowance of 16.6 hours of fun, the Busy   8
Class watches time expenditures carefully. Just like businesses do
while making bids, normal people calculate travel time for leisure
activities. If two tram rides away, a friendly squash game loses
out. One time-efficient woman even formulated a mathematical
theorem: fun per mile quotient. Before accepting any social
invitation, she adds up travel costs, figures out the time spent
laughing, drinking and eating. If the latter exceeds the former, she
accepts. It doesn't matter who asks.

Downtime. Borrowed from the world of heavy equipment   9
and sleek computers, downtime is a professional-sounding word
meaning the damn thing broke, wait around until it's fixed.
Translated into real life, downtime counts as neither work nor
play, but a maddening no-man's land where nothing happens!
Like lining up for the ski-lift, or commuting without a car phone,
or waiting a while for the mechanic's diagnosis. Beware: people
who keep track of their downtime probably indulge in less than
16 hours of leisure.

Family time. In addition to 60-hour weeks, aerobics and dinner   10
parties, some people make time for their children. When asked to
brunch, a young couple will reply, "We're sorry but that's our
family time." A variant of quality time, it's Sunday afternoon
between lunch and the Disney Hour when nannies frequent
Filipino restaurants. In an effort to entertain their children without
exposure to sex and violence, the family attends craft fairs,
animated matinees or tree-tapping demonstrations. There, they
converge with masses of family units spending time alone with
the kids. After a noisy, sticky afternoon, parents gladly punch
the clock come Monday.

Quiet time. Overwhelmed by their schedules, some people   11
try to recapture the magic of childhood when they watched
clouds for hours on end. Sophisticated grown-ups have
rediscovered the quiet time of kindergarten days. They unplug
the phone (not the answering machine), clutch a book and try
not to think about work. But without teachers to enforce it, quiet
doesn't last. The clock ticks too loudly. As a computer fanatic
said, after being entertained at 16 megahertz, sitting still to watch
a sunset pales by comparison.

As it continues to increase in value, time will surely divide   12
into even smaller units. And people will share only the tiniest
amounts with each other. Hey, brother, can you spare a minute?
Got a second? A nanosecond?

UNDERSTANDING DETAILS

1. Summarize the various categories into which Cross divides time. How many categories does she believe used to exist?
2. Why do busy people divide time into so many different categories?
3. What technological innovations does Cross mention that have allowed us to "maximize our efficient use of time"?

ANALYZING MEANING

1. What is Cross's purpose in this essay? To what extent does she achieve this purpose?
2. What is responsible for our measuring time in smaller and smaller units? What implications does this have for the way we live?
3. Why has increased efficiency resulted in less leisure time?

DISCOVERING RHETORICAL STRATEGIES

1. While Cross's main division is that of time, she also divides people into groups. On what basis has she divided each of these subjects?
2. How would you describe the tone that Cross adopts in this essay? How does she feel about the "Busy Class" and the categories of time they have created? How do you know this?
3. Humour and unexpected phrasing are used effectively in describing the people that are featured in this essay and the different categories of time. Which details are particularly effective in conveying Cross's point of view?

MAKING CONNECTIONS

1. Amy Willard Cross identifies several types of time in her essay. Imagine a conversation between Cross and Tomson Highway ("What a Certain Visionary Once Said"). Do you think these two writers would view time the same way? Explain why or why not.
2. David Foot ("Boomers Dance to a New Beat") discusses the role of demographics in societal trends. How is Cross's division of time a reflection of the generation to which she belongs?
3. Amy Willard Cross identifies each of the categories in her essay with a clear heading. How does this compare to the strategies

used by Susan Swan ("Nine Ways of Looking at a Critic") and Gwynne Dyer ("Flagging Attention")? Why has each author chosen his or her respective approach?

IDEAS FOR DISCUSSION/WRITING

Preparing to Write

Write freely about the effects of technology. What technological developments have made us more efficient? What expectations have changed as a result of changing technology? What positive effects do you see from things such as computers, cellular telephones, and fax machines? What negative consequences have these pieces of equipment had on our lives?

Choosing a Topic

1. In a short essay, outline the ways in which some technological development has changed your life. Before you start writing, make sure that you choose a purpose and a particular point of view.
2. The way time is viewed varies greatly across cultures. Write an essay, to be distributed at an international conference on education, that gives teachers from a variety of different countries an idea of how a typical Canadian student spends her/his time. Use a clear system of division to convey your message effectively.
3. Write an essay in which you classify the various people you know into categories. First, decide on a principle for classification, and then use specific detail to explain where individuals are placed.

WEBSITES

www.chatelaine.com
Enter "Amy Willard Cross" in the search field to find other articles by this writer.

www.globeandmail.ca
The Globe and Mail is the source of this article.

GWYNNE DYER

Flagging Attention

Gwynne Dyer is described on the CBC *Ideas* website as "one of Canada's media renaissance men, an outstanding journalist, broadcaster, producer, author, and filmmaker." Dyer was born in St. John's, Newfoundland, in 1943, and has earned degrees from Memorial University of Newfoundland (B.A., history), Rice University in Houston (M.A., military history), and King's College, University of London (Ph.D., military and Middle Eastern history). That education, along with his experience serving in the Royal Canadian Naval Reserve, the U.S. Naval Reserve, and the British Royal Naval Reserve and reporting on the Gulf War has prepared Dyer well for the writing, producing, directing, and hosting of a multitude of radio productions, films, and television series, mainly dealing with topics related to war, defence, militarism, international conflict, and human politics. Dyer also writes a twice-weekly syndicated column on international affairs that appears in about 150 papers in approximately 30 countries.

Preparing to Read

The following essay, taken from *enRoute* (Air Canada's in-flight magazine), discusses the range of flags that exists and the qualities that allow us to categorize them. As you prepare to read this article, think about flags. What do flags represent? Who designs flags? What rules of conduct govern people's behaviour in relation to flags? What does it mean to burn a flag? Where are flags typically displayed? At what times of year or at what events are flags typically highly visible?

If you want to see my favourite flag in the whole world—more 1
bizarre than the Nepalese flag, which looks like two scraps of red bikini fluttering in the wind; more literal-minded even than Cyprus's flag, which consists of an orange map of Cyprus on a white background—you don't have to go that far. Just go to Vancouver.

I spent some time in the Navy during the late Jurassic, and 2
reservists I knew from Vancouver would actually boast about it. It was the flag of Her Majesty's Canadian Ship Discovery (which is actually a building, or "stone frigate"). How will you

know which one that is? Easy. It's a neat little circle nestled in the crotch of a large letter "Y." Or to put it another way: It is a "disc over" a "Y."

Visual puns are to ordinary puns as Ebola fever is to measles. 3 A long time ago (back when I had pimples) I used to collect visual puns, but after HMCS Discovery I just gave up. You can search the front and back pages of any dictionary you like, and no flag in the world even begins to approach it for sheer awfulness. Though they do try.

All this stuff about flags came up after my six-year-old, Kate, 4 saw *Mulan* and wanted to know what the Chinese flag looked like. So out with the trusty dictionary, and there it was in all its minimalist splendour: a plain red flag with some stars in the corner.

She seemed a bit disappointed by China's flag, so to cheer 5 her up I started making fun of some of the more lurid flags that jostled alongside it on the page. Brazil's, for example, has the slogan of a dead political movement—*Ordem e Progresso* (Order and Progress)—written on a white band stretched like an equator across a blue globe with the southern night sky superimposed on it, and the whole mess being contained within a yellow diamond on a green background. Kate was riveted.

While there were about 50 flags at the back of the dictionary 6 when I was a kid, there are now close to 200, and the style has changed.

Boring old horizontal or vertical stripes are out. Diagonal 7 slashes, nested triangles and heraldic animals are in, and any flag with less than five colours just isn't in the running. I get around a lot, but I haven't seen even half of them in real life— except maybe outside the United Nations building in New York, where the flagpoles are now crowded so closely together that you can't make anything out.

What struck both me and my daughter was that there are 8 obviously three quite different kinds of flags. There are the traditional ones, with a few dignified stripes and maybe some stars or a crest. There are the designer ones, ranging from ad-agency flash to play-school messy. And there are the ones that are just trying too hard, like Mozambique's flag: crossed black hoe and AK-47 superimposed on an open white book, all on a yellow star, which is, in turn, on a red triangle, with broad green, thin white, broad black, thin white and broad yellow stripes off to the right. (Yes, I know it's all symbolic, but even so ...)

Canada's flag falls into the designer category. Three vertical 9
stripes, red-white-red, still look quite traditional, and if you were
feeling bold you might even get away with having a discreet
little shield or badge on the middle stripe—in fact, more than
half the flags of Latin America follow exactly that pattern—but
the maple leaf is just too big and in-your-face to qualify as
traditional. This is a flag halfway to being a logo. Well, good.
The whole idea of a new Canadian flag, back in the '60s, was to
re-brand the country, and it has worked a treat: Everybody now
understands that we're not British, we're Canadian. Québec went
through a similar exercise 15 years before, adopting the old pre-
revolutionary French flag in colour-reverse, with an equally
satisfactory rise in the recognition factor.

If it works, don't knock it. But what you notice, looking across 10
the pages and pages of flags, is that (a) most of the good ideas
were taken some time ago; (b) the smaller the country, the more
elaborate the flag; and (c) there are fashions in flags, as in
everything else. The new South African flag, for example, looks
like a collision between Jamaica's and Vanuatu's. After 200 other
countries have dipped into the pot, there aren't any elegant
designs left. While Japan (pop. 125 million) has made do with a
plain red circle on a white background for over 1,000 years,
latecomer Grenada (pop. 101,000) wound up with a multi-
coloured extravaganza involving stars, circles, triangles,
rectangles and what appears to be a leaf shape.

As for fashion, it's not just Muslim countries putting crescent 11
moons on their flags, or half the countries of Africa going in for
stars. For some reason, it has become de rigueur among small
island states—Trinidad and Tobago, St. Kitts-Nevis, the Marshall
Islands, the Solomon Islands—to put bold diagonal slashes on
their flags.

But no matter how gaudy or silly the flag, somewhere a 12
bunch of school kids or army conscripts is being taught to love it,
pledge allegiance to it, maybe even kill or die for it. Now, I
understand the need for a sense of unity and community, and I
realize that people need symbols. In my time, I have served in
various people's navies and saluted their flags without feeling
abused or humiliated. It's just part of the package. Once, in the
Canadian Navy, I was the guy out in front with the sword and
shiny boots when we did the Sunset Ceremony, and even felt a
surge of emotion myself at the climax of the ceremony.

We are all tribesmen under the skin, and there's no point in   13
beating ourselves up about it. But we don't have to fall for it
either; we are not *only* tribesmen. I'll pledge allegiance to any
flag you like if it will keep me out of jail. But frankly, I'd rather
pledge allegiance to a bedspread.

UNDERSTANDING DETAILS

1. What are the three categories of flags that Dyer identifies? What
   characterizes each of these categories? Into which category does
   the Canadian flag fall? Why?
2. In paragraph 3, Dyer discussed visual puns. What is a visual
   pun? How does Dyer feel about them?
3. What is the purpose of a national flag? What need or needs
   does it fulfill?

ANALYZING MEANING

1. Dyer ends his essay by saying, "We are all tribesmen under the
   skin ... [but] we are not *only* tribesmen. I'll pledge allegiance to
   any flag you like if it will keep me out of jail. But frankly, I'd
   rather pledge allegiance to a bedspread." Explain what Dyer
   means in this conclusion.
2. In paragraph 6, Dyer comments on the increase in the number
   of flags and the change in their style. Why is there such an
   increase in the number of flags, and what accounts for the stylistic changes in flag design?
3. Dyer has an M.A. and a Ph.D. in military history. In addition, the
   focus of his writing, films, and broadcasting has been militarism
   and war in many different nations. Why is it the curiosity of
   his six-year-old daughter that alerts him to the variety of flags
   and their significance?

DISCOVERING RHETORICAL STRATEGIES

1. How would you describe the tone that Dyer adopts in this
   essay? How has Dyer created this tone?
2. Throughout his essay, Dyer makes several interesting word
   choices and uses several figures of speech. Identify at least four
   examples of this type of language usage and explain the effect
   they have on Dyer's essay.

3. Dyer makes a few references to belonging to the navy. What role do these references play in his essay?

MAKING CONNECTIONS

1. Anita Rau Badami ("My Canada") writes about characteristic features and images that represent the values of Canada. How are the images and values Badami evokes reflected in the flags that Dyer describes?
2. How does Dyer's attitude toward patriotism compare to that of Allen Abel in "A Home at the End of the Journey" or of Steven Heighton in "Elegy in Stone"?

IDEAS FOR DISCUSSION/WRITING

Preparing to Write

Write freely about patriotism. In what ways do people demonstrate their patriotism? Why do people feel such strong loyalty to their countries? In what ways is patriotism created? How is it maintained? What types of behaviour are considered particularly patriotic? What is the opposite of being patriotic?

Choosing a Topic

1. Write an essay in which you classify specific examples of behaviour into those that are distinctly patriotic and those that are counter to patriotism. Be clear about your attitude toward each category of behaviour.
2. Assume that you are responsible for another "rebranding of Canada." Describe the flag that you would design and its significance. What new aspects of Canada are you hoping to convey with this flag?
3. National anthems are another symbol of a country intended to inspire patriotism and reflect the values of a nation. In the same way that Dyer has categorized flags, categorize a range of national anthems with which you are familiar.

WEBSITES

radio.cbc.ca/programs/ideas/millenn/dyerbio.html
A CBC biography of Gwynne Dyer.

www.crwflags.com/fotw/flags
Flags of the world.

aurora.icaap.org/archive/dyer.html
An *Aurora Online* interview with Gwynne Dyer.

www.dfait-maeci.gc.ca/skelton/dyer_bio-e.asp
The Canadian Department of Foreign Affairs biography of
Gwynne Dyer.

SUSAN SWAN

Nine Ways of Looking at a Critic

"Swan has a gift for the provocative ...," says Joe Hooper of *Mirabella*, and in the essay that appears here, Swan does not shy away from provoking her audience.

Born in Midland, Ontario, in 1945, Swan was a student at Havergal College in Toronto in the early 1960s and received a B.A. from McGill University in 1967. In the 1970s Swan became involved in theatre, both writing and performing. She is now a novelist, a journalist, a script writer, a faculty member for the Humber School for Writers' correspondence program, and a professor of humanities at York University in Toronto.

Susan Swan's novels include *The Biggest Modern Woman in the World* (1983), the story of a giantess who exhibited with P.T. Barnum; *The Last of the Golden Girls* (1989); and *The Wives of Bath* (1993), about a murder in a girls' boarding school. Swan's most recent book is *Stupid Boys Are Good to Relax With* (1998) and she is currently working on a novel called *What Casanova Told Me*. While Swan has received a very positive response to her work, as evidenced by her nominations for Canada's Governor General's Award, the U.K. Guardian Award, and Ontario's Trillium Award, she has also created controversy as sexuality figures prominently in all of her novels. Suanne Kelman, in a 1994 story about "Can Lit's bad girls" in *Chatelaine* magazine, summarizes Swan's attitude as follows: "Swan writes the way she thinks: raised to be a pillar of society, she's still trying to free herself—and her readers—from what she sees as a phony concept of female virtue."

Preparing to Read

In this humorous essay, which originally appeared in *The Globe and Mail*, Susan Swan divides book reviewers into nine different categories. Before you begin reading, think about the job of a reviewer, whether that person is reviewing books, movies, restaurants, concerts, or any other work or performance. Who is the audience the reviewer is targeting? What is the goal of a reviewer? Are there reviewers whose opinions you particularly value? Are there reviewers with whom you disagree? What makes a good reviewer? How do you think reviewers are perceived by those whose work they review?

A s a writer, I naturally have some idealistic notions about book   1
reviewing. For instance, I admire Alexander Pope's list of
necessary qualities for a critic—integrity, modesty, tact, courage
and an awareness of the critic's own limitations. I also like Matthew
Arnold's claim that a critic should possess an eager, open mind
and the ability to rise above a sect or clique.

But a reviewer with these qualities is not a person most   2
authors get to meet very often, no matter how much we might
long for an intelligent review. The more books I write and the
more reviews I receive (whether good, bad or indifferent), the
more I see how elusive this ideal reviewer is. What I notice
instead are the clearly recognizable types of unsatisfactory
reviewers no author can avoid meeting in the pages of our
newspapers and magazines. I'm not talking so much about
academic journals, although you can probably spot my reviewing
types there too.

The following is a list of eight types of less-than-ideal   3
reviewers I've met in my 20 years of writing fiction and 30 years
of reviewing.

Number one are The Masturbators, a common category.   4
These are the reviewers who feel they could have written a better
book on the subject, given half the chance. In their eyes, the
author got it all wrong, and the only value in the book is that it
reminds the reviewers that they have superb and untested writing
skills which, for one reason or another, they haven't got around
to putting into practice.

Sometimes, the direction these reviewers suggest the book   5
take are strange and hilarious. For instance, G.K. Chesterton was
fond of quoting the reviewer who liked Charles Dickens's novel
Martin Chuzzlewit, but complained that it shed no light on the
marital customs of Norway.

Number two are The Spankers. Canada, which has an   6
abundance of good writers, also teems with Spankers, who are
out to administer discipline over anything from ill-conceived
plot-lines to misplaced commas. If Spankers are male, they often
display a macho zest—"a real man calls crap crap." If they are
female, Spankers can indulge in a scolding, martyred tone—as in,
"I have better things to do, but for the good of literature I will
dirty my hands in pronouncing this book not worth the reader's
time."

Once in a while, in my writerly paranoia, I think the   7
Canadian style *is* to punish and admonish. After all, Canadians

tend to look suspiciously at anyone who upholds what is good. Like our pioneers, who distrusted emotions and the body—viz. French-Canadian Jansenism and English-Canadian Calvinism— we prefer the canny so-and-so who won't be fooled by what is bad.

But Spankers can be found anywhere, particularly if the book 8 tries to tackle sexuality. "D.H. Lawrence has a diseased mind. He is obsessed with sex ... we have no doubt that he will be ostracized by all except the most degenerate coteries in the literary world," an English reviewer once wrote in *John Bull*.

The third category, closely aligned with Spankers, is The 9 Young (and Old) Turk. This group sees the review solely as an opportunity to demonstrate its literary superiority and above-average intelligence. (Not only was I once one of these— dismissing older, established writers in a few sentences—I have been the victim of Young Turks, too. This may be my karma for assuming earlier that my limited life experience and barely developed writing skills were the very qualities that allowed me to see the tinny emptiness of the older writer's celebrity.)

It's probably a good thing Turks can sometimes leave us 10 with memorable witticisms that may be remembered long after the book they reviewed. Who can forget Oscar Wilde's riposte that it took a heart of stone to read of the death of Little Nell without laughing?

The fourth category is Gushers: They skip over discussion 11 of the book; they just want to communicate the enjoyment of reading it. The best example of Gushers can be found in the book ads of publications like *The New York Times Book Review*, where phrases lifted from reviews proclaim: "major"; "ground-breaking"; "compulsively readable"; "new genius that will change the face of literature"; "the first truly great novel since Tolstoy," and so on. Americans excel at the use of superlatives, trotting out for different authors the same laudatory manifestos of praise week after week. Few writers will object to this habit, for obvious reasons.

The fifth category is The Diviners, a sympathetic but 12 misguided lot. Diviners claim to know the author's reasons for writing the book. They may even deliver an up-to-the-minute and totally fabricated psychological analysis of the author as an incest victim or recovering alcoholic as evidence for their position. (Authors are wise to hold their tongues when confronted with these well-wisher divinations.)

Sixth are The Puritans, who don't like a book if they think 13
its characters have bad morals. They have trouble separating the
author from the people in the story.

Seventh come The Grumps, who may like the book but 14
begrudge its author too much praise. Grumps are fond of making
congratulatory noises and then lingering for much of their review
over typos and small mistakes as if they were major boo-boos
that undermined the book's credibility. Most authors I know
would feel grateful (although embarrassed) if the reviewer
pointed out a major mistake. But to be taken to task for tiny errors
by reviewers who say they love the book is the sort of thing that
can make a writer want to take up brick-laying.

My eighth and final category—to date—is that of The 15
Flat-Earthers. These reviewers believe all fiction should be true-
to-life, relying, like non-fiction, on fact. Flat-Earthers tend to say
things like, "This would never happen so it's no good." In this
category, a film like *Thelma and Louise* would be a failure because
how often have you heard of two women driving their car over
a cliff into the Grand Canyon?

Flat-Earthers also have an astonishing ability to know what 16
life is really like. I don't mean the reviewer who is upset by a
writer sloppily sticking wrong details into a piece of fictional
realism, like putting palm trees on Baffin Island. The Flat-Earther
has more hubris than that; a book must support his or her
definition of what it's like to be alive, as he or she knows it. The
idea that fiction can present a reality altogether different from
the life the reviewer knows is unheard of to a Flat-Earther.

All right. I've told you about the types of reviewers writers 17
often meet. But if a writer like me could construct the ideal critic
the way I make up a character, what qualities would I give this
creature? First of all, most writers I know want professional
standards. Curiously enough, many reviewers aren't
knowledgeable about literature. Nor are they experienced enough
with reviewing to know what they're doing. Would you let your
child take English lessons from somebody newly arrived from
a non-English-speaking country? Canada now has an abundance
of good writers, but the quality of our reviewers hasn't kept up
with the quality of our books. Much of the blame for this belongs
to the media, which has eliminated space for book reviews and
is still paying reviewers roughly what it did when I started
reviewing back in the late 1960s.

No other profession I know could get away with such sub-   18
standard pay. A good reviewer needs credentials and a living
wage, otherwise getting your book reviewed is like having your
teeth pulled in the Wild West. Instead of a trained dentist, you
face the equivalent of a drunken cowboy with pliers, who has
the confidence to think he can do a good job. The idea that he
might leave a hole in your head for the rest of your life doesn't
occur.

As Pope said, a writer appreciates a reviewer who is brave   19
enough to declare a bias. Why review Jane Austen if you are a
Jack Kerouac fan who hates 19th-century British writers, unless
you are going to admit up front that Austen isn't your cup of
tea? (Book columnists are an exception because readers get to
know their taste and can put their judgments in perspective.)

"Says who?," I often think, reading reviewers with no   20
particular credentials to engage the book's subject, or who lack the
courage to admit that a certain style isn't their specialty.

By contrast, good reviews will represent the book (without   21
lapsing into long-winded plot summaries) so the reader gets a
sense of what the book is like whether the reviewer likes it or
not. And the best reviews offer an informed reading that will
provide an interesting or revealing point of view from which the
book can be perceived. In other words, a well-written review
gives us not only the reviewer's personal reaction, it adds to our
knowledge of the book.

Pure opinion is a cheat; it belongs to talk radio stations, not   22
reviews. In some ways, personal reaction is the most uninteresting
thing a reviewer has to offer.

UNDERSTANDING DETAILS

1. List the types of critics Swan identifies. Explain the apparent
   contradiction between the title, which prepares you for nine
   groupings, and the sentence in paragraph 3 that introduces
   eight types of critics.
2. According to Swan, what is the difference between a good
   review and a bad review?
3. Into which category of reviewer does Swan put herself? Does
   she believe she still belongs in this category? Why or why not?

ANALYZING MEANING

1. Explain why Swan has chosen the name "The Flat-Earthers" for the category of reviewers who "believe all fiction should be true-to-life"? Is this an effective name for this group?
2. In this essay, Swan refers to a variety of people ranging from Alexander Pope to Jack Kerouac. Who are the people she mentions and why has she made reference to them in this essay?
3. Explain which of the eight types of "less-than-desirable" reviewers you think would be the worst in the opinion of most writers. Which would be the best? Why?

DISCOVERING RHETORICAL STRATEGIES

1. Why do you think that Susan Swan has written this essay? What is her purpose? Where is this made clear?
2. Who is the intended audience of this essay? Explain why you have identified this group of people.
3. Explain the effectiveness of Swan's introduction and conclusion. How has she linked the beginning and end of her essay?

MAKING CONNECTIONS

1. In this essay Swan identifies one category as being particularly Canadian and another as being typically American. How do these qualities compare to the contrasts between Canadians and Americans that are pointed out by Allen Abel ("A Home at the End of the Journey")?
2. In "The Babar Factor," Evan Solomon reviews video games by comparing them to Babar books. In Swan's terms, what category does Solomon fit into as a reviewer?
3. Compare and contrast the way Swan organizes her topic with the organizational techniques used by Gwynne Dyer in "Flagging Attention" and by Amy Willard Cross in "Life in the Stopwatch Lane."

IDEAS FOR WRITING/DISCUSSION

Preparing to Write

Write freely about a book you have read. What was the book about? Did you like it? What was good about it? What didn't you like? Was there anything about it that confused you? Would you read other books by the same author? What would you say to the author if you met him or her? How would you rate the book overall? Would you recommend it to others?

Choosing a Topic

1. In this essay Swan divides book reviewers into different categories. Write an essay in which you divide movie reviewers into a series of appropriate categories.
2. Using the internet or periodical indexes, find a review of one of Swan's books. Read the review and then decide in which of Swan's categories the reviewer best fits. Explain why the reviewer fits the category you have chosen.
3. Stores classify their merchandise into various categories to help shoppers locate the things they are looking for. Think of a type of store where things are often difficult to find, and propose a new system of classification that you think would be more effective. You might choose a music store, a grocery store, a hardware store, a department store, or some other type of store with which you are familiar.

WEBSITES

www.arts.yorku.ca/english/people/gradFaculty/swan.html
Read York University's biography of Susan Swan.

www.wall-of-fiction.com/swan/author.html
Read a review as well as an interview with Susan Swan about her novel *Stupid Boys Are Good to Relax With*.

CHAPTER 6

COMPARISON/ CONTRAST

Discovering Similarities and Differences

Making comparisons is such a natural and necessary part of our everyday lives that we often do so without conscious effort. When we were children, we compared our toys with those of our friends, we contrasted our height and physical development to other children's, and we constantly evaluated our happiness in comparison with that evidenced by our parents and childhood companions. As we grew older, we habitually compared our dates, teachers, parents, friends, cars, and physical attributes. In college or university, we learn about anthropology by writing essays on the similarities and differences between two African tribes, about political science by contrasting the Liberal and Alliance platforms, about business by comparing annual production rates, and about literature by comparing Atwood with Ondaatje or Shakespeare with Marlowe. Comparing and contrasting various elements in our lives helps us make decisions, such as which course to take or which house to buy, and it justifies preferences that we already hold, such as liking one city more than another or loving one person more than the next. In these ways and in many others, the skillful use of comparison and contrast is clearly essential to our social and professional lives.

Defining Comparison/Contrast

Comparison and contrast allow us to understand one subject by putting it next to another. Comparing involves discovering likenesses or similarities, whereas contrasting is based on finding differences. Like division and classification, comparison and contrast are generally considered part of the same process, because we usually have no reason for comparing unless some contrast is also involved. Each technique implies the existence of the other. For this reason, the word *compare* is often used to mean both techniques.

Comparison and contrast are most profitably applied to two items that have something in common, such as cats and dogs, or cars and motorcycles. A discussion of cats and motorcycles, for example, would probably not be very rewarding or stimulating, because they do not have much in common. If more than two items are compared in an essay, they are still most profitably discussed in pairs: for instance, motorcycles and cars, cars and bicycles, or bicycles and motorcycles.

An analogy is an extended, sustained comparison. Often used to explain unfamiliar, abstract, or complicated thoughts, this rhetorical technique adds energy and vividness to a wide variety of college-level writing. The process of analogy differs slightly from comparison/contrast in three important ways: Comparison/contrast begins with subjects from the same class and places equal weight on both of them. In addition, it addresses both the similarities and the differences of these subjects. Analogy, conversely, seldom explores subjects from the same class, and it focuses principally on one familiar subject in an attempt to explain another, more complex one. Furthermore, it deals only with similarities, not with contrasts. A comparison/contrast essay, for example, might study two veterans' ways of coping with the trauma of the Gulf War by pointing out the differences in their methods as well as the similarities. An analogy essay might use the familiar notion of a fireworks display to reveal the chilling horror of the lonely hours after dark during this war: "Nights in the Persian Gulf were similar to a loud, unending fireworks display. We had no idea when the next blast was coming, how loud it would be, or how close. We cringed in terror after dark, hoping the next surprise would not be our own death." In this example, rather than simply hearing about an event, we participate in it through this highly refined form of comparison.

The following student paragraph compares and contrasts married and single life. As you read it, notice how the author compares similar social states and, in the process, justifies her current lifestyle:

> Recently I saw a bumper sticker that read, "It used to be wine, women, and song, and now it's beer, the old lady, and TV." Much truth may be found in this comparison of single and married lifestyles. When my husband and I used to date, for example, we'd go out for dinner and drinks and then maybe see a play or concert. Our discussions were intelligent, often ranging over global politics, science, literature, and other lofty topics. He would open doors for me, buy me flowers, and make sure I was comfortable and happy. Now, three years later, after marriage and a child, the baby bottle has replaced the wine bottle, the smell of diapers wipes out the scent of roses, and our nights on the town are infrequent, cherished events. But that's OK. A little bit of the excitement and mystery may be gone, but these intangible qualities have given way to a sturdy, dependable trust in each other and a quiet confidence about our future together.

Thinking Critically by Using Comparison/Contrast

Comparison and contrast are basic to a number of different thought processes. We compare and contrast quite naturally on a daily basis, but all of us would benefit greatly from being more aware of these companion strategies in our own writing. They help us not only in perceiving our environment but also in understanding and organizing large amounts of information.

The basic skill of finding similarities and differences will enhance your ability to create accurate descriptions, to cite appropriate examples, to present a full process analysis, and, of course, to classify and label subjects. It is a pattern of thought that is essential to more complex thinking strategies, so perfecting the ability to use it is an important step in your efforts to improve your critical thinking.

Once again, we are going to practise this strategy in isolation to get a strong sense of its mechanics before we combine it with other rhetorical modes. Isolating this mode will make your reading and writing even stronger than they are now, because the individual parts of the thinking process will be more vigorous and effective, thus making your academic performance more powerful than ever.

1. Find magazine ads that use comparison/contrast to make a point or sell a product. What is the basis of each comparison? How effective or ineffective is each comparison?

2. Compare or contrast the experience of spending time with a special person to another type of experience (e.g., a roller-coaster ride, sleeping, or a trip across Canada). Be as specific as possible in your comparison.

3. Have you ever been to the same place twice? Think for a moment about how the first and second visits to this place differed. How were they similar? What were the primary reasons for the similarities and differences in your perceptions of these visits?

Reading and Writing Comparison/ Contrast Essays

Many established guidelines regulate the development of a comparison/contrast essay and should be taken into account from both the reading and the writing perspectives. All good comparative studies serve a specific purpose. They attempt either to examine their subjects separately or to demonstrate the superiority of one over the other. In evaluating two different types of cars, for example, a writer might point out the amazing gas mileage of one model and the smooth handling qualities of the other, or the superiority of one car's gas consumption over that of the other. Whatever the intent, comparison/contrast essays need to be clear and logical and to have a precise purpose.

How to Read a Comparison/Contrast Essay

Preparing to Read. As you begin reading this chapter, pull together as much preliminary material as possible for each essay so you can focus your attention and have the benefit of prior knowledge before you start to read. In particular, you are trying to discover what is being compared or contrasted and why. What does Will Ferguson's title ("The Sudbury Syndrome") suggest to you? From the title of his essay, can you tell what Michael McKinley is comparing in "Opera Night in Canada"?

From glancing at the essay itself and reading the synopsis in the Rhetorical Table of Contents, what does Gloria Steinem's essay try to accomplish?

Also, before you begin to read these essays, try to discover information about the author and about the conditions under which each essay was written. Why is Bissoondath qualified to write about spirituality and religious faith? Does he reveal his background in his essay? What is Monte Hummel's job? To what extent do you expect this to colour his comparison of a natural environment at two different times?

Finally, just before you begin to read, answer the Preparing to Read questions, and then make some free associations with the general topic of each essay. For example, what are some of the similarities and differences between hockey and opera (Michael McKinley)? What is your general view on women's bodybuilding (Gloria Steinem)?

Reading. As you read each comparison/contrast essay for the first time, be sure to record your own feelings and opinions. Some of the issues presented in this chapter are highly controversial. You will often have strong reactions to them, which you should try to write down as soon as possible.

In addition, you may want to comment on the relationship between the preliminary essay material, the author's stance in the essay, and the content of the essay itself. For example, what motivated Solomon to write "The Babar Factor"? Who was his primary audience? What is Ferguson's tone in "The Sudbury Syndrome," and how does it further his purpose? Answers to questions such as these will provide you with a context for your first reading of these essays and will assist you in preparing to analyze the essays in more depth on your second reading.

At this point in the chapter, you should make certain you understand each author's thesis and then take a close look at his or her principal method of organization: Is the essay arranged (1) point by point, (2) subject by subject, (3) as a combination of these two, or (4) as separate discussions of similarities and differences between two subjects? (See the chart on page 264 for an illustration of these options.) Last, preview the questions that follow the essay before you read it again.

Rereading. When you read these essays a second time, you should look at the comparison or contrast much more closely than you have up to now. First, look in detail at the writer's method of organization (see the chart on page 264). How effective is it in advancing the writer's thesis?

Next, you should consider whether each essay is fully developed and balanced: Does McKinley compare similar items? Does Solomon discuss the same qualities for his subjects? Does Bissoondath deal with all aspects of the comparison between spirituality and religious faith? Is Steinem's treatment of her two subjects well balanced? And does Ferguson give his audience enough specific details to clarify the extent of his comparison? Do all the writers in this chapter use well-chosen transitions so you can move smoothly from one point to the next? Also, what other rhetorical modes support each comparison/contrast in this chapter? Finally, answering the questions after each selection will let you evaluate your understanding of the essay and help you analyze its contents in preparation for the discussion/writing topics that follow.

For a more thorough inventory of the reading process, you should turn to pages 17–18 in the Introduction.

How to Write a Comparison/Contrast Essay

Preparing to Write. As you consider various topics for a comparison/contrast essay, you should answer the Preparing to Write questions that precede the assignments and then use the prewriting techniques explained in the Introduction to generate even more ideas on these topics.

As you focus your attention on a particular topic, keep the following suggestions in mind:

1. Compare/contrast items in the same category (e.g., compare two professors, but not a professor and a swimming pool).

2. Have a specific purpose or reason for writing your essay.

3. Discuss the same qualities of each subject (if you evaluate the teaching techniques of one professor, do so for the other professor as well).

4. Use as many pertinent details as possible to expand your comparison/contrast and to accomplish your stated purpose.

5. Deal with all aspects of the comparison that are relevant to the purpose.

6. Balance the treatment of the different subjects of your comparison (i.e., don't spend more time on one than on another).

7. Determine your audience's background and knowledge so that you will know how much of your comparison should be explained in detail and how much can be skimmed over.

Next, in preparation for a comparison/contrast project, you might list all the elements of both subjects that you want to compare. This list can then help you give your essay structure as well as substance. At this stage in the writing process, the task may seem similar to pure description, but a discussion of two subjects in relation to one another rapidly changes the assignment from description to comparison.

Writing. The introduction of your comparison/contrast essay should (1) clearly identify your subjects, (2) explain the basis of your comparison/contrast, and (3) state your purpose and the overall limits of your particular study. Identifying your subject is, of course, a necessary and important task in any essay. Similarly, justifying the elements you will be comparing and contrasting creates reader interest and gives your audience some specifics to look for in the essay. Finally, your statement of purpose or thesis (for example, to prove that one professor is superior to another) should include the boundaries of your discussion. You cannot cover all the reasons for your preference in one short essay, so you must limit your consideration to three or four basic categories (perhaps teaching techniques, the clarity of the assignments given, classroom attitude, and grading standards). The introduction is the place to make all these limits known.

You can organize the body of your paper in one of four ways: (1) a point-by-point, or alternating, comparison; (2) a subject-by-subject, or divided, comparison; (3) a combination of these two methods; or (4) a division between the similarities and differences. (See the chart on page 264.)

The point-by-point comparison evaluates both subjects in terms of each category. If the issue, for example, is which of two cars to buy, you might discuss both models' gasoline consumption first; then, their horsepower; next, their ease in handling; and, finally, their standard equipment. Following the second method of organization, subject by subject, you would discuss the gasoline consumption, horsepower, ease in handling, and standard equipment of car A first and then follow the same format for car B. The third option would allow you to introduce, say, the interior design of each car point by point (or car by car) and then explain the mechanical features of the automobiles

Methods of Organization

Point by Point
km/L, car A
km/L, car B
horsepower, car A
horsepower, car B
handling, car A
handling, car B
equipment, car A
equipment, car B

Subject by Subject
km/L, car A
horsepower, car A
handling, car A
equipment, car A
km/L, car B
horsepower, car B
handling, car B
equipment, car B

Combination
interior, car A
interior, car B
———
km/L, car A
horsepower, car A
km/L, car B
horsepower, car B

Similarities/Differences
similarities:
km/L, cars A & B
differences:
horsepower, cars A & B
handling, cars A & B
equipment, cars A & B

(kilometres per litre, horsepower, gear ratio, and braking system) subject by subject. To use the last method of organization, you might discuss the similarities between the two models first and the differences second (or vice versa). If the cars you are comparing have similar kilometres-per-litre (km/L) ratings but completely different horsepower, steering systems, and optional equipment, you could discuss the gasoline consumption first and then emphasize the differences by mentioning them later in the essay. If, instead, you are trying to emphasize the fact that the km/L ratings of these models remain consistent despite their differences, then reverse the order of your essay.

When confronted with the task of choosing a method of organization for a comparison/contrast essay, you need to find the pattern that best suits your purpose. If you want single items to stand out in a discussion, for instance, the best choice will be the point-by-point system; it is especially appropriate for long essays, but has a tendency to turn into an exercise in making lists if you don't pay careful attention to your transitions. If, however, the subjects themselves (rather than the itemized points) are the most interesting feature of your essay, you should use the subject-by-subject comparison; this system is particularly good for short essays in which the readers can retain what was said about one subject while they read about a second subject. Through this second system of organization, each subject becomes a unified whole, an approach to an essay that is generally effective unless the theme becomes awkwardly divided into two separate parts. You must also remember, if you choose this second method of organization, that the second (or last) subject is in the most emphatic position because that is what your readers will have seen most recently. The final two options for organizing a comparison/contrast essay give you some built-in flexibility so that you can create emphasis and attempt to manipulate reader opinion simply by the structure of your essay.

Using logical transitions in your comparison/contrast essays will establish clear relationships between the items in your comparisons and will also move your readers smoothly from one topic to the next. If you wish to indicate comparisons, use such words as *like, as, also, in like manner, similarly,* and *in addition;* to signal contrasts, try *but, in contrast to, unlike, whereas,* and *on the one hand/on the other hand.*

The conclusion of a comparison/contrast essay summarizes the main points and states the deductions drawn from those points. As you choose your method of organization, remember not to get locked into a formulaic approach to your subjects, which will adversely affect the readability of your essay. To avoid making your reader feel like a spectator at a verbal table tennis match, be straightforward, honest, and patient as you discover and recount the details of your comparison.

Rewriting. When you review the draft of your comparison/contrast essay, you need once again to make sure that you communicate your purpose as effectively as possible to your intended audience. Two guidelines previously mentioned should help you accomplish this goal:

- Do you identify your subjects clearly?
- Does your thesis clearly state the purpose and overall limits of your particular study?

You will also need to pay close attention to the development of your essay:

- Are you attempting to compare/contrast items from the same general category?
- Do you discuss the same qualities of each subject?
- Do you balance the treatment of the different subjects of your essay?
- Did you organize your topic as effectively as possible?
- Does your conclusion contain a summary and analysis of your main points?

For further information on writing and revising your comparison/contrast essays, consult the checklists on pages 29–30 of the Introduction.

Student Essay: Comparison/Contrast at Work

The following student essay compares the advantages and disadvantages of macaroni and cheese versus tacos in the life of a harried first-year college or university student. As you read it, notice that the writer states his intention in the first paragraph and then expands his discussion with appropriate details to produce a balanced essay. Also, try to determine what effect he creates by using two methods of organization: first subject by subject, then point by point.

Student Chef

To this day, I will not eat either macaroni and cheese or tacos. No, it's not because of any allergy; it's because during my first year at college, I prepared one or the other of these scrumptious dishes more times than I care to remember. However, my choice of which culinary delight to cook on any given night was not as simple a decision as one might imagine.

Macaroni and cheese has numerous advantages for the student chef. First of all, it is inexpensive. No matter how poor one may be, there's probably enough change under the couch cushion to buy a box at the market. All that starch for only 89¢. What a bargain! Second, it can be prepared in just one pan. This is especially important given the meagre resources of the average

Marginal annotations:

Topics

Basis of comparison

Thesis statement: Purpose and limits of comparison

Paragraph on Subject A: Macaroni and cheese

Point 1 (Price)

Point 2 (Preparation)

Point 3
(Odour)

student's kitchen. <u>Third, and perhaps most important, macaroni and cheese is odourless.</u> By odourless, I mean that no one else can smell it. It is a well-known fact that students hate to cook and that they love nothing better than to wander dejectedly around the kitchen with big, sad eyes after someone else has been cooking. But with macaroni and cheese, no enticing aromas are going to find their way into the nose of any would-be mooch.

Paragraph
on
Subject B:
Tacos

Tacos, <u>on the other hand</u>, are a different matter altogether. For the student cook, <u>the most significant difference is obviously the price</u>. To enjoy tacos for dinner, the adventurous student gourmet must purchase no fewer than five ingredients from the market: corn tortillas, beef, lettuce, tomatoes, and cheese. Needless to say, this is a major expenditure. <u>Second, the chef must adroitly shuffle these ingredients back and forth among his very limited supply of pans and bowls. And finally, tacos smell great.</u> That wouldn't be a problem if the tacos didn't also smell great to about twenty of the cook's newest—if not closest—friends, who appear with those same pathetic, starving eyes mentioned earlier. When this happens, the cook will be lucky to get more than two of his own creations.

Transition

Point 1 (Price)

Point 2
(Preparation)

Point 3
(Odour)

Subject B
Paragraph
on Point 4:
Taste

<u>Tacos, then,</u> wouldn't stand much of a chance if they didn't outdo <u>macaroni and cheese</u> in one area: taste. Taste is almost— but not quite—an optional requirement in the opinion of a frugal student hash-slinger. Taste is just important enough so that tacos are occasionally prepared, despite their disadvantages.

Transition
Subject A

Transition
Paragraph
on Point 5:
Colour

<u>But tacos</u> have other advantages besides their taste. With their enticing, colourful ingredients, they even look good. The only thing that can be said about the colour of <u>macaroni and cheese</u> is that it's a colour not found in nature.

Subject B

Subject A

Transition
Paragraph
on Point 6:
Time

<u>On the other hand, macaroni and cheese</u> is quick. It can be pre- pared in about ten minutes, while <u>tacos</u> take more than twice as long. And there are occasions—such as final exam week—when time is a scarce and precious resource.

Subject A
Subject B

Transition
Analysis

<u>As you can see,</u> quite a bit of thinking went into my choice of food in my younger years. These two dishes essentially got me through my first year and indirectly taught me how to make im- portant decisions (like what to eat). <u>But I still feel a certain revul- sion when I hear their names today.</u>

Summary

Concluding
statement

Some Final Thoughts on Comparison/Contrast

The essays in this section demonstrate various methods of organization as well as a number of distinct stylistic approaches to writing a comparison/contrast essay. As you read these selections, pay particular attention to the clear, well-focused introductions; the different logical methods of organization; and the smooth transitions between sentences and paragraphs.

Comparison/Contrast in Review

Reading Comparison/Contrast Essays

Preparing to Read .

- What assumptions can you make from the essay's title?
- Can you guess what the general mood of the essay is?
- What is the essay's purpose and audience?
- What does the synopsis in the Rhetorical Table of Contents tell you about the essay?
- What can you learn from the author's biography?
- Can you guess what the author's point of view toward the subject is?
- What are your responses to the Preparing to Read questions?

Reading

- What is the author's thesis?
- How is the essay organized: Point by point? Subject by subject? As a combination of the two? As separate discussions of similarities and differences between two subjects?
- Did you preview the questions that follow the essay?

Rereading

- Is the writer's method of organization effective for advancing the essay's thesis?
- Is the essay fully developed?

- What other rhetorical strategies does the author use to support the essay's purpose?
- What are your responses to the questions after the essay?

Writing Comparison/Contrast Essays

Preparing to Write

- What are your responses to the Preparing to Write questions?
- What is your purpose?
- Are you comparing/contrasting items in the same category (e.g., two professors, but not a professor and a swimming pool)?
- Do you have a specific purpose or reason for writing your essay?
- Are you going to discuss the same qualities of each subject?
- Have you generated as many pertinent details as possible to expand your comparison/contrast and to accomplish your stated purpose?

Writing

- Does your introduction (1) clearly identify your subjects, (2) explain the basis of your comparison/contrast, and (3) state your purpose and the overall limits of your particular study?
- Does your thesis include the boundaries of your discussion?
- Have you limited your discussion to three or four basic categories?
- Is your paper organized in one of the following ways: point by point, subject by subject, as a combination of the two, or as separate discussions of similarities and differences between two subjects?
- Does your conclusion summarize your main points and state the deductions you made from those points?

Rewriting

- Do you identify your subjects clearly?
- Does your thesis clearly state the purpose and overall limits of your particular study?

- Are you attempting to compare/contrast items from the same general category?
- Do you discuss the same qualities of each subject?
- Do you balance the treatment of the different subjects of your essay?
- Have you organized your topic as effectively as possible?
- Does your conclusion contain a summary and analysis of your main points?

MONTE HUMMEL

A Passion for the Environment: Two Accounts

The Order of Canada recognizes "outstanding achievement and service in various fields of human endeavour." Monte Hummel's appointment as an Officer of the Order of Canada in 2000 reflects the difference he has made to Canada in the realm of the environment.

Born in Toronto in 1947, Monte Hummel spent his childhood in White Dog Falls in Northern Ontario, and then moved back south to attend high school and university. At the University of Toronto, Hummel earned a B.A., an M.A., and an M.Sc. in forestry; he has spent his career in various environmental advocacy roles ranging from Executive Director and Chairman of Pollution Probe (which he co-founded) to his current role (held since 1985) as president of the World Wildlife Fund Canada.

Hummel's strong commitment to environmental preservation is evidenced as well by his service on the boards of several conservation organizations, both Canadian and international, and many government advisory councils. In addition Hummel has written five books—*Arctic Wildlife*, *Endangered Spaces*, *Wild Hunters* (co-authored with his wife, Sherry Pettigrew), *Protecting Canada's Endangered Spaces*, and *Wintergreen: Reflections from Loon Lake*—and several articles for popular and scientific publications.

Now a resident of Beeton, Ontario, Hummel continues to win recognition for his efforts to preserve the Canadian landscape from organizations including the Canadian Parks and Wilderness Society and the University of Toronto.

"A Passion for the Environment" first appeared in the *Queen's Quarterly* in 2000.

Preparing to Read

Before reading Hummel's essay, think about changes to the natural environment. What changes have you observed in your lifetime? Are those changes positive or negative? What has caused those changes? What future changes do you anticipate? What value do you attach to preservation of the natural environment? Where should this fit in governmental, societal, and commercial priorities?

On a sunny day in August 1959, my honey-coloured spaniel   1
Roxy and I went fishing. At the time, my family lived in a
hydro camp at White Dog Falls, north of Kenora in northwestern
Ontario. Roxy and I scrambled over familiar rocks along the river
bank, caught frogs for bait, shared a sandwich for lunch, landed a
couple of medium-sized pike out of dark swirling pools below
the rapids, and rested looking up through pines at osprey who
were also fishing these northern waters. Two men noticed us, and
asked if I would show them where I caught the fish, which I was
pleased to do if they would let me fillet anything they caught at 25
cents each. It was truly a Huck Finn kind of upbringing, and deeply
formative of "a passion for the environment."

On a sunny day in August 1969, I returned to visit my home   2
river of those halcyon boyhood days, with the ink barely dry on
a university degree. Memories welled up as I picked my way
down to the shore to see what a small sign said, posted right by
the water. "Fish for Fun Only." This message was screened
against the background of a skull and crossbones, by authority of
the Government of Ontario. The English-Wabigoon river system
had become tragically contaminated by mercury from an
upstream chlor-alkali plant associated with the pulp and paper
industry. The fish were no longer fit to eat. The Ojibway kids I
went to school with had lost their commercial white-fish fishery
and jobs guiding sport anglers, so the economic base of their
reserve was in tatters. So was my Huck Finn upbringing. On that
day, "a passion for the environment" came crisply into focus.

UNDERSTANDING DETAILS

1. What is Hummel comparing and contrasting?
2. What served as the economic base of the Ojibway reserve in
   1959?
3. What changes to his childhood home does Hummel find when
   he returns from university? What was responsible for these
   changes?

ANALYZING MEANING

1. Explain Hummel's purpose in this essay. What is his thesis?
2. Hummel refers to his "Huck Finn upbringing." Explain this
   reference.

3. Now in his fifties, Hummel chooses to relate incidents from several decades earlier. Why has this experience had such a strong impact on Hummel? Given his range of experience related to the environment, why hasn't Hummel focused on a more current example?

DISCOVERING RHETORICAL STRATEGIES

1. Find three examples of repetition of phrases in Hummel's essay. What is the effect of this repetition?
2. Has Hummel organized his comparison/contrast to focus on one side at a time or point by point? Is this an effective choice? Why or why not?
3. Hummel uses several specific examples in his essay. Explain the effect of the incorporation of these examples.

MAKING CONNECTIONS

1. The title of Hummel's essay clearly indicates his attitude toward the environment. How does his stance toward the environment compare to that of Tomson Highway ("What a Certain Visionary Once Said") or Sharon Butala ("The Myth: The Prairies Are Flat")?
2. Hummel and David Adams Richards ("My Old Newcastle") both write about their recollections of their childhood homes. Compare and contrast their experiences of returning to the place where they grew up.
3. Hummel's essay appeared as part of a series in the *Queen's Quarterly* about people's passions. How does Hummel's portrayal of his passion compare to that of Marguerite Andersen ("Passion for Language")?

IDEAS FOR DISCUSSION/WRITING

Preparing to Write

What do you feel passionate about? What has created that passion in you? What continues to fuel that passion? How is that passion expressed? How do others respond to your passion? Have your passions changed over time or remained consistent?

Choosing a Topic

1. Write about your passion. What has created your passion and how is your passion expressed?
2. Imagine you are a representative for the chlor-alkali plant that has caused the changes to the English-Wabigoon river system. Write an essay in which you justify the actions taken by your company and explain the benefits that have resulted from your company's industry in this area.
3. Think of a particular interest that you pursued at one point in your life that has significantly diminished or heightened in importance to you. This might be a sport, a hobby, a community issue, or a social/political cause. Write a comparison and contrast essay in which you compare your engagement in this interest at different stages of your life, and account for the change over time.

WEBSITES

www.cpaws.org/aboutus/harkin-hummel.html
Monte Hummel is the 2001 recipient of the Harkin Award, recognizing his lifelong career contribution to wilderness protection.

www.wwfcanada.org
Hummel is the president of the World Wildlife Fund Canada.

www.queensu.ca/quarterly
Hummel's essay comes from the *Queen's Quarterly* journal.

WILL FERGUSON

The Sudbury Syndrome

Originally from Fort Vermilion in northern Alberta, Will Ferguson (1964–)
has lived and worked in a wide variety of places both in Canada and
abroad, including five years in Japan. These experiences provide the basis
for the books he has written and the commentary he occasionally provides on CBC radio. Ferguson's *I Was a Teenage Katima-Victim* (1998) is a
memoir of the period he spent participating in the national Katimavik
volunteer program that brought together young people from across the
country to work on various projects in different communities. *Hokkaido
Highway Blues: Hitchhiking Japan* (1998) and *The Hitchhiker's Guide to Japan*
(1998) are both products of Ferguson's 1996 hitchhiking trip over the
length of Japan. The book from which the selection here was taken is *Why
I Hate Canadians* (1997), a humorous analysis of what Canada is and the
meaning of being Canadian. A graduate of York University with a B.F.A.
in film studies, Ferguson now lives with his wife and sons in Calgary,
Alberta. His recent works include *Bastards and Boneheads* (1998), *Canadian
History for Dummies* (2000), and *How to Be a Canadian (Even If You Already
Are One)*, co-written with his brother.

Preparing to Read

In this essay, Ferguson introduces Sudbury as one of Canada's "scars"
rather than one of its "smiles." Before you read Ferguson's essay, think
about a specific place that you would characterize as a "scar" instead of
a "smile." Why is it a scar? What specific details illustrate its ugliness or
lack of appeal? Does it have any redeeming qualities? Does it seem to be
improving or getting worse?

So far we have been discussing Canada largely in the abstract.   1
Let's now take a closer look at some of the places and spaces we
occupy. Canada on the street corner of a specific town or city is
far different from the Canada of the imagination. With that in
mind, I give you the city of Sudbury. And remember as you read
this that (A) I love Sudbury, and (B) our scars define us every bit
as much as our smiles, and our *collective* scars define us even further. Plastic surgery is *not* the answer.

England may have the White Cliffs of Dover, but Canada 2
has the Black Cliffs of Sudbury. And unlike the cliffs of Dover,
which are really more of an *off*-white, the cliffs of Sudbury are
black. Even better, they are man-made.

You see the cliffs as you drive into town, Sudbury's slag-pile 3
glaciers, the scorched tailings of the city's infamous nickel mines.
Rail-cars roll up to the edge, then pause, tilt and pour out the
molten slag, casting an orange echo against the sky, like the castle
defences of a medieval siege. The slag cools into a crust, then
blackens, and is in turn covered.

No animal can live off its own waste. This is a basic rule of 4
biology, and yet Sudbury, a city of 90,000 in the scrub-backed
land of the Canadian Shield, seems to defy this. Folk singer
Murray McLaughlin called it a "hard-rock town." Others have
been less charitable. But if Sudbury has a bad reputation, it came
by it honestly. It may be ugly, but it was a damn sight uglier and
nastier just a few years ago. (*Suggested town motto:* You think it
stinks now, you should have seen it before!)

Sudbury started in 1883 as a muddy, backwoods rail town at 5
the junction of two main lines. With the discovery of the world's
richest nickel deposits came an economic boom. Two companies
blasted their way to the top of the slag pile and stayed there:
Falconbridge Mines and the almighty American-based
International Nickel Company, now known simply as INCO.

INCO ruled Sudbury for almost eighty years. As final courts 6
of appeal, there was God, Ottawa and INCO, but not necessarily
in that order. As late as 1964, the mayor of Sudbury was
cheerfully informing newcomers to the city: "INCO calls the
shots around here, and don't ever forget it."

> Oh the girls are out to bingo,
>   and the boys are gettin' stink-o,
> And we'll think no more of INCO
>   on a Sudbury Saturday night.

So sang Stompin' Tom Connors, and the words ring true of 7
a company town that ate its own. The pollution was horrific.
Every dollar earned was wrestled from the earth, carved, blasted,
crushed, melted down and skimmed off. For miles around the
vegetation was dead, the land was barren and sullied. Lung
cancer, acid rain, lakes turned to vinegar, bedrock torched bare:

Sudbury had it all. It was—and still is—a hard-drinking, blue-collar place, with a rowdy mix of French and English. An archetypal mining town, a sorrowful and sickly place.

And yet never were a people so proud of their town. The 8 good citizens of Sudbury will defend their rocky home amid the smokestacks with the same fierce stubbornness that a parent defends a particularly ugly child. It's a town with a chip on its shoulder, and so it should. If you were the brunt of innumerable jokes, if in high school you were always voted most likely to die of industrial disease, you too would get pissed off at writers like me who come into town, shake their heads and declare it a "sorrowful and sickly place."

Later, INCO built Superstack, the tallest chimney in the 9 world, to throw the emissions out higher and over a larger area. This massive, spewing smokestack is a symbol of Sudbury as much as the Giant Nickel on the road into town. (In his travel book *Last Train to Toronto*, Terry Pindell recalls meeting Miss Nude Canada, the amply endowed Kathy Stack, in her home town of Sudbury. Her stage name was XTC, but everyone around town called her Superstack, though I believe this nickname may not have been in reference to the INCO chimney.)

The glory of nude dancing aside, Sudbury went into free- 10 fall sometime around 1980 and just kept tumbling. A series of bitter strikes and layoffs was followed hard by recession and terminal unemployment and the apocalyptic INCO strike. The picket lines, the cutbacks, the false minibooms that came and went like death spasms, all weighed heavy on the City That Nickel Built.

The story of Sudbury doesn't end there, though by all logic 11 it should; it was a one-industry town and its time had run out. But then, like a minor miracle, the clouds broke and the Sudbury Renaissance began. A streak of civic pride, as deep as any nickel core, saved them. (That and millions of dollars in federal and corporate aid.) The strategy was simply, the mantra short: diversify or die.

And what do you think they decided to base their recovery 12 on? You'll never guess. Never. They decided to make Sudbury a centre for *tourism*. That's right, tourism. "I don't know, honey, this year it's either Paris or Sudbury, I just can't decide." The crazy thing is, it worked. Tourism is now a major, multimillion-dollar industry in Sudbury and one of the cornerstones of the city's recovery plan.

INCO donated $5 million towards the construction of Science   13
North, a tourist-orientated interactive centre. It was the biggest
single corporate donation to a community project in Canadian
history—something which INCO never tires of pointing out.

Science North is "science beyond the classroom." The   14
buildings are designed in the shape of snowflakes, *stainless steel*
snowflakes, that are connected via bedrock tunnels. And how
do they entice you to come to the complex? With the promise
that you will *"Pet a tarantula! Hold a porcupine! and lie on a bed of
nails!"* Tarantulas? Bed of nails? Just how does this tour end? Do
they poke you in the eye with a stick and set your hair on fire? In
fact, Science North is a lot of fun. And yes, as I discovered, you
can pet a porcupine. His name is Ralf, he likes to have his belly
rubbed, and no, his quills don't come off. Unless he's angry. So
you should try to stay on his good side.

Sudbury has reinvented itself, and with tourism now   15
booming, people are actually ending up in Sudbury *on purpose!*
The city's concentrated tree-planting and beautification project
finally paid off when *Chatelaine* magazine—that purveyor of
good taste—ranked Sudbury as one of the ten best Canadian
cities to live in. *Crowds cheer! Balloons fly! Parades parade!*

Now then, let's not go overboard. Sudbury, no matter how   16
many trees you plant is still, well, Sudbury. Many of the newly
built and much ballyhooed residential complexes were really
just the generic Canadian Suburb transplanted whole into what
was once, and still is, a rough northern town. All the trees by
the side of the road are not going to hide the rock and refineries.
(*Suggested motto:* As far as industrial wastelands go, we're not
that bad!)

It's true, the United Nations Environment Committee has   17
applauded Sudbury's urban renewal efforts. (*Crowds cheer,
balloons fly*, etc. etc.) Do you remember back in grade school,
when the teacher used to give special silver stars to that slow
kid who tried really, really hard but was still a bit thick? They
called the award Most Improved. Well, Sudbury is that student,
and she wears her star proudly.

From the top of the hill, beside the giant stainless steel nickel,   18
she proclaims, like Scarlett O'Hara in *Gone with the Wind*, "As
God is my witness, I will never be ugly again!"

And on the other side, across the hill, the slag cars rumble   19
and roll, pouring the fire that slides down like lava and cools
into blackness on the edge of town.

Tucked in within Sudbury's Copper Cliff townsite is a place   20
called Little Italy. Built by migrant workers to resemble the
mountain villages of their native land, it is a small enclave of
narrow random streets and oddly angled houses. From Little
Italy to the Giant Nickel, from the Black Cliffs to the Superstack
itself, Sudbury has stories to tell. Love her or hate her, there is no
place quite like her. Sudbury *is* ugly. It is a city with a past, a
city covered with scars, but it is also a city with that elusive
quality we call *character*, and character is not something you can
buy. But it is something you can lose.

Every time you pass through Sudbury, you will notice the   21
encroaching sameness of suburbia. It is happening across Canada.
I call it the Sudbury Syndrome: the desire to eradicate the scars
and birthmarks of a place and import instead the shiny surfaces
and retail clones of a common urban/suburban culture. It is
nothing short of the Blanding of Canada. Local character and
diversity is slowly being watered down, and our cities and towns
are fast becoming as interchangeable as shopping malls.

The town of Sudbury, with its gritty working-class roots and   22
nickel-plated pride, epitomizes this. A campaign has been under
way since the early 1990s to change Sudbury's image, to make it
more like every other town, to make it as innocuous as possible.
To make it as nice as everybody else.

Let me take you now to Saint John, New Brunswick, or, as I   23
like to call it, Sudbury-by-the-sea. Living as I do in the fey little
town of St. Andrews, I have come to rely on Saint John
(population: 79,000) as my pipeline to consumer goods, import
foods, cinemas, and adult sex shoppes (*sic*).

St. Andrews, with a population less than 1,300, has a mind-   24
boggling variety all its own, a riffraff collection of greying hippies,
faded back-to-the-landers, imported salmon researchers, restless
college kids, price-gouging landlords, wealthy elders and assorted
craftspeople. The town has also, wisely and with more than a
little smugness, decided to resist the drift towards mass
commercialization. The town stewards have kept fast-food chains
and discount department stores at bay and the result is an
expensive but largely unspoiled town. Quaint. Historic.
Narcoleptic.

The city of Saint John, an hour and a half down the road, is   25
a world away from St. Andrews, and the two coexist like a
dowager aunt and a tattooed dock-worker: uneasily.

Let's be frank. Saint John is a functionally illiterate city.   26
Trying to find a decent used bookstore in Saint John is like trying
to find a decent restaurant in Regina. Much like Sudbury, Saint
John is a blue-collar, gaseous, foul-smelling, knocked-about town.
And just as Sudbury has been cursed and blessed—but to my
mind, mostly cursed—by the presence of INCO, so has Saint
John suffered at the hands of its own capitalist overlords: the
Clan Irving.

To me, the Irvings have always seemed to be old-school   27
caricatures: cigar-smoking, round-bellied, union-busting
capitalists of nineteenth-century America. Except it isn't the
nineteenth century any more (a fact which no one has had the
nerve to tell the Irvings) and Saint John remains a city in thrall.

Have you ever started packing to move, and you start out   28
by boxing and labelling everything and then arranging them
carefully by content and size, but by the time you are done you
are throwing things into boxes and shoving them wherever the
hell they can fit? Well, it's the same with Saint John. There may
have been a plan way back when, but the city is now a stack of
random boxes jumbled along the bedrock, wedged in among
highway overpasses and Irving shipyards. With its one-way
streets and sadistic bypasses, Saint John is an unforgiving city;
take a wrong turn and it's *Hello Moncton*!

And yet, for all that—because of that—I love Saint John. It's   29
a great place. The Old City is filled with surprises and the people
are as raw and real as they come. Whether you're eating the
meatloaf sandwich and spicy fries at Reggie's Diner or waiting for
the Reversing (yawn) Falls to do their stench-side trick, it is hard
not to feel a begrudging admiration for Saint John. Like Sudbury,
it has a character all its own. Which makes it all the more
depressing that it was in Saint John that I experienced my worst
case of Urban Amnesia ever.

Fredericton, meanwhile, is a government town. Inhabited   30
largely by bureaucrats, poets and students, Fredericton can't
quite make up its mind if it wants to be eccentric or snooty and
has settled on a kind of eccentric snootiness that puzzles as much
as it captivates. Like most Canadian cities, Fredericton
(population: 45,000) is inflicted with a perimeter rim of shopping
malls and fast-food emporiums. Like Saint John, Fredericton is
about an hour and a half from St. Andrews.

Where Saint John is pure grit, Fredericton is pampered and   31
refined. Where Saint John is masculine, Fredericton is feminine.

Where Saint John is dark, Fredericton is light. It's yin, it's yang. It's the fiddle vs. the violin. It's diner coffee vs. cappuccino. Saint John is unforgiving, Fredericton is welcoming.

The two cities are as different as any two could be, and yet, 32 during a grey winter outing as I wandered down a hermetically sealed shopping mall corridor, I suddenly lost all sense of place. I couldn't remember if I was in Saint John or Fredericton. Everything was completely familiar—and yet I had absolutely no idea where I was. It must be the way a victim of amnesia feels.

Which city was I in? Fredericton? Saint John? There was 33 nothing to distinguish it either way. Shopping malls, like suburbs, have no character. They are, by their very nature, generic.

It turned out I was in Saint John, which I discovered only 34 after I stopped someone and asked. (And boy, did I get a funny look.) It was a heart-sinking moment to realize just how standardized modern Canadian culture has become. It is cheerful and clean and comfortable. And soulless.

What this country needs is more Sudburys and fewer 35 shopping malls.

UNDERSTANDING DETAILS

1. How has Sudbury changed between the 1980s and the late 1990s when Ferguson's essay was written? Give specific examples that show the progression.
2. How are Saint John and Fredericton similar? In what ways do they differ?
3. What force has been primarily responsible for the establishment and development of Sudbury?

ANALYZING MEANING

1. In this essay Ferguson introduces a trend he labels "the Blanding of Canada." Explain exactly what "the Blanding of Canada" is. What is Ferguson's attitude toward this trend?
2. How does Ferguson feel about his hometown of St. Andrews, New Brunswick? Is his attitude consistent with the characteristics he uses to introduce St. Andrews? Explain the apparent contradiction in Ferguson's approach.
3. Ferguson concludes his essay with a call for more Sudburys and fewer shopping malls. Explain why Ferguson sees this as the ideal.

DISCOVERING RHETORICAL STRATEGIES

1. Which of the four patterns of organization has Ferguson chosen in this essay?
2. Reading reviews of *Why I Hate Canadians*, in which this essay first appeared, shows that Ferguson offends many readers with his views about Canada and Canadians. The tone that Ferguson uses and his tendency to exaggerate to make a point may exacerbate this reaction. Explain why Ferguson hasn't adopted a more diplomatic, even tone in conveying the ideas he has about his subject matter.
3. Ferguson uses many metaphors and similes to make his writing interesting and vivid. Find four examples of Ferguson's use of these figures of speech. Which do you find the most effective? Why?

MAKING CONNECTIONS

1. Ferguson concludes his essay by saying that "[w]hat this country needs is more Sudburys and fewer shopping malls." Imagine that Ferguson is having a conversation about Canada with Anita Rau Badami ("My Canada"), Sharon Butala ("The Myth: The Prairies Are Flat"), and Tomson Highway ("What a Certain Visionary Once Said"). Who in this group do you think would agree with Ferguson? Who would disagree? Who would you most closely agree with?
2. In "Kris King Looks Terrible," Dave Bidini writes about a section of Hong Kong. How does Bidini's depiction of Hong Kong compare to Ferguson's depiction of St. Andrews? Would Bidini describe Hong Kong as a "scar" or a "smile" on the face of China?
3. Ferguson uses an informal and humorous tone in this essay. Identify the specific techniques he employs to achieve this tone. How do those techniques compare to the strategies used by Drew Hayden Taylor ("Pretty Like a White Boy")?

IDEAS FOR DISCUSSION/WRITING

Preparing to Write

In "The Sudbury Syndrome" Ferguson writes about the value of character in a place. Write freely about a place you know that has character. What makes this place unique? Is it generally viewed positively or negatively? Why? Are the elements of character valued? How has this place changed over time? Has that enhanced its character or diminished it?

Choosing a Topic

1. Think about a city or town you know well. Compare and contrast what that place is like today with what it was like when you first knew it. Using specific examples, show how it has changed. In your view, has the change been an improvement or a deterioration?
2. Ferguson laments the uniformity and consistency of shopping malls and the lack of unique character that they possess. Using specific examples with which you are familiar, write an essay in which you either advance Ferguson's view or counter it with a defence of shopping malls.
3. Choose two people who work in the same field and compare and contrast their approaches to the job. You might consider two teachers, two newscasters, two DJs, two store clerks, two servers in a restaurant, or two politicians.

WEBSITES

www.januarymagazine.com/profiles/ferguson.html
A *January Magazine* interview with Will Ferguson.

www.globebooks.com/interviews/fergusonwill.html
A *Globe and Mail* interview with Will Ferguson.

www.yorku.ca/ycom/profiles/past/aug98/current/dept/ gprofile/gprofile3.htm
A profile of York University alumnus Will Ferguson.

GLORIA STEINEM

The Politics of Muscle

Once described as a writer with "unpretentious clarity and forceful expression," Gloria Steinem is one of the foremost organizers and champions of the modern women's movement. She was born in Toledo, Ohio, in 1934, earned a B.A. at Smith College, and pursued graduate work in political science at the universities of Delhi and Calcutta in India before returning to America to begin a freelance career in journalism. One of her earliest and best-known articles, "I Was a Playboy Bunny," was a witty exposé of the entire Playboy operation written in 1963 after she had worked undercover for two weeks in the New York City Playboy Club. In 1968 she and Clay Felker founded *New York* magazine; then, in 1972, they started *Ms.* magazine. Steinem's subsequent publications have included *Outrageous Acts and Everyday Rebellions* (1983), *Marilyn: Norma Jean* (1986), *Bedside Book of Self-Esteem* (1989), and *Moving Beyond Words* (1994). She has also written several television scripts and is a frequent contributor to such periodicals as *Esquire, Vogue, Cosmopolitan, Seventeen,* and *Life.* An articulate and passionate spokesperson for feminist causes, Steinem has been honoured nine times by the *World Almanac* as one of the 25 most influential women in America.

Preparing to Read

Taken from the author's newest book, *Moving Beyond Words*, "The Politics of Muscle" is actually an introduction to a longer essay entitled "The Strongest Woman in the World," which celebrates the virtues of women's bodybuilding champion Bev Francis. In this introductory essay, Steinem examines the sexual politics of women's weightlifting and the extent to which a "new beauty standard" has begun to evolve because of pioneers in the sport like Francis. As you prepare to read this essay, examine for a few minutes your own thoughts about the associations people make with weakness and strength in both men and women: Which sex do you think of as stronger? In our society, what does strength have to do with accomplishment? With failure? Do these associations vary for men and women? What does weakness suggest in North American culture? Do these suggestions vary for men and women? What are the positive values North Americans associate with muscles and strength? With helplessness and weakness? What are the negative values North Americans associate with muscles and strength? With helplessness and weakness? From your experience, what connections have you made between physical strength and gender roles?

Icome from a generation who didn't do sports. Being a cheer-   1
leader or a drum majorette was as far as our imaginations or
role models could take us. Oh yes, there was also being a
strutter—one of a group of girls (and we were girls then) who
marched and danced and turned cartwheels in front of the high
school band at football games. Did you know that big football universities actually gave strutting scholarships? That shouldn't sound
any more bizarre than football scholarships, yet somehow it does.
Gender politics strikes again.

But even winning one of those rare positions, the stuff that   2
dreams were made of, was more about body display than about
the considerable skill they required. You could forget about trying
out for them if you didn't have the right face and figure, and my
high school was full of girls who had learned to do back flips
and twirl flaming batons, all to no avail. Winning wasn't about
being the best in an objective competition or achieving a personal
best, or even about becoming healthy or fit. It was about *being
chosen*.

That's one of many reasons why I and other women of my   3
generation grew up believing—as many girls still do—that the
most important thing about a female body is not what it does
but how it looks. The power lies not within us but in the gaze
of the observer. In retrospect, I feel sorry for the protofeminist
gym teachers who tried so hard to interest us in half-court
basketball and other team sports thought suitable for girls in my
high school, while we worried about the hairdo we'd slept on
rollers all night to achieve. Gym was just a stupid requirement
you tried to get out of, with ugly gym suits whose very freedom
felt odd on bodies accustomed to being constricted for viewing.
My blue-collar neighborhood didn't help much either, for it
convinced me that sports like tennis or golf were as remote as
the country clubs where they were played—mostly by men
anyway. That left tap dancing and ballet as my only exercise,
and though my dancing school farmed us out to supermarket
openings and local nightclubs, where we danced our hearts out
in homemade costumes, those events were about display too,
about smiling and pleasing and, even during the rigors of ballet,
about looking ethereal and hiding any muscles or strength.

My sports avoidance continued into college, where I went   4
through shock about class and wrongly assumed athletics were
only for well-to-do prep school girls like those who brought their

own lacrosse sticks and riding horses to school. With no sports training to carry over from childhood—and no place to become childlike, as we must when we belatedly learn basic skills—I clung to my familiar limits. Even at the casual softball games where *Ms.* played the staffs of other magazines, I confined myself to cheering. As the *Ms.* No Stars, we prided ourselves on keeping the same lineup, win or lose, and otherwise disobeying the rules of the jockocracy, so I contented myself with upsetting the men on the opposing team by cheering for their female team members. It's amazing how upset those accustomed to conventional divisions can become when others refuse to be divided by them.

In my case, an interest in the politics of strength had come not   5
from my own experience but from observing the mysterious changes in many women around me. Several of my unathletic friends had deserted me by joining gyms, becoming joggers, or discovering the pleasure of learning to yell and kick in self-defense class. Others who had young daughters described the unexpected thrill of seeing them learn to throw a ball or run with a freedom that hadn't been part of our lives in conscious memory. On campuses, I listened to formerly anorexic young women who said their obsession with dieting had diminished when they discovered strength as a third alternative to the usual fat-versus-thin dichotomy. Suddenly, a skinny, androgynous, "boyish" body was no longer the only way to escape the soft, female, "victim" bodies they associated with their mothers' fates. Added together, these examples of before-and-after strength changes were so dramatic that the only male analogues I could find were Vietnam amputees whose confidence was bolstered when they entered marathons in wheelchairs or on artificial legs, or paralyzed accident survivors whose sense of themselves was changed when they learned to play wheelchair basketball. Compared to their handicapped female counterparts, however, even those men seemed to be less transformed. Within each category, women had been less encouraged to develop whatever muscle and skills we had.

Since my old habits of ignoring my body and living inside my   6
head weren't that easy to break, it was difficult to change my nonathletic ways. Instead, I continued to learn secondhand from watching my friends, from reading about female strength in other cultures, and from asking questions wherever I traveled.

Though cultural differences were many, there were political   7
similarities in the way women's bodies were treated that went as

deep as patriarchy itself. Whether achieved through law and social policy, as in this and other industrialized countries, or by way of tribal practice and religious ritual, as in older cultures, an individual woman's body was far more subject to other people's rules than was that of her male counterpart. Women always seemed to be owned to some degree as the means of reproduction. And as possessions, women's bodies then became symbols of men's status, with a value that was often determined by what was rare. Thus, rich cultures valued thin women, and poor cultures valued fat women. Yet all patriarchal cultures valued weakness in women. How else could male dominance survive? In my own country, for example, women who "belong" to rich white men are often thinner (as in "You can never be too rich or too thin") than those who "belong" to poor men of color; yet those very different groups of males tend to come together in their belief that women are supposed to be weaker than men; that muscles and strength aren't "feminine."

If I had any doubts about the psychological importance of 8 cultural emphasis on male/female strength difference, listening to arguments about equality put them to rest. Sooner or later, even the most intellectual discussion came down to men's supposedly superior strength as a justification for inequality, whether the person arguing regretted or celebrated it. What no one seemed to explore, however, was the inadequacy of physical strength as a way of explaining oppression in other cases. Men of European origin hadn't ruled in South Africa because they were stronger than African men, and blacks hadn't been kept in slavery or bad jobs in the United States because whites had more muscles. On the contrary, males of the "wrong" class or color were often confined to laboring positions precisely because of their supposedly greater strength, just as the lower pay females received was often rationalized by their supposedly lesser strength. Oppression has no logic—just a self-fulfilling prophecy, justified by a self-perpetuating system.

The more I learned, the more I realized that belief in great 9 strength differences between women and men was itself part of the gender mind-game. In fact, we can't really know what those differences might be, because they are so enshrined, perpetuated, and exaggerated by culture. They seem to be greatest during the childbearing years (when men as a group have more speed and upper-body strength, and women have better balance, endurance, and flexibility) but only marginal during early childhood and old age (when females and males seem to have about the same degree of physical strength). Even during those middle years, the range of difference *among* men and *among* women is far greater than the generalized difference *between* males and females as groups. In multiracial societies like ours, where males of some races are smaller than females of others, judgments based on sex make even less sense. Yet we go right on assuming and praising female weakness and male strength.

But there is a problem about keeping women weak, even in   10
a patriarchy. Women are workers, as well as the means of reproduction. Lower-class women are especially likely to do hard physical labor. So the problem becomes: How to make sure female strength is used for work but not for rebellion? The answer is: Make women ashamed of it. Though hard work requires lower-class women to be stronger than their upper-class sisters, for example, those strong women are made to envy and imitate the weakness of women who "belong" to, and are the means of reproduction for, upper-class men—and so must be kept even *more* physically restricted if the lines of race and inheritance are to be kept "pure." That's why restrictive dress, from the chadors, or full-body veils, of the Middle East to metal ankle and neck rings in Africa, from nineteenth-century hoop skirts in Europe to corsets and high heels here, started among upper-class women and then sifted downward as poor women were encouraged to envy or imitate them. So did such bodily restrictions as bound feet in China, or clitoridectomies and infibulations in much of the Middle East and Africa, both of which practices began with women whose bodies were the means of reproduction for the powerful, and gradually became generalized symbols of femininity. In this country, the self-starvation known as anorexia nervosa is mostly a white, upper-middle class, young-female phenomenon, but all women are encouraged to envy a white and impossibly thin ideal.

Sexual politics are also reflected through differing emphases   11
on the reproductive parts of women's bodies. Whenever a patriarchy wants females to populate a new territory or replenish an old one, big breasts and hips become admirable. Think of the bosomy ideal of this country's frontier days, or the *zaftig*, Marilyn Monroe–type figure that became popular after the population losses of World War II. As soon as increased population wasn't

desirable or necessary, hips and breasts were deemphasized. Think of the Twiggy look that arrived in the 1960s.

But whether bosomy or flat, *zaftig* or thin, the female ideal 12 remains weak, and it stays that way unless women ourselves organize to change it. Suffragists shed the unhealthy corsets that produced such a tiny-waisted, big-breasted look that fainting and smelling salts became routine. Instead, they brought in bloomers and bicycling. Feminists of today are struggling against social pressures that exalt siliconed breasts but otherwise stick-thin silhouettes. Introducing health and fitness has already led to a fashion industry effort to reintroduce weakness with the waif look, but at least it's being protested. The point is: Only when women rebel against patriarchal standards does female muscle become more accepted.

For these very political reasons, I've gradually come to believe 13 that society's acceptance of muscular women may be one of the most intimate, visceral measures of change. Yes, we need progress everywhere, but an increase in our physical strength could have more impact on the everyday lives of most women than the occasional role model in the boardroom or in the White House.

UNDERSTANDING DETAILS

1. According to Steinem, what is "gender politics" (paragraph 1)?
2. In what ways does Steinem equate "winning" with "being chosen" (paragraph 2)? Why is this an important premise for her essay?
3. What does Steinem mean when she says, "Oppression has no logic" (paragraph 8)? Explain your answer in detail.
4. In what ways does "power" lie with the observer rather than within the female?

ANALYZING MEANING

1. Why does Steinem call the female body a "victim" body (paragraph 5)? What did girls' mothers have to do with this association?
2. Do you agree with the author that a woman's body is "far more subject to other people's rules than [is] that of her male counterpart" (paragraph 7)? Explain your answer, giving examples from your own experience.

3. What is Steinem implying about the political overtones connected with female weakness and male strength? According to Steinem, why are these judgments so ingrained in North American social and cultural mores?

4. What are Steinem's reasons for saying that "society's acceptance of muscular women may be one of the most intimate, visceral measures of change" (paragraph 13)? Do you agree with this statement or not? Explain your reaction in detail.

DISCOVERING RHETORICAL STRATEGIES

1. Who do you think is Steinem's intended audience for this essay? On what evidence do you base your answer?

2. In your opinion, what is Steinem's primary purpose in this essay? Explain your answer in detail.

3. How appropriate is the title of this essay? What would be some possible alternative titles?

4. What rhetorical modes support the author's comparison/contrast? Give examples of each.

MAKING CONNECTIONS

1. To what extent would Laura Robinson ("Starving for the Gold") agree with Gloria Steinem's assertion that many girls still believe that "the most important thing about a female body is not what it does but how it looks" (paragraph 3)? Do you agree or disagree with this assertion? Give at least three reasons for your opinion.

2. If Steinem is correct that American women have not traditionally found power in their muscles, where have they found it? If you were able to ask Naheed Mustafa ("My Body Is My Own Business") this same question, what do you think her answer would be?

3. Steinem's essay explores women in a realm that is traditionally male-dominated. How does her presentation of the experience of women in bodybuilding compare to Judy Rebick's position about women in a world that is traditionally male-dominated? What elements make a difference in these experiences?

IDEAS FOR DISCUSSION/WRITING

Preparing to Write

Write freely about the definition and role of strength and weakness in North American society: What does strength generally mean in our society? What does weakness mean? What association do you have with both modes of behaviour? Where do these associations come from? What are the political implications of these associations? The social implications? In what ways are strength and weakness basic to the value system in North American culture?

Choosing a Topic

1. Compare two different approaches to the process of succeeding in a specific job or activity. Develop your own guidelines for making the comparison; then write an essay for your fellow students about the similarities and differences you have observed between these two different approaches. Be sure to decide on a purpose and a point of view before you begin to write.

2. Interview your mother and father about their views on physical strength in their separate family backgrounds. If you have grandparents or step-parents, interview them as well. Then compare and contrast these various influences in your life. Which of them are alike? Which are different? How have you personally dealt with these similarities and differences? Be sure to decide on a purpose and a point of view before you begin to write.

3. In her essay, Steinem argues that "an increase in our [women's] physical strength could have more impact on the everyday lives of most women than the occasional role model in the boardroom or in the White House" (paragraph 13). Do you agree with the author? Write an essay to be published in your local newspaper explaining your views on this issue.

WEBSITES

 www.greatwomen.org/women.php?action=viewone&id=150
Find biographical information about Steinem at the National Women's Hall of Fame.

 www.femalemuscle.com
Lori Victoria Braun's musclezine focuses on athletic and powerful women.

 www.motherjones.com/mother_jones/ND95/gorney.html
Read an interview of Gloria Steinem by Cynthia Gorney in *Mother Jones* magazine.

MICHAEL McKINLEY

Opera Night in Canada

Michael McKinley is a screenwriter, journalist, and author of three books about hockey. *Hockey Hall of Fame Legends, Putting a Roof on Winter*, and *Etched in Ice* are all sports history books that reflect McKinley's love of this traditional Canadian game. In addition, McKinley, who graduated from the University of British Columbia and Oxford University, wrote and produced *Sacred Ballot*, a documentary on papal elections, for CBC's *Witness*. In his role as a journalist, McKinley has written for many publications, including the *Chicago Sun-Times*, the *New York Daily News*, the *Daily Mail* (London), the *Guardian* (London), the *Los Angeles Times*, the *New York Observer, Saturday Night*, and *Sports Illustrated*. McKinley, who lives in Vancouver, is the program director for the Cambridge Tradition, an international academic program.

Preparing to Read

"Opera Night in Canada" first appeared in *Saturday Night* magazine with the subtitle "hockey and opera are more similar than you think, which is bad news for hockey." In this essay Michael McKinley shows the commonalities between these two apparently disparate forms of entertainment. What are your thoughts about hockey? Do you play hockey? Do you like to watch hockey? Do you attend hockey games? Do you like opera? Have you ever attended an opera? To what types of people do these forms of entertainment typically appeal? Why do you think McKinley sees the similarities between hockey and opera as bad news for hockey?

In late August, a new opera by composer Leslie Uyeda and 1 librettist Tom Cone debuted at Festival Vancouver, an international showcase for music. Of course, the premiere of an opera at a music festival is hardly newsworthy, but the subject matter of this opera was: *Game Misconduct* is an opera about hockey.

The ninety-minute opera takes place in the seventh game of 2 a playoff series between a Canadian team and their American rivals, and follows eight characters over three periods, plus overtime, as they watch the action from the bleachers. Each character represents a theme: there's Larry, a hot-dog and popcorn vendor, who will lose his job of twenty years when the arena is torn down; Rita, a fan whom Larry loves; Rene, the father of the Canadian team's goalie; Blossom, who loves hockey for the fighting; Snake and Sylvia, for whom hockey fills the gaps in their relationship; Hugo, an obnoxious fan from Anaheim; and Trish, a hockey virgin at her first game.

For those of us who love both hockey and opera, the idea of   3
these two art forms being united after all this time is as shocking as Pinkerton returning to marry Madame Butterfly or the Leafs being united with the Stanley Cup. Hockey and opera would seem to exist on opposite ends of the cultural spectrum; a closer look, however, reveals that they have a lot in common. Hockey has three periods; most operas have three acts. Hockey has six positions—a centre, two wingers, two defencemen, and the goalie—while opera has six major "positions"—soprano, mezzo, contralto, tenor, baritone, and bass. Opera's favourite themes are love and death, and hockey echoes these themes, giving us something to love (the game) in the season of death (winter).

Perhaps the most interesting parallel, though, is that both   4
opera and hockey were, in the early stages of their development, hugely popular, and populist, forms of entertainment. Venice saw the world's first public opera house open in 1637, and by 1670, the city had twenty of them. Opera houses had also sprouted up in Rome, Florence, Genoa, Bologna, and Modena. In fact, all across Europe, "real people" were piling in to see tragedy and comedy set to a few good tunes, even if they couldn't understand the Italian, an oversight that Mozart addressed in 1791 when he wrote *The Magic Flute* in his native language of German—a move that brought even more common folk into the stalls.

A century later, opera enjoyed a similar flowering on this   5
side of the Atlantic. Places as far-flung as Dawson City built ice rinks in the service of hockey—but an opera house was just as important to a Canadian small town. Indeed, the country's towns and cities did not consider themselves civilized until they had an opera house to call their own, and both urban Brahmin and rugged frontiersman would think nothing of going to the opera one night and a hockey game the next. When the Kenora Thistles won the Stanley Cup in 1907, the team from the smallest town ever to win the trophy (population 10,000) could only hold their civic reception in a place as hallowed as the ice rink: the Kenora

Opera House. The champion Thistles sat in the opera boxes, their faces reflecting the "barricade of silverware"—including the Cup—that lined the stage as the ecstatic townspeople serenaded their heroes with speeches and song. The occasion itself was operatic.

Nearly a quarter of a century later, Conn Smythe was inventing the Maple Leafs as "Canada's Team" (or English Canada's Team) and looking to raise them a temple at Carlton and Church Streets. He wanted to build a place that could not only house the Stanley Cup champions to come, but where people could also dress as though they were going to the opera. On November 12, 1931, 13,000 people—many of them in evening dress, as if at *Siegfried* (or later, under Harold Ballard, at *I Pagliacci*)—turned out for the Gardens opening. As speeches droned on at centre ice, impatient shouts of "Play hockey!" roared down from the rafters, where sat many of the men who had built the place, eager to see if the one-dollar MLG common shares they had taken were going to be worth anything.

The image of proles in the cheap seats shouting "Get on with it" recalls the vocal passion of early opera audiences, but it also highlights the downward trajectory of opera in the twentieth century. Movies, radio, and eventually television rendered a night at the opera a largely upper-class pursuit; the importance of opera to the common folk was confined to that parodic phrase beloved of sports announcers: "It ain't over until the fat lady sings." Opera drifted from its populist roots, becoming rarefied, culturally adrift, and, arguably, irrelevant, at least to the public at large.

Opera's current cultural relevance—or lack of same—is one of the reasons that *Game Misconduct*'s composer chose to tackle hockey as a theme. "'Contemporary' has become a frightening word to a lot of people," Uyeda says. "I don't understand why people don't want to see themselves reflected [in opera]. And that is exactly the reason that I went for this theme of hockey, because it has something to do with me, and with this great country."

Ironically, just as people no longer see themselves reflected in opera, it may not be long before they no longer see themselves reflected in hockey. Just as opera has its corporate-sponsorship drives, the NHL now fights for the corporate patron with its mega-arenas bearing corporate logos and perks like wine cellars and humidors and, at the Staples Center in Los Angeles, fireplaces in the corporate boxes. In fact, top tickets for a Maple Leafs game cost a whopping $325 each, or almost three times what you'd pay to sit in the front row at a Canadian Opera Company performance.

When the swank Air Canada Centre opened in Toronto, Leafs   10
coach Pat Quinn saw the future of hockey—and it was not good. Asked if he feared losing the blue-collar fan, Quinn said, "We've already lost the blue-collar fan. I'm worried about the white-collar fan." It's something that *Game Misconduct* worries about too. Opera, once central, lost touch with the common fan. In the ultimate irony of the hockey-opera relationship, the fat lady may be singing for the national game as well.

UNDERSTANDING DETAILS

1. The differences between opera and hockey are obvious; McKinley focuses on similarities. List the similarities he identifies.
2. Why did Uyeda choose to create an opera about hockey?
3. Why has the popularity of opera diminished over time? What effects have these forces had on hockey?

ANALYZING MEANING

1. Why has McKinley chosen to compare opera and hockey? What is his purpose in this essay?
2. Explain the "parodic phrase beloved of sports announcers: 'It ain't over until the fat lady sings.'" What does McKinley mean by his reference to this phrase in the final sentence of his essay?
3. Is McKinley's outlook for the future of hockey optimistic or pessimistic? Explain.

DISCOVERING RHETORICAL STRATEGIES

1. Which of the four main methods of organizing a comparison and contrast essay has McKinley used? Why do you think he has made this choice?
2. In addition to comparison and contrast, what rhetorical strategies has McKinley employed in his essay? Where do you see evidence of these strategies?
3. How does McKinley give his essay cohesiveness? What details link the conclusion back to the beginning of the essay?

MAKING CONNECTIONS

1. Michael McKinley and Dave Bidini ("Kris King Looks Terrible") both write about hockey. If they were to attend a hockey game together, on what aspects of the experience do you think they would agree? Where might their views differ?
2. David Foot ("Boomers Dance to a New Beat") attributes various social trends to changing demographics. How do changing demographics contribute to the changing nature of the experience of attending a hockey game?
3. Imagine that McKinley and Evan Solomon ("The Babar Factor") are having a discussion about popular entertainment. What does hockey have in common with the stories about Babar the elephant? What about opera in comparison to Babar?

IDEAS FOR DISCUSSION/WRITING

Preparing to Write

Michael McKinley writes about the popular and populist beginnings of both opera and hockey, but he suggests that both have become "rarefied" or inaccessible to the public at large. Write freely about entertainment events and their appeal. What types of events have the broadest public appeal? Where do they take place? What type of events do you like to attend? To what do you attribute their appeal? What type of audience do those events tend to attract? Is there a cost associated with those events? Are there types of entertainment events that you avoid? If so, why? How do you learn about events that are happening in your community? Are there types of events you have attended in the past but that have now become inaccessible?

Choosing a Topic

1. Write an essay for a group of your classmates in which you propose attending an event or participating in an activity that won't have immediate appeal. To convince them to participate, show the similarities between this type of event or activity and another that you know they enjoy.
2. Write an essay in which you compare and contrast two events that you have attended. Make sure you point out both similarities and differences, and clarify for your audience which one you preferred.

3. Hockey is often considered the national sport of Canada (although that title is officially shared with lacrosse). Compare and contrast the role of hockey in Canada to the role of baseball in the United States, football in Brazil or Italy, cricket in the West Indies, tae kwon do in Korea, or sumo wrestling in Japan. Have the roles of these respective sports changed over time? If so, in what way?

WEBSITES

www.douglas-mcintyre.com/book_details.asp?b=713
Douglas & McIntyre has descriptions of a selection of McKinley's books as well as a short biography.

www.nsnews.com/issues99/w052499/opera.html
Read an article in the *North Shore News* about how the opera *Game Misconduct* came to be.

EVAN SOLOMON

The Babar Factor

A graduate of McGill University with degrees in English literature and religious studies, Evan Solomon (1968–) is the cofounder and executive editor of *Shift* magazine, a freelance journalist, and a fiction writer. For four years he was the host of a weekly show on CBC Newsworld called *Futureworld* and he is now the host of Newsworld's *Hot Type* and *Masters of Technology*, a series that explores "the ideas and lives of some of today's most influential innovators," as well as co-host of *CBC News: Sunday*—a weekly news and current affairs magazine. He has also worked as a reporter for the *South China Morning Post* and is a regular contributor to CBC's *The National* as a guest host and a contributor of cultural essays. Solomon's success is evidenced, in part, by the fact that he has received three Gemini nominations for *Futureworld* and has been named "one of the top 100 people to watch" by *Maclean's* magazine. His first novel, *Crossing the Distance*, the story of two brothers, was published in 1999.

Preparing to Read

"The Babar Factor" first appeared in *Shift* magazine in the spring of 1994. In this essay Evan Solomon looks at the distinctions between the stories of childhood and the enormously popular video games that have made a fairly recent appearance. In preparing to read this essay, think about the stories that you remember from your own childhood. Do you remember reading books or having them read to you? Were stories told to you by the adults in your life? Are there characters from traditional stories that you can recall? Do you remember any specific stories that you particularly liked? What role did stories and books play in your childhood?

*P*eople come from all over the world to Celesteville-on-the-Sea. It has   1
the most beautiful beach in the land of the elephants.

And so begins another adventure with Jean de Brunhoff's   2 noble elephant-king Babar. Remember him? He was a great hero. So were Curious George, Madeline, Mike Mulligan and his steam shovel Mary Anne. This is a memorial to them. This is a memorial to popular stories without interactive characters.

Super Mario sets foot in the door ...   3

Accompanied by a catchy digital melody, these lines begin   4
another adventure in the ongoing saga of that noble video game
plumber Mario. Do you know him? Apparently, he's a great
hero. So is Sonic the Hedgehog and Dino Man. This is a memorial
to them. This a memorial to popular video game characters who
have yet to be forgotten.

Listen: 5

Two very interesting documents were recently made public.   6
One is called the Nintendo Co. 1993 *Annual Report* and the other
is the year-end numbers for Sega Canada. Both are filled with
extraordinary figures like this:

1. Over 75% of the 9.9 million households in Canada own
   video games.

2. The video game market is worth $400 million in Canada
   and $6 billion worldwide.

3. Nintendo has sold more than 100 million Mario video
   games worldwide.

Dazzling figures. So dazzling that they induce me to throw   7
away my Luddite bias and embark on a quest to understand
why video games are popular.

Because my background is filled with books rather than video   8
games, I decide to measure the quality of the games by the Babar
factor. Is a game more interesting than a story about Babar? Are
the graphics more compelling than Jean de Brunhoff's famous
watercolours? Is there more action, are the characters better
developed? In short, what would I rather do, play with a game or
read a Babar?

I begin by playing those games which boil CRTC chief Keith   9
Spicer's lobster. First there's Night Trap, an adventure where
vampire-like gentlemen in black costumes stalk women and suck
out their blood. Called a "live action game" because it contains
video images complete with incredibly bad acting, this beauty
is now available from 3DO. Translation: The company 3DO uses
better graphics than the much touted 16-bit machines from Sega
and so the women's blood is more visible.

Cheers from the vidiots, jeers from the worry-warts.   10
Summary: an altogether dreary game with less graphic violence
than the Ren and Stimpy show (stay with me now as I connect
with these cultural touchstones). Definitely less interesting than
a Babar story—even those which focus too much on Babar's
pesky nephew Arthur—but only slightly more sexist.

Then there's the controversial Mortal Kombat, details of 11
which I will spare you, but needless to say, it revolves around
a tournament where players fight to the death. With a multicultural cast of sadistic characters, this action-packed thriller is
clearly fluent in the vernacular of fun.

Home versions of the game don't allow players to see 12
essentials like blood spurting from a decapitated corpse, and
that has some customers crying foul. But what these customers
don't realize is that every home unit of the Sega system is, in
fact, secretly encoded with a way to unleash Mortal Kombat's
gory potential. Here is that secret code. Move your joy stick in the
following sequence: Down, Up, Left, Left, press button A, then
Right, and finally Down. Now, I'm no expert in mnemonics, but
there is an easy way to remember the code. The first letters spell
the word DULLARD. Go check. Is this a profound semiotic irony
or merely hacker humour that I don't get? I decide to rate Mortal
Kombat highly. While not as strong on narrative as Brunhoff's
work, the game is far more compelling. Just think, if only Celeste
had ripped out Babar's tusks in a bloody domestic dispute. What
a read! And those would have been watercolours worth saving.

But enough of the violent games. What of Mario and Sonic, 13
the real driving forces behind the video game explosion? Getting
to know them is slightly more difficult. First Mario. Resides in
Brooklyn. Plumber. First appeared as "Jumpman" in the 1981
version of Donkey Kong. Nimble of foot. On a mission to save one
of his three lovers. Last year Mario slipped the surly bonds of
the video game world and became a movie star. Played by the
irrepressible Bob Hoskins, Mario emerges as a bumbling fool
with a good heart. Bob did such a fine job effacing any nuance in
Mario's character that children went wild and a sequel went into
production.

And then Sonic, Sega's champion character. Sonic: video 14
game star, Saturday morning cartoon hero, leader of an
interactive video empire worth an estimated 3.5 billion dollars.
And the recent Q-score independent research ratings in the States
concluded that Sonic is more recognizable than Mickey Mouse.
Hmm, makes you look twice at this hedgehog.

And if you do look twice, here is what you will find. Not 15
only are Mario and Sonic childishly underdeveloped characters,
they do not even function within a narrative framework. But
because of a sophisticated marketing campaign, the lines between

story and game have become blurred. And so we mistake these exercises in hand-eye coordination for valuable narratives.

The campaign to blur these lines begins in promotional 16 literature. "Fun is an international language," a Nintendo report says, and then continues, "and Mario helps kids experience fun." Loaded words like "language" and "experience" are used to enrich the basic idea of fun, while positive characteristics such as bravery and loyalty are grafted onto one-dimensional game characters. By dressing up chase-games in the garb of story, marketing possibilities are exponentially greater. After all, it's easier to sell a person than a pixel.

And so, Mario the game piece becomes Mario the lovable 17 hero, and Sonic the blue graphic becomes Sonic the precocious child. Now they can be sold as role models. It's interactive literature, the press releases say, and the kids relate to it, don't you see? I, for one, don't see. Because despite the cartoons, the movies, and the proliferation of games, no real narrative structure exists at all. And everyone in the industry knows it.

"Mario is goofy and awkward, but he works hard and thus 18 can do superhuman things like flying and leaping over buildings," says Nintendo marketing vice president Peter Main, desperate to give Mario some depth. Notice how Main is not compelled to justify Mario's actions in a coherent way. Rather, the *non sequitur*—"he works hard therefore he can fly"—suffices. It suffices because the games move too fast for anyone to notice.

But contrast this shallow imaginative universe to that of 19 Babar. Babar, whose mother is tragically gunned down in front of him. Babar, who unites the elephants after the old king dies from poison. Babar who builds a city, fights enemies and teaches his children valuable, hard-learned lessons.

Because video games have no story, they are unable to create 20 or sustain dramatic tension. The excitement generated by overcoming obstacles is not dramatic because players can always replay the game if they fail. Nothing of value is ever won or lost. In Babar, on the other hand, there is always the potential for tragedy. Each story is compelling because we rely on the eminently mortal Babar to save the situation. But in video games, the "Play Again" factor is the prevailing eschatology, dulling the pleasures derived from emotional uncertainty.

Ultimately, this debases our understanding of the heroic. 21 Mario and Sonic are no more than Pavlovian dogs, conditioned to either pursue or retreat. Nothing they do requires risk or choice. The fact that Pavlov's bell has been substituted by a quarter and the dog biscuit by a princess should not fool us. Mario and Sonic are neither heroes nor role models, they are cute exercise tools that amuse, distract and ultimately bore.

As video games continue to grow in popularity, our 22 imaginative universe continues to shrink. While classic forms of entertainment like Babar demand a willing suspension of disbelief, video games only demand a willing suspension—that is to say, the choice to believe or disbelieve is irrelevant because there is nothing to believe or disbelieve in. With no context, there is no way to explore the heights and depths of human experience, which, after all, is the fundamental task of stories. In the end, all there is left to do is unplug the mind, plug in the game and play.

I don't like to wax nostalgic for books. I keep up with 23 developments in CD-ROMs. Heck, I just recently got myself an e-mail address. But when it comes to Mario and Sonic, I have simple advice: turn back from these wicked ways and read your holy Babar.

UNDERSTANDING DETAILS

1. What is Solomon comparing and contrasting (a) specifically and (b) generally?
2. Who is Babar? Who are Super Mario and Sonic?
3. Why does Solomon choose to measure the appeal of video games against a story about Babar?

ANALYZING MEANING

1. What is the essential difference between video games and stories?
2. Explain the popularity of video games such as Mortal Kombat and Super Mario.
3. Explain Solomon's conclusion. What do books have to offer that video games do not?

DISCOVERING RHETORICAL STRATEGIES

1. Describe Solomon's tone in this essay. Point out specific examples that create this tone.
2. In addition to comparison and contrast, what rhetorical modes has Solomon used in "The Babar Factor"?

3. Explain what strategies Solomon uses to make his introduction particularly effective.

MAKING CONNECTIONS

1. Evan Solomon and Will Ferguson ("The Sudbury Syndrome") are contemporaries who are both writing about change. In both cases the authors conclude that the original is preferable to the newer, although many people see the newer form (video games or shopping malls) as more desirable. Why do these writers advocate for resisting the change and returning to what has gone before? Do you agree with their positions?
2. In addition to being writers, Solomon, Coren ("Dogs and Monsters"), and Rebick ("The Culture of Overwork") are all television hosts. Is there anything in their writing that reflects their TV style?
3. Much of Solomon's essay considers the impact of new technology. Imagine a conversation between Evan Solomon and Ken Wiwa ("Say It With Numbers") about the impact of new technology on our society. How do the views of these two men compare? Do you believe they would essentially agree or disagree? How does your view fit into the conversation?

IDEAS FOR DISCUSSION/WRITING

Preparing to Write

In this essay Solomon cites statistics that demonstrate the overwhelming popularity of video games. Write freely about the role that video games play in our lives. Who plays video games? When and where are they played? What is their appeal? What accounts for their success? Do you think that their popularity will last?

Choosing a Topic

1. Choose two forms of entertainment and write an essay in which you compare and contrast them. Use your examination of their similarities and differences to determine which is the better option.
2. Choose a character from a story that you think resembles you or someone you know in appearance and/or character. You might

choose a childhood story or one that you have read as an adult. Write an essay in which you describe the similarities between your two subjects.

3. Your student council is going to purchase a new video game for the student lounge at your school. Write an essay in which you compare and contrast two of the available games in order to make a recommendation about which one they should purchase.

WEBSITES

www.januarymagazine.com/profiles/solomon.html
A *January Magazine* interview with Solomon.

www.cbc.ca/programs/sites/hottype_bio.html
CBC profile of Solomon.

www.speakers.ca/esolomon.html
Speakers' Spotlight profile of Solomon.

NEIL BISSOONDATH

Religious Faith Versus Spirituality

Neil Bissoondath (1955–) is the Trinidadian-born Canadian author of
three novels and two collections of short stories. Known internationally for
his fiction, Bissoondath has probably become best known in Canada for
his contentious views on multiculturalism as put forth in his first non-
fiction book, *Selling Illusions: The Cult of Multiculturalism in Canada*. The
essay included here was part of a series solicited by CBC at the end of
1999, in which a variety of Canadian writers were asked to reflect on the
new millennium.

Preparing to Read

In this essay Bissoondath compares spirituality with religious faith. Before
reading his perspective, think about your own experience of religion and
spirituality. In your mind are the two the same or distinct? Do you
consider yourself a religious person? A spiritual person? What has made
you religious or spiritual (or both or neither)? How do you respond to
the expression of religious faith in others?

Wait till someone you love dies. You'll see. You'll know God exists. 1
You'll want Him to.

The prediction, repeated with minimal variation through the 2
years by believers challenged by my non-belief, was never offered
as a promise but as a vague threat, and always with a sense of
satisfied superiority, as if the speakers relished the thought that
one day I would get my comeuppance.

They were, without exception, enthusiastic practitioners of 3
their respective faiths—Roman Catholics, Presbyterians, Hindus,
Muslims. God-fearing people all. Which was, to me, precisely
the problem: Why all this fear?

And then one day, without warning, my mother died. Hers 4
was the first death to touch me to the quick. Her cremation was
done in the traditional Hindu manner. Under the direction of a
pundit, my brother and I performed the ceremony, preparing

the body with our bare hands, a contact more intimate than we'd ever had when she was alive.

As I walked away from her flaming pyre, I felt myself soaring 5 with a lightness I'd never known before. I was suddenly freed from days of physical and emotional lassitude, my first inkling of the healing power of ritual, the solace that ceremony can bring.

Still, despite the pain and the unspeakable sense of loss, the 6 oft-predicted discovery of faith eluded me. I remained, as I do today, a non-believer, but I have no doubt that I underwent a deeply spiritual experience. This was when I began to understand that religious faith and spirituality do not necessarily have anything to do with each other—not that they are incompatible but that they are often mutually exclusive.

Western civilization has spent two thousand years blurring 7 the distinction between the two, and as we enter the third millennium we are hardly more at peace with ourselves than people were a thousand years ago. Appreciating the distinction could help soothe our anxieties about the days to come.

Spirituality is the individual's ability to wonder at, and 8 delight in, the indecipherable, like a baby marvelling at the wiggling of its own toes. It is to be at ease with speculation, asking the unanswerable question and accepting that any answer would necessarily be incomplete, even false. It is recognizing that if scientific inquiry has inevitable limits, so too do religious explanations, which base themselves on unquestioning acceptance of the unprovable: neither can ever fully satisfy.

A sense of the spiritual comes from staring deep into the 9 formation of a rose or a hibiscus and being astonished at the intricate delicacy of its symmetry without needing to see behind its perfection of form the fashioning hand of deity.

It comes from watching your child being born and gazing 10 for the first time into those newly opened eyes, from holding that child against your chest and feeling his or her heartbeat melding with yours.

It comes from gazing up into the sparkling solitude of a clear 11 midnight sky, secure in the knowledge that, no matter how alone you may feel at moments, the message of the stars appears to be that you most indisputably are not.

At such moments, you need no dogma to tell you that the 12 world seen or unseen, near or distant, is a wonderful and mysterious place.

Spirituality, then, requires neither science nor religion, both   13
of which hunger after answers and reassurance—while the
essence of spirituality lies in the opening up of the individual to
dazzlement. Spirituality entails no worship.

At the very moment of my mother's cremation, her brother,   14
trapped thousands of miles away in England by airline schedules,
got out his photographs of her and spread them on his coffee
table. He reread her old letters and spent some time meditating
on the life that had been lived—his way, at the very moment
flames consumed her body, of celebrating the life and saying
farewell, his way of engaging with the spiritual.

UNDERSTANDING DETAILS

1. According to Bissoondath, what distinguishes religious faith
   from spirituality?
2. What is the effect on Bissoondath of the traditional Hindu death
   ceremony performed when his mother died?
3. In Bissoondath's opinion, what gives a person a sense of the
   spiritual?

ANALYZING MEANING

1. What is Bissoondath's thesis in this essay? How effectively does
   he develop his central idea?
2. Bissoondath claims that "Western civilization has spent two
   thousand years blurring the distinction between [religious faith
   and spirituality]." Explain what he means by this statement.
   Do you agree or disagree? Explain.
3. Why does Bissoondath feel the need to distinguish between
   religious faith and spirituality? Why do you think he has
   chosen this focus for an essay on the new millennium?

DISCOVERING RHETORICAL STRATEGIES

1. In addition to comparison and contrast, what rhetorical strategies has Bissoondath used in this essay?
2. Describe the tone of Bissoondath's essay. How does he achieve
   this tone?
3. Explain how Bissoondath gets the reader's attention in the
   introduction of his essay. How does the conclusion of the essay
   link back to the introduction?

MAKING CONNECTIONS

1. Like Bissoondath, Tomson Highway ("What a Certain Visionary Once Said") chooses the spiritual distinct from religious faith. In what ways does Bissoondath's description of the spiritual show up in Highway's description of the north?
2. In his essay Bissoondath describes the effect of the Hindu death ceremony performed when his mother dies. How would Kim Pittaway ("Dead Wrong") explain Bissoondath's experience? How would the experience of Bissoondath's uncle fit into Pittaway's ideas?
3. Bissoondath chooses spirituality over religious faith while Matt Cohen ("Zada's Hanukkah Legacy") writes about the role of religious faith in his life. How do you think Cohen would respond to Bissoondath's argument? On what points might the two writers agree? On what points do you expect they would disagree?

IDEAS FOR DISCUSSION/WRITING

Preparing to Write

Write freely about religion. What religions are you aware of? What role does religion play in your life or the lives of people you know? What religious practices are you familiar with? What is your reaction to these practices? What role should religion play in society? Are there instances where religious traditions or practices should supersede existing laws?

Choosing a Topic

1. Religion is often the motivation for action that is violent or hateful. Write an essay in which you explain why religious affiliation or belief sometimes causes people to act in extreme ways.
2. When his mother dies, Bissoondath finds solace in the Hindu death ceremony. Write an essay about your experience of a ceremony or ritual that you found healing or comforting at a difficult time.
3. Write an essay in which you compare and contrast two distinct religions. In addition to specific beliefs and practices, you may want to consider the history of each religion, regional variations, and the changes it has undergone over time.

WEBSITES

www.cbc.ca/millennium/authors/bissoondath.html
Neil Bissoondath on the millennium.

www.schoolnet.ca/greatquestions/e/q2_intro.html
On the Great Canadian Questions site you'll find two essays by
Bissoondath, as well as a biography and bibliography.

CHAPTER 7

DEFINITION

Limiting the Frame of Reference

Definitions help us function smoothly in a complex world. All effective communication, in fact, is continuously dependent on our unique human ability to understand and employ accurate definitions of a wide range of words, phrases, and abstract ideas. If we did not work from a set of shared definitions, we would not be able to carry on coherent conversations, write comprehensible letters, or respond to even the simplest radio and television programs. Definitions help us understand basic concrete terms (such as automobiles, laser beams, and the gross national product), discuss various events in our lives (such as snowboarding, legal proceedings, and a New Year's celebration), and grasp difficult abstract ideas (such as the concepts of democracy, ambition, and resentment). The ability to comprehend definitions and use them effectively helps us keep our oral and written level of communication accurate and accessible to a wide variety of people.

Defining Definition

Definition is the process of explaining a word, object, or idea in such a way that the reader (or listener) knows as precisely as possible what we mean. A good definition sets up intellectual boundaries by focusing on the special qualities of a word or phrase that set it apart from other similar words or phrases. Clear definitions always give the writer and the reader a mutual starting point on the sometimes bumpy road to successful communication.

Definitions vary from short, dictionary-length summaries to longer, extended accounts that determine the form of an entire essay. Words or ideas that require expanded definitions are usually abstract, complex, or unavoidably controversial; they generally bear many related meanings or many shades of meaning. Definitions can be *objective* (technically precise and generally dry) or *subjective* (coloured with personal opinion), and they can be used to instruct or entertain, or to accomplish a combination of these two fundamental rhetorical goals.

In the following excerpt, a student defines *childhood* by putting it into perspective with other important stages of life. Though mostly entertaining, the paragraph is also instructive as the student objectively captures the essence of this phase of human development:

> Childhood is a stage of growth somewhere between infancy and adolescence. Just as each developmental period in our lives brings new changes and concerns, childhood serves as the threshold to puberty—the time we learn to discriminate between good and bad, right and wrong, love and lust. Childhood is neither a time of irresponsible infancy nor responsible adulthood. Rather, it is marked by duties that we don't really want, challenges that excite us, feelings that puzzle and frighten us, and limitless opportunities that help us explore the world around us. Childhood is a time when we solidify our personalities in spite of pressures to be someone else.

Thinking Critically by Using Definition

Definitions are building blocks in communication that help us make certain we are functioning from the same understanding of terms and ideas. They give us a foundation to work from in both reading and writing. Definitions force us to think about meanings and word associations that make other thinking strategies stronger and easier to work with.

The process of thinking through our definitions forces us to come to some understanding about a particular term or concept we are mentally wrestling with. Articulating that definition helps us move to other modes of thought and higher levels of understanding. Practising definitions in isolation to get a feel for them is much like separating the skill of pedalling from the process of riding a bike. The better you get at pedalling, the more natural the rest of the cycling process becomes. The following exercises ask you to practise definitions in a number of different ways. Being more conscious of what definition entails will make it more useful to you in both your reading and your writing.

1. Define one of the concrete words and one of the abstract words listed here in one or two sentences. What were some of the differences between the processes you went through to explain the concrete word and the abstract word? What can you conclude from this brief exercise about the differences in defining abstract and concrete words? Concrete: *cattle, book, ranch, water, gum.* Abstract: *freedom, progress, equality, fairness, boredom.*

2. Define the word *grammar.* Consult a dictionary, several handbooks, and maybe even some friends to get their views on the subject. Then, write a humorous definition of *grammar* that consolidates all these views into a single definition.

3. In what ways can you "define" yourself? What qualities or characteristics are crucial to an understanding of you as a person?

Reading and Writing Definition Essays

Extended definitions, which usually range from two or three paragraphs to an entire essay, seldom follow a set pattern of development or organization. Instead, as you will see from the examples in this chapter, they draw on a number of different techniques to help explain a word, object, term, concept, or phenomenon.

How to Read a Definition Essay

Preparing to Read. As you begin to read each of the definition essays in this chapter, take some time to consider the author's title and the synopsis of the essay in the Rhetorical Table of Contents: What is Michael Clugston's attitude toward lightning in "Twice Struck"? What do you sense is the general mood of Lawrence Hill's "Don't Call Me That Word"?

Equally important as you prepare to read is scanning an essay and finding information from its preliminary material about the author and the circumstances surrounding the composition of the essay. What do you think is Wayson Choy's purpose in his definition of "banana"? And what can you learn about Drew Hayden Taylor and his qualifications for writing "Pretty Like a White Boy"?

Last, as you prepare to read these essays, answer the pre-reading questions before each essay, and then spend a few minutes thinking freely about the general subject of the essay at hand: What role does your appearance play in your life (Taylor)? What information do you need about Alphanumerish (Wiwa)? What is your reaction to the word *nigger* (Hill)?

Reading. As you read a definition essay, as with all essays, be sure to record your initial reactions to your reading material. What are some of your thoughts or associations in relation to each essay?

As you get more involved in the essay, reconsider the preliminary material so you can create a context within which to analyze what the writer is saying: Who do you think is Taylor's primary audience? Do you think his essay will effectively reach that group of people? In what ways is Wayson Choy qualified to write about being a "banana"?

Also, determine at this point whether the author's treatment of his or her subject is predominantly objective or subjective. Then, make sure you understand the main points of the essay on the literal, interpretive, and analytical levels by reading the questions that follow.

Rereading. When you read these definition essays for a second time, check to see how each writer actually sets forth his or her definition: Does the writer put each item in a specific category with clear boundaries? Do you understand how the item being defined is different from other items in the same category? Did the author name the various components of the item, explain its etymology (linguistic origin and history), discuss what it is not, or perform a combination of these tasks?

To evaluate the effectiveness of a definition essay, you need to reconsider the essay's primary purpose and audience. If Taylor is trying to get the general reader to understand the experience of not "looking the part," how effective is he in doing so? In like manner, is Clugston successful in explaining the nature of lightning and humans' understanding of it? Especially applicable is the question of what other rhetorical strategies help the author communicate this purpose. Through what other modes does Wiwa enhance your understanding of Alphanumerish?

For an inventory of the reading process, you can review the guidelines on pages 17–18 of the Introduction.

How to Write a Definition Essay

Preparing to Write. As with other essays, you should begin the task of writing a definition essay by answering the prewriting questions featured in this text and then by exploring your subject and generating other ideas. (See the explanation of various prewriting techniques on pages 19–25 of the Introduction.) Be sure you know what you are going to define and how you will approach your definition. You should then focus on a specific audience and purpose as you approach the writing assignment.

Writing. The next step toward developing a definition essay is usually to describe the general category to which the word belongs and then to contrast the word with all other words in that group. To define *exposition*, for example, you might say that it is a type of writing. Then, to differentiate it from other types of writing, you could go on to say that its main purpose is to "expose," or present information, as opposed to rhetorical modes such as description and narration, which describe and tell stories. In addition, you might want to cite some expository methods, such as example, process analysis, division/classification, and comparison/contrast.

Yet another way to begin a definition essay is to provide a term's etymology. Tracing a word's origin often illuminates its current meaning and usage as well. *Exposition*, for example, comes from the Latin *exponere*, meaning "to put forth, set forth, display, declare, or publish" (*ex* = out; *ponere* = to put or place). This information can generally be found in any good dictionary or in a good encyclopedia.

Another approach to defining a term is to explain what it does not mean. For example, *exposition* is not creative writing. By limiting the readers' frame of reference in these various ways, you are helping to establish a working definition for the term under consideration.

Finally, rhetorical methods that we have already studied, such as description, narration, example, process analysis, division/classification, and comparison/contrast, are particularly useful to writers in expanding their definitions. To clarify the term *exposition*, you might **describe** the details of an expository theme, **narrate** a story about the wide use of the term in today's classroom, or **give examples** of assignments that would produce good expository writing. In other situations, you could **analyze** various writing assignments and discuss the **process** of producing an expository essay, **classify** exposition apart from creative writing and then **divide** it into categories similar to the headings of this book, or **compare** and **contrast** it with creative writing. Writers also use definition quite often to support other rhetorical modes.

Rewriting. Reviewing and revising a definition essay is a relatively straightforward task:

- Have you chosen an effective beginning for your paper?
- Did you create a reasonable context for your definition?
- Have you used appropriate rhetorical strategies to develop your ideas?
- Have you achieved your overall purpose as effectively as possible?

Other guidelines to direct your writing and revising appear on pages 29–30 of the Introduction.

Student Essay: Definition at Work

In the following essay, a student defines "the perfect yuppie." Notice how the writer puts this term in a category and then explains the limits of that category and the uniqueness of this term within the category. To further inform her audience of the features of "yuppiedom," the student calls on the word's etymology, its dictionary definition, an itemization of the term's basic characteristics, a number of examples that explain those characteristics, and, finally, a general discussion of causes and effects that regulate a yuppie's behaviour.

The Perfect Yuppie

Etymology/ dictionary definition — Many people already know that <u>the letters YUP stand for "young urban professional."</u> *Young* in this context is understood to mean thirtyish; *urban* often means suburban; and *professional* means most **[General category of word being defined]** definitely college-educated. Double the *P* and add an *I* and an *E* at

Subject — the end, and you get <u>*yuppie*</u>—that 1980s bourgeois, the marketers' darling, and the 1960s' inheritance. But let's not generalize. <u>Not</u> **[Why the dictionary definition is inadequate]**

Limitations set — <u>every thirty-year-old suburban college graduate qualifies as a yuppie. Nor is every yuppie in his or her thirties.</u> True yuppiness involves much more than the words that make up the acronym.

Writer's credibility — Being the little sister of a couple of yups, I am in an especially good position to define the perfect yuppie. I watched two develop.

The essence of yuppiness is generally <u>new money</u>. In the [General characteristic] yuppie's defence, I will admit that most yuppies have worked hard for their money and social status. [Cause/Effect] Moreover, the baby boom of which they are a part has caused a glut of job seekers in their age bracket, forcing them to be competitive if they want all the nice [General characteristic] things retailers have designed for them. But with new money comes <u>an interesting combination of wealth, naiveté, and pretentiousness</u>.

For example, most yuppies worthy of the title have long ago [Specific example] <u>traded in their fringed suede jackets for fancy fur coats</u>. Although they were animal rights activists in the 1960s, they will not notice [Cause/effect] the irony of this change. In fact, they may be shameless enough to <u>parade in their fur coats—fashion-show style—for friends and [Specific example] family</u>. Because of their "innocence," yuppies generally will not see the vulgarity of their actions.

[General characteristic] Because they are often quite wealthy, yuppies <u>tend to have a lot of "things."</u> They are simply overwhelmed by the responsibility of spending all that money. For example, <u>one yup I know has [Specific example] fourteen pairs of sunglasses and seven watches</u>. She, her husband, and their three children own at least <u>twenty collections of every- [Specific example] thing from comic books to Civil War memorabilia</u>. Most yuppies have so much money that I often wonder why the word "yuppie" does not have a dollar sign in it somewhere.

Perhaps in an effort to rid themselves of this financial burden, [Cause/effect] [General characteristic] <u>all good yuppies go to Europe</u> as soon as possible. Not Germany or France or Portugal, mind you, but Europe. They do not know what they are doing there and thus generally spend much more [Cause/effect] money than they need to—but, after all, no yuppie ever claimed to [General characteristic] be frugal. Most important, they <u>bring home slides of Europe and show them</u> to everyone they know. A really good yuppie will forget and show you his or her slides more than once. Incidentally, when everyone has seen the slides of Europe twice, the yuppie's next stop is Australia.

[General characteristic] A favourite pastime of yuppies is having <u>wine-tasting parties</u> for their yuppie friends. At these parties, they must <u>make a great [Specific example] to-do about tasting the wine</u>, cupping their faces over the glass with their palms (as if they were having a facial), and even sniffing the cork, for goodness sake. I once knew a yuppie who <u>did [Specific example] not understand that a bottle of wine could not be rejected simply</u>

Specific example | because he found he "did not like that kind." Another enjoyed making a show of having his wife choose and taste the wine occasionally, which they both thought was adorable.

What it is not | Some yuppie wanna-be's drive red or black BMWs, but don't let them fool you. A genuine, hard-core yuppie will usually own a gold or silver Volvo station wagon. In this yuppie-mobile, the *(General characteristic)* yuppie wife will chauffeur her young yupettes to and from their modelling classes, track meets, ballet, the manicurist, and boy

Specific examples | scouts, for the young yuppie is generally as competitive and socially active as his or her parents. On the same topic, one particularly annoying trait of yuppie parents is bragging about their yupettes. You will know yuppies by the fact that they have the

General characteristic | smartest, most talented children in the world. They will show you their kids' report cards, making sure you notice any improvements from last term. *(Specific example)*

Division/ classification | Perhaps I have been harsh in my portrayal of the perfect yuppie, and, certainly, I will be accused by some of stereotyping. But consider this: I never classify people as yuppies who do not so classify themselves. The ultimate criterion for being yuppies is that they will always proudly label themselves as such. *(General characteristic and concluding statement)*

Some Final Thoughts on Definition

The following selections feature extended definitions whose main purpose is to explain a specific term or idea to their readers. Each essay in its own way helps the audience identify with various parts of its definitions, and each successfully communicates the unique qualities of the term or idea in question. Notice what approaches to definition each writer takes and how these approaches limit the readers' frame of reference in the process of effective communication.

Definition in Review

Reading Definition Essays

Preparing to Read

- What assumptions can you make from the essay's title?
- Can you guess what the general mood of the essay is?
- What is the essay's purpose and audience?

- What does the synopsis in the Rhetorical Table of Contents tell you about the essay?
- What can you learn from the author's biography?
- Can you guess what the author's point of view toward the subject is?
- What are your responses to the Preparing to Read questions?

Reading

- Have you recorded your reactions to the essay?
- Is the author's treatment of the subject predominantly subjective or objective?
- Did you preview the questions that follow the essay?

Rereading

- How does the author lay out the definition?
- What is the essay's main purpose and audience?
- What other rhetorical strategies does the author use to support the essay's purpose?
- What are your responses to the questions after the essay?

Writing Definition Essays

Preparing to Write

- What are your responses to the Preparing to Write questions?
- Do you know what you are going to define and how you will approach your topic?
- Who is your audience?

Writing

- Does the beginning of your essay suit your purpose?
- Do you use effective strategies to define your word or concept?
- What rhetorical strategies do you use to expand your definition essay?

Rewriting

- Have you chosen an effective beginning for your paper?
- Did you create a reasonable context for your definition?
- Have you used appropriate rhetorical strategies to develop your ideas?
- Have you achieved your overall purpose as well as possible?

KEN WIWA

Say It With Numbers

In the Shadow of a Saint is Ken Wiwa's memoir about his father, Ken Saro-Wiwa, a Nigerian writer and political activist who was executed in 1995 by the Nigerian government, and the legacy his father has left him. He later produced a documentary with the same title, about his father, for CBC TV. Wiwa's work, however, extends far beyond these accomplishments. In addition to being a writer and journalist, Wiwa is the Managing Director of Saros International, a Nigerian-based company that specializes in community development projects.

Ken Wiwa now lives in Toronto with his wife and son, but he grew up in Nigeria and England and was educated in Britain. Originally intending to be a sportswriter, Wiwa has, in fact, become an international journalist whose work has appeared in newspapers and magazines around the world. A former journalist and editor at *The Guardian*, he now writes for *The Globe and Mail*, has been a senior resident writer at Massey College, University of Toronto, and is currently Saul Rae Fellow at the Munk Centre for International Studies at the University of Toronto.

In 2002 Wiwa was nominated for a National Newspaper Award for feature writing.

Preparing to Read

"Say It With Numbers" is taken from *The Globe and Mail*'s Workopolis website, a site for job seekers. Before reading the essay, think about the language of work. In what ways is the language you use in work situations different from the language you use elsewhere? How has the language of the workplace changed in the last decade? How have communication systems within business and industry changed since the 1980s? What changes do you anticipate over the next ten or twenty years? What do you think of these changes?

Forget French, English, Chinese or any other language for that   1
matter because the future is Alphanumerish. Not as yet an officially recognized language, Alphanumerish has no country, no grammar, or dictionary—but we all use it, and many of us are fluent in the language.

The origins of Alphanumerish are obscure and possibly   2
undocumented, but as its etymology suggests, the language
evolved out of Alphanumeric. According to on-line encyclopedia
Webopedia, Alphanumeric is the "combined set of all letters in
the alphabet and the numbers 0 through 9. Sometimes additional
characters are considered alphanumeric."

Most of us are already familiar with the language because   3
Alphanumerish is not just a combination of letters and numbers.
Whenever you are caught in the maze of an organization's
recorded phone message you will probably require some
knowledge of Alphanumeric—"#"—to navigate the system.

But the most instantly recognizable symbol of the   4
Alphanumerish alphabet is of course the "@" sign.

For a symbol that was once largely redundant on a keyboard,   5
@ has come a long way. It still doesn't have a name, but it is now
more recognizable than its more illustrious cousins, *, & and ~
(asterisk, ampersand and tilde). @ is the cornerstone of Alphanumerish.

In a sense, @ is the Trojan horse in a Peloponnesian war   6
between computer technology and language. Lurking above the
2 on the Qwerty keyboard, @ has coughed up an army of symbols
and shorthand that make up Alphanumerish—the everyday argot
of techno-loving teenagers and rap bands.

Alphanumerish is the preferred language of cyberspace,   7
enabling teenagers on Internet chat, e-mail, cellphones, pagers
and palm tops to speak volumes in text messages. Like CB radio
before it, text messaging has spawned a lexicon. Because of the
limits of space and bandwidth, a text message is restricted to 141
characters, and this has spawned a dictionary of Alphanumeric
words that make up the new language.

Words like gr8 (great), sum1 (someone) and 2moro   8
(tomorrow) are the primary colours of Alphanumerish. And then
there are those colourful symbols like :-(which take the language
to a new level, enabling users to emote alphanumerically.

There is a whole army of Web-heads creating new emoticons,   9
adding new words and phrases to Alphanumerish. Enter the
word *smiley* on your search engine and you will see what I mean.
Your basic inoffensive smiley—:)—has evolved into an all-
singing, all-dancing character that makes writing in
Alphanumerish read like Tom Wolfe on crack cocaine.

It was Prince, who had long written songs with titles like   10
Nothing Compares 2 U and *When 2 R in Love*, who inadvertently

launched a whole new dialect of Alphanumerish. The singer turned the Fugitive's existentialist yell on its head when he declared that he was a symbol—the infamous "glyph"—and not a free man, in protest against his recording contract. What the Artist could not have known was that rap acts (DMX), boybands ('NSYNC) and Jennifer Lopez (J-Lo) would soon be offering him coded support.

The beauty of Alphanumerish is that, like sign language or sheet music, it offers the tantalising possibility of a Canadian in Moosejaw communicating fluently with a Congolese in Kikwit. Years after the inventors of Esperanto failed in their attempt to create a universal language, Alphanumerish is poised to emerge as the next lingua franca.   11

All of this should be no surprise to students of language. The alphabet is only a collection of symbols. The Roman alphabet, at 26 letters, is one of the shorter versions of the collection of symbols that man has invented to communicate. Clunky languages like Sumerian, which had a head-spinning 600 letters, would never have survived in the era of the text message. But with the coming of Alphanumerish we can now compress messages and emotions in the window of a cellphone.   12

And so we come full circle, because of course cave men were the first to use Alphanumerish, expressing themselves on rocks.   13

And just in case you were wondering whether this new language is a retrograde step for mankind, consider that when Nasa's scientists were trying to figure out how to write a concise message in case any other life forms stumbled across Voyager, they settled for a coded message made up of symbols.   14

In years to come, these scribblings will be viewed in the same way as cave paintings, primitive attempts at Alphanumerish.   15

So U C, th fUtR is 2day. ;=)   16

UNDERSTANDING DETAILS

1. What is Alphanumerish? Where does it come from? Who uses it?
2. What are the following Alphanumerish characters called? #, *, ~, &, @, :-)
3. Explain the role of musicians in the development of Alphanumerish.

ANALYZING MEANING

1. Why has Alphanumerish developed?
2. Explain the place of Alphanumerish in the history of languages. What parameters govern its form?
3. What is Wiwa's attitude toward his subject? How can you tell this?

DISCOVERING RHETORICAL STRATEGIES

1. Characterize the tone of Wiwa's essay. How does he achieve this tone?
2. In "Say It With Numbers," Wiwa makes reference to Tom Wolfe, Prince, and the Trojan horse in a Peloponnesian war. Explain the function of these references in this essay.
3. Explain what other rhetorical modes Wiwa has employed in developing his definition of Alphanumerish.

MAKING CONNECTIONS

1. Both Wiwa and Stanley Coren ("Dogs and Monsters") outline a kind of evolution in their essays. Compare the strategies they use for depicting the development of their respective topics.
2. Evan Solomon ("The Babar Factor") finds video games wanting when compared with traditional children's stories. What do you think Solomon would say about the use of Alphanumerish?
3. David Foot ("Boomers Dance to a New Beat") writes about demographics and the changes they create. In what way is the development of Alphanumerish affected by demographics?

IDEAS FOR DISCUSSION/WRITING

Preparing to Write

Before beginning to write, think about the language that you regularly use. What changes have you observed in language? What new vocabulary has been introduced? What words have different meanings now than they had in the past? What jargon or specialized language can you think of that has been introduced into usage as a result of new technology? Is change in language a positive development?

Choosing a Topic

1. Select a paragraph from one of the essays in this book (other than Wiwa's) and translate it into Alphanumerish. How much shorter is the new version? Give your translation to at least one other person and see if he or she can understand it.
2. Write an essay in which you argue for the acceptance of Alphanumerish as a language to be taught in school.
3. Wiwa claims that "Alphanumerish is poised to emerge as the next lingua franca." Write an essay in which you clearly define *lingua franca*. In your essay, make it clear whether you believe that Alphanumerish has the potential to be "the next lingua franca."

WEBSITES

radio.cbc.ca/programs/asithappens/international/kenwiwa.html
An *As It Happens* feature interview with Ken Wiwa on CBC radio.

www.randomhouse.ca/catalog/display.pperl?isbn=0-676-97173-3#desc
The Random House description of Wiwa's book, *In the Shadow of a Saint*.

www.workopolis.ca
Wiwa's essay comes from the Workopolis website.

DREW HAYDEN TAYLOR

Pretty Like a White Boy: The Adventures of a Blue-Eyed Ojibway

Living in Toronto, but originally from the Curve Lake Reserve near Peterborough, Ontario, Drew Hayden Taylor (1962–) is quoted in a profile from the Montreal *Gazette* as follows: "I hate the technical part of writing ... I hate it with a passion." And yet he had achieved enviable success by his early thirties—as a writer.

Since graduating from the broadcasting program at Seneca College, Taylor has worked as a radio reporter, a sound recordist for a film company, a trainee producer with the CBC, a promoter at the Canadian Native Arts Foundation, and a freelance writer. In addition to articles and stories that have appeared in *Maclean's, The Globe and Mail, This Magazine, Anishinabek News, Cinema Canada,* and *Windspeaker,* Taylor has written episodes for *The Beachcombers* and *Street Legal.* He is also an award-winning playwright who has served as the writer-in-residence for the Native Earth Performing Arts Theatre. His published works include several plays (*Toronto at Dreamer's Rock, Someday, Only Drunks and Children Tell the Truth,* and *The Baby Blues*), a collection of essays (*Funny, You Don't Look Like One: Observations from a Blue-Eyed Ojibway*), and a book of short stories (*Fearless Warriors*). Taylor's most recent works include *The Boy in the Treehouse/Girl Who Loved Her Horses* (2000), *alterNatives* (2000), and *The Buz'Gem Blues,* the third play in his *Blues Quartet* (2002).

Taylor brings a strong sense of humour to his work, which centres primarily around Native issues. One of his aspirations is described in a quotation from a profile in *Windspeaker*: "With Native People writing their own stories, Canadians and people in other countries may get a more accurate view of (our people)," says Taylor. "It may help abolish the popular concept that Indians are all the same ..." The essay "Pretty Like a White Boy: The Adventures of a Blue-Eyed Ojibway" conveys Taylor's frustrating experiences of not "looking the part."

Preparing to Read

In this essay, Drew Hayden Taylor presents examples from his own life that illustrate the problems that occur as we categorize and define people by their heritage and appearance. Taylor's definition of a new term that accurately defines who he is provides a concluding summary to his discussion of stereotypes and the difficulties of not fitting neatly into the already existing categories. As you prepare to read, consider the terms *Indians, Native people,* and *white man.* What associations do you have with each of these? Are they positive labels or negative ones? How do you distinguish people from these groups? What does an Indian look like? In what way does a white person differ in appearance? What does the title of this essay tell you about the author's attitude toward his topic?

In this big, huge world, with all its billions and billions of people, 1 it's safe to say that everybody will eventually come across personalities and individuals that will touch them in some peculiar yet poignant way. Individuals that in some way represent and help define who you are. I'm no different, mine was Kermit the Frog. Not just because Natives have a long tradition of savouring Frogs' legs, but because of his music. If you all may remember, Kermit is quite famous for his rendition of "It's Not Easy Being Green." I can relate. If I could sing, my song would be "It's Not Easy Having Blue Eyes in a Brown Eyed Village."

Yes, I'm afraid it's true. The author happens to be a card- 2 carrying Indian. Once you get past the aforementioned eyes, the fair skin, the light brown hair, and noticeable lack of cheekbones, there lies the heart and spirit of an Ojibway storyteller. Honest Injun, or as the more politically correct term may be, honest aboriginal.

You see, I'm the product of a white father I never knew, and 3 an Ojibway woman who evidently couldn't run fast enough. As a kid I knew I looked a bit different. But, then again, all kids are paranoid when it comes to their peers. I had a fairly happy childhood, frolicking through the bulrushes. But there were certain things that, even then, made me notice my unusual appearance. Whenever we played cowboys and Indians, guess who had to be the bad guy, the cowboy.

It wasn't until I left the Reserve for the big bad city, that I 4 became more aware of the role people expected me to play, and the fact that physically I didn't fit in. Everybody seemed to have this preconceived idea of how every Indian looked and acted. One guy, on my first day of college, asked me what kind of horse I preferred. I didn't have the heart to tell him "hobby."

I've often tried to be philosophical about the whole thing. I 5 have both white and red blood in me, I guess that makes me pink. I am a "Pink" man. Try to imagine this, I'm walking around on any typical Reserve in Canada, my head held high, proudly announcing to everyone "I am a Pink Man." It's a good thing I ran track in school.

My pinkness is constantly being pointed out to me over and over and over again. "You don't look Indian?" "You're not Indian, are you?" "Really?!?" I got questions like that from both white and Native people, for a while I debated having my status card tattooed on my forehead.   6

And like most insecure people and specially a blue-eyed Native writer, I went through a particularly severe identity crisis at one point. In fact, I admit it, one depressing spring evening, I dyed my hair black. Pitch black.   7

The reason for such a dramatic act, you may ask? Show Business. You see, for the last eight years or so, I've worked in various capacities in the performing arts, and as a result I'd always get calls to be an extra or even try out for an important role in some Native oriented movie. This anonymous voice would phone, having been given my number, and ask if I would be interested in trying out for a movie. Being a naturally ambitious, curious, and greedy young man, I would always readily agree, stardom flashing in my eyes and hunger pains from my wallet.   8

A few days later I would show up for the audition, and that was always an experience. What kind of experience you may ask? Picture this, the picture calls for the casting of seventeenth-century Mohawk warriors living in a traditional longhouse. The casting director calls the name "Drew Hayden Taylor" and I enter.   9

The casting director, the producer, and the film's director look up from the table and see my face, blue eyes flashing in anticipation. I once was described as a slightly chubby beachboy. But even beachboys have tans. Anyway, there would be a quick flush of confusion, a recheck of the papers, and a hesitant "Mr. Taylor?" Then they would ask if I was at the right audition. It was always the same. By the way, I never got any of the parts I tried for, except for a few anonymous crowd shots. Politics tells me it's because of the way I look, reality tells me it's probably because I can't act. I'm not sure which is better.   10

It's not just film people either. Recently I've become quite involved in Theatre, Native theatre to be exact. And one cold October day I was happily attending the Toronto leg of a province-wide tour of my first play, *Toronto at Dreamer's Rock*. The place was sold out, the audience very receptive and the   11 performance was wonderful. Ironically one of the actors was also half white.

The director later told me he had been talking with the actor's father, an older non-Native type chap. Evidently he had asked a few questions about me, and how I did my research. This made the director curious and he asked about his interest. He replied "He's got an amazing grasp of the Native situation for a white person." 12

Not all these incidents are work related either. One time a friend and I were coming out of a rather upscale bar (we were out Yuppie watching) and managed to catch a cab. We thanked the cab driver for being so comfortably close on such a cold night, he shrugged and nonchalantly talked about knowing what bars to drive around. "If you're not careful, all you'll get is drunk Indians." I hiccuped. 13

Another time this cab driver droned on and on about the government. He started out by criticizing Mulroney, and eventually his handling of the Oka crisis. This perked up my ears, until he said "If it were me, I'd have tear-gassed the place by the second day. No more problem." He got a dime tip. A few incidents like this and I'm convinced I'd make a great undercover agent for one of the Native political organizations. 14

But then again, even Native people have been known to look at me with a fair amount of suspicion. Many years ago when I was a young man, I was working on a documentary on Native culture up in the wilds of Northern Ontario. We were at an isolated cabin filming a trapper woman and her kids. This one particular nine-year-old girl seemed to take a shine to me. She followed me around for two days both annoying me and endearing herself to me. But she absolutely refused to believe that I was Indian. The whole film crew tried to tell her but to no avail. She was certain I was white. 15

Then one day as I was loading up the car with film equipment, she asked me if I wanted some tea. Being in a hurry I declined the tea. She immediately smiled with victory crying out "See, you're not Indian, all Indians drink tea!" 16

Frustrated and a little hurt I whipped out my Status card and thrust it at her. Now there I was, standing in a Northern Ontario winter, showing my Status card to a nine-year-old non-status Indian girl who had no idea what one was. Looking back, this may not have been one of my brighter moves. 17

But I must admit, it was a Native woman that boiled   18
everything down in one simple sentence. You may know that
woman, Marianne Jones from "The Beachcombers" television
series. We were working on a film together out west and we got
to gossiping. Eventually we got around to talking about our
respective villages. Hers on the Queen Charlotte Islands, or Haida
Gwaii as the Haida call them, and mine in central Ontario.

Eventually childhood on the Reserve was being discussed   19
and I made a comment about the way I look. She studied me for
a moment, smiled, and said "Do you know what the old women
in my village would call you?" Hesitant but curious, I shook my
head. "They'd say you were pretty like a white boy." To this day
I'm still not sure if I like that.

Now some may argue that I am simply a Métis with a Status   20
card. I disagree, I failed French in grade 11. And the Métis as
everyone knows have their own separate and honourable culture,
particularly in western Canada. And of course I am well aware
that I am not the only person with my physical characteristics.

I remember once looking at a video tape of a drum group,   21
shot on a Reserve up near Manitoulin Island. I noticed one of
the drummers seemed quite fairhaired, almost blond. I mentioned
this to my girlfriend of the time and she shrugged saying "Well,
that's to be expected. The highway runs right through the
Reserve."

Perhaps I'm being too critical. There's a lot to be said for   22
both cultures. For example, on the left hand, you have the Native
respect for Elders. They understand the concept of wisdom and
insight coming with age.

On the white hand, there's Italian food. I mean I really love   23
my mother and family but seriously, does anything really beat
good Veal Scaloppine? Most of my aboriginal friends share my
fondness for this particular brand of food. Wasn't there a warrior
at Oka named Lasagna? I found it ironic, though curiously logical,
that Columbus was Italian. A connection I wonder?

Also Native people have this wonderful respect and love for   24
the land. They believe they are part of it, a mere link in the cycle
of existence. Now as many of you know, this conflicts with the
accepted Judeo-Christian i.e. western view of land management.
I even believe somewhere in the first chapters of the Bible it says
something about God giving man dominion over Nature. Check
it out, Genesis 4:?, "Thou shalt clear cut." So I grew up

understanding that everything around me is important and alive. My Native heritage gave me that.

And again, on the white hand, there's breast implants. Darn 25 clever them white people. That's something Indians would never have invented, seriously. We're not ambitious enough. We just take what the Creator decides to give us, but no, not the white man. Just imagine it, some serious looking white man, and let's face it people, we know it was a man who invented them, don't we? So just imagine some serious looking white doctor sitting around in his laboratory muttering to himself, "Big tits, big tits, hmmm, how do I make big tits?" If it was an Indian, it would be "Big tits, big tits, white women sure got big tits" and leave it at that.

So where does that leave me on the big philosophical 26 scoreboard? What exactly are my choices again? Indians—respect for Elders, love of the land. White people—food and big tits. In order to live in both cultures I guess I'd have to find an Indian woman with big tits who lives with her grandmother in a cabin out in the woods and can make Fettuccini Alfredo on a wood stove.

Now let me make this clear, I'm not writing this for 27 sympathy, or out of anger, or even some need for self-glorification. I am just setting the facts straight. For as you read this, a new Nation is born. This is a declaration of independence, my declaration of independence.

I've spent too many years explaining who and what I am 28 repeatedly, so as of this moment, I officially secede from both races. I plan to start my own separate nation. Because I am half Ojibway and half Caucasian, we will be called the Occasions. And I of course, since I'm founding the new nation, will be a Special Occasion.

UNDERSTANDING DETAILS

1. Does Drew Hayden Taylor affiliate himself more closely with Native or white culture? Give specific examples to support your answer.
2. What advantages does Taylor associate with being Native? What advantages does he link with being white?
3. According to Taylor, why would he make a great undercover agent for a Native political organization?

ANALYZING MEANING

1. What is the author's purpose in this essay? Does he take an objective or a subjective approach in defining his subject?
2. Explain why Drew Hayden Taylor does not consider himself to be Métis.
3. Why do you think that Taylor did not get the parts in the films for which he auditioned?

DISCOVERING RHETORICAL STRATEGIES

1. What tone is established in this essay? How does Taylor create this tone? Is it effective?
2. What rhetorical strategies is Taylor employing in this essay in addition to definition? Give specific examples to support your answer.
3. Why does Taylor settle on the term "Special Occasion" rather than "Pink Man" as a way to define himself? What definition strategy has resulted in his final title?

MAKING CONNECTIONS

1. Drew Hayden Taylor credits Tomson Highway ("What a Certain Visionary Once Said") with "helping him to get his feet wet" in Native theatre. What similarities are there between Taylor's essay and Highway's?
2. Imagine Cecil Foster ("Why Blacks Get Mad") and Drew Hayden Taylor having a conversation about their experiences of being judged based on their appearance. In what respects are their experiences similar? How do they differ? Do the two respond to appearance-based judgment in the same way? Give specific examples to support your answer.
3. Drew Hayden Taylor has chosen humour as a vehicle for making a difficult subject more palatable to his readers. Compare this strategy to that of Laura Robinson ("Starving for the Gold") or Lawrence Hill ("Don't Call Me That Word"). Explain which you think is the more effective approach.

IDEAS FOR DISCUSSION/WRITING

Preparing to Write

Write freely about your ethnic background, race, or heritage. How would you define yourself? Do existing categories work for you or do you feel the need to create a new category to capture who you are? What physical characteristics define you as part of the group you have identified? What personality characteristics affiliate you with this group? How would you categorize children of mixed heritage?

Choosing a Topic

1. Think of a term to define yourself in a way that reflects various aspects of your heritage/background. Others may belong to this group, but focus on the aspects that make you unique from other, already existing categories. Write an essay for a general interest magazine in which you define your term using examples from your own life to make your definition clear.
2. Often our expectations are not borne out by reality. Write an essay for college or university students in which you define a particular job or profession based on your knowledge of someone in that position.
3. In paragraph 1, Taylor refers to "[i]ndividuals that in some way represent and help define who you are." Describe one such individual in your life and explain how he or she has contributed to making you who you are.

WEBSITES

www.canadiantheatre.com/dict.pl?term=Drew%20Hayden%20Taylor
A *Canadian Theatre Encyclopedia* profile of Taylor.

www.operation-dialogue.com/lafontaine-baldwin/e/2001_article_gm_taylor.html
"Seeing Red Over Myths": an essay by Drew Hayden Taylor.

www.ipl.org/cgi/ref/native/browse.pl/A185
Native American Authors Project: Drew Hayden Taylor.

www.thescream.ca/bios/2002/d_taylor.shtml
Drew Hayden Taylor participated in the 2002 Scream in High Park.

WAYSON CHOY

I'm a Banana and Proud of It

Now a teacher of English at Toronto's Humber College and a faculty member at the Humber School for Writers, Wayson Choy (1939–) was born and raised in British Columbia, where he was the first Chinese Canadian to enroll in the University of British Columbia's creative writing program. Since that time, Choy has won the 1996 Trillium Award and the 1996 Vancouver City Book Award for his first novel, *The Jade Peony*, which is about Vancouver's Chinatown during the Depression and World War II. Choy followed *The Jade Peony* with the critically acclaimed *Paper Shadows: A Chinatown Childhood*, a memoir about his own experiences growing up in Vancouver's Chinatown and the discovery of hidden truths about his childhood. Choy describes his childhood as being "like a Chinese box that opens in a variety of different ways, revealing different levels, each sliding compartment a secret"; in *Paper Shadows*, he explores the challenges of growing up with his Chinese heritage often in conflict with the influences of the North American culture in which he was living.

Choy is currently working on a new novel, a sequel to *The Jade Peony* called *The Ten Thousand Things*.

Preparing to Read

In this essay, which first appeared in *The Globe and Mail*'s "Facts & Arguments" column, Wayson Choy proudly defines himself as a "banana," an affectionate nickname for integrated North American children of Chinese parents. Before reading this essay think about nicknames and the role that they play in our lives. Who assigns nicknames? Who uses them? What makes some nicknames stick and others fade? Are nicknames positive or negative? Do you have a nickname? Do you like it? Does it appropriately reflect who you are?

Because both my parents came from China, I took Chinese. But   1
I cannot read or write Chinese and barely speak it. I love my North American citizenship. I don't mind being called a "banana," yellow on the outside and white inside. I'm proud I'm a banana.

After all, in Canada and the United States, native Indians   2
are "apples" (red outside, white inside); blacks are "Oreo cookies"

(black and white); and Chinese are "bananas." These metaphors assume, both rightly and wrongly, that the culture here has been primarily anglo-white. Cultural history made me a banana.

History: My father and mother arrived separately to the B.C. 3 coast in the early part of the century. They came as unwanted "aliens." Better to be an alien here than to be dead of starvation in China. But after the Chinese Exclusion laws were passed in North America (late 1800s, early 1900s), no Chinese immigrants were granted citizenship in either Canada or the United States.

Like those Old China village men from *Toi San* who, in the 4 1850s, laid down cliff-edge train tracks through the Rockies and the Sierras, or like those first women who came as mail-order wives or concubines and who as bond-slaves were turned into cheaper labourers or even prostitutes—like many of those men and women, my father and mother survived ugly, unjust times. In 1917, two hours after he got off the boat from Hong Kong, my father was called "chink" and told to go back to China. "Chink" is a hateful racist term, stereotyping the shape of Asian eyes: "a chink in the armour," an undesirable slit. For the Elders, the past was humiliating. Eventually, the Second World War changed hostile attitudes toward the Chinese.

During the war, Chinese men volunteered and lost their lives 5 as members of the American and Canadian military. When hostilities ended, many more were proudly in uniform waiting to go overseas. Record Chinatown dollars were raised to buy War Bonds. After 1945, challenged by such money and ultimate sacrifices, the Exclusion laws in both Canada and the United States were revoked. Chinatown residents claimed their citizenship and sent for their families.

By 1949, after the Communists took over China, those of us 6 who arrived here as young children, or were born here, stayed. No longer "aliens," we became legal citizens of North America. Many of us also became "bananas."

Historically, "banana" is not a racist term. Although it 7 clumsily stereotypes many of the children and grandchildren of the Old Chinatowns, the term actually follows the old Chinese tendency to assign endearing nicknames to replace formal names, semicomic names to keep one humble. Thus, "banana" describes the generations who assimilated so well into North American life.

In fact, our families encouraged members of my generation 8 in the 1950s and sixties to "get ahead," to get an English education, to get a job with good pay and prestige. "Don't work like me," Chinatown parents said. "Work in an office!" The *lao wah-kiu* (the Chinatown old-timers) also warned, "Never forget— you still be Chinese!"

None of us ever forgot. The mirror never lied.   9

Many Chinatown teen-agers felt we didn't quite belong in   10
any one world. We looked Chinese, but thought and behaved North American. Impatient Chinatown parents wanted the best of both worlds for us, but they bluntly labelled their children and grandchildren *"juk-sing"* or even *"mo no."* Not that we were totally "shallow bamboo butt-ends" or entirely "no brain," but we had less and less understanding of Old China traditions, and less and less interest in their village histories. Father used to say we lacked Taoist ritual, Taoist manners. We were, he said, *"mo li."*

This was true. Chinatown's younger brains, like everyone   11
else's of whatever race, were being colonized by "white bread" U.S. family television programs. We began to feel Chinese home life was inferior. We co-operated with English-language magazines that showed us how to act and what to buy. Seductive Hollywood movies made some of us secretly weep that we did not have movie-star faces. American music made Chinese music sound like noise.

By the 1970s and eighties, many of us had consciously or   12
unconsciously distanced ourselves from our Chinatown histories. We became bananas.

Finally, for me, in my 40s or 50s, with the death first of my   13
mother, then my father, I realized I did not belong anywhere unless I could understand the past. I needed to find the foundation of my Chinese-ness. I needed roots.

I spent my college holidays researching the past. I read   14
Chinatown oral histories, located documents, searched out early articles. Those early citizens came back to life for me. Their long toil and blood sacrifices, the proud record of their patient, legal challenges, gave us all our present rights as citizens. Canadian and American Chinatowns set aside their family tongue differences and encouraged each other to fight injustice. There were no borders. "After all," they affirmed, *"Daaih ga tohng yahn ...* We are all Chinese!"

In my book, *The Jade Peony*, I tried to recreate this past, to   15
explore the beginnings of the conflicts trapped within myself, the struggle between being Chinese and being North American.

I discovered a truth: these "between world" struggles are universal.

In every human being, there is "the Other"—something that 16
makes each of us feel how different we are to everyone else, even
to family members. Yet, ironically, we are all the same, wanting
the same security and happiness. I know this now.

I think the early Chinese pioneers actually started "going 17
bananas" from the moment they first settled upon the West Coast.
They had no choice. They adapted. They initiated assimilation. If
they had not, they and their family would have starved to death.
I might even suggest that all surviving Chinatown citizens
eventually became bananas. Only some, of course, were more
ripe than others.

That's why I'm proudly a banana: I accept the paradox of 18
being both Chinese and not Chinese.

Now at last, whenever I look in the mirror or hear ghost 19
voices shouting, "You still Chinese!," I smile.

I know another truth: In immigrant North America, we are all 20
Chinese.

UNDERSTANDING DETAILS

1. What does the term *banana* mean? How is this different from *apple* and *Oreo cookie*?
2. Describe the experience of Choy's parents coming to Canada.
3. What motivated Choy to research the past? What type of research did he do? Did he find what he was looking for?

ANALYZING MEANING

1. Choy differentiates between racist terms and nicknames. What is the difference between them? Can a term be both a racist term and a nickname? Can it move from being one to the other?
2. In the 1950s and '60s, why did Chinatown parents encourage their children to assimilate?
3. Explain Choy's discovery of the "... truth [that] these 'between world' struggles are universal" (paragraph 15).

DISCOVERING RHETORICAL STRATEGIES

1. Choy centres his essay around the use of the term *banana*. How does he extend this metaphor in his essay?

2. What is Choy's thesis? Where is it found?
3. Who is Choy's intended audience?

MAKING CONNECTIONS

1. Choy defines the term *banana* as an affectionate nickname which he groups with the metaphors "apple" and "Oreo cookie." Imagine Choy is having a conversation with Cecil Foster ("Why Blacks Get Mad") about the use of these terms. On what points would the two agree? Are there areas where they would disagree?
2. Choy's essay is one of self-definition. In what ways is "I'm a Banana and Proud of It" similar to Drew Hayden Taylor's "Pretty Like a White Boy"? What differences do you find in the strategies these two writers use to define themselves?
3. In "I'm a Banana and Proud of It," Wayson Choy talks about the importance of understanding the past. Steven Heighton ("Elegy in Stone") also recognizes value in understanding the past. Why is an understanding of our history important to our sense of belonging in the present? How does the larger context enrich our lives in the present?

IDEAS FOR DISCUSSION/WRITING

Preparing to Write

Wayson Choy talks in this essay about what the Chinatown parents wanted for their children. Write freely about parental aspirations or dreams for their children. What dreams did your parents have for you as you were growing up? Were these messages conveyed explicitly or implicitly? Did you share these aspirations? What hopes would you have for your children if you were a parent?

Choosing a Topic

1. Think of a nickname you have now or have had in the past, and write an essay in which you explain how this nickname defines you.
2. Wayson Choy, in writing *The Jade Peony* as an exploration of his roots, discovered the combination in every human being of "the Other" and the desire for the same security and

happiness. Using your own personal history, write a narrative essay showing this combination of elements in a person or people you know.

3. In this essay, Wayson Choy introduces a food metaphor that defines many North Americans. Write an essay in which you use an animal metaphor to describe the various members of your family. Make sure you keep your metaphor consistent.

WEBSITES

www.cbc.ca/millennium/authors/choy.html
Wayson Choy writing on the millennium.

www.banffcentre.ca/press/contributors/abc/choy_w
Banff Centre profile of Choy.

MICHAEL CLUGSTON

Twice Struck

A Canadian journalist, Michael Clugston has had articles published in a variety of magazines, including *Equinox*, from which this essay was taken; *Reader's Digest; The Globe and Mail's Destinations*; and *Canadian Geographic*, where he was an editor until 1996. After spending almost five years as a news editor in Japan, where he grew up, Clugston is now living in Gatineau, Quebec.

Preparing to Read

In *Equinox*, where "Twice Struck" originally appeared in 1991, Clugston's essay is accompanied by a picture of a spectacular bolt of lightning. Before you begin reading, think about lightning and thunderstorms. How do you feel about thunderstorms? Have you ever been frightened by a crack of thunder or a flash of lightning? What kind of emotions do thunder and lightning typically evoke in people? In animals? What associations do you have with thunder and lightning in movies you have seen or stories you have read? What gives Clugston's subject its lasting appeal and interest?

Tennyson called it a "flying game." Benjamin Franklin termed it a "sudden and terrible mischief." In Roman mythology, the god Jupiter used spiky thunderbolts as letters to the editor when he chose to show displeasure with the poor mortals below. 1

By whatever name, lightning is a spectacular natural event. Captured in photographs, its grandeur and beauty are safely petrified in static portraits of primal energy. In reality, at 24,000 to 28,000 degrees C, it is four times hotter than the surface of the sun. It can vaporize steel, plough up fields, shatter giant trees and scatter livid incendiary sparks over vast forests. Each day, it kills 20 people. 2

Its horror is the haphazard nature of its violence, a random Russian-roulette threat beyond control. If you are caught out in the open during a thunderstorm, it can look like oncoming headlights of celestial chaos. Lightning can terrify you, charm 3 you with its beauty, fry you, or, prosaically enough, bring on asthma, drowsiness and other discomforting side effects from the ionized air it creates.

Ask a scientist what lightning is, and he or she will most 4 likely remind you of the electric kiss you get indoors on a dry winter day when you walk across a carpet and then touch an electric switch or another person. That nasty little jolt is the micro version of the heaven-sent tracery that can look as delicate as needlepoint while travelling between 100,000 and 300,000 kilometres per second.

But the scientist will also tell you that there is still a 5 considerable mystery to lightning. "In some areas, we really don't know what's happening up there," says Andrew Podgorski, a senior research officer at the National Research Council of Canada in Ottawa and head of the Electromagnetic Interference/ Electromagnetic Compatibility Programme. "It's very difficult to predict where the lightning is being initiated and how the lightning channels are defined. Nor do we know how the lightning bolt itself can grow so quickly to the huge channel that we perceive."

What is known, though, is fascinating enough. If nature 6 abhors a vacuum, electricity abhors imbalance. Like water, which seeks its own level, electricity tries to even out the imbalance on charges between two neighbouring bodies by leaping the gap with a bright spark. However, when we see that spark in the form of lightning, what we see is not what we think we see.

The colossal structures we know as thunderheads are giant 7 electrical generators. They occur when weather conditions create rapid updrafts of warm, moist air that travel high in the atmosphere. Furious updrafts and downfalls of water and ice particles create regions of positive and negative charge. Lightning can travel between the opposite charges within the clouds or between the cloud and ground. The negative base of a thunderhead creates a positive charge in the ground immediately below and sets the scene for the gaudy short circuits overhead.

Majestic bolts such as those pictured here* were probably 8 preceded by a weak electrical spark that descended from the negatively charged clouds to the positively charged earth. The weak spark is called the "stepped leader," named for its rootlike branchings. Near the earth, the spindly leader intersects with a

* See Preparing to Read on the previous page.

shorter leader rising from the ground to meet it. This creates a conductive pathway of ionized air—a bridge of ions from heaven to earth. The stage is then set for the real business to begin.

A few millionths of a second later, a bright channel of light   9 and heat—a lightning bolt—leaps back up the bridge, but the human eye is not fast enough to distinguish the leader from the bolt. If lightning appears to be branched downward, it is because the upward-moving charge flows through all the ionized side routes established by the leader. It is the return stroke that causes most of the thunder we hear.

Last year, Podgorski conducted lightning experiments inside   10 the top of Toronto's CN Tower during a thunderstorm. "I thought about Ben Franklin while I was up there," he says. "But the tip is protected by metal, so I didn't even realize lightning was striking the tower while I was inside."

Franklin, the Philadelphian Renaissance man, flew his famous   11 kite in 1752 to prove that clouds were electrified, an experiment which led him to the invention of lightning rods. By 1782, the only building in Philadelphia that did not sport one of Franklin's rods was the French Embassy. One official died when it was struck by lightning that year.

Ever since Franklin's experiment and well into the 1800s,   12 lightning, and protection against it, has caught the public imagination. For a few years, people could be seen carrying lightning-rod umbrellas, which lofted a sharp metal rod on top and trailed ground wires behind them.

While we may think of such a device as a silly momentary   13 fad, it was a big step forward in understanding from the Middle Ages in Europe. Then people believed that ringing church bells in thunderstorms kept the lightning from striking nearby buildings. In this way, the call of duty sent hundreds of bell ringers on sudden ascensions to heaven before the curious custom belatedly became unpopular. The words *fulgura frango* ("I break the lightning") can still be found on some medieval bells.

We still cannot "break" lightning, but we can study it.   14 Experiments have shown that lightning saturates the air with positive ions—atoms that have lost one or more electrons. The heat of lightning produces ions by searing electrons away from the atoms in its path. For some people, these can bring on a host of unpleasant effects. "Weather-sensitive people have reported insomnia, irritability, tension, chills, sweats, dizziness and loss of balance, migraines and other types of headaches, visual disturbances, nausea and vomiting," writes bacteriologist Julius Fast in his book of reactions.

But whatever the folklore or science of the day, our   15 perception of lightning remains rooted in the universal reactions of wonder and respect.

UNDERSTANDING DETAILS

1. In your own words, define lightning.
2. List the various effects that lightning can have.
3. Explain the words *fulgura frango* that can be found on some medieval church bells.

ANALYZING MEANING

1. In "Twice Struck," Clugston cites scientific knowledge about lightning as well as folklore on this subject. What is the relationship between these two realms of understanding our world?
2. Explain why Clugston says that wonder and respect are universal reactions to lightning.
3. In the Middle Ages people rang church bells to ward off lightning; in the 1800s they carried lightning rod umbrellas. What do people today do to protect themselves against the "flying flames"? Are these practices based on science or folklore?

DISCOVERING RHETORICAL STRATEGIES

1. Is Clugston's definition objective or subjective? Explain your answer.
2. In his essay, Clugston cites Benjamin Franklin, Andrew Podgorski, Julius Fast, and Alfred Lord Tennyson. Who is each of these people and why is each mentioned in "Twice Struck"?
3. Reread paragraph 3 of "Twice Struck." Identify all the examples of figurative language that you can find in this paragraph. What effect do these uses of language have on you as a reader?

MAKING CONNECTIONS

1. Michael Clugston cites other people in his essay as do Judy Rebick ("The Culture of Overwork") and Malcolm Gladwell ("Is the Belgian Coca-Cola Hysteria the Real Thing?"). Explain

why these authors have incorporated quotations from others into each of their essays.

2. In "Twice Struck" Clugston describes a particular natural phenomenon and our reactions to it. How do the responses to lightning that Clugston details compare to the reactions to other natural processes such as that described by Lesley Choyce ("Thin Edge of the Wedge")?

3. Michael Clugston says that wonder and respect are universal reactions to lightning. How do you think Tomson Highway ("What a Certain Visionary Once Said") would respond to this assertion? Explain your answer.

IDEAS FOR DISCUSSION/WRITING

Preparing to Write

Write freely about the weather. In what ways does the weather affect your life? How are our lives generally governed by weather? What is the most severe storm you have ever experienced? How did you react to it? Why do we consider weather predictions important? What need sustains whole television stations devoted to weather?

Choosing a Topic

1. While science has come a long way in explaining lightning, there are still some things we don't know. Traditionally, myths and legends have been invented to explain events that we don't entirely understand. Write a myth to explain a particular weather phenomenon.

2. Write an essay in which you explain how the weather that you experience in your region of the country has contributed to defining you as a person.

3. Weather is often said to influence people's behaviour in fairly significant ways. This might be an ongoing condition like Seasonal Affective Disorder (SAD) or it might be a more specific behaviour related to a dramatic change in temperature or humidity or a phase of the moon. Write an essay in which you explore the connection between people's behaviour and the weather.

WEBSITES

www.horsburgh.com/h_bolt.html
This site has some impressive photographs of lightning.

www.lightningsafety.com
Visit the National Lightning Safety Institute.

sln.fi.edu/franklin/rotten.html
The World of Benjamin Franklin.

LAWRENCE HILL

Don't Call Me That Word

Racial identity is a recurring theme in the work of Lawrence Hill (1957–). Hill grew up in a suburb of Toronto, Ontario, in the 1960s grappling with his identity as the child of a black father and a white mother. This experience informs much of the writing, teaching, and speaking that he does today.

With a B.A. in economics from Laval University in Quebec City and an M.A. in writing from Johns Hopkins University in Baltimore, Hill is a writer of both fiction and non-fiction. His work has been published in literary anthologies, magazines, and newspapers including *Toronto Life*, the *Toronto Star*, and *West Coast Line*. Hill has also published two books about black history, and one novel (*Any Known Blood*), and he is currently working on a second one (*Migration*). His non-fiction book *Black Berry, Sweet Juice: On Being Black and White in Canada* examines what it is like to grow up as a mixed-race person in Canada.

Hill, who speaks French and Spanish in addition to English, has lived and worked across Canada, in the U.S., Spain, and France. As a volunteer with Canadian Crossroads International, Hill has led cultural exchanges in Niger, Cameroon, and Mali, and he volunteers with a variety of other Canadian black history and writers' groups.

Hill has also taught writing through organizations such as Ryerson University, Johns Hopkins University, and the Writers in Electronic Residence program of the Writers' Trust of Canada, and he runs a small writing consultant business from Oakville, where he now lives with his family.

Preparing to Read

Hill's essay comes from *Maclean's* magazine. Before you begin reading, think about name calling. What is the effect of being called a name that has negative connotations? Have you ever been called names as a child or as an adult? If so, what were those names? How did those names make you feel? Have you ever called others names with negative overtones? If so, why did you use those names? What was the intended effect on your audience? What negative names specifically relate to race or ethnicity?

Growing up in the 1960s in the affluent, almost all-white Don   1
Mills, Ont., I was told by my black father that education and
professional achievement were the only viable options for black
people in North America. He laid down three rules as if they had
been received from the mouth of God: 1) I was to study like the
dickens; 2) anything less than complete success in school or at
work was to be regarded as failure; 3) if anybody called me "nigger," I was to beat the hell out of him.

This is the legacy of being black in Canada. You over-   2
compensate for the fluke of your ancestry, and stand on guard
against those who would knock you down. Over 400 years of
black history here, we have had to overcome numerous
challenges: the chains of slave vessels, the wrath of slave owners,
the rules of segregation, the killing ways of police bullets, our
own murderous infighting, and all the modern vicissitudes of
polite Canadian oppression.

Blacks in Canada, like our metaphorical brothers and sisters   3
all over the world, have a vivid collective memory. We know
what our ancestors have been through, and we know what our
children still face. Most of us cringe when we hear the word
"nigger." No other word in the English language distills hatred
so effectively, and evokes such a long and bloody history.

These days, more people than ever are talking about the   4
word "nigger," as a result of the publication this year of the book
Nigger: The Strange Career of a Troublesome Word, by Randall
Kennedy, a black American law professor at Harvard University.
It's a fascinating read, but it raises a troublesome argument that
I ultimately reject: Kennedy praises "African American
innovators" (by which he means comedians and hip hop stylists)
for "taming, civilizing, and transmuting 'the filthiest, dirtiest,
nastiest word in the English language.'"

Some misguided white people have bought into this same   5
way of thinking. We have hit the pinnacle of absurdity when
white teenagers sling their arms around black friends and ask,
"Whassup my nigger?" And some white people seem to want a
piece of that word, and feel the need to apply it to their own
difficult experiences. The Irish have been referred to as "the
niggers of Europe." In the 1970s, Québécois writer Pierre Vallieres
titled one of his books *White Niggers of America*. And just the
other night, when I visited a drop-in centre catering mostly to
black junior high and high school students in Toronto's

Kensington Market area, a white teenager decked out in baggy pants and parroting what he imagined to be blackspeak complained that some kids accused him of being a "wigger"—an insulting term for whites who are trying to act black. Whatever that means.

As Randall Kennedy rightly asserts, the word abounds in   6 contemporary black urban culture. True, when it crops up in hip hop lyrics, it's not intended to carry the hate of the racist. It signals an in-group, brotherly, friendly trash talk. This is well known in American culture but it has penetrated black Canadian culture, too. Choclair, a leading black Canadian hip hop artist, uses the word "nigga"—a derivation of "nigger"—frequently in his lyrics.

Some people might say that the N-word is making a   7 comeback. That the old-style, racist use of the word has faded into history and that it's now kosher to use the word in ordinary conversation. This argument fails on two counts. First, racists and racism haven't disappeared from the Canadian landscape. The comeback argument also fails because it suggests that reappropriating the word reflects a new linguistic trend. This is naive. As a way of playing with the English language's most hateful word, black people—mostly young black males—have called themselves "nigger" for generations. The difference now is that these same young blacks have broadcast the word, via music and TV, to the whole world. In the middle-class black cultures I've encountered in Canada and the United States, such a young man usually gets slapped or tongue-lashed by his mother, at just about that point, and he learns that the only time it's safe to use that word is when he's chilling on the street with his buddies. Black people use the word "nigger" precisely because it hurts so much that we need to dance with our own pain, in the same way that blues music dives straight into bad luck and heartbreak. This is very much part of the black North American experience: we don't run from our pain, we roll it into our art.

But does that take the sting out of the word? No. And what's   8 the proof of that? We don't use the word around our mothers, our teachers, the people we fall in love with, or our children. "Nigger" is a word that young black men use on each other. But the word still pains most black Canadians. Let me share an image of just how much the word hurts. A friend of mine—a black woman, community activist and graduate student—was dying to read Kennedy's book. She bought it last week, but couldn't bring herself to start devouring it on the subway to work until she had ripped off the cover: she wouldn't allow herself to be seen on the subway with the word "nigger" splashed on the cover of a book, so close to her face.

UNDERSTANDING DETAILS

1. What is the word to which Hill refers in his title? How, physically, is it set apart in the text of the essay?
2. Describe Randall Kennedy's view of the word "nigger."
3. Hill points out that "[s]ome people might say that the N-word is making a comeback. That the old-style, racist use of the word has faded into history and that it's now kosher to use the word in ordinary conversation" (paragraph 7). Does Hill agree with this position? Why or why not?

ANALYZING MEANING

1. Explain the difference between the word "nigger" being used by young black men among themselves and by anyone else.
2. Why do some people believe that "the N-word is making a comeback" (paragraph 7)? Do you agree with them? Explain.
3. Why is the word "nigger" "the English language's most hateful word"? What other words have a similar impact?

DISCOVERING RHETORICAL STRATEGIES

1. How effective is the title of Hill's essay? What is the effect of using "That Word" rather than "Nigger"?
2. What is Hill's purpose in writing this essay? Has he successfully achieved his purpose?
3. Is Hill's definition primarily an objective or a subjective one? Explain your conclusion.

MAKING CONNECTIONS

1. Wayson Choy ("I'm a Banana and Proud of It") and Lawrence Hill both talk about terms that label people based on their race or ethnicity. In what ways are the terms "nigger" and "banana" similar? In what respects do they differ?
2. Lawrence Hill and Cecil Foster both write about their experiences as black Canadians. In what ways are their experiences common?

IDEAS FOR DISCUSSION/WRITING

Preparing to Write

Hill says of the black North American experience: "we don't run from our pain, we roll it into our art." Write freely about rolling pain into art. What does it mean to roll your pain into your art? What types of pain take form in art? What forms of art reflect people's pain?

Choosing a Topic

1. Write an essay in which you explore the meaning of a name given to people of a community to which you belong. This community might be one distinguished by race, ethnicity, socio-economic status, residence, religion, age, sexual orientation, or political stance. Be clear about your attitude toward the term you are defining.
2. Many musicians such as Choclair cause controversy by using language that is commonly considered offensive. Write an essay about the inclusion of such language in the work of contemporary musicians.
3. What is the attraction of art (e.g., music, visual art, dance) that reflects pain? Write an essay defining the appeal of such work.

WEBSITES

www.lawrencehill.com
Visit Lawrence Hill's personal website for biographical and bibliographical information as well as reviews and samples of Hill's writing.

www.wier.ca/lhill.html
Lawrence Hill is a participant in the Writers in Electronic Residence program.

www.macleans.ca
Hill's essay was first published in *Maclean's* magazine.

CHAPTER 8

CAUSE/EFFECT

Tracing Reasons and Results

Wanting to know why things happen is one of our earliest, most basic instincts: Why can't I go out, Mommy? Why are you laughing? Why won't the dog stop barking? Why can't I swim faster than my big brother? These questions, and many more like them, reflect the innately inquisitive nature that dwells within each of us. Closely related to this desire to understand *why* is our interest in *what* will happen in the future as a result of some particular action: What will I feel like tomorrow if I stay up late tonight? How will I perform in the track meet Saturday if I practise all week? What will be the result if I mix together these two potent chemicals? What will happen if I turn in my next English assignment two days early?

A daily awareness of this intimate relationship between causes and effects allows us to begin to understand the complex and interrelated series of events that make up our lives and the lives of others. For example, trying to understand the various causes of the conflict in the Middle East teaches us about international relations; knowing our biological reactions to certain foods helps us make decisions about what to eat; understanding the interrelated reasons for the outbreak of World War II offers us insight into historical trends and human nature; knowing the effects of sunshine on various parts of our bodies helps us make decisions about how much ultraviolet exposure we can tolerate and what sunscreen lotion to use; and understanding the causes of Canada's most recent recession will help us respond appropriately to the next economic crisis we encounter. More than anything else, tracing causes and effects teaches us how to think clearly and react intelligently to our multifaceted environment.

In college or university, you will often be asked to use this natural interest in causes and effects to analyze particular situations and to discern general principles. For example, you might be asked some of the following questions on essay exams in different courses:

Anthropology: Why did the Mayan culture disintegrate?

Psychology: Why do humans respond to fear in different ways?

Biology: How do lab rats react to caffeine?

History: What were the positive effects of building the Trans-Canada Highway?

Business: Why did so many computer manufacturing companies go bankrupt in the early 1980s?

Your ability to answer such questions will depend in large part on your skill at writing a cause/effect essay.

Defining Cause/Effect

Cause/effect analysis requires the ability to look for connections between different elements and to analyze the reasons for those connections. As the name implies, this rhetorical mode has two separate components: cause and effect. A particular essay might concentrate on cause (Why do you live on campus?), on effect (What are the resulting advantages and disadvantages of living on campus?), or on some combination of the two. In working with causes, we are searching for any circumstances from the past that may have caused a single event; in looking for effects, we seek occurrences that took place after a particular event and resulted from that event. Like process analysis, cause/effect makes use of our intellectual ability to analyze. Process analysis addresses *how* something happens, whereas causal analysis discusses *why* it happened and *what* the result was. A process analysis paper, for example, might explain how to advertise more effectively to increase sales, whereas a cause/effect study would discover that three specific elements contributed to an increase in sales: effective advertising, personal service, and selective discounts. The study of causes and effects, therefore, provides many different and helpful ways for humans to make sense of and clarify their views of the world.

Looking for causes and effects requires an advanced form of thinking. It is more complex than most rhetorical strategies we have studied because it can exist on a number of different and progressively more difficult levels. The most accurate and effective causal analysis accrues from digging for the real or ultimate causes or effects, as opposed to those that are merely superficial or immediate. Actress Angela Lansbury would have been out of work on an episode of the television show *Murder, She Wrote*, for example, if her character had stopped her investigation at the immediate cause of death (slipping in the bathtub) rather than searching diligently for the real cause (an overdose of cocaine administered by an angry companion, which resulted in the slip in the tub). Similarly, voters would be easy to manipulate if they considered only the immediate effects of a tax increase (a slightly higher tax bill) rather than the ultimate benefits that would result (the many years of improved education that our children would receive because of the specialized programs created by such an increase). Only the discovery of the actual reasons for an event or an idea will lead to the logical and accurate analysis of causes and effects important to a basic understanding of various aspects of our lives.

Faulty reasoning assigns causes to a sequence of actions without adequate justification. One such logical fallacy is called *post hoc, ergo propter hoc* (after this, therefore because of this): The fact that someone lost a job after walking under a ladder does not mean that the two events are causally related; by the same token, if we get up every morning at 5:30 a.m., just before the sun rises, we cannot therefore conclude that the sun rises *because* we get up (no matter how self-centred we are!). Faulty reasoning also occurs when we oversimplify a particular situation. Most events are connected to a multitude of causes and effects. Sometimes one effect has many causes: A student may fail a history exam because she's been working two part-time jobs, she was sick, she didn't study hard enough, and she found the instructor very boring. One cause may also have many effects. If a house burns down, the people who lived in it will be out of a home. If we look at such a tragic scene more closely, however, we may also note that the fire traumatized a child who lived there, helped the family learn what good friends they had, encouraged the family to double their future fire insurance, and provided the happy stimulus that they needed to make a long-dreamed-of move to another city. One event has thus resulted in many interrelated effects. Building an argument on insecure foundations or oversimplifying the causes or effects connected with an event will seriously hinder the construction of a rational essay. No matter what the nature of the cause/effect analysis, it must always be based on clear observation, accurate facts, and rigorous logic.

In the following paragraph, a student writer analyzes some of the causes and effects connected with the controversial issue of euthanasia. Notice how he makes connections and then analyzes those connections as he consistently explores the immediate and ultimate effects of being able to stretch life beyond its normal limits through new medical technology:

> Along with the many recent startling advances in medical technology have come a number of complex moral, ethical, and spiritual questions that beg to be answered. We now have the ability to prolong the life of the human body for a very long time. But what rights do patients and their families have to curtail cruel and unusual medical treatment that stretches life beyond its normal limits? This dilemma has produced a ripple effect in society. Is the extension of life an unquestionable goal in itself, regardless of the quality of that life? Modern scientific technology has forced doctors to re-evaluate the exact meaning and purpose of their profession. For example, many medical schools and undergraduate university programs now routinely offer classes on medical ethics—an esoteric and infrequently taught subject only a few years ago. Doctors and scholars alike are realizing that medical personnel alone cannot be expected to decide on the exact parameters of life. In like manner, the judicial process must now evaluate the legal complexities of mercy killings and the rights of patients to die with dignity and without unnecessary medical intervention. The insurance business, too, wrestles with the catastrophic effects of new technology on the costs of today's hospital care. In short, medical progress entails more than microscopes, chemicals, and high-tech instruments. If we are to develop as a thoughtful, just, and merciful society, we must consider not only the physical well-being of our nation's patients, but their emotional, spiritual, and financial status as well.

Thinking Critically by Using Cause/Effect

Thinking about causes and effects is one of the most advanced mental activities that we perform. It involves complex operations that we must think through carefully, making sure all connections are reasonable and accurate. Unlike other rhetorical patterns, cause/effect thinking requires us to see specific relationships between two or more items. To practise this strategy, we need to look for items or events that are causally related—that is, one that has caused the other. Then, we can focus on either the causes (the initial stimulus), the effects (the results), or a combination of the two.

Searching out causes and effects requires a great deal of digging that is not necessary for most of the other modes. Cause/effect necessitates the ultimate in investigative work. The mental exertion associated with this thinking strategy is sometimes exhausting, but it is always worth going through when you discover relationships that you never saw before or you uncover links in your reasoning that were previously unknown or obscure to you.

If you've ever had the secret desire to be a private eye or an investigator of any sort, practising cause/effect reasoning can be lots of fun. It forces you to see relationships among multiple items and then to make sense of those connections. Completing exercises in this skill will help you perfect the logistics of cause/effect thinking before you mix and match it with several other thinking strategies.

1. Choose a major problem you see in our society, and list what you think are the main causes of this problem on one side of a piece of paper and the effects on the other side. Compare the two lists to see how they differ. Then, compare and contrast your lists with those written by other students.

2. What "caused" you to become a student? What influences led you to this choice at this point in your life? How has being a student affected your life? List several overall effects.

3. List the effects of one of the following: getting a speeding ticket, winning an Olympic medal, graduating from college or university, or watching TV until the early hours of the morning.

Reading and Writing Cause/Effect Essays

Causal analysis is usually employed for one of three main purposes: (1) to prove a specific point (such as the necessity of tighter airport security), in which case the writer generally deals totally with facts and with conclusions drawn from those facts;

(2) to argue against a widely accepted belief (for example, the assertion that cocaine is addictive), in which case the writer relies principally on facts, with perhaps some pertinent opinions; or (3) to speculate on a theory (for instance, why the crime rate is higher in most major cities than it is in rural areas), in which case the writer probably presents hypotheses and opinions along with facts. This section will explore these purposes in cause/effect essays from the standpoint of both reading and writing.

How to Read a Cause/Effect Essay

Preparing to Read. As you set out to read the essays in this chapter, begin by focusing your attention on the title and the synopsis of the essay you are about to read and by scanning the essay itself: What do you think Stephen King is going to talk about in "Why We Crave Horror Movies"? What does the synopsis in the Rhetorical Table of Contents tell you about Laura Robinson's "Starving for the Gold"?

Also, at this stage in the reading process, you should try to learn as much as you can about the author of the essay and the reasons he or she wrote it. Ask yourself questions like the following: What is King's intention in "Why We Crave Horror Movies"? Who is Kim Pittaway's intended audience in "Dead Wrong"? And what is Trina McQueen's point of view in "Why We Crave Hot Stuff"?

Finally, before you begin to read, answer the prereading questions for each essay and then consider the proposed essay topic from a variety of perspectives: For example, concerning Pittaway's topic, have you ever attended a celebrity funeral or watched one on TV? Do you read tabloid news stories (McQueen)? Have you participated in competitive sports (Robinson)? Was it a positive or negative experience? What do you want to know about eating disorders from Evelyn Lau?

Reading. As you read each essay in this chapter for the first time, record your spontaneous reactions to it, drawing as often as possible on the preliminary material you already know: What do you think of horror movies (King)? Why did Pittaway choose the title she did? What is McQueen suggesting about "hot stuff" stories? Whenever you can, try to create a context for your reading: What is the tone of Robinson's discussion about young female athletes? How does this tone help her communicate with her audience? What do you think Robinson's purpose is in her essay on athletes and eating disorders? How clearly does she get this purpose across to you?

Also, during this reading, note the essay's thesis and check to see if the writer thoroughly explores all possibilities before settling on the primary causes and/or effects of a particular situation; in addition, determine whether the writer clearly states the assertions that naturally evolve from a discussion of the topic. Finally, read the questions following each essay to get a sense of the main issues and strategies in the selection.

Rereading. When you reread these essays, you should focus mainly on the writer's craft. Notice how the authors narrow and focus their material, how they make clear and logical connections between ideas in their essays, how they support their conclusions with concrete examples, how they use other rhetorical modes to accomplish their cause/effect analysis, and how they employ logical transitions to move us smoothly from one point to another. Most important, however, ask yourself if the writer actually discusses the real causes and/or effects of a particular circumstance: What does King say are the primary reasons people crave horror movies? What does McQueen consider the main cause of the appeal of "hot stuff" stories? What are the primary causes and effects of eating disorders?

For a thorough outline of the reading process, consult the checklist on pages 17–18 of the Introduction.

How to Write a Cause/Effect Essay

Preparing to Write. Beginning a cause/effect essay requires— as does any other essay—exploring and limiting your subject, specifying a purpose, and identifying an audience. The Preparing to Write questions before the essay assignments, coupled with the prewriting techniques outlined in the Introduction, encourage you to consider specific issues related to your reading. The assignments themselves will then help you limit your topic and determine a particular purpose and audience for your message. For cause/effect essays, determining a purpose is even more important than usual because your readers can get hopelessly lost unless your analysis is clearly focused.

Writing. For all its conceptual complexity, a cause/effect essay can be organized quite simply. The introduction generally presents the subject(s) and states the purpose of the analysis in a clear thesis. The body of the paper then explores all relevant causes and/or effects, typically progressing either from least to most influential or from most to least influential. Finally, the concluding section summarizes the various cause-and-effect relationships established in the body of the paper and clearly states the conclusions that can be drawn from those relationships.

The following additional guidelines should assist you in producing an effective cause/effect essay in all academic disciplines:

- Narrow and focus your material as much as possible.
- Consider all possibilities before assigning real or ultimate causes or effects.
- Show connections between ideas by using transitions and key words—such as *because, reasons, results, effects,* and *consequences*—to guide your readers smoothly through your essay.
- Support all inferences with concrete evidence.
- Be as objective as possible in your analysis so that you don't distort logic with personal biases.
- Understand your audience's opinions and convictions, so that you know what to emphasize in your essay.
- Qualify your assertions to avoid overstatement and oversimplification.

These suggestions apply to both cause/effect essay assignments and exam questions.

Rewriting. As you revise your cause/effect essays, ask yourself the following important questions:

- Is your thesis stated clearly at the outset of your paper?
- Does it include your subject and your purpose?
- Do you accomplish your purpose as effectively as possible for your particular audience?
- Do you use logical reasoning throughout the essay?
- Do you carefully explore all relevant causes and/or effects, searching for the real (as opposed to the immediate) reasons in each case?
- Do you state clearly the conclusions that can be drawn from your paper?

More specific guidelines for writing and revising your essays appear on pages 29–30 of the Introduction.

Student Essay: Cause/Effect at Work

In the following essay, the student writer analyzes the effects of contemporary TV soap operas on young people: Notice that she states her subject and purpose at the beginning of the essay and then presents a combination of facts and opinions in her exploration of the topic. Notice also that, in her analysis, the writer is careful to draw clear connections between her perceptions of the issue and various objective details in an attempt to trace the effects of this medium in our society today. At the end of her essay, look at her summary of the logical relationships she establishes in the body of the essay and her statements about the conclusions she draws from these relationships.

Distortions of Reality

Background Television's contributions to society, positive and negative, have been debated continually since this piece of technology invaded the average Canadian household in the 1950s. Television has brought an unlimited influx of new information, ideas, and cultures into our homes. However, based on my observations of my thirteen-year-old cousin, Katie, and her friends, I think we need to take a closer look at the effects of soap operas on adolescents today. The distortions of reality portrayed on these programs are frighten- Thesis ingly misleading and, in my opinion, can be very confusing to statement young people.

Transition   During the early 1990s, the lifestyle of the typical soap opera "family" has been radically transformed from comfortable pretentiousness to blatant and unrealistic decadence. The characters neither live nor dress like the majority of their viewers, who are generally middle-class Canadians. These television families live First in large, majestic homes that are flawlessly decorated. The actors distortion of reality are often adorned in beautiful designer clothing, fur coats, and Concrete examples expensive jewellery, and this opulent lifestyle is sustained by people with no visible means of income. Very few of the characters seem to "work" for a living. When they do, upward mobility—without the benefit of the proper education or suitable training—and a well-planned marriage come quickly.

Transition   <u>From this constant barrage of conspicuous consumption, my</u>   First effect
<u>cousin and her friends seem to have a distorted view of everyday</u>
<u>economic realities</u>. I see Katie and her group becoming obsessed
with the appearance of their clothes and possessions. I frequently
Concrete   hear them berate their parents' jobs and modest homes. With no-
examples   ticeable arrogance, these young adolescents seem to view their
parents' lives as "failures" when compared to the effortless, lux-
urious lifestyles portrayed in the soaps.

Transition   <u>One of the most alluring features of this genre is its masterful use</u>
<u>of deception</u>. Conflicts between characters in soap operas are based
on secrecy and misinformation. Failure to tell the truth and to per-
Concrete   form honourable deeds further complicates the entangled lives
examples   and love affairs of the participants. <u>But when the truth finally</u>   Second
<u>comes out and all mistakes and misdeeds become public, the</u>   distortion
<u>culprits and offenders hardly ever suffer for their actions</u>. In fact,   of reality
they appear to leave the scene of the crime guilt-free.

Transition   <u>Regrettably,</u> Katie and her friends consistently express alarming
Concrete   indifference to this lack of moral integrity. In their daily viewing, they
examples   shrug off underhanded scenes of scheming and conniving, and they
marvel at how the characters manipulate each other into positions
of powerlessness or grapple in distasteful love scenes. <u>I can only</u>   Second
<u>conclude that continued exposure to this amoral behaviour is erod-</u>   effect
<u>ing the fundamental values of truth and fidelity in these kids</u>.

Transition   <u>Also in the soaps, the powers-that-be conveniently disregard</u>   Third
<u>any sense of responsibility for wrongdoing</u>. Characters serve jail   distortion
Concrete   terms quickly and in relative comfort. Drug or alcohol abuse does   of reality
examples   not mar anyone's physical appearance or behaviour, and poverty
is virtually non-existent. Usually, the wrongdoer's position, wealth,
and prestige are quickly restored—with little pain and suffering.

<u>Adolescents are clearly learning that people can act without re-</u>   Third effect
<u>gard for the harmful effects of their actions on themselves and</u>
<u>others when they see this type of behaviour go unpunished</u>. Again,
I notice the result of this delusion in my cousin. Recently, when a
businessman in our community was convicted of embezzling large
sums of money from his clients, Katie was outraged because he
Concrete   was sentenced to five years in prison, unlike her daytime TV
examples   "heartthrob," who had been given a suspended sentence for a
similar crime. With righteous indignation, Katie claimed that the
victims, many of whom had lost their entire savings, should have
realized that any business investment involves risk and the threat
of loss. Logic and common sense evaded Katie's reasoning as she
insisted on comparing television justice with real-life scruples.

The writers and producers of soap operas argue that the shows are designed to entertain viewers and are not meant to be reflections of reality. Theoretically, this may be true, but I can actually see how these soap operas are affecting my cousin and her crowd. Although my personal observations are limited, I cannot believe they are unique or unusual. <u>Too many young people think that they can amass wealth and material possessions without an edu-</u> **Ultimate** <u>cation, hard work, or careful financial planning; that material</u> **effect** <u>goods are the sole measure of a person's success in life; and that honesty and integrity are not necessarily admirable qualities.</u>

Proposed <u>Soap operas should demonstrate a realistic lifestyle and a re-</u> **solution** <u>sponsible sense of behaviour.</u> The many hours adolescents spend in front of the television can obviously influence their view of the world. As a society, we cannot afford the consequences resulting from the distortions of reality portrayed every day in these shows.

Some Final Thoughts on Cause/Effect

The essays in this chapter deal with both causes and effects in a variety of ways. As you read each essay, try to discover its primary purpose and the ultimate causes and/or effects of the issue under discussion. Note also the clear causal relationships that each author sets forth on solid foundations supported by logical reasoning. Although the subjects of these essays vary dramatically, each essay exhibits the basic elements of effective causal analysis.

Cause/Effect in Review

Reading Cause/Effect Essays

Preparing to Read

- What assumptions can you make from the essay's title?
- Can you guess what the general mood of the essay is?
- What is the essay's purpose and audience?
- What does the synopsis in the Rhetorical Table of Contents tell you about the essay?
- What can you learn from the author's biography?

- Can you guess what the author's point of view toward the subject is?
- What are your responses to the Preparing to Read questions?

Reading

- What is the author's thesis?
- What are the primary causes and/or effects in the essay?
- Did you preview the questions that follow the essay?

Rereading

- How does the writer narrow and focus the essay?
- Does the writer make clear and logical connections between the ideas in the essay?
- What concrete examples support the author's conclusions?
- Does the writer discuss the real causes and effects?
- What are your responses to the questions after the essay?

Writing Cause/Effect Essays

Preparing to Write

- What are your responses to the Preparing to Write questions?
- What is your purpose?
- Who is your audience?

Writing

- Do you narrow and focus your material as much as possible?
- Do you consider all possibilities before assigning real or ultimate causes or effects?
- Do you show connections between ideas by using transitions and key words?
- Do you support all inferences with concrete evidence?
- Are you as objective as possible in your analysis so that you don't distort logic with personal biases?
- Do you understand your audience's opinions and convictions, so that you know what to emphasize in your essay?

- Do you qualify your assertions to avoid overstatement and oversimplification?

Rewriting

- Is your thesis stated clearly at the outset of your paper?
- Does it include your subject and your purpose?
- Do you accomplish your purpose as effectively as possible for your particular audience?
- Do you use logical reasoning throughout the essay?
- Do you carefully explore all relevant causes and/or effects, searching for the real (as opposed to the immediate) reasons in each case?
- Do you state clearly the conclusions that can be drawn from your paper?

STEPHEN KING

Why We Crave Horror Movies

"People's appetites for terror seem insatiable," Stephen King once remarked, an insight which may help justify his phenomenal success as a writer of horror fiction since the mid-1970s. His books have sold over one hundred million copies, and the movies made from them have generated more income than the gross domestic product of several small countries. After early jobs as a janitor, a laundry worker, and a high school English teacher in Portland, Maine, King turned to writing full time following the spectacular sales of his first novel, *Carrie* (1974), which focuses on a shy, socially ostracized young girl who takes revenge on her cruel classmates through newly developed telekinetic powers. King's subsequent books have included *The Shining* (1976), *Firestarter* (1980), *Cujo* (1981), *Pet Sematary* (1983), *Misery* (1987), *The Stand* (1990), *The Waste Lands* (1992), *Dolores Claiborne* (1993), *Rose Madder* (1995), *Desperation* (1996), *Bag of Bones* (1998), and *Dreamcatcher* (2001). Asked to explain why readers and moviegoers are so attracted to his tales of horror, King recently explained that most people's lives "are full of fears—that their marriage isn't working, that they aren't going to make it on the job, that society is crumbling all around them. But we're really not supposed to talk about things like that, and so they don't have any outlets for all those scary feelings. But the horror writer can give them a place to put their fears, and it's ok to be afraid then, because nothing is real, and you can blow it all away when it's over." A cheerful though somewhat superstitious person, King, who now lives in Bangor, Maine, admits to doing most of his best writing during the morning hours. "You think I want to write this stuff at night?" he once asked a reviewer.

Preparing to Read

As you prepare to read this article, consider your thoughts on our society's emotional condition: How emotionally healthy are Canadians? Were they more emotionally healthy twenty years ago? A century ago? What makes a society emotionally healthy? Emotionally unhealthy? How can a society maintain good health? What is the relationship between emotional health and a civilized society?

I think that we're all mentally ill; those of us outside the asylums   1
only hide it a little better—and maybe not all that much better,
after all. We've all known people who talk to themselves, people
who sometimes squinch their faces into horrible grimaces when
they believe no one is watching, people who have some hysterical
fear—of snakes, the dark, the tight place, the long drop ... and, of
course, those final worms and grubs that are waiting so patiently
underground.

When we pay our four or five bucks and seat ourselves at   2
tenth-row center in a theater showing a horror movie, we are
daring the nightmare.

Why? Some of the reasons are simple and obvious. To show   3
that we can, that we are not afraid, that we can ride this roller
coaster. Which is not to say that a really good horror movie may
not surprise a scream out of us at some point, the way we may
scream when the roller coaster twists through a complete 360 or
plows through a lake at the bottom of the drop. And horror
movies, like roller coasters, have always been the special province
of the young; by the time one turns 40 or 50, one's appetite for
double twists or 360-degree loops may be considerably depleted.

We also go to reestablish our feelings of essential normality;   4
the horror movie is innately conservative, even reactionary. Freda
Jackson as the horrible melting woman in *Die, Monster, Die!*
confirms for us that no matter how far we may be removed from
the beauty of a Robert Redford or a Diana Ross, we are still light-
years from true ugliness.

And we go to have fun.   5

Ah, but this is where the ground starts to slope away, isn't it?   6
Because this is a very peculiar sort of fun, indeed. The fun comes
from seeing others menaced—sometimes killed. One critic has
suggested that if pro football has become the voyeur's version
of combat, then the horror film has become the modern version
of the public lynching.

It is true that the mythic, "fairy-tale" horror film intends to   7
take away the shades of gray. ... It urges us to put away our more
civilized and adult penchant for analysis and to become children
again, seeing things in pure blacks and whites. It may be that
horror movies provide psychic relief on this level because this
invitation to lapse into simplicity, irrationality, and even outright
madness is extended so rarely. We are told we may allow our
emotions a free rein ... or no rein at all.

If we are all insane, then sanity becomes a matter of degree. 8
If your insanity leads you to carve up women, like Jack the Ripper
or the Cleveland Torso Murderer, we clap you away in the funny
farm (but neither of those two amateur-night surgeons was ever
caught, heh-heh-heh); if, on the other hand, your insanity leads
you only to talk to yourself when you're under stress or to pick
your nose on your morning bus, then you are left alone to go
about your business ... though it is doubtful that you will ever be
invited to the best parties.

The potential lyncher is in almost all of us (excluding saints, 9
past and present; but then, most saints have been crazy in their
own ways), and every now and then, he has to be let loose to
scream and roll around in the grass. Our emotions and our fears
form their own body, and we recognize that it demands its own
exercise to maintain proper muscle tone. Certain of these
emotional muscles are accepted—even exalted—in civilized
society; they are, of course, the emotions that tend to maintain the
status quo of civilization itself. Love, friendship, loyalty,
kindness—these are all the emotions that we applaud, emotions
that have been immortalized in the couplets of Hallmark cards
and in the verses (I don't dare call it poetry) of Leonard Nimoy.

When we exhibit these emotions, society showers us with 10
positive reinforcement; we learn this even before we get out of
diapers. When, as children, we hug our rotten little puke of a
sister and give her a kiss, all the aunts and uncles smile and twit
and cry, "Isn't he the sweetest little thing?" Such coveted treats
as chocolate-covered graham crackers often follow. But if we
deliberately slam the rotten little puke of a sister's fingers in the
door, sanctions follow—angry remonstrance from parents, aunts
and uncles; instead of a chocolate-covered graham cracker, a
spanking.

But anticivilization emotions don't go away, and they 11
demand periodic exercise. We have such "sick" jokes as, "What's
the difference between a truckload of bowling balls and a
truckload of dead babies?" (You can't unload a truckload of
bowling balls with a pitchfork ... a joke, by the way, that I heard
originally from a ten-year-old.) Such a joke may surprise a laugh
or a grin out of us even as we recoil, a possibility that confirms the
thesis: If we share a brotherhood of man, then we also share an
insanity of man. None of which is intended as a defense of either
the sick joke or insanity but merely as an explanation of why the

best horror films, like the best fairy tales, manage to be reactionary, anarchistic, and revolutionary all at the same time.

The mythic horror movie, like the sick joke, has a dirty job to do. It deliberately appeals to all that is worst in us. It is morbidity unchained, our most base instincts let free, our nastiest fantasies realized ... and it all happens, fittingly enough, in the dark. For those reasons, good liberals often shy away from horror films. For myself, I like to see the most aggressive of them—*Dawn of the Dead*, for instance—as lifting a trap door in the civilized forebrain and throwing a basket of raw meat to the hungry alligators swimming around in that subterranean river beneath.   12

Why bother? Because it keeps them from getting out, man. It keeps them down there and me up here. It was Lennon and McCartney who said that all you need is love, and I would agree with that.   13

As long as you keep the gators fed.   14

UNDERSTANDING DETAILS

1. Why, in King's opinion, do civilized people enjoy horror movies?
2. According to King, in what ways are horror movies like roller coasters?
3. According to King, how are horror films like public lynchings?
4. What is the difference between "emotions that tend to maintain the status quo of civilization" (paragraph 9) and "anticivilization emotions" (paragraph 11)?

ANALYZING MEANING

1. How can horror movies "reestablish our feelings of essential normality" (paragraph 4)?
2. What is "reactionary, anarchistic, and revolutionary" (paragraph 11) about fairy tales? About horror films?
3. Why does the author think we need to exercise our anticivilization emotions? What are some other ways we might confront these emotions?
4. Explain the last line of King's essay: "As long as you keep the gators fed" (paragraph 14).

DISCOVERING RHETORICAL STRATEGIES

1. What is the cause/effect relationship King notes in society between horror movies and sanity?
2. Why does King begin his essay with such a dramatic statement as "I think that we're all mentally ill" (paragraph 1)?
3. Who do you think is the author's intended audience for this essay? Describe them in detail. How did you come to this conclusion?
4. What different rhetorical strategies does King use to support his cause/effect analysis? Give examples of each.

MAKING CONNECTIONS

1. Apply Stephen King's definition of the appeal of horror to such experiences as attending a celebrity funeral (Pittaway, "Dead Wrong"). In what way does participating in the ritual of death compare to watching a horror movie? What are the principal differences between watching a horror movie and living through a real-life celebrity death?
2. The effect of a horror movie can be contagious, like the hysterical behaviour described by Malcolm Gladwell ("Is the Belgian Coca-Cola Hysteria the Real Thing?"). In what way might a horror movie trigger mass hysteria?
3. Compare King's comments about fear with similar insights into fear by other authors such as Laura Robinson ("Starving for the Gold") and Evelyn Lau ("More and More"). How would each of these writers define the term differently? With which author's definition would you most likely agree? Explain your answer.

IDEAS FOR DISCUSSION/WRITING

Preparing to Write

Write freely about how most people maintain a healthy emotional attitude: How would you define emotional well-being? When are people most emotionally healthy? Most emotionally unhealthy? What do your friends and relatives do to maintain a healthy emotional life? What do you do to maintain emotional health? What is the connection between our individual emotional health and the extent to which our society is civilized?

Choosing a Topic

1. Think of a release other than horror films for our most violent emotions. Is it an acceptable release? Write an essay for the general public explaining the relationship between this particular release and our "civilized" society.

2. If you accept King's analysis of horror movies, what role in society do you think other types of movies play (e.g., love stories, science fiction, and comedies)? Choose one type, and explain its role to your composition class.

3. Your psychology instructor has asked you to explain your opinions on the degree of sanity or insanity in Canada at present. In what ways are we sane? In what ways are we insane? Write an essay for your psychology instructor explaining in detail your observations along these lines.

WEBSITES

www.stephenking.com
Visit Stephen King's official website.

www.horrorking.com
This site offers extensive biographical information on Stephen King.

www.stephenkingnews.com
Find updated information about Stephen King at this site.

TRINA McQUEEN

Why We Crave Hot Stuff

Trina McQueen (1943–) has been head of news at CBC, president of the Discovery Channel, and president and COO of CTV Inc. She started her career as an on-air reporter. She is a member of the Canadian News Hall of Fame and the Canadian Broadcast Hall of Fame. She is chair of the Governor General's Performing Arts Awards and serves on the boards of the Canadian Journalism Foundation and the Canadian Television Fund. The essay that appears here was published in *The Globe and Mail* and is an adaptation of a piece that appears in a collection of essays, entitled *Journalism in the New Millennium*, published to commemorate the opening of the University of British Columbia's Sing Tao School of Journalism.

Preparing to Read

In this essay, Trina McQueen considers the role of journalism in our lives and presents an argument for the appeal of "tabloid" news stories. Before you begin reading, consider the appeal of stories about people such as Bill Clinton, O.J. Simpson, Princess Diana, Pamela Anderson, and Britney Spears. Why are we fascinated by the lives of people who are "beset by extremely interesting personal demons"? What kinds of items in the news catch your attention? What kinds of items do you ignore?

Journalism about ethics reminds me of those "thin book" jokes. 1
There isn't much of it. Even when an event seems to have a moral centre, journalists will report around, over, under and through the moral issue.

One case in point: the controversy over providing financial 2 aid to people who had contracted hepatitis C from tainted blood. The controversy was hugely reported. The facts of the matter were well documented. There was extensive background analysis of surrounding issues. What got very little ink and air time were the principles that a society might use in deciding whether compensation was justified. Much was made of the tears streaming down the face of a dissident Liberal who voted with the government. But how had she come to her original decision that compensation was a moral duty? And how had she balanced those principles against the principles used in deciding her political duty? In mainstream journalism, the moral issues were mostly edited out or weren't even there to be edited.

But before we consider what's left out, let's consider what   3
is lately there: Princess Diana, Bill Clinton, Margaret Trudeau, O.J. Simpson, Mr. and Mrs. Matthew Barrett, Pamela Anderson. Beautiful, rich and sensational, their characters are redolent of power and sexuality, and all are beset by extremely interesting personal demons.

Many academics and journalists wonder why there is so   4
much in newspapers, magazines and television about these folks and so little about Chiapas and hydroelectric restructuring. They argue about it at conferences; they write books and columns and theses. It's called the "tabloidization of news." Some of this tabloidization is wild rumour and some of it is outright lies. It is acknowledged that this is deplorable. It is also agreed that some tabloid journalism is true but there is too much of it.

Today, tabloid journalism may have reached terminal   5
velocity. The next U.S. president,* for example, cannot reasonably be expected to provide the wealth of embarrassingly riveting intimate material that the current one does. Yet we can predict that attempts will be made and that the coverage of them will be exuberant.

What distresses some media thinkers about tabloid news is   6
that it fits uncomfortably into the usually accepted noble purposes of news. The word "noble" is not being used sarcastically here. The practice of journalism has, in most democracies, special protections and rights because it is one of the people's defences against tyranny and injustice. Tabloid stories—let's call them hot-stuff stories—are not likely to inspire the people to rise against their oppressors.

So hot stuff is not part of the core competencies of journalism: 7
politics and business. It has no advice for us on our democratic responsibilities and duties. It may tell us something of the character of powerful people, but it is silent on the systems and processes that rule us. It deep-backgrounds not nor does it spin.

Nor is hot stuff related to another accepted use of journalism: 8
to determine whether we are safe. Stories about war, crime,

---

* Bill Clinton was president of the U.S. when this essay was written.

disasters and the environment are all said to answer these important questions. Is my family safe? Is my community safe? Is my world safe? But few of us can learn much that we did not know about safety from Diana's death. We had already decided whether to do up our seat belts and ask our chauffeurs to slow down in Paris tunnels.

Hot stuff is not "news you can use," as are stories about 9 health, consumerism, hobbies and education. And I would argue that hot stuff is not truly human interest, as are features about feisty centenarians and champion pumpkin carvers. The characters in hot stuff are truly characters; the demonic killers, the fabulous babes, the hot commander-in-chief and the angelic princess. They are dramatis personae.

Hot stuff certainly fills one of the chief purposes of 10 journalism, which is to sell copies and increase ratings. *The Columbia Journalism Review*, in an issue devoted to what it calls "money lust," opines that "more so than at any other moment in journalism's history, the news product that lands on newsstands, doorsteps and television screens is hurt by a heightened, unseemly lust at many companies for ever greater profits." The periodical warns that today's "diminished and deracinated journalism ... could lead to a fatal erosion of the ancient bond between journalists and the public."

Certainly if profits are the question, hot stuff is one terrific 11 answer. In the past five years, hot stuff has produced all the ecstatic revenue moments of the news business. From the first shot of the white Bronco on the freeway, O.J. drove CNN ratings, revenue and stock prices. *Time* and *Newsweek* covers on Diana— two each in a row—produced the biggest newsstand sales in the magazines' histories. CBC Newsworld drew huge audiences even at midnight the night Diana died. The numbers for her funeral service were as much as 60 times higher than normal.

The Diana phenomenon was the breathtaking culmination 12 of a change in news choices that had begun years before. The *Times* of London probably shows that change most dramatically. *The Economist* has noted that in a newspaper historically celebrated for its international news (Stanley finds Livingstone, the Charge of the Light Brigade), the *Times'* front page recently had only one foreign piece: it was about Leonardo DiCaprio's new girlfriend.

Rupert Murdoch—he of Fox TV and sensational tabloids— 13 had a heretical vision. Like many other heretical visions, it has become commonplace. The Project for Excellence in Journalism analyzed stories on television, newsmagazines and front pages and concluded that stories of celebrity, gossip and scandal took up 43 per cent of the total space—three times more than 20 years ago. It all seems to have worked out nicely. Profits at most newspaper chains are showing healthy gains, and television news departments have become profit centres.

None of these choices and changes would have been made if 14 the public had not responded. Hot stuff sells. Right now I'm reading every word of *The Globe and Mail*'s comprehensive and straight-faced coverage of the trial of a dominatrix in Richmond Hill, Ont.

There are many theories about why scandal and gossip are so 15 popular.

Margaret Thatcher said "there is no such thing as society: 16 only individuals and their families." In her time, politicians, associations and even nation states began to be seen as ineffective and even irrelevant (incorrectly seen so, in my view). Philosopher Mark Kingwell in his book *Better Living* says this is an age in which "the individual is granted an unprecedented moral, political and epistemological influence." So it is hardly surprising that the intensely personal becomes an important subject of journalism.

A simpler theory is that ordinary people are rather stupid, 17 moving their lips as they read the latest about Brad Pitt. Although there is a definite bozo factor in the population, it is my experience that most people want to expand their experience. Working at the Discovery Channel, where a hot-stuff story is the uncovering of a new dinosaur skeleton, I'm constantly humbled by the knowledge and the intelligence of our public. But Discovery Channel's ratings hit their lowest the week of Aug. 31, 1997. Our viewers had the same fascination for the Diana story as everyone else.

And it was a Story. That is the attraction of hot stuff. Most of 18 it has the pure and elemental force of story. There is a narrative; there are characters. Storytelling is simply the most powerful form of human communication. We are wired to absorb and comprehend the world through constructing, telling and hearing stories.

But journalism is more than storytelling. It is about 19 witnessing faithfully and intelligently, it is about recording carefully, it is about hard questioning and intense listening, and it is about skepticism and empathy. But when all of that is done, there is still a story to tell. And in most traditional journalism, from daily news to documentaries, this is the element most forgotten.

There are dangers to journalistic storytelling: Sometimes the   20
facts won't fit a neat narrative; bits have to be crammed in or left out. But the story rules, and unless journalists are willing to study the craft of storytelling so they can apply it to subjects that are difficult and foreign but relevant, they will fight a losing battle against the natural story. And why should the Devil have all the good tunes?

It is important to consider also that hot-stuff journalism   21
brings the storyteller and audience directly together. Political, business or labour reporters all want and need the respect of those about whom they write. The result is often a kind of insider writing that puts the onus on the viewer or reader to fight his or her way into the inner sanctum where the reporter and subject live. In much of hot-stuff reporting, that's not so. No journalist really cared what Monica Lewinsky or Louise Woodward thought about their press. The reporters were free to think only about the viewers and their needs.

Hot stuff, however, has another appeal: the moral questions   22
it raises. When I was a young journalist, idealistic, arrogant and hopeful, I thought my profession might change the world— expose injustice, inspire citizenship, provoke thought, preserve democracy, increase decency.

I have read a survey of people who described the uses they   23
made of journalism. They found news to be very important in their lives, but they did not say they used it to help them fulfill the duties of citizenship or to decide their economic courses of action or to galvanize themselves into political action. They used the news as something to talk about. How trivial, I thought, raging. They see the world as small talk.

I now think that using the news as something to talk about is   24
terribly important. I think it may even be the way of linking information to personal decisions, what U.S. cultural critic Neil Postman might call adding wisdom to data.

And I suspect that one of the appeals of hot-stuff journalism   25
is that it gives people a simple and effective opportunity to explore and discuss morals and ethics, to test their own standards and principles, to answer Socrates' question, "What is the life that is worth living?"

We make many more ethical decisions than we do political 26 ones. We will be called on to vote perhaps once a year. But every day we face moral decisions, big and small: Should I give money to a squeegee kid? Should I walk back four blocks to return the extra $10 the cashier gave me? Is that man lying on the street drunk or sick? And there are horrific dilemmas: My unborn child is deformed; my dying father begs me to help him go sooner. Or how do we deal with a nasty neighbour, a daughter-in-law of a different religion, a drug-addicted friend? What does it mean to be a good parent, spouse, child or employee? Perhaps when we gather in the lunchroom to discuss O.J. or Paul Bernardo or Paula Jones or Alan Eagleson or Diana, we are really discussing our moral options and ourselves.

There is a paradox here: People clearly seek out and desire 27 information about morality; and they are just as clearly rejecting more of the traditional sources of that information.

But mainstream journalism is curiously absent from this 28 arena. It offers "news you can use" on almost every subject: RRSPs, removing stains, starting a neighbourhood action group, writing a résumé, taking vitamins. It educates us endlessly on politics, personal finance and health. But on ethics and spirituality, the great presses and the great networks can offer only whispers. There are a few religion columns and essays. Business ethics receive some attention, and journalistic ethics are covered. CBC Newsworld, in fact, will begin airing a new program titled *The Moral Divide* in the new year. It is probably the first of its kind. Perhaps it is the first of a trend.

It makes me squeamish to try to "sell" journalism about 29 ethics, but I think it is possible to find utility as well as virtue in the subject.

The more we consider the importance—the value and the 30 wonderful stories of moral and ethical decisions—the more curious the lack of their presence in journalism is. The Greeks had a word for those unacquainted with ethics: *idiot*.

UNDERSTANDING DETAILS

1. Explain the term "tabloidization of news" (paragraph 4).
2. What are the noble purposes of journalism identified by McQueen? What element does she say is forgotten (paragraph 19)? How has her view of the profession of journalism shifted over time?

3. In McQueen's opinion, what is the attraction of "hot stuff" stories?

ANALYZING MEANING

1. McQueen repeatedly uses the example of Princess Diana in her essay. Why is this example particularly significant?
2. Describe McQueen's attitude toward journalistic storytelling. Do you agree with her position?
3. To what extent do you think news stories shape behaviour and public opinion on socially relevant issues? According to McQueen, why is journalism about ethics so rare (paragraph 28)?

DISCOVERING RHETORICAL STRATEGIES

1. In this essay McQueen uses many examples to illustrate the points she is making. Why has she employed so many examples in her essay? Which examples are the most effective?
2. Characterize the tone McQueen uses in this essay. Why has she made this choice? How is the tone appropriate for the subject matter and the audience she is addressing?
3. Explain McQueen's conclusion to this essay. What comment is she making about the importance of ethics in our lives?

MAKING CONNECTIONS

1. McQueen's title has obvious similarities to the title of Stephen King's essay ("Why We Crave Horror Movies"). What do the topics they have chosen to write about have in common?
2. McQueen attributes some of the attraction of "hot stuff" to the appeal of story. How would Michael McKinley ("Opera Night in Canada") respond to McQueen's position? What about Evan Solomon ("The Babar Factor")?
3. Imagine a conversation between Trina McQueen and David Foot ("Boomers Dance to a New Beat"). How do you think Foot would account for the appeal and the growing prevalence of "hot stuff" stories? On what points do you think McQueen and Foot would agree? Where might they disagree? Whose view is closer to your own?

IDEAS FOR DISCUSSION/WRITING

Preparing to Write

Write freely about a major news topic that has captured your attention over the last year. How much detail do you have about this topic? What about it attracted your attention? What retained your interest? What made it a "newsworthy" event? Did your friends or family members share your interest in this story? Why or why not?

Choosing a Topic

1. Editors and producers of news stories constantly have decisions to make about what kinds of stories to pursue and report on as well as what angle should be taken on a story. Write an essay for your school newspaper in which you discuss the role you believe that journalism should play in our society.

2. McQueen suggests that using the news as something to talk about may be a way of exploring personal morals and ethics. Choose a well-known news story such as that of Monica Lewinsky, former Enron executive Michael J. Kopper, former B.C. Premier Gordon Campbell, or Gary Condit and Chandra Levy, and write an essay in which you discuss how you support the behaviour of one of the participants in the story, or argue that he or she should have behaved differently.

3. One of the questions McQueen poses in her essay is "What does it mean to be a good parent, spouse, child or employee?" Choose one of these roles and write an essay in which you answer this question. Include specific details and examples to support your argument.

WEBSITES

www.museum.tv/archives/etv/M/htmlM/mcqueentrin/mcqueentrin.htm
Biographical page on Trina McQueen.

magazine.carleton.ca/2000_Winter/134.htm
Trina McQueen won the A.D. Dunton Award in 1999.

www.rcc.ryerson.ca/ccf/personal/hof/mcquee_t.html
McQueen is a member of the Canadian Association of Broadcasters Hall of Fame.

 www.journalism.ubc.ca/publications.html
Read a review of McQueen's book *Journalism in the New Millennium.*

LAURA ROBINSON

Starving for the Gold

A former member of Canada's national cycling and Nordic skiing teams, Laura Robinson (1958–) is known for her articles on sports and recreation, and particularly women athletes. Her commentaries have appeared in the *Toronto Star*, *The Globe and Mail*, *Canadian Living*, *Toronto Life*, *Saturday Night*, *NOW Magazine*, and *Up Here*, and she wrote a play called *FrontRunners* in her year as writer-in-residence at the University of Calgary. She has also published *She Shoots, She Scores: Canadian Perspectives on Women in Sport* (1997), *Crossing the Line: Sexual Assault in Canada's National Sport* (1998), a book that details the abuse in the world of minor league hockey, and *Black Tights: Women, Sport and Sexuality* (2002). Robinson no longer participates in sports competitively. Instead, she enjoys recreational ski racing, cycling, and running. In this article Robinson portrays a frightening picture of the way young female athletes are treated by their male coaches.

Preparing to Read

As you prepare to read, think about competitive sports and athletes. What does it take for someone to become a top athlete? How does pursuing this level of achievement influence the lives of those athletes? What is the appeal of competitive sports, both to the participants and to the observers? What benefits does one enjoy as a top athlete? What disadvantages or drawbacks might there be? In international competitions, such as the Olympic Games, why are some countries consistently winners in particular sports? Think specifically of sports such as gymnastics and figure skating, where many young women compete. As either a participant or a spectator, what role do you see coaches playing in competitive sports?

Imagine for a moment you are an Olympic athlete. If you   1
pictured a male athlete, try again. Actually, you are a woman, engaged in rigorous year-round training. Now, imagine that your body-fat percentage is less than half the average for a reasonably active woman your age. As a result, your menstrual cycle has stopped; you no longer have a period. You are a textbook case of anorexia nervosa, obsessed with weight and body shape. Perhaps

you are bulimic, and resort to compulsive binge eating, followed by violent purging—vomiting, fasting or the taking of laxatives and diuretics. If you are a junior athlete, in your early teens, you are effectively delaying the onset of puberty and stunting normal growth.

A rational observer would conclude that you are seriously ill. 2 A rational observer would not suspect that you had been driven to these life-threatening disorders by your coach.

According to five women, former members of Canada's 3 national sports teams, their coaches' insistence on excessive thinness threatened their physical health. The athletes' identities have been disguised for reasons that will presently be made clear.

The first woman, while still a junior, was told by her coach 4 that she should "think about" losing weight. "I was 5-foot-5 and weighed 135, but he said, 'Look, all the top women, all the senior women are thin.' So I thought, 'Maybe I am a little chubby.' I started to train for the Calgary Olympics. By late 1987, I weighed less than 110. I was constantly hungry, but I told myself, 'This is a good feeling.' I lost another five pounds the week before our qualifying competition, but I felt extremely weak and didn't make the team." Her standing began to suffer, and two years later she retired from active competition.

Says another woman, "Looking back, I can see how stupid it 5 was. The coaches were saying, 'Hey, we've got the thinnest team around, the girls are looking great.' We didn't have great results, but that didn't seem to matter. I was just a teenager, and a coach's attitude means everything when you're young. Now, I'm angry. They screwed up my mind, and I'll never be able to look at food again the way I did before."

A third athlete, now attending university, wrote in a study of 6 athletic amenorrhea (cessation of the menstrual period): "Pressure was always felt to be lean, and considerable emphasis was placed on being beneath 12 percent body fat. It seemed that the primary goal was to maintain a low body-fat composition. Often, it was felt this was more important than actual performance."

This pressure was applied in unmistakable ways. One coach 7 held contests to see who could leave the most food uneaten on her plate at training camp. Yet another athlete experienced anxiety attacks over the caliper tests and pool dunking (total submersion in order to accurately gauge a subject's body fat). "After the tests, we'd compare results," she says. "Our coach would announce at dinner who had the lowest fat percentage, and the roller-coaster eating would start all over again."

One's first reaction to these charges is a measure of disbelief. 8
We hesitate to think that coaches would do such things—but not so long ago, our athletes were supplied with anabolic steroids because it was "necessary" in order to win, because "everyone else did it." A conspiracy of silence surrounded these activities. Ben Johnson's and Angella Issajenko's physiques were obviously artificial: the changes in their bodies couldn't be attributed to natural causes. Every athlete, every sports journalist and sports official had ample cause for suspicion. No one spoke up.

Next, one might ask: Where are the women coaches, who 9
presumably wouldn't participate in this nonsense? An answer is suggested by the dismissal in February of Ken Porter, Athletics Canada's former director of track and field technical programs. Mr. Porter claimed that he was fired in part because he wished to promote black and women coaches, and deplored the relegation of women to "a ghetto-type position as team chaperone."

Third, why hasn't coaching malfeasance come to light? Well, 10
it has. The Dubin Report, commissioned after Ben Johnson tested positive for anabolic steroids at the 1988 Seoul Olympics, concluded that coaches must assume responsibility for the "health, welfare, moral education and preparation for life of the athlete." Since then, another report, prepared for the federal Minister of Fitness and Amateur Sport, found that athletes feel they are coerced into "harmful practices ... and believe their concerns on the subject of personal harm are ignored." A third report, undertaken on behalf of the same ministry, is due within the next month. It is said to address the issue of physical and sexual abuse.

The reports stack up, the problems are studied to death, and 11
the bad-apple coaches are seldom weeded out.

According to Marion Lay, manager of the Women's Program 12
at Sport Canada (the funding agent for our national teams), "Coaches who manipulate through food and body image are robbing women of their self-esteem and self-respect. But what safe place is there for an athlete who feels abused?"

The women who confided in me asked for anonymity 13
because some of them intend to work within the system; but even those who maintain only a casual interest fear that if they speak out they will be perceived as "traitors" to sport. Ms. Lay's

reaction says it all: "Of course, they can't reveal their identities. There's no mechanism to protect them."

Why this particular form of abuse? Helen Lenskyj, a sports 14 sociologist at the Ontario Institute for Studies in Education, cites the emergence during the 1970s of a prepubescent body type— the very young, very thin gymnast, minus hips and breasts, whose appearance continues to influence judges when it comes to awarding points for artistic merit in the so-called esthetic sports. As a result, coaches everywhere decided that their athletes should look like Soviet gymnast Olga Korbut. In fact, leanness is a factor in both esthetic and endurance sports—to a point. Athletes shouldn't carry extra pounds. The trouble is that not everyone is prepubescent and can't possibly look that way, no matter what she does.

Another factor, according to Marion Lay, is simply resistance 15 to change. The last two decades have seen a dramatic increase in the number of female competitors. Ms. Lay feels that often coaches haven't come to terms with this fact: "There's an attitude of, 'Yes, we'll let you in, but you have to play the game our way, look the way we want you to look.' Women have to give things up in order to enter sports." In other words, the predominant view (because men control sports) is that sports are male. If a woman is going to take part, she'd better resemble a man. If she's got womanly hips, she can't really be an athlete, because real athletes aren't women—and so on, all round the vicious circle.

Little wonder that even so cautious an organization as the 16 Coaching Association of Canada (CAC) raises the shocking notion that nearly one-third of all women athletes have some sort of eating disorder. This figure, culled from unspecified studies, appears in the National Coaching Certification Program's Level III Course—mandatory at a national-team level. The course describes the symptoms of anorexia and bulimia, and provides checklists for their detection, but assumes that the person studying the materials isn't the source of the difficulty. According to Tom Kinsman, the CAC's executive director, "These are problems that weren't talked about before, so we didn't write about them. I hope a new awareness will go a long way in helping people raise the issues with dignity and security. But I can tell you the process won't be nice, clean and clear-cut."

Apparently not. In fact, these issues were under discussion 17 when I began competing over 20 years ago. One of the problems has always been, as Mr. Kinsman admits, if a coach acts improperly, it's up to the sport's governing body, not the CAC, to discipline him—an unlikely scenario if athletes are too intimidated to lodge complaints, and "believe their concerns are ignored" when and if they do so.

It is important not to trivialize the issue here. Demeaning   18 comments and sexist behaviour aren't confined to the world of sports. Yes, it's crude and counterproductive to criticize an athlete in front of her peers. If a coach's first reaction to every woman who passes by is "What a lardass," the message sinks in. These things are wounding, but women everywhere face similar indignities daily. Nor do I suggest that every coach is like Charlie Francis, Ben Johnson's steroid supplier.

A skeptic would argue that plenty of non-athletic teenagers   19 are anorectic, that countless women punish their bodies for doubtful ends (silicone implants and face-lifts spring to mind), that a certain number of women athletes would succumb to eating disorders even with the most supportive and caring coach. As well, an athlete places such extraordinary demands on her body that it's hard to pinpoint cause and effect.

All this may be so. But it can't be denied that Canada's most   20 senior coaches are exacerbating—if not creating—a problem of terrible magnitude.

With devastating results. First, long-term amenorrheics are   21 susceptible to a loss in bone density or osteoporosis (abnormally porous or weakened bones). If these conditions persist, one in three such athletes will suffer a fracture. A 1985 study found that even athletes with irregular (as opposed to nonexistent) periods were nearly four times more prone to stress fractures than those whose periods were uninterrupted.

Next, and more serious, is the fact that athletes engage in   22 regular aerobic activity, which reduces low-density lipoprotein-cholestrol. So far, so good—LDL-C is a contributing factor in coronary ailments. But because an amenorrheic woman's estrogen secretions are low, this positive effect is reversed. Up go the LDL-C levels; up goes the risk of heart disease.

Lastly, it's been predicted that almost 15 per cent of anorectics   23 and bulimics will die over the course of 30 years as a direct result of their disorders. There hasn't been a verifiable instance yet among Canadian athletes—but these are early days.

So the question remains. Why would a coach encourage such   24 dangerous behaviour? Anorectic athletes are too unhealthy to do well over the long haul; you can't compete at the international level if you're starving yourself. Many athletes eventually break down and disappear from view. Unless they're household names, no one notices. They're interchangeable, there are plenty more where they came from.

One answer has been suggested by Ms. Lenskyj, the OISE   25 sports psychologist: it's imitative crime. In addition to underage gymnasts like Olga Korbut, a fair number of older European athletes are much too thin. I could name an entire cycling team whose members are plainly anorectic. They're fast on the road, but they're burning out even faster. Watch for them at the Barcelona Olympics, because they won't be competing in a couple of years.

But Marion Lay's comments earlier about forced make-overs   26 may be closer to the mark. Notes Karin Jasper, a Toronto psychotherapist, "The athletic look is lean with narrow hips, and we have learned that women dislike the size of their hips, stomachs and thighs, those areas most connected with pregnancy." Constant harping on these areas—the first ones to catch a male coach's eye—is enough to stir up instant insecurity. "The ideal male athlete has narrow hips, but that's not normal for women," says Ms. Lenskyj. "Dieting can't change skeletal structure. Only a few girls have bodies that correspond to a male's in terms of leanness. If coaches use weight and fat percentages as a tool to manipulate athletes, it is a form of sexual abuse."

The inescapable conclusion is that the coach, unused to   27 women in sport, wants them to look like boys. Or, failing that, like little girls. This syndrome assumes even more ominous overtones when you consider the inordinate number of women athletes and coaches who wind up as romantic items. I remember a Canadian national team where every member was living with or married to her coach or technical adviser. One hesitates to speculate on these unions. According to Karin Jasper, an unfortunate side-effect of self-starvation is often a loss of sexual drive. The coach gets less than he bargained for in that department. The other possibility is that his fondest wish has come true—he has found someone who's lost all outward signs of womanhood—no breasts, no hips, no period. It makes you wonder whether he might not be happier coaching little boys.

The real imperative here is obviously control over someone   28 less powerful, someone malleable and eager to please. Given that girls begin their athletic careers very young, they don't get a chance to develop into well-rounded human beings in any sense. I personally believe that many male coaches don't like, and are ill-equipped to deal with, grown women. There's no other explanation for the ceaseless humiliation and ridicule— the construction of a closed system where trauma becomes a tool to produce great-looking girls, the thinnest team around.

Is change possible in the world of organized sports? Let's 29 give coaches the benefit of the doubt. Maybe they think that all these things will actually help us bring home lots of medals. Remember the outcry when Canada's skaters "failed" to win Gold and had to "settle for" Bronze. Third-best in the world translated as "not good enough." (The logical extension of this sort of thinking is that, whatever an athlete's body is like, it's never right. It's too fat, too thin, too this or too that.)

When our athletes, being human, made mistakes, they were 30 savagely criticized by the media. As a result, every athlete, man or woman, becomes a performance machine. Karin Jasper is not surprised: "We talk to girls and women about overcoming perfectionism, about not basing their evaluation of themselves on all-or-nothing standards. But athletes are taught to see themselves this way. Either they win, or they don't. When their entire value is based on performance, they won't be viewed as a whole person, they're one-dimensional."

Under these conditions, even an influx of women coaches 31 would do little good. Until the system asks what's best for a given person, not an athlete, it's stuck in the all-or-nothing groove. For male coaches to change, they'd have to re-examine their priorities, their own sexuality, their entire basis for coaching. That's not going to happen.

The real tragedy is that sports can feel so good, so refreshing 32 and exciting and freeing. I entered organized sports when I was 14. I was lucky. I had people who made sure I got to the races on time, but also gave me plenty of books to read. Still, I couldn't help but be affected to some degree. I was obsessed with exercise; I overtrained. That was my response to the pressure, and it wasn't healthy. Even now, I tend to avoid scales. I have to think twice if someone asks me if I consider myself thin. I escaped the worst of it, but my attitudes remain.

One of the women whose own sad story I recounted earlier 33 has started to coach girls between the ages of 12 and 16. "They ask me if they're overweight," she says, "and I tell them, 'If you think you can work with your weight, then you're fine. This is the body God has given you, so enjoy it.'" That's encouraging, as far as it goes—although the fact that 12-year-old athletes anguish about their weight is food for thought. But, because of her experiences, this woman is incapable of saying, "This is the body God has given me, so I'll enjoy it." That has been taken from her and nothing can compensate her for such a loss.

UNDERSTANDING DETAILS

1. Why, in Robinson's opinion, are male coaches starving their female athletes?
2. Why don't the athletes challenge the coaches about their food consumption?
3. According to Robinson, what is necessary for this unhealthy pattern to be broken?

ANALYZING MEANING

1. What does the title tell you about the tone of this article?
2. Do you agree that the use of weight and fat percentages as a tool to manipulate athletes is a form of sexual abuse (paragraph 26)? Why or why not?
3. In her discussion of this problem, Robinson identifies a chain of reaction. She considers both the causes and effects of the coaches' behaviour and the causes and effects of the athletes' behaviour. Rank these four categories according to the amount of attention Robinson gives to each. Which ranks the highest? Why has Robinson chosen this focus?

DISCOVERING RHETORICAL STRATEGIES

1. What is Robinson's main purpose in this essay? Has she achieved her goal? Explain.
2. Describe Robinson's intended audience.
3. At what points in this essay does Robinson analyze the causes of this problem? When does she study the effects? Is a pattern apparent?

MAKING CONNECTIONS

1. Imagine a conversation between Gloria Steinem ("The Politics of Muscle") and Laura Robinson about the role of sport in women's lives. On what points do you think they would agree?

Where might they disagree? Whose view would you most closely agree with?

2. Laura Robinson, Naheed Mustafa ("My Body Is My Own Business"), and Evelyn Lau ("More and More") all discuss body image in their essays. Compare and contrast the views of these three writers.

3. In this essay Laura Robinson discusses her own experience, but she also includes many quotations from others and cites many experts in the field of sports psychology, coaching, and psychotherapy. How does this approach compare to that used by Cecil Foster ("Why Blacks Get Mad") and Judy Rebick ("The Culture of Overwork")?

IDEAS FOR DISCUSSION/WRITING

Preparing to Write

Write freely about participation in sports. Do you participate in any sports? If so, what sports? Do individual sports or team sports hold more appeal? Would you rather be involved in sports recreationally or competitively? What sports do you like to watch? Do sports play a role in your school life now? Should participation in sports be mandatory in elementary school? In secondary school? Why or why not?

Choosing a Topic

1. In an article for a fashion magazine, promote participation in sports for the beneficial effects that it can have. Provide specific examples to generate a convincing argument.

2. Body image is a major concern, particularly for young women. Why do females, especially, work so hard to achieve a certain prescribed image? What effects does this obsession with appearance have? Write an essay for teenagers that points out the problems of striving to be something that does not come naturally.

3. Think of a situation in which your behaviour was influenced either positively or negatively by the expectations of another individual, such as a parent, friend, teacher, or other relative. Write an essay for that person in which you outline and explain the effects of those expectations.

WEBSITES

www.competitor.com
Competitor is an online, interactive sports magazine.

www.sfwed.org/default.php
"Something Fishy," an eating disorder site, provides extensive information on various eating disorders.

KIM PITTAWAY

Dead Wrong

As managing editor and columnist for *Chatelaine* magazine, Kim Pittaway (1964–) tackles a broad range of subjects of concern, particularly to Canadian women. In addition, Pittaway sits on the editorial board of *This Magazine* and the board of directors of the National Magazine Awards Foundation.

Preparing to Read

The following essay, taken from *Chatelaine* magazine, maintains a clear position on our society's attitudes about grieving and reactions to death. As you prepare to read this article, think for a few minutes about funeral customs in our society: Have you attended a funeral service recently? Which rituals seemed particularly vivid to you? Who else attended the funeral? What relationship did the people there have to the deceased? How do people typically react to the death of a family member or close friend? What provisions are made at your school or workplace to deal with the death of a friend or relative? How do you react to the death of celebrities who you don't know personally?

The pundits can't condemn them loudly enough: the celebrity- 1
death rituals of the 1990s, with their flowery shrines and on-camera weeping by complete strangers. It's distasteful, they say. A symptom of our obsession with media-manufactured personalities, when even the kid next door can end up in *People* magazine if she's unlucky enough to be caught in the crossfire of the latest school shooting. A sign of the times, when we feel closer to JFK Jr. or Princess Di or a murdered child than to the people in our own homes.

The naysayers heap scorn on those who line up to leave 2
flowers, bad poetry and children's drawings in remembrance and they mutter about the empty lives of those who have time to indulge in all this artificial grief. They, of course, are too busy being interviewed about the "problem" on yet another current affairs program to have time for such nonsense.

And they're dead wrong.   3

I'll admit that I once agreed with the cynics on the issue of   4
public grieving. I'm not proud to admit it now, but I once took a
side trip to Graceland for the sole purpose of laughing at the
kitschiness of it all and snickered at the visitors crying and leaving
letters at Elvis's grave. (Though Graceland was pretty kitschy,
what with the Jungle Room and its shag-carpeted floors and
ceilings. And, really, when someone says the King is buried in the
backyard, I think "dog" not "rock 'n' roll legend." But there he
was, with his mom, baby brother and Colonel Parker.)

But time and, perhaps more important, personal experiences   5
with grief have made me change my mind. We live in a society
where publicly mourning our personal losses is discouraged.
Your best friend dies? Use a vacation day for the funeral; no,
actually, use half a vacation day—and be back to work after
lunch. Lose your mom or a child? Check your company policy or
collective agreement and you'll likely find you get three days
off. Then move on—and try not to depress your friends and
coworkers with the details. Miscarry? Well, that one doesn't
count at all. After all, you can try again soon.

Still feeling the pain of your loss months later? Get the   6
mourning-after pill: Prozac should take the edge off that grief.
You'll be back on your feet—and back to work—in no time. And
if you must cry, do it quietly in a washroom stall where you
won't disturb others. Death makes people uncomfortable—and
distracts them from their work.

Death has never been a laugh-a-minute conversation starter.   7
But we've become less and less able to talk about it. We let others
prepare our loved ones' bodies for burial. We contract out the
wake. We insist on "happy" funerals, celebrations where wailing
is frowned upon and any sign that this is a grim affair is
discouraged. And if we dress entirely in black, it's only because
we live in Toronto, where dressing entirely in black is compulsory
year-round. We've turned grieving into an industry with
consultants and counselors and books to tell us how to do it
(quick: what stage am I in now?).

Part of that is because, these days, many of us have   8
surprisingly little personal experience with death. Thanks to
modern medicine and the luck of being born Canadian in the
latter half of the 20th century, we haven't lost siblings to smallpox
or flu or uncles and brothers and fathers to war or mothers and

aunts to childbirth. I'm amazed at how many people my age—35—have never even been to a funeral.

So, when a public figure dies or a tragedy like Littleton or Taber turns someone like us into a public figure, we mourn. Why? If we've been lucky enough to be largely untouched by death in our own lives, we get to practise. It's virtual death: we're imagining what it would be like to be Caroline, a sister without a brother, or William and Harry, sons without a mother, or the minister and his wife in Taber, parents coping bravely with the loss of a son.   9

If we've got personal griefs of our own, we vent them vicariously. We talk death to our friends, discuss the unfairness of a life cut short, share our fears about our own mortality—all of the things we wanted to talk about but couldn't when our own loved ones died. And we cry, we buy flowers, we even pen a bad poem or two.   10

I've shed lots of tears for celebrities in the past couple of years. And with each one, I've thought of my friends Catherine and Keitha, my colleague Jim, my grandparents Kay, Edna and Tom, my childhood friends Suzie, Billy, Rhonda, and Michael. Yes, I've mourned those I never knew. But, more important, each time I've remembered those I did.   11

UNDERSTANDING DETAILS

1. What is Pittaway's position on the "celebrity-death rituals" she refers to in paragraph 1? What purpose does Pittaway see these rituals performing?
2. According to Pittaway, what is our society's attitude toward mourning? What evidence does she give to support this point of view?
3. Pittaway claims "these days, many of us have surprisingly little personal experience with death" (paragraph 8). Why is this the case?

ANALYZING MEANING

1. What is Pittaway's purpose in writing this essay? Is she hoping to change people's behaviour or attitudes? Explain your answer.
2. Why do people have the need to mourn when someone dies? Why have we "become less and less able to talk" about death?

3. Explain the title of this essay. In what respect does it have a double meaning?

DISCOVERING RHETORICAL STRATEGIES

1. What tone does Pittaway establish in her essay? What is her reason for creating this particular tone? What is your reaction to it?
2. In paragraphs 1, 4, 9, and 11, Pittaway mentions specific people and places. Who are these people she mentions? What is the effect of the incorporation of these examples?
3. A *euphemism* is the substitution of a deceptively pleasant term for a straightforward, less pleasant one (e.g., "he has gone to a better place" rather than "he died"). Has Pittaway used euphemisms or straightforward terms in her essay? What effect does this choice have?

MAKING CONNECTIONS

1. In "Why We Crave Hot Stuff," Trina McQueen mentions some of the same celebrity examples that Pittaway cites in "Dead Wrong." Is McQueen's attitude to these examples consistent with Pittaway's, or is McQueen one of the people whose attitude Pittaway considers "dead wrong"?
2. Pittaway makes a case for acknowledging grief and not limiting our range of emotions to those that are considered acceptable by our society. How does this compare to Evelyn Lau's comments ("More and More") on socially unacceptable behaviour?
3. Stephen King ("Why We Crave Horror Movies") argues that horror movies are an outlet for our less socially acceptable emotions. How do you think King would respond to Pittaway's position on "celebrity-death rituals"? Do you see the "flowery shrines and on-camera weeping by complete strangers" to be a comparable outlet for less socially acceptable emotions? Why or why not?

IDEAS FOR DISCUSSION/WRITING

Preparing to Write

Write freely about celebrities. What role do celebrities play in your life? What celebrities do you particularly admire? Why?

How do you learn the details about the lives of celebrities? How do you respond to the life events that happen to celebrities? Have you ever visited a celebrity home? To what lengths would you go to meet a celebrity you admired? What type of behaviour crosses the line between admiration and obsession?

Choosing a Topic

1. Celebrities often have profound effects on our lives, either through their behaviour or through things that happen to them. Write an essay in which you outline the effects on you of the actions or the fate of a particular celebrity.
2. The deaths resulting from the September 11, 2001, terrorist attacks on the United States caused an international outpouring of response. Write an essay in which you discuss how those attacks personally affected you or someone you know.
3. In an essay directed to your colleagues, explain the effect of a school or workplace policy that you believe doesn't respond adequately to the needs of the people it governs. Make it clear how consequent behaviour demonstrates the inadequacy of this policy.

WEBSITES

www.chatelaine.com
Pittaway's essay originally appeared in *Chatelaine* magazine.

radio.cbc.ca/programs/ideas/shows/grief/index.html
"Meditations on Grief" was broadcast on CBC's *Ideas* in 1996.

EVELYN LAU

More and More

In *Reference West: A Monthly Review of Books for BC Readers*, poet Robin Skelton said that each of Lau's books merits "attention for its artistry, its vision, and its pure intelligence." An online profile by Anders Blichfeldt identifies "the soul-mark of Evelyn Lau's writing: poignancy and a sense of deep emotional disorientation, at once subtle and nightmarish." Lau (1971–) has typically focused her artistry, her vision, and her poignant portrayals of characters and situations on the dark fringes of society, but she says, "I have always wanted to move from the 'margin' to the 'centre' in my writing; I want to train my powers of observation and imagery on more 'normal' lives than I have previously been able to chronicle."

The hard, gritty details of Evelyn Lau's life first became familiar to many with the success of her book, *Runaway: Diary of a Street Kid*, published in 1989. This autobiographical work that was, five years later, made into a television movie, chronicles Lau's experiences as a 14-year-old runaway who became a prostitute and a junkie on the way to becoming a writer. She has also published three books of poetry, including *Oedipal Dreams* (1992)—which made her the youngest nominee ever for the Governor General's Award for poetry—two books of short stories entitled *Fresh Girls and Other Stories* (1983) and *Choose Me* (1999), and a novel, *Other Women* (1985). Lau's most recent book is *Inside Out: Reflections on a Life So Far*, a collection of personal essays.

Preparing to Read

In this selection, taken from a book entitled *In the Belly of the Beast*, a collection of essays about addiction, Evelyn Lau writes about her childhood addiction to sweets. Before you begin reading, think about the foods that you particularly enjoy. Are there foods for which you get cravings? What typically creates those cravings? How do you respond when you feel cravings for particular foods? Do you deny yourself foods you desire or do you satisfy those desires? At what point does a craving become an addiction?

When did it begin? The sensation of a depthless hole 1 opening up inside me, a cavernous feeling of need. The surrendering to compulsion, which was like getting on a treadmill and not being able to get off. The craving for perfection, so that if I slipped and had one of something "bad," then the day had fallen into disarray, and I had to keep having another and another until the darkness fell.

It began in childhood, innocently. My normal child's greed 2 for candy magnified until it became all-consuming, until the thought of the next candy crowded out every other thought in my mind—though there was little pleasure in eating it beyond the first sweet jolt on the tongue. After that moment it could have been soap or sawdust, but the urge to consume grew in me as steadily as an anxiety attack. The craving was compounded by secrecy, fuelled by being forbidden; this was the most direct route I could see to escaping the control my mother exerted over me, to sabotaging her constant vigilance. Eating surreptitiously was a way of rebelling, of declaring my body my own. I chewed smuggled sweets in bed, tossing the wrappers into the darkness behind the nearby sofa until one day, to my mortification, my father pulled the furniture away from the wall to vacuum and found the dusty, crumpled evidence. I disowned responsibility the way only a child could, claiming I didn't know how the wrappers could have gotten there, it had nothing to do with me.

Once, very early on, this desire for more must have had 3 something to do with pleasure. Once I must have enjoyed a piece of cake or a scoop of ice cream and only wanted more of that enjoyment. But I can no longer remember such a time. I remember instead the growing panic, the desperate need that was a kind of clawing inside me. My quest for satiation blotted out everything in its path. When I was caught stealing a chocolate bar at a local drugstore, my mother screamed and hit at me wildly the moment I came home—was the food she cooked not good enough for me? Did I want people to think she was starving me? I had stolen two chocolate bars that day, but the store detective, emptying out my schoolbag, had found only one—the other had slipped between the pages of a textbook and lodged there. I hid the second bar in a drawer that afternoon, eager to get rid of it but unable to throw it away. The next day I shoved pieces of it into my mouth, fearful and ashamed, chewing miserably until it was gone. The chocolate was dark, it was bitter, it tasted like despair.

I hid sweets in my desk drawers, between the pages of books, 4 even sometimes tucked inside my underwear when I came home from school, so that when my mother searched my pockets for contraband she would come up empty-handed. The food I ate became one of the few things my parents could not always supervise. Whenever they left me alone in the house I hurried to the orange kitchen as soon as I heard the door close behind them. Heart racing, palms sweaty, I ransacked the cupboards, consuming bits of food—a biscuit, a handful of nuts, a mouthful of whisky—that I hoped would not be missed. My mother had begun keeping meticulous track of the food in the house and forcing me every week onto the bathroom scale, which had the opposite effect of what she wanted. I was twelve, thirteen, humiliated by her mocking comments as she peered at the dial on the scale; though I was never more than ten pounds overweight, I must have seemed impossibly fleshy next to her own ninety-pound frame. When she asked me to undress, when she slapped my thighs or pinched my waist or criticized my large breasts, I detached in my mind the same way I would years later when strangers ran their hands over my body. I dreaded these intrusions, and my compulsive behaviour grew in direct proportion to her increasingly frantic efforts to monitor every aspect of my life.

Sometimes I would scurry down to the basement, where I   5 would scoop up spoonfuls of sugar from the sacks in storage, gagging on the crystals lining my tongue. From my mother's purse I stole dimes and quarters that bought greasy paper bags of day-old cookies and doughnuts from the bakery on the way home from school. I still remember the taste of two dozen stale shortbread cookies consumed in a matter of blocks, the thick buttery dust of them in my throat, the nausea that pressed up inside me. I remember hiding behind a tree to finish the cookies before turning the corner onto the block where we lived, cramming them into my mouth; within moments I had reached a sugar and carbohydrate plateau where the clamour inside me dulled and my head felt thick, dazed. The storm of anxiety, of helpless rage, had passed for the time being. The frustration of never being good enough, of knowing I could never please my parents by winning a scholarship to medical school, of realizing that the life they wanted for me was not one I was capable of living. This happened day after day, bags of candies and pastries tearfully choked down along the corridor of streets between school and home. An hour later I would have to eat dinner, feeling so full I could hardly breathe, and that night in bed I would vow never to binge again; the next day I would wake up and be perfect at last.

But the next day I would wake in darkness, not perfect at 6 all, and I knew I would do it again. I was driven by something larger than myself, some force I could hardly explain, let alone fight against. The tension that filled our household after my father lost his job, my mother's obsessive calibration of groceries and finances, my parents' expectations for my future ... These things overpowered me and somehow manifested themselves in my need to keep eating until I was physically incapable of continuing.

It was as if I were trying to reach someplace that didn't exist, 7 except in sleep or death. A perfect blankness, a white light. The search for this obliteration began with food, but later it wouldn't matter if it was food or alcohol or drugs or sleeping with men for money—the feeling was the same one I'd had as a child behind the shut door of my bedroom, gobbling up one candy, barely tasting it, so I could reach for the next, and the next. The urge was to keep going until the anxiety and rage stopped, until as a teenager I threw up or passed out or felt so blank that I no longer was myself.

One afternoon when I was sixteen or seventeen, years after I had 8 run away from home, I sat sullenly in my psychiatrist's office with my parents. I wore a leather jacket and a miniskirt and was barely able to look at them across the room, my father's face lowered in pain and bewilderment, my mother twisting the strap of her purse between her thin fingers. My doctor was coaxing my father into telling me that he loved me.

"Chinese people don't talk about these things," my father 9 tried to explain, haltingly. "It's not our tradition. But she knows. My wife—her mother—even when we couldn't afford any food, she would always have a cup of hot water waiting for her when she came home from school."

"She needs to hear you say it, Dad. Can you look at her and 10 tell her?"

In a moment of what, even then, I knew was bravery worthy 11 of a medal, my father lifted his face and looked straight at me. "Of course I love you," he said.

That was a moment I would remember from the session, 12 though at the time I stared back at him hard-eyed. Also his mention of the hot water, how I winced at the pathos of that, and how my mother clutched my arm as my parents left the doctor's office and tried to persuade me to come home with them for dinner. Was it so simple as food equalling love? Was it their love I was after, in all the years of my life when I threw one thing after another into that bottomless well, and all of those things— food, drugs, alcohol, men—simply fell in and disappeared? What happened in the beginning that caused this? Something my mother did when I was an infant at her breast? Did she not come when I cried, did she hold me too tightly or turn her back when she should have stayed? Was there a chemical deficiency in my brain, a lack of serotonin, a predisposition toward these moods and impulses and compulsions? Was it a milder version of the mental illnesses that had stunted the lives of several of my mother's sisters, consigning them to a lifetime of antipsychotic medications and hospitals? Was it nature or nurture, creation or circumstance?

One substance replaced another, changing with the seasons. I   13
gave up food for drugs, cigarettes for alcohol, moved fluidly back and forth, tried various combinations. As a teenager it was marijuana, LSD, tranquilizers, painkillers and cocaine. I binged on these drugs, finding a more complete oblivion through chemicals, a more extensive loss of self, of memory and pain. Candy is dandy, but liquor is quicker ... and nothing is so quick as a few lines of white glitter, a syringe dripping with a morphine derivative. Even when the acid gave me bad trips, even when the world morphed into a greater nightmare than it already seemed, being high was still better than staying inside myself. I sought through drugs to be somebody else—anybody else.

   At nineteen, when I stopped smoking three packs of   14
cigarettes a day, I began my mornings instead with a drink in hand. That drink led to another and another, as the day devolved and the sun spiralled down in the sky. I no longer used street drugs, but started to mix alcohol with the prescription tranquilizers—Halcion, Ativan, Xanax—I obtained from various men, including the middle-aged married psychiatrist with whom I had a destructive yearlong affair. Twenty was a lost year, a calendar of blackout evenings, mornings where I could remember nothing of what I had said or done the night before, or how I had gotten home in the end. When I stopped taking pills, the bulimia that had come and gone in earlier times became one long

unbroken stretch of binging and purging. I was throwing up seven or eight times a day and spending nearly as much on food as I had on drugs or alcohol.

Once, in my early twenties, I went out for lunch with two of   15 my aunts. I was hungover from the night before. I could barely touch the greasy dim sum, and I lost my temper when one of them kept insisting that I eat. When we were ready to leave, I said I'd wait for them outside while they used the washroom. A few minutes later I changed my mind and went to use the bathroom myself; as soon as I opened the door I could hear them talking about me behind the closed doors of their stalls.

"I know why she's the way she is," one aunt declared, in   16 Chinese. "It's not her fault. Her mother stayed in bed too long when she was pregnant, she didn't move around enough. I think it did something to Evelyn's brain, that's why she's like this. She can't help it, she's disturbed ..."

I turned on my heel and slammed the door on my way out,   17 enraged. How dare she assume there was something wrong with me? I refused to believe it myself. Yet that was how my whole family had dealt with my running away and becoming involved in drugs and prostitution—I was "mentally ill," which, in an odd way, absolved me of blame and responsibility. Once, to my psychiatrist's amusement, he received a phone call from this aunt, who insisted that I must be hearing voices; it was the only explanation for my behaviour. In her way, she believed I was pure, that none of it was my choice, that no one sane would choose such a life.

Was it a choice? Many people believe addicts are weak, that their   18 suffering stems from a lack of willpower, that an addiction or a dependency can be overcome by strength of character alone. Intellectually I lean toward this belief as well, but emotionally it is a different story. I think of how many people would like to have more than one cookie out of the bag they bring home from the supermarket. Some of them do have several cookies, savouring them, then place the rest of the bag in the cupboard. Others have a harder time doing that; they eat too many cookies, half the package perhaps, then feel repentant and disgusted with themselves. But imagine ratcheting that urge up further. Imagine that you are unable to sleep because of the cookies in your cupboard, that you can't work or read or leave the house knowing the uneaten cookies are there. That a feeling of anxiety begins to build in you, a desperation and a kind of anger, until you break down and cram the cookies into your mouth several at a time, devouring them until you throw up. If, after you throw up, there are still some cookies left in the bag, you have to keep eating them, even though by then you are sick of their taste and texture. If there are ten bags of cookies and no way that you can eat them all, you will have to bury the rest of them immediately at the bottom of the garbage pail—first crushing them and soaking them in water, say, to prevent your retrieving them later—in order to be rid of them.

Is this behaviour something that can be changed by force of   19
will? The feelings behind that scenario: what are they? Are they symptoms of some other hunger, some emotional lack or faulty wiring in the brain? I don't know, but I have lived with those feelings, those uncontrollable impulses, all my life.

I don't like the word "addiction." It conjures up dismal   20
pictures of sober or lapsed strangers sitting together talking about their dependencies week after week, year after year, mired in the language of abstinence and recovery. I find myself impatient with people who identify themselves so closely with their affliction. There is something in me that scorns the weak-chinned, bleary-eyed, sad-sack faces of recovering addicts whose lives and vocabulary have been overtaken by their illness. And yet the emotions they cycle through, the force that dictates their behaviour, must not be so different from mine.

Sometime toward my mid-twenties, the fog began to clear.   21
Your body tires, your life changes, you climb out of the whirlpool and onto dry land. Certainly there were still days when I ate or drank to the point of vomiting, there were unhealthy relationships to become obsessed with, but I didn't lose myself in the same way any more. With adulthood came the knowledge that emotions and experiences that seemed decimating at the time would pass, and sooner rather than later. I was no longer always facing the end of the world.

I became like everyone around me, with a mortgage and   22
RRSPs and responsibilities, and if there were nights when I went out and drank too many martinis or glasses of wine, then stayed up all night throwing up in the bathroom—well, who didn't?

Now I'm almost thirty, the once unimaginable age. "Time to give   23
up childish things," my psychiatrist chides. Once in a while I still binge and purge, but one lapse no longer triggers a six-month

cycle as it used to. I often eat too much to quell some anxiety or emptiness, but now I can usually stop it from escalating into the sort of frenzy that leads to forced vomiting. Sometimes I drink vast quantities of alcohol and lose myself, but this is no different from the behaviour of many people I know. It's never a problem for me to have only one glass of wine at dinner, or to keep alcohol around the apartment without consuming it, or to go for days without a drink. Illegal drugs haven't interested me for a decade, and pills—well, there are vials of tranquilizers in my drawer that have lain there untouched for eight years. But a little part of me is still glad when I get a headache. Even the small amount of codeine in several Tylenol 1's makes me feel more confident and slightly elevated. So, after all these years of almost never taking a sleeping pill or a painkiller, I must still be cautious. The old desire for oblivion is not gone, only lying dormant, as are the temptation to slip into sleep rather than live through a difficult emotion and the longing to give in. And yet I know that if I give in, the next day will be harder as a result. That in the morning the previous day's anxiety, temporarily muffled by pills, will be back—tripled, quadrupled. That my hands will shake, my nerves will be frayed, and I will be less armoured than before.

The compulsions, the feelings of need and lack, are still there. 24 They are always there. At one time, it was worth any price to get away from them—to feel bright and confident, to find the clearing in the forest where the sun streamed down and I was complete. I think now that these urges will stay with me for the rest of my life. The feelings will ebb and flow; maybe one day things will be a lot easier, and maybe they won't. At least I no longer wake up every morning expecting to be perfect, then destroying myself if I am not. Though I would never have believed it as a teenager, you do move beyond things, outgrow the person you were. Sometimes, just by staying alive, you find you have become someone who can live in the world after all.

UNDERSTANDING DETAILS

1. What are the immediate reasons that Evelyn Lau begins overeating as a child?
2. How does Lau's family respond to her eating behaviour?
3. Explain why Lau's father has difficulty telling his daughter that he loves her.

ANALYZING MEANING

1. Why does Lau overeat? How does it make her feel? What are the effects of her overeating?
2. In what way is Lau's overeating in childhood connected to her drinking, drug use, and promiscuity later in her life? What causes all these behaviours?
3. At her current age is Lau an addict? Why or why not?

DISCOVERING RHETORICAL STRATEGIES

1. Lau uses many specific examples in her essay. Explain the effect of these examples on the overall effectiveness of "More and More."
2. Identify Lau's intended audience in this essay. What leads you to this conclusion?
3. Describe the tone of Lau's essay. Is this an appropriate tone for an essay on this topic? What language choices contribute to creating this tone?

MAKING CONNECTIONS

1. Evelyn Lau, Steven Heighton ("Elegy in Stone"), and Karen Connelly ("Touch the Dragon") are all poets as well as writers of prose. What aspects of their essays reflect their poetic interests?
2. Evelyn Lau and Laura Robinson ("Starving for the Gold") both address the topic of eating disorders in girls. What do these two women have in common in writing about this topic? Imagine they were having a conversation about the causes of eating disorders in girls. Do you think they would generally agree with each other, or are there significant differences in the causes they see for eating disorders?
3. Compare the cause/effect strategies used by Lau with those used by Kim Pittaway ("Dead Wrong") or Trina McQueen ("Why We Crave Hot Stuff"). Which essay do you find the most effective? Explain why.

IDEAS FOR DISCUSSION/WRITING

Preparing to Write

Write freely about addiction. What is an addiction? What causes addiction? What types of things do people become addicted to? How is addiction generally viewed in our society? How can a person overcome an addiction?

Choosing a Topic

1. Write about a type of addiction you have experienced personally or that you've witnessed in someone else. Explain the causes of the addiction and the effects both on the addict and on others.
2. Lau says that she doesn't like the word *addiction*. From your own perspective explain the effect of the word *addiction* or *addict*. Is there an alternative word that has less negative connotations?
3. Lau's addictive behaviour begins with food. Write an essay about the role of food in your family. How is food viewed? What emotions are attached to food? What associations or expectations accompany food in your family?

WEBSITES

www.nwpassages.com/bios/lau.asp
This site provides a biography of Evelyn Lau, as well as a list of books published by Northwest Passages.

www.januarymagazine.com/profiles/lau.html
A *January Magazine* interview with Lau.

www.coolwomen.org/coolwomen/cwsite.nsf/f85b4e3889247adc 8525645600629c11/1f13e01c95b6cfe3852565d2005c4055?Open Document&Highlight=0,Evelyn
In-depth biography of Evelyn Lau.

CHAPTER 9

ARGUMENT/ PERSUASION

Inciting People to Thought or Action

Almost everything we do or say is an attempt to persuade. Whether we dress up to impress a potential employer or argue openly with a friend about an upcoming election, we are trying to convince various people to see the world our way. Some aspects of life are particularly dependent upon persuasion. Think, for example, of all the television, magazine, and billboard ads we see urging us to buy certain products, or of the many impassioned appeals we read and hear on such controversial issues as school dress codes, abortion, gun control, and nuclear energy. Religious leaders devote their professional lives to convincing people to live a certain way and believe in certain religious truths, whereas scientists and mathematicians use rigorous logic and natural law to convince us of various hypotheses. Politicians make their living persuading voters to elect them and then support them throughout their terms of office. In fact, anyone who wants something from another person or agency, ranging from federal money for a research project to a new bicycle for Christmas, must use some form of persuasion to get what he or she desires. The success or failure of this type of communication is easily determined: If the people being addressed change their actions or attitudes in favour of the writer or speaker, the attempt at persuasion has been successful.

Defining Argument/Persuasion

The terms *argument* and *persuasion* are often used interchangeably, but one is actually a subdivision of the other. Persuasion names a purpose for writing. To persuade your readers is to convince them to think, act, or feel a certain way. Much of the writing you have been doing in this book has persuasion as one of its goals: A description of an African tribe has a "dominant impression" you want your readers to accept; in an essay comparing various ways of celebrating the New Year, you are trying to convince your readers to believe that these similarities and differences actually exist; and in writing an essay exam on the causes of the strife in the Middle East, you are trying to convince your instructor that your reasoning is clear and your conclusions sound. In a sense, some degree of persuasion propels all writing.

More specifically, however, the process of persuasion involves appealing to one or more of the following: to reason, to emotion, or to a sense of ethics. An argument is an appeal predominantly to your readers' reason and intellect. You are working in the realm of argument when you deal with complex issues that are debatable; opposing views (either explicit or implicit) are a basic requirement of argumentation. But argument and persuasion are taught together because good writers are constantly blending these three appeals and adjusting them to the purpose and audience of a particular writing task. Although reason and logic are the focus of this chapter, you need to learn to use all three methods of persuasion as skillfully as possible to write effective essays.

An appeal to reason relies upon logic and intellect and is usually most effective when you are expecting your readers to disagree with you in any way. This type of appeal can help you change your readers' opinions or influence their future actions through the sheer strength of logical validity. If you wanted to argue, for example, that pregnant women should refrain from smoking cigarettes, you could cite abundant statistical evidence that babies born to mothers who smoke have lower birth weights, more respiratory problems, and a higher incidence of sudden infant death syndrome than the children of nonsmoking mothers. Because smoking clearly endangers the health of the unborn child, reason dictates that mothers who wish to give birth to the healthiest possible babies should avoid smoking during pregnancy.

Emotional appeals, however, attempt to arouse your readers' feelings, instincts, senses, and biases. Used most profitably when your readers already agree with you, this type of essay generally validates, reinforces, and/or incites in an effort to get your readers to share your feelings or ideas. In order to urge our lawmakers to impose stricter jail sentences for alcohol abuse, you might describe a recent tragic accident involving a local twelve-year-old girl who was killed by a drunk driver as she rode her bicycle to school one morning. By focusing on such poignant visual details as the condition of her mangled bike, the bright blood stains on her white dress, and the anguish on the faces of parents and friends, you could build a powerfully persuasive essay that would be much more effective than a dull recitation of impersonal facts and nationwide statistics.

An appeal to ethics, the third technique writers often use to encourage readers to agree with them, involves cultivating a sincere, honest tone that will establish your reputation as a reliable, qualified, experienced, well-informed, and knowledge-able person whose opinions on the topic under discussion are believable because they are ethically sound. Such an approach is often used in conjunction with logical or emotional appeals to foster a verbal environment that will result in minimal resistance from its readers. Michael Jordan, former Chicago Bulls basketball star, is an absolute master at creating this ethical, trustworthy persona as he, along with Tweety Bird, coaxes his television viewers to purchase the latest long distance calling plan. In fact, the old gag question "Would you buy a used car from this man?" is our instinctive response to all forms of attempted persuasion, whether the salesperson is trying to sell us Puppy Chow or gun control, hair spray or school prayer. The more believable we are as human beings, the better chance we will have of convincing our audience.

The following student paragraph is directed primarily toward the audience's logical reasoning ability. Notice that the writer states her assertion and then gives reasons to convince her readers to change their ways. The student writer also brings both emotion and ethics into the argument by choosing her words and examples with great precision.

> Have you ever watched a pair of chunky thighs, a jiggling posterior, and an extra-large sweatshirt straining to cover a beer belly and thought, "Thank God I don't look like that! I'm in pretty good

shape ... for someone my age." Well, before you become too smug and self-righteous, consider what kind of shape you're really in. Just because you don't look like Shamu the Whale doesn't mean you're in good condition. What's missing, you ask? Exercise. You can diet all day, wear the latest slim-cut designer jeans, and still be in worse shape than someone twice your age if you don't get a strong physical workout at least three times a week. Exercise is not only good for you, but it can also be fun—especially if you find a sport that makes you happy while you sweat. Your activity need not be expensive: Jogging, walking, basketball, tennis, and handball are not costly, unless you're seduced by the glossy sheen of the latest sporting fashions and accessories. Most of all, however, regular exercise is important for your health. You can just as easily drop dead from a sudden heart attack in the middle of a restaurant when you're slim and trim as when you're a slob. Your heart and lungs need regular workouts to stay healthy. So do yourself a favour and add some form of exercise to your schedule. You'll feel better and live longer, and your looks will improve, too!

Thinking Critically by Using Argument/Persuasion

Argument and persuasion require you to present your views on an issue through logic, emotion, and good character in such a way that you convince an audience of your point of view. This rhetorical mode comes at the end of this book because it is an extremely complex and sophisticated method of reasoning. The more proficient you become in this strategy of thinking and presenting your views, the more you will get what you want out of life (and out of school). Winning arguments means getting the pay raises you need, the refund you deserve, and the grades you've worked so hard for.

In a successful argument, your logic must be flawless. Your conclusions should be based on clear evidence, and your evidence must be organized in such a way that it builds to an effective, convincing conclusion. You should constantly have your purpose and audience in mind as you build your case; at the same time, issues of emotion and good character should support the flow of your logic.

Exercising your best logical skills is extremely important to all phases of your daily survival—in and out of the classroom. Following a logical argument in your reading and presenting a logical response to your course work are the hallmarks of a good student. Right now, put your best logic forward and work on your reasoning and persuasive abilities in the series of exercises below. Isolate argument and persuasion from the other rhetorical strategies so that you can practise them and strengthen your ability to argue before you combine them with other methods.

1. Bring to class two magazine ads—one ad that tries to sell a product and another that tries to convince the reader that a particular action or product is wrong or bad (unhealthy, misinterpreted, politically incorrect, etc.). How does each ad appeal to the reader's logic? How does the advertiser use emotion and character in his or her appeal?

2. Think of a recent book you have read. How could you persuade a friend either to read or not to read this book?

3. Fill in the following blanks: The best way to _____ is to _____ . (For example, "The best way to <u>lose weight</u> is to <u>exercise</u>.") Then, list ways you might persuade a reader to see your point of view in this statement.

Reading and Writing Persuasive Essays

Although persuasive writing can be approached essentially in three different ways—logically, emotionally, and/or ethically—our stress in this chapter is on logic and reason because they are at the heart of most college writing. As a reader, you will see how various forms of reasoning and different methods of organization affect your reaction to an essay. Your stand on a particular issue will control the way you process information in argument and persuasion essays. As you read the essays in this chapter, you will also learn to recognize emotional and ethical appeals and the different effects they create. In your role as writer, you need to be fully aware of the options available to you as you compose. Although the basis of your writing will be logical argument, you will see that you can learn to control your readers' responses to your essays by choosing your evidence carefully, organizing it wisely, and seasoning it with the right amount of emotion and ethics—depending on your purpose and audience.

How to Read Persuasive Essays

Preparing to Read. As you prepare to read the essays in this chapter, spend a few minutes browsing through the preliminary material for each selection: What does Judy Rebick's title, "The Culture of Overwork," prepare you for? What can you learn from scanning Jennifer Cowan's essay, "TV Me Alone," and reading its synopsis in the Rhetorical Table of Contents?

Also, you should bring to your reading as much information as you can from the authors' biographies: Why do you think Jennifer Cowan writes about keeping television out of public places in "TV Me Alone"? Does she have the appropriate qualifications to teach us about the proper time and place for TV? What is the source of Juanita Polegi's interest in "There's a Better Environmental Way to Farm"? For the essays in this chapter that present two sides of an argument, what biographical details prepare us for each writer's stand on the issue? Who were the original audiences for these pro and con arguments?

Last, before you read these essays, try to generate some ideas on each topic so that you can take the role of an active reader. In this text, the Preparing to Read questions will ready you for this task. Then, you should speculate further on the general subject of the essay: Do you believe that the collection of personal data is dangerous or desirable (Lawrence Solomon, "Too Much Privacy Can Be Hazardous to the Person")? What do you want to know from Rebick about workaholics?

Reading. Be sure to record your spontaneous reactions to the persuasive essays in this chapter as you read them for the first time: What are your opinions on each subject? Why do you hold these opinions? Be especially aware of your responses to the essays representing opposing viewpoints at the end of the chapter; know where you stand in relation to each side of the issues here.

Use the preliminary material before an essay to help you create a framework for your responses to it: Who was Jennifer Cowan's primary audience when her essay was first published? In what ways is the tone of her essay appropriate for that audience? What motivated Rebick to publish her arguments on the problem of workaholism? Why is Stein so interested in Canada's ability to speak up and make a difference? Which argument do you find most convincing?

Your main job at this stage of reading is to determine each author's primary assertion or proposition (thesis statement) and to create an inquisitive environment for thinking critically about the essay's ideas. In addition, take a look at the questions after each selection to make sure you are picking up the major points of the essay.

Rereading. As you reread these persuasive essays, notice how the writers integrate their appeals to logic, to emotion, and to ethics. Also, pay attention to the emphasis the writers place on one or more appeals at certain strategic points in the essays: How does Cowan integrate these three appeals in "TV Me Alone"? Which of these appeals does she rely on to help bring her essay to a close? How persuasive is her final appeal? What combination of appeals does Rebick use in "The Culture of Overwork"? In what ways does the tone of her writing support what she is saying? How does she establish the tone?

Also, determine what other rhetorical strategies help these writers make their primary points. How do these strategies enable each writer to establish a unified essay with a beginning, a middle, and an end?

Then, answer the questions after each reading selection to make certain you understand the essay on the literal, interpretive, and analytical levels in preparation for the discussion/writing assignments that follow.

For a list of guidelines for the entire reading process, see the checklists on pages 17–18 of the Introduction.

How to Write Persuasive Essays

Preparing to Write. The first stage of writing an essay of this sort involves, as usual, exploring and then limiting your topic. As you prepare to write your persuasive paper, first try to generate as many ideas as possible—regardless of whether they appeal to logic, emotion, or ethics. To do this, review the prewriting techniques in the Introduction and answer the Preparing to Write questions. Then, choose a topic. Next, focus on a purpose and a specific audience before you begin to write.

Writing. Most persuasive essays should begin with an assertion or a proposition stating what you believe about a certain issue. This thesis should generally be phrased as a debatable statement, such as, "If the national government instituted a guaranteed income supplement for seasonal workers, it would provide security for workers in the natural resource sectors of the economy and minimize the draw on the Employment Insurance Fund." At this point in your essay, you should also justify the significance of the issue you will be discussing: "Such a program would help to support workers in industries vital to Canada's economy, would help to maintain the EI fund for people who become unexpectedly out of work, and would improve the image of seasonal workers among Canadians."

The essay should then support your thesis in a variety of ways. This support may take the form of facts, figures, examples, or opinions by recognized authorities, case histories, narratives/anecdotes, comparisons, contrasts, or cause/effect studies. This evidence is most effectively organized from least to most important when you are confronted with a hostile audience (so that you can lead your readers through the reasoning step by step) and from most to least important when you are facing a supportive audience (so that you can build on their loyalty and enthusiasm as you advance your thesis). In fact, you will be able to engineer your best support if you know your audience's opinions, feelings, and background before you write your essay, so that your intended "target" is as clear as possible. The body of your essay will undoubtedly consist of a combination of logical, emotional, and ethical appeals—all leading to some final summation or recommendation.

The concluding paragraph of a persuasive essay should restate your main assertion (in slightly different terms from those in your original statement) and should offer some constructive recommendations about the problem you have been discussing (if you haven't already done so). This section of your paper should clearly bring your argument to a close in one final attempt to move your audience to accept or act on the viewpoint you present. Let's look more closely now at each of the three types of appeals used in such essays: logical, emotional, and ethical.

To construct a *logical* argument, you have two principal patterns available to you: inductive reasoning or deductive reasoning. The first encourages an audience to make what is called an "inductive leap" from several particular examples to a single, useful generalization. In the case of a guaranteed income supplement, you might cite a number of examples, figures, facts, and case studies illustrating the effectiveness of a guaranteed income supplement plan, thereby leading to your firm belief that implementation of this program is essential to the survival of many of Canada's core industries. Used most often by detectives, scientists, and lawyers, the process of inductive reasoning addresses the audience's ability to think logically by moving it systematically from an assortment of selected evidence to a rational and ordered conclusion.

In contrast, deductive reasoning moves its audience from a broad, general statement to particular examples supporting that statement. In writing such an essay, you would present your thesis statement about a guaranteed income supplement first and then offer clear, orderly evidence to support that belief. Although the mental process we go through in creating a deductive argument is quite sophisticated, it is based on a three-step form of reasoning called the *syllogism*, which most logicians believe is the foundation of logical thinking. The traditional syllogism has:

a major premise: Seasonal workers are essential to the Canadian economy;

a minor premise: All workers must make enough money, through wages and/or supplements, to support themselves year round;

and a conclusion: Therefore, for the survival of the Canadian economy, seasonal workers need to receive enough money, through wages and/or supplements, to live adequately for the entire year.

As you might suspect, this type of reasoning is only as accurate as its original premises, so you need to be careful with the truth of the premises as well as with the logical validity of your argument.

In constructing a logical argument, you should take great care to avoid the two types of fallacies in reasoning found most frequently in college papers: giving too few examples to support an assertion and citing examples that do not represent the assertion fairly. If you build your argument on true statements and abundant, accurate evidence, your essay will be effective.

Persuading through *emotion* necessitates controlling your readers' instinctive reactions to what you are saying. You can accomplish this goal in two different ways: (1) by choosing your words with even greater care than usual and (2) by using figurative language whenever appropriate. In the first case, you must be especially conscious of using words that have the same general denotative (or dictionary) meaning but bear decidedly favourable or unfavourable connotative (or implicit) meanings. For example, notice the difference between *slender* and *scrawny*, *patriotic* and *chauvinistic*, or *compliment* and *flattery*. Your careful attention to the choice of such words can help readers form visual images with certain positive or negative associations that subtly encourage them to follow your argument and adopt your opinions. Second, the effective use of figurative language—especially similes and metaphors—makes your writing more vivid, thus triggering your readers' senses and encouraging them to accept your views. Both of these techniques will help you manipulate your readers into the position of agreeing with your ideas.

Ethical appeals, which establish you as a reliable, well-informed person, are accomplished through (1) the tone of your essay and (2) the number and type of examples you cite. Tone is created through deliberate word choice: Careful attention to the mood implied in the words you use can convince your readers that you are serious, friendly, authoritative, jovial, or methodical—depending on your intended purpose. In like manner, the examples you supply to support your assertions can encourage readers to see you as experienced, insightful, relaxed, or intense. In both of these cases, winning favour for yourself will usually also gain approval for your opinions.

Rewriting. To rework your persuasive essays, you should play the role of your readers and impartially evaluate the different appeals you have used to accomplish your purpose:

- Is your thesis statement clear?
- Is the main thrust of your essay argumentative (an appeal to reason)?
- Will the balance of these appeals effectively accomplish your purpose with your intended audience?
- Does your conclusion restate your argument, make a recommendation, and bring your essay to a close?

You should also look closely at the way your appeals work together in your essay:

- When you use logic, is that section of your paper arranged through either inductive or deductive reasoning?
- Is that the most effective order to achieve your purpose?
- In appealing to the emotions, have you chosen your words with proper attention to their denotative and connotative effects?

- Have you chosen examples carefully to support your thesis statement?
- Are these examples suitable for your purpose and your audience?

Any additional guidance you may need as you write and revise your persuasive essays is furnished on pages 29–30 of the Introduction.

Student Essay: Argument/Persuasion at Work

The following essay, written by an American student, uses all three appeals to make its point about the power of language in shaping our view of the world. First, the writer sets forth her character references (ethical appeal) in the first paragraph, after which she presents her thesis and its significance in paragraph 2. The support for her thesis is a combination of logical and emotional appeals, heavy on the logical, as the writer moves her paragraphs from general to particular in an effort to convince her readers to adopt her point of view and adjust their language use accordingly.

The Language of Equal Rights

Ethical appeal Up front, I admit it. <u>I've been a card-carrying feminist since junior high school. I want to see an Equal Rights Amendment to the U.S. Constitution, equal pay for equal—and comparable—work, and I go dutch on dates. Furthermore, I am quite prickly on the subject of language. I'm one of those women who bristles at terms like</u> Emotional appeal <u>*lady doctor* (you know they don't mean a gynecologist), *female policeman* (a paradox), and *mankind* instead of *humanity* (are they really talking about me?).</u>

Many people ask "How important are mere words, anyway? You know what we really mean." A question like this ignores the symbolic and psychological importance of language. <u>What words</u> Assertion <u>"mean" can go beyond what a speaker or writer consciously in-</u> or thesis <u>tends, reflecting personal and cultural biases that run so deep that</u> statement <u>most of the time we aren't even aware they exist. "Mere words" are</u>
Significance <u>incredibly important: They are our framework for seeing and un-</u>
of assertion <u>derstanding the world.</u>

Logical appeal

Man, we are told, means woman as well as man, just as *mankind* supposedly stands for all of humanity. In the introduction of a sociology textbook I recently read, the author was anxious to demonstrate his awareness of the controversy over sexist language and to assure his female readers that, despite his use of non-inclusive terms, he was not forgetting the existence or importance of women in society. He was making a conscious decision to continue to use *man* and *mankind* instead of *people, humanity*, etc., for ease of expression and aesthetic reasons. "Man" simply sounds better, he explained. I flipped through the table of contents and found "Man and Society," "Man and Nature," "Man and Technology," and, near the end, "Man and Woman." At what point did *Man* quit meaning people and start meaning men again? The writer was obviously unaware of the answer to this question, because it is one he would never think to ask. Having consciously addressed the issue only to dismiss it, he reverted to form.

Examples organized deductively

Emotional appeal

Logical appeal

The very ambiguity of *man* as the generic word for our species ought to be enough to combat any arguments that we keep it because we all "know what it means" or because it is both traditional and sounds better. And does it really sound all that much better, or are we just more used to it, more comfortable? Our own national history proves that we can be comfortable with a host of words and attitudes that strike us as unjust and ugly today. A lot of white folks probably thought that Negroes were getting pretty stuffy and picky when they began to insist on being called blacks. After all, weren't there more important things to worry about, like civil rights? But black activists recognized the emotional and symbolic significance of having a name that was parallel to the name that the dominant race used for itself—a name equal in dignity, lacking that vaguely alien, anthropological sound. After all, whites were called *Caucasians* only in police reports, textbooks, and autopsies. *Negro* may have sounded better to people in the bad old days of blatant racial bigotry, but we adjusted to the word *black* and have now moved on to African American, and more and more people of each race are adjusting to the wider implications and demands of practical, as well as verbal labels.

Examples organized deductively

Emotional appeal

Logical appeal

In a world where *man* and *human* are offered as synonymous terms, I don't think it is a coincidence that women are still vastly underrepresented in positions of money, power, and respect. Children grow up learning a language that makes maleness the norm for anything that isn't explicitly designated as female, giving little girls a very limited corner of the universe to picture themselves in. Indeed, the language that nonfeminists today claim to be inclusive was never intended to cover women in the first place. "One man, one vote" and "All men are created equal" meant just that. Women had to fight for decades to be included even as an afterthought; it took constitutional amendments to convince the government and the courts that women are human, too.

Examples organized deductively

Conclusion/ restatement
The message is clear. <u>We have to start speaking about people, not men, if we are going to start thinking in terms of both women and men. A "female man" will never be the equal of her brother</u>.

Some Final Thoughts on Argument/Persuasion

As you can tell from the selections that follow, the three different types of persuasive appeals usually complement each other in practice. Most good persuasive essays use a combination of these methods to achieve their purposes. Good persuasive essays also rely on various rhetorical modes we have already studied—such as example, process analysis, division/classification, comparison/ contrast, definition, and cause/effect—to advance their arguments. In the following essays, you will see a combination of appeals at work and a number of different rhetorical modes furthering the arguments.

Argument/Persuasion in Review

Reading Argument and Persuasion Essays

Preparing to Read

- What assumptions can you make from the essay's title?
- Can you guess what the general mood of the essay is?
- What is the essay's purpose and audience?
- What does the synopsis in the Rhetorical Table of Contents tell you about the essay?
- What can you learn from the author's biography?
- Can you guess what the author's point of view toward the subject is?
- What are your responses to the Preparing to Read questions?

Reading

- What is the author's main assertion or thesis?
- What are the primary appeals at work in the essay?
- Did you preview the questions that follow the essay?

Rereading

- How does the writer integrate the appeals in the essay?
- What is the tone of the essay? How does the author establish this tone?
- What other rhetorical strategies does the author use to support the essay's purpose?
- What are your responses to the questions after the essay?

Writing Argument and Persuasion Essays

Preparing to Write

- What are your responses to the Preparing to Write questions?
- Do you narrow and focus your material as much as possible?
- What is your purpose?
- Who is your audience?

Writing

- Is your thesis a debatable question?
- Do you justify the organization of your essay?
- Is your essay organized effectively for what you are trying to accomplish?
- Does the body of your essay directly support your thesis?
- Do you understand your audience's opinions, convictions, and backgrounds so that you know what to emphasize?
- Does your conclusion restate your main intention and offer some constructive recommendations?

Rewriting

- Is your thesis statement clear?
- Is the main thrust of your essay argumentative (an appeal to reason)?

- Will the balance of these appeals effectively accomplish your purpose with your intended audience?
- Does your conclusion restate your argument, make a recommendation, and bring your essay to a close?
- When you use logic, is that section of your paper arranged through either inductive or deductive reasoning? Is that the most effective order to achieve your purpose?
- In appealing to the emotions, have you chosen your words with proper attention to their denotative and connotative effects?
- Have you chosen examples carefully to support your thesis statement?
- Is this tone suitable for your purpose and your audience?

JENNIFER COWAN

TV Me Alone

Jennifer Cowan (1965–) has spent more than a decade as a pop culture commentator, writer, director, and producer. Since graduating with a journalism degree from Carleton University in Ottawa, Cowan has become a regular contributor to *Wired*, CBC Stereo's *Realtime*, and *Shift*, from which this selection was taken. Also, in 1995 Cowan produced and directed the documentary *Douglas Coupland: Close Personal Friend*, which has been broadcast and screened at festivals across North America and Europe. Cowan's advice for writers: Have fun, be nice, and do good work.

Cowan's television experience has included work on the drama *Traders, Bob & Margaret, Edgemont, mediatelevision,* and *Wired for Sex* (a CBC *Witness* documentary). Cowan makes television, but in "TV Me Alone," she argues for keeping TV out of public places.

Preparing to Read

Jennifer Cowan's essay first appeared in *Shift* in the summer of 1995. Written on an overnight flight from Los Angeles to Toronto, "TV Me Alone" argues that television does not belong in public places. Before reading her argument, think about television and the role that it plays in your life. What do you watch on TV? What is your favourite program? What do you like least on TV? When do you watch television? Where do you watch it? What do you think of television in public places? Could you live without television?

I recently had the scrumptious opportunity to take the red-eye from Los Angeles to Toronto. Buoyed by the three-hour stopover in Chicago, I swiped a mini-puft-pillow and set out to catch some sleep in the departure lounge. Sadly, the hum of 5 a.m. airport traffic was drowned out by the incessant loop of CNN airport television. Instead of some much needed zzzzs, I was repeatedly subjected to life-enhancing information on the nutritional value of stamps (two to eight calories per lick if you must know) and tips for the solo traveller (when in San Francisco rent a car and drive down the coast).

TV in public and quasi-public places has become as   2
ubiquitous as the word ubiquitous. Flight attendants no longer
demo oxygen masks or point out exits with choreographed
precision. Instead, pop-out screens serve up sanitized corporate
videos with a unisex Benetton cast. And while you have to pony
up a few bucks to see an inflight movie, you can freely access
the ABC and NBC news-feeds on short hauls.

Airports are not the only venue plagued by monitor   3
multiplication. Try banks. If being watched by their security
cameras while picking underwear out of your bum wasn't
enough media scrutiny, now financial institutions want to watch
you as you watch them. So during the recent RSP blitz, they
played video loops of sailing, sunset strolls on the beach and
other dishy retirement options for the canny investor.

At the HMV music stores, the garish interiors and sadistic   4
display practices aren't the only consumer bonus. Toronto's
Yonge Street mausoleum is fronted by a 20-foot video wall
programmed with HMV's promotional choices of the moment.

Nary a retail space is free of TV. Used to be if you wanted to   5
watch TV in a department store, you had to go to the home
entertainment section. Now a detour through the men's wear in
Eaton's includes a how-to-open-an-umbrella TV demonstration
courtesy of the Totes galoshes people. No doubt the women's
accessories department plugs 50 ways to use a scarf clip. There are
even TVs, according to *Entertainment Tonight*, tucked into gas
pumps, so you can stay tuned while filling your car. The notion
that TV is mindless and relaxing, I've discovered, has become
as obsolete as manual channel-changing.

Even when there's nothing to see, televisions have taken on an   6
omniscient aura, staring like a Cyclops at the cultural psyche. On
a recent visit to a bar, three overhead monitors screened the film
Blood Simple, just in case my companion failed to provide enough
visual enticement. Not to be outdone, a few blocks down, at the
neighbouring Bovine Sex Club (where the interior design meshes
chicken wire, doll parts and TVs), four big screens emanated
everything from *Much Music* and anime to *Tommy* and *Night of
the Living Dead*. Bloodshot eyes were glued. Even I found myself
staring lemming-like, transfixed by the stream of cathode rays.

Don't get me wrong. I'm not trying to pull a Neil Postman. I   7
don't think TV will topple civilization and make us stop reading
or talking or screwing. I love TV! Hell, I make TV. But I think

TV has a time and a place—a personal time and a private place. No more.

When TV left our homes and went public, something curious   8 happened. It went from home appliance to tool of compliance. And TV continues to make inroads into the public domain because it reinforces our commonality. Or more specifically, our communality. This is good. I know I'm not alone in relishing mid–*Melrose Place* phone calls from friends dissing Amanda's roots, or Kimberly's lunacy. However, droning news packages, investment tips and how-to-dress techniques served up in buzzing public places don't inspire communal awe among strangers. The only thing I had in common with my fellow travellers at O'Hare during our airport television experience was peckishness and crankiness. United Airlines had united us in disdain, hardly the yummiest form of community.

Pundits keep spewing hoopla about the glowing blue   9 future-direct broadcast satellites, the 500-channel universe, video-on-demand—and we all blink in bewilderment. But if we open our eyes, we'll notice the 500-channel universe is already upon us, and someone else is holding the remote control! The TV nation is little more than a sea of TVs in every environment conceivable.

The fact is, TV should not be in airports or retail stores or   10 banks. TV should not be in doctors' waiting rooms (as the defunct Medical News Network discovered). And there's no need for it in supermarket checkouts. The power and wonder of TV is that it has an ability to create a community. It gives us things to laugh about, cry about and bitch about. But when it is forced upon us, all the things that give it power—intimacy, insularity, intensity—are deadened.

Moving through daily life should not be a battle to avoid the   11 relentless electronic assault. TV deserves so much more.

UNDERSTANDING DETAILS

1. List the range of public places Cowan mentions where TV can be found. Are there others you can add to this list?
2. What is Cowan's thesis or main point in this essay? Where in the essay can it be found?
3. What aspects of TV give it its power?

ANALYZING MEANING

1. How and why does television reinforce a sense of community? What other activities fill this role of creating and maintaining community?
2. Discuss the different reasons that various businesses and corporations have introduced TV into their public spaces.
3. Cowan says that the "notion that TV is mindless and relaxing ... has become as obsolete as manual channel-changing" (paragraph 5). Explain what view has replaced this antiquated notion.

DISCOVERING RHETORICAL STRATEGIES

1. Explain Cowan's perspective on the subject of this essay. What credentials does she have to write on this topic?
2. One strategy Cowan uses to strengthen her argument is specific, vivid examples. Identify four such examples and explain how they enhance her argument.
3. Cowan has made some careful deliberate word choices in "TV Me Alone." What is the effect of each of the following vocabulary choices: *mausoleum* (paragraph 4), *plagued* (paragraph 3), *lemming-like* (paragraph 6), and *zzzzs* (paragraph 1)?

MAKING CONNECTIONS

1. What similarities are there between the tone in Cowan's essay and that used by Kim Pittaway ("Dead Wrong")? What language choices has each author made to create her tone? Are their choices effective for the topics they are writing about?
2. Cowan's essay first appeared in *Shift* magazine as did "The Babar Factor" by Evan Solomon. From these two essays, what conclusions might you draw about the readers of *Shift*? What other essay in this book is also likely to appeal to this audience? Explain your answer.
3. Analyze the balance in Cowan's essay between logical, emotional, and ethical appeals. How is this balance different from that found in Judy Rebick's "The Culture of Overwork"? Which author uses more of an emotional appeal? Who uses more logic? Who relies most on ethical appeal? In what way does the mixture of appeals in each of these essays determine how convincing they are to you?

IDEAS FOR DISCUSSION/WRITING

Preparing to Write

Cowan says that one of the positive things TV has to offer is its ability to create a sense of community. Write freely about other shared aspects of life that create a sense of community. What filled this role before television was invented? What other things achieve this purpose today? How has TV contributed to the idea of the global community?

Choosing a Topic

1. Cowan loves TV, but she thinks TV has a time and a place. Write about a particular setting or time where you find television annoying. Explain clearly to your readers why television does not belong in that place or why it is not appropriate at that time.
2. In "TV Me Alone" Cowan says that TV's power is deadened when it is forced upon us. Choose another example of something that loses its power when it is forced on people, and write an essay in which you argue against its imposition.
3. TV is subject to a lot of criticism. Write an essay for *TV Guide* in which you present the benefits that TV has to offer its viewers.

WEBSITES

www.wired.com/wired/archive/1.06/citytv.html
"The Sheer Force of Attitude," about CityTV and Moses Znaimer, is another of Cowan's articles from *Wired*.

www.mtr.org
Visit the Museum of Television and Radio.

JUANITA POLEGI

There's a Better Environmental Way to Farm

Juanita Polegi is an agrologist ("one who is qualified to teach or practise the science and art of agriculture or to conduct related scientific experiments and research") with Saskatchewan's Soil Conservation Association in Yorkton, Saskatchewan. Her argument about soil conservation was initially broadcast on *Commentary* on CBC radio.

Preparing to Read

Before you begin reading this essay, think about organic food. What makes food "organic"? What differences are there between food labelled organic and other foods? Does your local grocery store sell organic food? Do you buy food labelled organic? Why or why not? What has motivated the organic food lobby?

All food is organic. But for some reason people seem to think 1 the "organic" label applies only to food grown without fertilizers or pesticides. The Canadian consumer has bought into the notion that "organic" foods are produced without harming the environment. Anything with chemicals is out. That idea is even in children's books. One nature story I read to my daughter ended with the author urging children to "buy organic produce" so the environment would be healthy for butterflies. That's so misguided. Farmers who refuse to use pesticides and fertilizers are not sin-free. Their production methods harm the precious topsoil.

To grow crops without pesticides, farmers have to use 2 intensive tillage to control weeds and diseases. Tillage has a terrible effect on the land. It leaves the soil bare. It creates and promotes soil erosion. Topsoil, rich in nutrients and organic matter, is blown or washed off the fields into ditches and streams. It's lost forever.

According to the United Nations' Food and Agriculture 3 Organization, soil erosion is one of the greatest environmental threats in the world. Tillage is not benign. It is the most destructive operation that can be done to soil.

Up until 15 years ago, I recall what would happen in dry, 4
windy springs like the one we are now experiencing. The entire
landscape seemed to be on the move. The air was so filled with
dust we called it a blackout. Driving could be dangerous. But
spring dust storms are not so common anymore. And they're
smaller than they used to be. It's because crops on about 40% of
the farmland in Saskatchewan are now seeded directly into last
year's stubble. Only one tillage operation is needed to put the
seed in the ground. The stubble anchors the soil against wind
and water. With minimal disturbance, the soil is healthier now
than it has been since the plow was first put to the land.

Conservation farmers do use commercial fertilizers and 5
pesticides. But the fertilizers, in combination with crop rotations
that include nitrogen-fixing legumes, maintain and enhance the
soil's fertility. Pesticides are applied judiciously, and at the
recommended rate.

Direct seeding is a better way to conserve our soil which is, 6
after all, a non-renewable resource. Direct seeding farmers are
true stewards of the land. It's important for Canadians to
recognize this and appreciate their conservation efforts.

The next time you visit the market and reach for produce 7
labelled "organic," remember how it was produced. Is the loss of
our topsoil really benefiting Mother Nature?

UNDERSTANDING DETAILS

1. What is organic food in the minds of most Canadians? How
   does Polegi define organic food?
2. Explain the problems created by not using pesticides and
   fertilizers.
3. Why have the dust storms in Saskatchewan declined?

ANALYZING MEANING

1. Why does Polegi have difficulty with farmers who don't use
   pesticides or fertilizers? Explain the larger issue at stake.
2. What is Polegi's main point? What is she trying to convince us
   of?
3. Polegi says that "Direct seeding farmers are true stewards of
   the land." What does it mean to be a "true steward of the land"?
   Do you agree with Polegi on this point?

DISCOVERING RHETORICAL STRATEGIES

1. Does Polegi use primarily emotional, logical, or ethical appeal in her essay?
2. Reread the conclusion of Polegi's essay. Do you find it effective? Why or why not?
3. How does Polegi establish credibility in making her argument?

MAKING CONNECTIONS

1. Polegi writes about the need to protect the land through conserving farming practices. Imagine Polegi in conversation with Monte Hummel ("A Passion for the Environment: Two Accounts") and Tomson Highway ("What a Certain Visionary Once Said"). On what points do you believe these three writers would agree? Is there anything on which you believe they would disagree?
2. Compare the images of "the prairies" created by Polegi and Sharon Butala ("The Myth: The Prairies Are Flat").
3. Polegi is presenting a somewhat controversial position in her essay as is Lawrence Solomon ("Too Much Privacy Can Be Hazardous to the Person"). Compare and contrast the strategies that these two writers have used to advance their positions and make their audiences more receptive to their views.

IDEAS FOR DISCUSSION/WRITING

Preparing to Write

Write freely about farming. What is the role of farmers in our country? How has that role changed in the last fifty years? What is your image of farmers? Should farmers be particularly responsible for preserving the environment?

Choosing a Topic

1. Write a persuasive essay in which you convince consumers to buy Canadian food products rather than their imported counterparts.
2. Think of a particular behaviour that will contribute to preserving the health of our environment. Write a "Commentary" of about 500 words that will be broadcast on national radio to

convince your audience to change their behaviour in order to benefit the environment.

3. The interests of environmentalists are often in conflict with the interests of business. Write an essay in which you make the case for the interests of one party needing to take priority over the needs of the other in one particular matter. You might, for example, focus on the disposal of waste material, access to natural resources as raw materials, or production processes that produce emissions that are harmful to the environment.

WEBSITES

ssca.usask.ca
Juanita Polegi works for the Saskatchewan Soil Conservation Association.

www.sia.sk.ca/index.html#branch
Learn more about agrology and agrologists.

www.cbc.ca/commentary
Polegi's essay was broadcast on CBC radio's *Commentary*.

LAWRENCE SOLOMON

Too Much Privacy Can Be Hazardous
to the Person

In addition to being the editor of (the now defunct) *The Next City*, Lawrence Solomon (1948–) has contributed to many publications including *The Globe and Mail* and *The Wall Street Journal*. Solomon's areas of expertise include public utilities, public-private partnerships, and regulation. Solomon is also noted as a leading environmentalist, and in the late 1970s he was an advisor to President Carter's Task Force on the Global Environment. In addition, his work on energy deregulation, as presented in his books *Energy Shock* (1980), *Breaking Up Ontario Hydro's Monopoly* (1982), and *Power at What Cost?* (1984), has served as a model for privatization of the electricity industry in several countries, including the United Kingdom.

Preparing to Read

"Too Much Privacy Can Be Hazardous to the Person" first appeared in *The Next City*, described in its masthead as "a solutions-oriented magazine that tackles issues confronting our new urban society." In this essay, Lawrence Solomon responds to the concern shared by many that electronic data collection and storage are an undesirable invasion of our privacy. Before you begin reading, think about the idea of privacy. What things do you consider private? Do others share your opinion about what things are private? In what ways have you had your privacy invaded? Do you ever refuse to give people information that you consider to be private? What is the risk associated with having private information shared with others?

W ith vast computer network data bases storing detailed   1
information about our private lives, many of us are becoming uneasy about invasions of privacy. Already, computers track our daily activities, time-stamping every credit and debit card transaction, monitoring who we call on the telephone or visit over the World Wide Web. Many businesses snoop on their employees, many municipalities film activities on city streets to

cut down on red-light runners and other violators. Soon, every highway will be tolled, recording our comings and goings; and so will every neighbourhood road—satellite technology today tracks the movement of London cabbies, the better to dispatch them; tomorrow these satellites will economically track private automobiles, the better to bill their owners.

Some privacy concerns revolve around bothersome junk mail   2 and unwanted telemarketing calls: Air mile and other cards let marketers analyze your personal shopping habits, opening you up to an avalanche of targeted offers. Other concerns—particularly access to your genetic code, which contains intimate details about you and your likely future life—are anything but frivolous. A recent study by the Federal Bureau of Investigation and the Computer Security Institute found that "most organizations are woefully unprepared ... [making] it easier for perpetrators to steal, spy, or sabotage without being noticed and with little culpability if they are." After sampling 400 sites, the study found 42 per cent had experienced an intrusion or unauthorized use over the past year. Even sophisticated agencies are vulnerable. Pentagon computers suffered 250,000 attacks by intruders in 1995, 65 per cent of whom gained entry to a computer network. That same year, the London *Sunday Times* reported that the contents of anyone's electronic health record could be purchased on the street for £150.

Because the dangers—ranging from financial exploitation   3 to, in the worst case, a police state—can be profound, legislation of various types is being proposed. Some argue that all personal information should be our own private property, to prevent marketers from storing and exchanging information about us without our consent; others would severely restrict or even prohibit the collection of sensitive personal data. These approaches miss the mark. The collection of data—the accumulation of knowledge—is almost always desirable. The relevant question is, when does the information belong in the public sphere and when in the private?

The claim that we somehow have property rights to our   4 personal information does not stand up to scrutiny. We all exchange information about others—"Did you see Andrea's new car?"; "I hear Jim got a promotion"—in our daily routines without requiring their consent, and a democratic society that respects free speech could not do otherwise. Even if we did enact laws to restrict or ban data banks from collecting information about us, it would generally backfire. Junk mail is unwanted precisely because it is indiscriminate and useless. If marketing succeeds in sending us useful, targeted information, many of us would have our goal of restricting unwanted mail. In one survey, 71 per cent of 18- to 20-year-olds wanted mail on products that interested them; in another, 52 per cent of consumers wanted to be profiled if that would lead to special offers. Those who don't want the mail or the offers will only need to make their views heard: Few companies would defy their customers by selling their names.

Valid restrictions governing free speech—such as slandering   5
others or violating their copyright on personal works—are properly limited. But we should add one other restriction—control over the use of our genetic code, where privacy should take precedence over free speech.

The field of genetic information promises to be the greatest   6
boon to science and medicine in human history. We suffer from at least 4,000 genetic diseases and conditions—everything from Huntington's disease to depression—that may one day be treated or cured as science unravels the mysteries of the human genome. Even today, reading our genes can guide us in making decisions about our future, revealing whether we have predispositions for cancers or alcoholism, medical conditions that preventative measures could ameliorate. The information in your genetic code amounts to a probabilistic future diary that describes an important part of a unique and personal character—not just about your physical and mental health but also about your family, especially your parents, siblings, and children.

Yet this field also promises to lead to invasions of privacy   7
unprecedented in their nature and scale. Unlike your personal diary, in which you might reveal your innermost secrets, the information in your genetic code may become known to strangers but not to you. From our own experiences, we know that there are no shortages of people with motives to acquire such information. Insurers and employers would value this information for business purposes. Political operatives might want to discredit opponents, as might combatants in divorces or other domestic disputes. Even where stakes aren't high, people may have malicious curiosities about their friends, neighbours, co-workers, or romantic rivals.

Until the turn of the century, our privacy was recognized as   8
a property right and consequently given great legal weight. Our

diaries and our secrets, particularly our medical secrets, were our own, in the United Kingdom as in North America. The genetic code, the epitome of that which is personal, is both a present document and a future diary. Giving each of us clear rights to our genetic code and requiring those who would use it to first obtain our consent would provide a necessary and indispensable ingredient to protecting our privacy.

Most day-to-day concerns that people have about privacy   9
will evaporate. Those who don't want consumer data collected on them can avoid Air Miles–type marketing. Those seeking anonymity in making a phone call or a toll road trip can purchase prepaid cards; other technologies will foil telemarketers and e-mail snoops. Those who value record keeping—primarily businesspeople who bill their time or track it for other purposes—will see this data collection as an added-value service. Most of us won't care much one way or the other.

In private spaces—banks, convenience stores, office   10
buildings—we have accepted cameras, taking little notice of them and worrying about their misuse even less. We understand the proprietor's motives—to protect his property and the security of those who use it—and accept them as valid. Though we want similar protection in our public spaces, we are less trusting here, not because we value public property and security less but because we know the proprietor—the state—may have mixed motives. Too often government officials have used privileged information—whether medical data or income tax files—for self-serving ends. We do need safeguards governing surveillance in public spaces to allay legitimate public fears over the advent of the police state. Less privacy, ironically, would be one such safeguard.

Many criminal lawyers believe the police state arrived some   11
time ago, that law enforcement authorities effectively frame individuals whom they believe to be guilty. Guy Paul Morin is a case in point: Convinced of his guilt, police fudged the facts. When conflicting evidence frustrated their efforts—Morin left work too late to have travelled the 30 miles home in time to have murdered 9-year-old Christine Jessop—police ingenuity overcame this shortcoming.

Morin has plenty of company—Donald Marshall, David   12
Milgaard, and countless others have been convicted of murder and lesser offences because they could not establish where they were at some fateful time. Put another way, they were victims of their privacy. The vacuum of reliable information about their

whereabouts created the opening for overzealous or overlazy police officers and prosecutors. Overzealous and overlazy authorities will always be with us, but vacuums of reliable information are increasingly becoming scarce. Had Jessop been murdered today, and had Morin travelled along an electronically tolled road such as Ontario's Highway 407, a record of when he got on and where he got off the highway would have established his whereabouts. The injustices perpetrated by the criminal justice system on this young man would never have occurred. Highway 407 was built too late to help Morin, but not for future travellers, whose record of their comings and goings—unbeknownst to them—adds a touch of security to their lives. So do new advances in DNA analysis, which eventually proved Morin innocent, as they are now doing for others around the world who were also falsely imprisoned.

A world in which we can verify our daily movements—the very world that has been unfolding for decades—diminishes the number of miscarriages of justice that can occur. To fill a void with false information has always been easy; to rewrite data showing that someone drove 30 miles at a particular time along a particular electronic toll road involves reconstructing an alternate route and time, which involves alternate billing, which involves replacing the old invoice with a new one, and on and on. The effort required to spin a web of false information and then overlay it upon an existing factual network without getting tangled up would be so daunting as to virtually never occur. The very data base networks that some fear will usher in the police state, in the end, are really the best protection against it. 13

UNDERSTANDING DETAILS

1. Itemize the privacy concerns that Solomon identifies in his essay. How many are there in total?
2. What is Solomon's position on the collection and sharing of personal genetic information?
3. In what ways is our daily activity monitored and tracked according to Solomon? What has led to this type of collection of information?

ANALYZING MEANING

1. Explain how Guy Paul Morin, Donald Marshall, and David Milgaard were "victims of their privacy."
2. Where does Solomon draw the line between the type of information that belongs in the public sphere and that which belongs in the private realm? Do you agree with him? Explain why or why not.
3. Explain why people are concerned about the collection of data. Are these concerns warranted? Why or why not?

DISCOVERING RHETORICAL STRATEGIES

1. In several places, Solomon uses statistics to help him advance his argument. Why does he incorporate survey and study results into his essay?
2. What is Solomon's thesis? Where in his essay does it appear? Why has he chosen to organize his argument in this way?
3. What type of appeal does Solomon primarily use in his essay? Is this an effective choice? Why or why not?

MAKING CONNECTIONS

1. Solomon discusses changes in our society that result from advances in technology. How are these changes similar to or different from the changes identified by Ken Wiwa ("Say It With Numbers") or Stanley Coren ("Dogs and Monsters")?
2. Electronic monitoring of our daily activities has the potential to affect our behaviour in many ways. How might electronic monitoring be used to combat racism (Cecil Foster, "Why Blacks Get Mad") or overwork (Judy Rebick, "The Culture of Overwork")?
3. Trina McQueen ("Why We Crave Hot Stuff") discusses the appeal of scandal, gossip, and stories about fascinating people. To what extent is information gathered through the types of electronic monitoring that Solomon describes fair game for media stories?

IDEAS FOR DISCUSSION/WRITING

Preparing to Write

Write freely about electronic monitoring of your daily activities. In what ways are your daily activities monitored? By whom? How do you feel about this monitoring? What are the consequences of the monitoring you have identified? Are these welcome outcomes or undesired consequences? Who should decide what activities are monitored?

Choosing a Topic

1. The electronic gathering of information about us enables marketers to send us unsolicited information or offers on various products and services. Write an essay in which you either promote the use of electronic gathering of data to support this activity or argue against the collection of this information to send "junk mail."
2. One person exercising the right to free speech may infringe on another's right to personal privacy. Write an essay in which you explain where the line should be drawn between free speech and personal privacy.
3. Solomon argues that the monitoring of our activities may protect us in many ways, but he has reservations about the collection of genetic data. Write an essay in which you either support or argue against the collection of genetic data. Make sure you include specific examples to support your argument.

WEBSITES

www.nextcity.com/main/town/4tolls.htm
Another article by Lawrence Solomon published in *The Next City*.

www.urban-renaissance.org/urbanren/index.cfm?DSP= larry&SubID=163
Read articles by Lawrence Solomon at the Urban Renaissance Institute.

JUDY REBICK

The Culture of Overwork

A noted feminist and political commentator, Judy Rebick (1945–) can currently be seen on CBC Newsworld's *Straight From the Hip* and was previously the cohost of CBC's *Face Off*, a national debate show. In addition, Rebick has appeared on a variety of TV and radio shows, including *The Journal*, *Prime Time News*, *Canada AM*, *CBC Midday*, and CBC's *Morningside*. Rebick also writes regular columns for *Elm Street*, *The Ottawa Citizen*, *The London Free Press*, and *CBC Online* and is the author of two books, *Politically Speaking* and *Imagine Democracy*.

A graduate of McGill University with a degree in psychology, Rebick worked as the director of special projects for the Canadian Hearing Society. From 1990 to 1993, she served as the president of Canada's largest women's organization, the National Action Committee on the Status of Women. Most recently Rebick has taken on the role of publisher of **rabble.ca**, an online community of rabble-rousers.

Preparing to Read

In "The Culture of Overwork," which first appeared in *Elm Street* magazine in the spring of 2001, Judy Rebick discusses the growing problem of overwork and the effects that it has on individuals and society. Before you begin reading, think about overwork. How often do you respond "Busy" when people ask how you are? Do you feel overworked? Are the general expectations of your workplace realistic or excessive? How many hours do you think the ideal workweek should be? How would you spend your remaining time? Who should determine the appropriate number of hours in a standard workweek? What is a workaholic?

The other day I sat down at the computer in my home office 1 and found that I just couldn't do any work. I was exhausted. At first I thought I was getting sick. Then I realized that I hadn't taken a day off in more than six weeks. I wound up sleeping and watching videos all weekend to recover. Still, I felt a little twinge of guilt that my work wasn't getting done even though years ago I had decided to break from the workaholic behaviour that was driving my life.

Overwork is becoming a cultural norm and it's bad for us.   2
Non-standard jobs, self-employment, cutbacks, weakened labour
standards, technology that permits us to work everywhere from
the car to the home, and the very male-defined norm that you
have to work endless hours to be a success are all contributing.

A Statistics Canada report from November 1999 says that   3
one-third of those aged 25 to 44 describe themselves as
workaholics. Studies show that long work hours are a major
contributor to stress, depression, burnout and a variety of other
illnesses. StatsCan data indicates that those who switched to a
workweek longer than 40 hours increased cigarette and alcohol
consumption and gained weight.

Irregular and long hours are stressful to families, too. A U.S.   4
study shows that family breakup is three to eight times more
likely in couples with children if one parent works nights or does
shift work. In Quebec, one parent works nights or weekends in
more than half of families.

But we don't just bring it on ourselves. In many of the fastest-   5
growing sectors, such as dot-coms, entertainment and business
services, small firms demand long hours and pay scant attention
to labour standards.

Two years ago, Tara Cleveland, now 25, got a job as a Web   6
page designer in a brand new dot-com business, so new that
they were working out of the owner's living room for a while. "I
worked 40 hours a week but they wanted more. They expected us
to stay late every night and on weekends, too. They were never
prepared to pay overtime." Cleveland, whose mother is a social
activist, refused the overtime and still kept the job. But "most
kids don't know what their rights are and they're just grateful
to have an interesting job," notes Cleveland.

If working long hours makes us unhappy and unhealthy,   7
why do we do it? Money is the obvious answer but, according to
StatsCan, most of the one-fifth of Canadians who worked
overtime during the first quarter of 1997 did so for free.

Chris Schenk, research director of the Ontario Federation of   8
Labour, says downsizing in the recession of the early 1990s meant
fewer people had to do more work. "It became an expectation
to work long hours and take work home, even in the broader
public sector," he explains. Just ask nurses or teachers how their
workload has increased.

Given these time stresses, you'd think that the length of a   9
workweek would be a major issue in Canada, but it wasn't even

mentioned in the recent federal election. Quebec—where the reality of women's lives seems to get more attention—has just reduced its legal workweek from 44 hours to 40 hours, joining four other provinces with a 40-hour week. But Ontario is going in the opposite direction with a proposal to extend the workweek to 60 hours if the employee and the employer agree.

In Europe, people want to live and work differently. France   10 adopted a legal 35-hour workweek last February. Norway just added a fifth week of paid vacation, Denmark a sixth. Last spring, the Netherlands passed a law permitting people who want to work a shorter week to request it from their employer, with the onus on the employer to explain why it couldn't be implemented. The same law permits part-time workers to request longer hours.

So what can we do about the situation at home? I'm going to   11 start booking time off in my agenda. We can challenge the culture of overwork by refusing overtime whenever possible and refusing to take work home. But individual action goes only so far. Women have to make overwork a major public policy issue. Let's look to Europe for the example and start demanding that the culture of work reflect the best interests of women and our families.

UNDERSTANDING DETAILS

1. What is "the culture of overwork"? According to Rebick, who and what is creating it?
2. What are the consequences of overwork?
3. How do the standards around working time in Europe compare with those in North America?

ANALYZING MEANING

1. How significant is the problem of overwork? Who does the culture of overwork affect to the greatest degree?
2. What is Rebick's thesis? What exactly is she advocating? Do you agree with this position? Why or why not?
3. Explain why people continue to work long hours despite the negative effects of this behaviour.

DISCOVERING RHETORICAL STRATEGIES

1. What is Rebick's purpose in writing this essay? Given the original source of this essay, who do you think is her intended audience?
2. In this essay, Rebick frequently uses statistics and quotations from authorities. Explain why she has incorporated these elements. How do they enhance her argument?
3. Is Rebick's essay an appeal primarily to logic, to emotion, or to ethics? Why do you think Rebick has made this choice?

MAKING CONNECTIONS

1. Amy Willard Cross writes about the demands on our time in "Life in the Stopwatch Lane." How do you think Cross would respond to Rebick's position about the culture of overwork?
2. In "Dead Wrong," Kim Pittaway talks about the intolerance for public grieving and says, "Death makes people uncomfortable, and distracts them from their work." How do you think Rebick would respond to this argument? In what way does Pittaway's essay support Rebick's argument?
3. Discuss the relative balance of the logical, emotional, and ethical appeals in the essays by Rebick, Janice Gross Stein ("Developing a National Voice"), and Lawrence Solomon ("Too Much Privacy Can Be Hazardous to the Person"). Which author uses logic most? Who relies most heavily on emotion? Whose ethical appeal is the strongest? What does the dominance of the appeal have to do with the subject matter of each essay?

IDEAS FOR DISCUSSION/WRITING

Preparing to Write

Write freely about changing societal expectations. How do you go about shifting attitudes toward an issue such as overwork? What kind of action is appropriate to encourage a change in attitudes or public policy? What kind of action is effective? Can an individual make a difference? Why or why not?

Choosing a Topic

1. Write a letter to the premier of your province or the prime minister of Canada about the problem of overwork. Be clear about what actions you are responding to and what you expect from your reader.
2. Rebick argues that we need to reduce the average workweek, but she mentions a proposal in one province to extend the workweek to sixty hours. In a coherent essay, persuade your colleagues that overwork is not a serious social problem and that the workweek should be lengthened.
3. Rebick concludes her essay with a call to action: "Let's look to Europe for the example and start demanding that the culture of work reflect the best interests of women and our families." Write an essay in which you either advance this argument or justify the culture of overwork that Rebick identifies.

WEBSITES

www.rabble.ca/columnists.shtml
Rebick is a columnist at **rabble.ca**.

www.cbc.ca/news/viewpoint/columns/rebick
Read Rebick's columns.

www.canspeak.com/speakers/rebick.htm
A profile of Rebick on the CanSpeak website.

www.salon.com/tech/feature/2001/03/01/white_collar_sweatshop/print.html
"The Age of Overwork" from *Salon* magazine.

JANICE GROSS STEIN

Developing a National Voice

Janice Gross Stein is the Harrowston Professor of Conflict Management in the Department of Political Science and the director of the Munk Centre for International Studies at the University of Toronto. She was educated at McGill and Yale universities in the 1960s and since 1996 has held the position of university professor. Stein also is a Fellow of the Royal Society of Canada. An expert on conflict resolution and international relations, particularly related to the Middle East, Stein has written more than eighty books and articles, including *We All Lost the Cold War* and *Citizen Engagement in Conflict Resolution: Lessons for Canada in International Experience.* She is also the winner of the Edgar Furniss Prize for outstanding contribution to the study of international security and civil-military education. In 2001 Stein delivered the Massey Lectures on "The Cult of Efficiency," and her lectures are now available in print. In addition Stein makes frequent television appearances on panels and comments on foreign policy issues on TVO's *Studio 2* and *Diplomatic Immunity* as well as CBC's *The National.* Stein has served as the chair of the Research Advisory Board to the Minister of Foreign Affairs and is currently a member of the International Security Committee of the American Academy of Science and the Committee on International Conflict Resolution of the National Academy of Sciences. She has two sons and lives in Toronto. Stein's essay reprinted here was originally printed as part of the Dominion Institute's ongoing Great Canadian Questions program (**www.greatquestions.com**), which provides high school, college, and university students with the opportunity to participate in an essay contest for a $2000 cash prize.

Preparing to Read

Janice Gross Stein's essay was originally written as part of a debate with Allan Gotlieb (Canada's former ambassador to the U.S.) on Canada and the world and the steps that Canada can take "to ensure a prominent voice in world affairs in the next century." Think about Canada's role in the international community. What position does Canada hold in this community? What should Canada's role be? What voice does Canada have on international issues? Is it sufficient? How would you characterize Canada's role in relation to other nations? What roles does Canada play in international organizations like the United Nations?

In a global economy, sovereignty is no longer what it was and   1
states no longer have the same power to protect, or to abuse,
their citizens. Canada is no exception: It is but a shadow of its
former self, with only a whisper for a voice. On this, Canadian
champions and the critics of "globalization" agree.

But both are wrong. Each underestimates the capacity Canada   2
retains to make a difference on global issues, even as the face of
sovereignty changes.

We can only make a difference, however, if we build the   3
domestic platform needed to participate effectively in a
knowledge-based global system; what we do at home shapes
our choices abroad.

In the post–Cold War world, powerful enemies are largely   4
absent and global market forces are ever present. In the global
marketplace, Canada is not as significant a player as it was 50
years ago, and it is likely to become even less important as China,
Brazil, Argentina and Indonesia mature. Canada also faces a
special challenge: it lives next door to the mighty United States.

The most serious threat to Canada's survival as a nation with   5
a distinct identity is no longer military attack, but the pull and
push of the U.S. economy and its entertainment industries. More
and more innovative, risk-acceptant young Canadians are being
drawn to the United States to work. More and more Canadians
are watching programs produced in the United States, listening
to music by American recording artists and reading books and
magazines written and edited in the United States.

It is no surprise that managing the Canada–U.S. relationship   6
is front and centre on our government's agenda. If there is to be
a Canada at all—much less a Canada that speaks with authority
on global issues—strategic choices must be made.

Ottawa, the provincial governments and the private sector   7
must invest strategically in educating a scientifically and
technically literate population and in promoting innovation. We
have just begun, for example, to renovate our decaying scientific
infrastructure through the Canadian Foundation for Innovation,
but far more must be done.

Telecommunications and computer companies, software   8
developers and biotechnology firms must partner with
universities, colleges and governments to provide world-class
opportunities for young Canadians. How Canada will fare in a
global knowledge-based economy will depend largely on the

skills of our citizens. Here we must do far better than in the past if Canada is to be a player in global markets.

But scientific and technical literacy alone will not provide a   9 sufficient platform for authoritative participation in world politics. Canadians know alarmingly little about their own history, and they are unfamiliar with the cultures and practices of their diverse fellow citizens. Our schools, post-secondary institutions and national public broadcaster must do significantly better in teaching Canadians about the richness of their past and the diversity of their present.

Participation in global politics is no longer restricted to a   10 cadre of trained experts, as it was half a century ago. In the future, larger and larger numbers of Canadians will move abroad, come home and move out again. If we do not know our history, we will quickly forget who we are as we spend more time away from home. Canadian identity will blur and Canada's voice will gradually become mute.

We will also be unable to exploit one of our most important   11 assets in global politics—our richly diverse population. Networks of immigrants now connect Canada around the globe. These networks are invaluable channels as Canada seeks to make its voice heard on international issues. We should lead in developing practices of multiple citizenship to strengthen these connections. Access to Canadian citizenship should be made easier rather than more difficult, and dual, even triple, citizenship should become possible. Canadians who move in and out of the country strengthen our international connections and help "brand" Canada to those who might not know us otherwise.

But even if we invest strategically in engineering a better   12 knowledge platform than we have in the past, living permanently in the shadow of the United States is still no easy task. It is even harder now, in this "unipolar" moment.

Canada must watch its economic back continuously. It does,   13 and should, devote a great deal of attention to monitoring and lobbying Washington. Officials must also use the dense networks of political, social, and economic connections between Canadians and Americans to promote Canadian interests in Washington. We must also continue to promote multilateral regimes and rules of fair play. Logic dictates that Canada will generally do better on a regulated multilateral playing field than in one-to-one contests with Washington. When there is no choice but to deal with an issue bilaterally, there will inevitably be conflict and compromise; Canada will win some, but lose more.

Above all, Canada must have a responsible, independent   14
voice in global politics. What Canada says and does globally helps us to define ourselves, and we have the power to speak strategically in several important ways. We can, for example, lead where the United States—particularly the executive branch—wishes it could go but sometimes cannot. We did so recently, for example, in Havana, and at the United Nations when sanctions against Iraq were once again on the agenda. In both cases, political constraints prevented the United States from exploring new openings. Despite rhetoric to the contrary in Congress, Canada's leadership was both helpful, and seen as helpful, in the American government.

Canada can also speak directly to some of the most difficult   15
problems bedevilling the global system. Ethnic and religious intolerance, governments unaccountable to their citizens, legal systems ungoverned by the rule of law, social inequity and the fracturing of communities in an age of global markets—all often spill over into violence. Canadian culture in its deepest sense—our habits of tolerance, our respect for human rights and our civility—provides the kind of expertise needed when the big powers or international institutions seek to prevent conflict or to reconstruct war-torn societies.

Canada has taken the lead on a basket of humanitarian   16
issues—the ban on land mines, the creation of an International Criminal Court—and has built a coalition of 12 states, including Norway and South Africa, committed to enhancing the protection of citizens, even, if necessary, against their own governments. Seizing the moment when sovereignty is in retreat, Canada has made a difference globally. We can continue to do so if we use our human resources well and choose our issues carefully. But this capacity for significant engagement in global politics will be impaired if we are reduced to echoing the United States. Unease with the weight of American economic, cultural, military and political power is not just a Canadian concern; Europe and Japan are worried as well, and they are not stilling their voices. On the right issues it is imperative that Canada have an independent voice, even if that voice occasionally irritates our neighbours.

The gravest threat, not only to our capacity to engage in the   17
world but also to our survival, is the tendency to whisper or echo when we can indeed speak and make a difference.

UNDERSTANDING DETAILS

1. Upon what does Stein say that Canadian champions and critics of globalization agree?
2. In what direction does Stein believe Canada should be moving? How does Stein propose this should be done? What direction has Canada been moving over the last 50 years? Why?
3. In global politics, where can Canada lead that the U.S. can't?

ANALYZING MEANING

1. Why does Stein believe Canada should have a louder voice in the global marketplace? How can Canada make a difference in global issues?
2. Why can Canada lead in areas where the U.S. can't?
3. This essay was originally written in 2000. Do you think Stein would view things differently now? Explain.

DISCOVERING RHETORICAL STRATEGIES

1. Who do you think is Stein's intended audience? Explain your conclusion.
2. Explain how Stein effectively frames her essay with the introduction and conclusion.
3. Is Stein's argument primarily an emotional, logical, or ethical one? Why has she chosen this approach?

MAKING CONNECTIONS

1. Anita Rau Badami ("My Canada") and Allen Abel ("A Home at the End of the Journey") both write about Canada in comparison to the U.S. How do you think they would respond to Janice Gross Stein's position that "The most serious threat to Canada's survival ... is the pull and push of the U.S. economy and its entertainment industries"?
2. Stein says, "Canadians know alarmingly little about their own history, and they are unfamiliar with the cultures and practices of their diverse fellow citizens." Imagine a conversation on this topic among Stein, Wayson Choy ("I'm a Banana and Proud of It"), Steven Heighton ("Elegy in Stone"), and Ross Kilpatrick ("Winnie-the-Pooh and the Canadian Connection"). On what points do you think the various writers would agree? In what areas might they disagree?

3. Compare the persuasive strategies employed by Stein, Lawrence Solomon ("Too Much Privacy Can Be Hazardous to the Person"), Judy Rebick ("The Culture of Overwork"), and Naheed Mustafa ("My Body Is My Own Business").

IDEAS FOR DISCUSSION/WRITING

Preparing to Write

Janice Gross Stein contends that the U.S. economy and the American entertainment industries are the greatest threat to Canada's survival. Write freely about the influence of the U.S. on Canada. In what areas do you believe U.S. influence is the strongest? Is U.S. influence a problem? What should Canadians do about this influence? What should the Canadian government do about this influence?

Choosing a Topic

1. In paragraph 15 Stein lists many of the "most difficult problems bedevilling the global system." Choose one of the problems she mentions and write an essay in which you take a strong persuasive stance on the position Canada should take on this issue in the international arena.

2. How much do you know about Canadian history? Write an essay in which you support or refute Janice Gross Stein's position that "Canadians know alarmingly little about their own history."

3. In paragraphs 7–9, Stein identifies a number of steps that she believes need to be taken to ensure that, going forward, there is a Canada that speaks with authority on global issues. Select one of the propositions Stein makes and write a persuasive essay in which you encourage the appropriate party or parties to follow Stein's recommended course of action.

WEBSITES

www.schoolnet.ca/greatquestions/e/bio_q4_stein.html
Read the Great Canadian Questions biography and bibliography of Janice Gross Stein.

www.utoronto.ca/provost/univprofs/Stein.htm
Read the University of Toronto biography of Janice Gross Stein.

www.schoolnet.ca/greatquestions/e/tools_4_0.html
Submit an entry to the Dominion Institute's Great Canadian Questions essay competition.

masseylectures.cbc.ca/index2001.html
Janice Gross Stein delivered the 2001 Massey Lecture on "The Cult of Efficiency."

NAHEED MUSTAFA

My Body Is My Own Business

Naheed Mustafa chose to voice her opinion about the traditional Muslim dress for women in an essay published in the "Facts & Arguments" column of *The Globe and Mail*. A graduate of the University of Toronto with a degree in political science and history, Mustafa went on to study journalism at Ryerson University. She makes the point in her essay that she grew up in Canada, although she has lived in Pakistan since her article was originally published in 1993. Since its original publication, this essay has been reproduced in several anthologies and on several websites.

Preparing to Read

In this essay, Naheed Mustafa discusses the ways in which appearance and clothing are related to the oppression of women. Before you read the essay, think about feminism and the oppression of women. What is feminism? Do you consider yourself a feminist? Why or why not? Traditionally, what aspects of society have oppressed women? Are there still barriers that women face today? How does the situation in Canada compare to that of other countries? What is the relationship between women's physical appearance and their oppression?

I often wonder whether people see me as a radical, fundamentalist Muslim terrorist packing an AK-47 assault rifle inside my jean jacket. Or maybe they see me as the poster girl for oppressed womanhood everywhere. I'm not sure which it is. 1

I get the whole gamut of strange looks, stares and covert glances. You see, I wear the *hijab*, a scarf that covers my head, neck and throat. I do this because I am a Muslim woman who believes her body is her own private concern. 2

Young Muslim women are reclaiming the *hijab*, reinterpreting it in light of its original purpose—to give back to women ultimate control of their own bodies. 3

The Koran teaches us that men and women are equal, that individuals should not be judged according to gender, beauty, wealth or privilege. The only thing that makes one person better than another is her or his character. 4

Nonetheless, people have a difficult time relating to me. After   5
all, I'm young, Canadian born and raised, university-educated—
why would I do this to myself, they ask.

Strangers speak to me in loud, slow English and often appear   6
to be playing charades. They politely inquire how I like living
in Canada and whether or not the cold bothers me. If I'm in the
right mood, it can be very amusing.

But why would I, a woman with all the advantages of a   7
North American upbringing, suddenly, at 21, want to cover
myself so that with the *hijab* and the other clothes I choose to
wear, only my face and hands show?

Because it gives me freedom.   8

Women are taught from early childhood that their worth is   9
proportional to their attractiveness. We feel compelled to pursue
abstract notions of beauty, half realizing that such a pursuit is
futile.

When women reject this form of oppression, they face ridicule   10
and contempt. Whether it's women who refuse to wear makeup
or to shave their legs or to expose their bodies, society, both men
and women, have trouble dealing with them.

In the Western world, the *hijab* has come to symbolize either   11
forced silence or radical, unconscionable militancy. Actually, it's
neither. It is simply a woman's assertion that judgment of her
physical person is to play no role whatsoever in social interaction.

Wearing the *hijab* has given me freedom from constant   12
attention to my physical self. Because my appearance is not
subjected to public scrutiny, my beauty, or perhaps lack of it,
has been removed from the realm of what can legitimately be
discussed.

No one knows whether my hair looks as if I just stepped out   13
of a salon, whether or not I can pinch an inch, or even if I have
unsightly stretch marks. And because no one knows, no one
cares.

Feeling that one has to meet the impossible male standards   14
of beauty is tiring and often humiliating. I should know, I spent
my entire teenage years trying to do it. I was a borderline bulimic
and spent a lot of money I didn't have on potions and lotions in
hopes of becoming the next Cindy Crawford.

The definition of beauty is ever-changing; waifish is good,   15
waifish is bad, athletic is good—sorry, athletic is bad. Narrow
hips? Great. Narrow hips? Too bad.

Women are not going to achieve equality with the right to   16
bare their breasts in public, as some people would like to have
you believe. That would only make us party to our own
objectification. True equality will be had only when women don't
need to display themselves to get attention and won't need to
defend their decision to keep their bodies to themselves.

UNDERSTANDING DETAILS

1. Why does Mustafa tell us that she has chosen to wear the hijab?
   What does the hijab represent to her?
2. How do people typically respond to Mustafa when she is wearing the hijab? How does she feel about their responses?
3. According to Mustafa, what will give women real freedom?

ANALYZING MEANING

1. Mustafa claims that "because no one knows [details of her physical appearance], no one cares" (paragraph 13). How strong is
   this argument?
2. What does wearing the hijab say about the respective roles of
   men and women, according to Mustafa?
3. Since this article was originally published in 1993, it has been
   extensively reproduced, both in anthologies and on various
   websites, and has been translated into other languages. Why
   does this essay have such broad appeal? Do you think it would
   be any different if Mustafa were writing it today?

DISCOVERING RHETORICAL STRATEGIES

1. Would you characterize Mustafa's argument as using logical,
   emotional, or ethical appeals? Support your response with
   specific examples.
2. Mustafa has personal characteristics that give her credibility in
   dealing with this subject. What aspects of the author's life
   strengthen her argument?
3. Mustafa uses figurative language to help convey her point effectively. Find three examples of figurative language (e.g.,
   metaphor, simile, alliteration) in this essay. What effect do these
   language choices have on the reader?

MAKING CONNECTIONS

1. Like Mustafa, Gloria Steinem ("The Politics of Muscle"), Barbara Kingsolver ("Life Without Go-Go Boots"), and Laura Robinson ("Starving for the Gold") all write about aspects of the appearance of women. On what points do you think these writers would agree? On which points would they disagree? Explain your answer.

2. Drew Hayden Taylor ("Pretty Like a White Boy") and Cecil Foster ("Why Blacks Get Mad") frequently run into difficult situations as people make assumptions based on their appearance. How is their experience similar to that of Naheed Mustafa? How do their experiences differ?

3. Naheed Mustafa writes about some of the conflicts that arise as two cultures meet. How is the situation she describes similar to the one that Wayson Choy presents in "I'm a Banana and Proud of It"?

IDEAS FOR DISCUSSION/WRITING

Preparing to Write

Write freely about clothing and the fashion industry. Why do we wear what we wear? What is the purpose of clothing? How do we choose the things that we wear? What does our clothing tell the world about us? Why do fashions change? Why is fashion such a major industry? What factors in our lives dictate the fashion choices we make?

Choosing a Topic

1. How do you respond when you see a woman wearing the hijab? Write an essay about the effect of the hijab on you and how you react to the person wearing it.

2. The imposition of the values of one culture on another is always a difficult issue. In promoting multiculturalism, many immigrants to Canada are encouraged to maintain some traditional practices and lifestyles. Which practices should be maintained from an old culture and which Canadian values should be imposed upon newcomers? Write an essay for a group of newcomers to Canada in which you explain which values or practices are appropriate to maintain, and which Canadian values or practices should replace the ones

with which they are familiar. Be sure that you present your argument in a clear, tactful, and diplomatic way.

3. The clothing we choose to wear tells the world a lot about who we are. Write an essay for a fashion magazine in which you explain how the fashion choices you make reflect your lifestyle and values.

WEBSITES

www.urbanmozaik.com/2002.march.issue/mar02_fea_chador.html
Read Emily Monroy's article "The Chador: A Western Woman's Perspective."

www.al-sunnah.com/principles.htm
This site gives detailed information about the principles of Islam.

Heroes and Symbols

Charlotte Gray (1948–) has been a regular contributor to three magazines: *Chatelaine* (a parenting column), *Saturday Night* (where her focus is national politics and for which she was the Ottawa editor), and the *Canadian Medical Association Journal* (in which she examines a wide scope of health-care-related issues). This range is testament to Gray's ability as a writer and her capacity to enable her reader to relate to many different experiences. Originally from Sheffield, U.K., Gray earned her B.A. from Oxford University in 1969, and went on to work as the assistant editor and then the editor of *Psychology Today* (U.K.). She is, in addition, the author of Governor General's Award nominee *Mrs. King: The Life & Times of Isabel Mackenzie King* (1997) (for which she won the Canadian Authors Association Birks Family Foundation Award for a biographical work about a Canadian by a Canadian) and *Sisters in the Wilderness: The Lives of Susanna Moodie and Catharine Parr Traill* (1999). The mother of three children, Gray lives and works in Ottawa and appears periodically on radio and television speaking on political issues. She has recently published *Flint and Feather*, a biography of the Mohawk poet E. Pauline Johnson.

Born in Vienna, Austria, in 1929, Peter C. Newman, came to Canada as a refugee in 1940 and enrolled as a "war guest" boarder at Upper Canada College four years later. Educated at the University of Toronto, he went on to a career as an author of over nineteen award-winning books, as a journalist, and a newspaper and magazine editor. He is currently senior contributing editor at *Maclean's*. Newman's books include a series on the Canadian Establishment, a history of the Hudson's Bay Company, and several profiles of Canadian politicians and business leaders.

In addition to being made Companion in the Order of Canada in 1990, Newman was elected to the Canadian News Hall of Fame (1992) and given a Lifetime Achievement Award by the Canadian Journalism Foundation in 1998.

Preparing to Read

The following pair of essays is part of a debate between Charlotte Gray and Peter C. Newman about Canadian heroes. The essays by Charlotte Gray and Peter C. Newman reprinted here were originally printed as part of the Dominion Institute's ongoing Great Canadian Questions program (**www.greatquestions.com**) that provides high school, college, and university students with the opportunity to participate in an essay contest for a $2000 cash prize. Before you read the essays, think about heroes in Canada. What Canadian heroes can you name? What qualifies them as heroes? Are the criteria for Canadian heroes the same as those for heroes in general? Generally, do you believe Canada does a good job of recognizing its heroes?

CHARLOTTE GRAY

No Idol Industry Here

Canada doesn't do heroes well. Look at our paper money for evidence of the scarcity of national symbols. The current series of bills features prime ministers and birds in their natural terrain—emblematic of the only two brands of psychological glue that bind Canada together: political culture and love of landscape. 1

Of course, there is the Queen, too, with her Mona Lisa smile gleaming out from the hallmarked paper. But the monarchy has always been included on Canadian money—a remnant of our colonial past. If she weren't part of the family furniture, Elizabeth II would have been dropped years ago. 2

Other countries have liberators, scientists, authors, saints, war heroes—outstanding figures from the past who are supposed to represent the nation's greatness. We have the loon on our $20 bill and William Lyon Mackenzie King on our $50 bill. King, prime minister for 22 years, may have been one of our better leaders (number one out of 20 on a recent ranking), but he is hardly the figure to make Canadian bosoms swell with national pride. 3

Why are we so hero-poor? At one level, the answers to this question are embedded in the nature of Canada itself. We live in a country that has a weak national culture and strong regional identities. As historian Daniel Francis pointed out in *National Dreams: Myth, Memory and Canadian History*: "In Canada, heroic figures have tended to emerge from the regions or from minority struggles against the status quo. By and large, they are sticks used by one part of the community to beat on another." 4

Louis Riel is a hero to Métis and francophones, and a mad troublemaker to anglophones. Even national figures are enmeshed in regional rivalries: Pierre Trudeau is the darling of Toronto's Liberal élite and a menace to Quebec nationalists and Alberta oilmen. 5

The majority of Canadians have only been in the country for two or three generations. Most of the first European arrivals carry far too much baggage. How can we glorify explorers like Jacques Cartier when they treated the First Nations as savages? 6

Or military heroes like Generals Wolfe and Montcalm when they fought each other? Finding common ground for home-grown heroes is a challenge. Countries with homogenous populations and histories stretching back beyond the printed word can pickle their heroes in the sweet vinegar of centuries.

Easy for the Brits to accept Boadicea as a heroine, or for the   7
French to revere the memory of Jeanne d'Arc: The mists of history have obscured Boadicea's murderous reputation and Jeanne d'Arc's psychiatric problems. Any women in Canadian history must stand much more brutal scrutiny, and measure up to 1990s values. So Susanna Moodie, whose *Roughing It in the Bush* is a vivid and gripping record of 19th-century pioneer life, fails as a hero because she expressed the snooty disdain of her class towards Irish immigrants. And Nellie McClung, the Western novelist who in the early years of this century fought for female suffrage, factory safety legislation and women's rights, doesn't cut it for contemporary feminists because she glorified the traditional family.

Most countries choose individuals with larger-than-life   8
qualities to mythologize: extraordinary imagination, against-the-odds bravery, brilliant creativity. There are colourful characters in our collective past who embody such qualities—think of Sir Sandford Fleming, inventor of Standard Time; Dr. Frederick Banting, co-discoverer of insulin; the fighter pilot Billy Bishop. Why aren't they on our money, instead of stuffy old Mackenzie King?

Fleming has never found an enthusiastic biographer, and   9
Banting and Bishop are too damn controversial for Canada. Neither displayed the humility that is the first requisite of Canadian heroism. Prime Minister King, on the other hand, is respected (by those who respect him) for qualities that are seen as quintessentially Canadian—his skill at compromise, his success in keeping the country unified. "He was an unheroic leader," suggests historian Norman Hillmer, "who understood the contradictions of an unheroic country."

So we do heroes badly. Moreover, we do hero worship really   10
badly. The United States has an idol industry for most of the founding fathers, plus a whole military-industrial complex for the Kennedys. British academics and writers churn out books on Churchill (and there is a blossoming Thatcher industry). France has myth-creation factories for both Napoleon Bonaparte and Charles de Gaulle. Each of these national heroes has sparked

several million feet of film and a gazillion written pages (over 15,000 books on Napoleon and still counting).

It is not only national leaders who are celebrated in these 11 countries: University library shelves groan with mega-bios and unpublished theses on Rockefeller, the American robber-baron; Florence Nightingale, the autocratic Englishwoman who revolutionized nursing; or the French intellectual, Jean-Paul Sartre. Each of these characters incarnates a trait of which their country is proud: American industry, British guts, French brains.

But anti-heroes, such as Mackenzie King, don't spark such 12 exuberant hero worship. Most Canadians are more interested in King's weird side—his interest in spiritualism and his penchant for table-tapping—than in his determination to strengthen Canadian independence or his intuitive grasp of how to make Canadians feel comfortable. In a fragmented country such as Canada, successful leaders embody modest virtues. But biographers looking for titans aren't interested in modest virtues. Cultural consumers only embrace these virtues when they are accompanied by extraordinary athletic prowess (come in, number 99) or teeth-gritting tragedy (Terry Fox).

There have been attempts to establish a pantheon of heroes— 13 iconic reflections of our past and our psyche. In the early years of this century, when we were still suffused with the Victorian assumption that bearded patriarchs made the best heroes, the Toronto publisher George Morang commissioned a series of volumes under the title *Makers of Canada*. The "Makers" in this 20-volume collection, published between 1908 and 1911, were all men, all either French- or English-speaking, and almost all involved in public life, as governors, politicians and premiers. There were three fur traders, but no entrepreneurs until the late addition of Sir William Van Horne, president of the Canadian Pacific Railway. There was not a single scholar, writer, artist, scientist or athlete.

Mr. Morang's reverential volumes never caught the public 14 imagination. They were out of step with the emerging Canadian sensibility. Their view of history was too restricted, and their style too prissy, for a young country hurtling towards a multicultural future.

The qualities that are celebrated in our national life today 15 are collective virtues—the bravery of our peacekeepers, the compassion of all Canadians for Manitoba's flood victims. Our best-known artists are the Group of Seven. When writers want to pump some adrenaline into our past or present, they capture groups rather than individuals. Pierre Berton wrote about the whole ruling class of Sir John A.'s day when he penned *The Last Spike*. Peter Newman has described the raw ambition and acquisitive urges of the business establishment as the 20th century has unfolded. The heroes of other nations are usually fiercely individualistic—but individualism has never been celebrated in Canada. It is not a useful quality for a loose federation perched on a magnificent and inhospitable landscape—a nation that sees survival as a collective enterprise.

PETER C. NEWMAN

We'd Rather Be Clark Kent

Heroes reflect the nations that anoint them, and Canada is no 1 exception. To the Americans, contemporary heroes tend to be androgynous, retroactive virgins, such as Ally McBeal, gum-chewing batters, such as Mark McGwire, or Monica Lewinsky, immortalized by her kneel-and-duck love life. Historically, the Yanks have benefited from the hero factory run by Walt Disney, who made demigods out of such frontier reprobates as Davy Crockett and Francis Marion, better known as "the swamp fox."

I have long argued that Canadian heroes—the few who have 2 retained that state of grace—share one essential qualification: They're dead.

In our peculiar way, we do not salute living heroes, even 3 when they deserve to be recognized, because that hints of boasting. This country is fuelled by envy and deference, qualities that rank heroism as an emotional extravagance reserved for Italian tenors and one-album country-and-western singers. If God had meant us to be heroic, he wouldn't have made us Canadians. This is the only country on Earth whose citizens dream of being Clark Kent, instead of Superman.

A good example is our reticence in decorating our military 4 heroes. Ottawa has actually struck three Canadian medals for bravery—our own versions of the Victoria Cross, the Star of Military Valour and the Medal of Military Valour—but none has ever been awarded.

From the beginning of Canadian history, there have been 5 some curious lapses in our choices. The St. Malo navigator Jacques Cartier is credited with Canada's "discovery" and is widely hailed, but John Cabot, that silk-clad Venetian dandy who had immigrated to England, made his landfall in Newfoundland or Cape Breton 37 years earlier. Until the recent celebration of the anniversary of his voyage, the only memorials to Cabot were the scenic trail looping northern Cape Breton Island and the plaque on a drafty baronial tower on Signal Hill in St. John's, better known as the location of Guglielmo Marconi's earliest transatlantic signal transmission. If Cabot had only landed in what is now the United States, he would have been as famous as Christopher Columbus. (The Americans celebrate the befuddled Spanish navigator as their discoverer, though he didn't even sight North America's coastline and mistook Haiti for Japan.)

James Wolfe, Louis-Joseph de Montcalm and Isaac Brock   6 were more appropriate Canadian heroes, since they died in battles without knowing their outcomes. And the memory of our most daring pirate, Antoine Laumet dit de Lamothe Cadillac, the privateer and fur trader who flourished in Quebec in 1691 and later founded Detroit, is perpetuated only by General Motors.

Except for Louis Riel, few of our deities have personified   7 ideals central to their time and place. Riel belongs to a category all his own. He became Canada's presiding martyr by refusing, at his trial for high treason, to hide behind a justified plea of insanity that might have saved his life. He thus personified the quintessential Canadian hero: a deluded mystic who died prematurely by pretending to be sane.

There is little consensus on the nature of Canadian heroes,   8 except that they're not politicians. We do not even officially mark the anniversary of our founding father, Sir John A. Macdonald, but celebrate instead Queen Victoria's birthday—long after it has been forgotten in the mother country. Of the modern crop, Pierre Trudeau, who most closely approached heroic status when he first boogied onto the scene in 1968, was quickly revealed as having an icicle for a heart, and was defeated in the 1979 election. By who? That's right—Joe Clark.

No Canadian politician ever lost his heroic aura faster than   9 Brian Mulroney—the man with the Gucci smile—who harvested more votes than Trudeau ever did, when he swept the nation in 1984. Within months, Mulroney was being blamed for every sparrow that fell from the sky, while mothers were using his name as a threat to force their kids to eat spinach.

A rare exemption to our anti-hero worship is the Group of   10 Seven, those determined hikers who glorified Ontario cottage country by turning it into derivative landscapes. (Most Canadians assume the Group of Seven was fronted by Tom Thomson—an authentic Canadian hero because he drowned under mysterious circumstances at the height of his fame. In fact, Thomson died three years before the Group was formed.)

Our anti-hero attitude extends even to our entertainers. If   11 they're successful, they can't be real. Anne Murray, one of our first world-class popular singing stars, received this back-handed tribute from the music critic Larry LeBlanc in *Saturday Night* magazine: "If you close your eyes, and think of a naked Anne Murray, parts of her always come up airbrushed."

The most conspicuously heroic Canadian of recent times was, 12 of course, Terry Fox, the young British Columbia athlete ravaged by cancer, who, in 1981, hobbled halfway between our coasts, before he collapsed. His heroic stature was confirmed when he was pinned with the Order of Canada on his deathbed. (What's-his-name, who followed Fox's path while suffering from the same affliction, actually completed his trek and raised millions for cancer research. But Steve Fonyo lived to tell the tale and has since been relegated to obscurity so chilling that he has felt compelled to commit a series of misdemeanours just to stay in print.)

Similarly, no one made much fuss about Dr. Norman Bethune 13 until 1939, when he was sanctified in his heroic status by dying from neglecting a cut finger after operating on an infected patient as a member of Mao Tse-Tung's Communist forces. (Wayne Gretzky retains his heroic stature only because he saw what was coming, and left the country.)

At another level, Canadians did not celebrate ambassador 14 Ken Taylor's heroism in smuggling six U.S. diplomats out of the Ayatollah's reach during the American-Persian confrontation. Ottawa exacted revenge on the unconventional diplomat, who broke the rules when he took a risk on behalf of freedom, by refusing to offer him an appropriately senior posting following his stint as consul-general in New York, thus forcing his resignation.

One of the few Canadians who took advantage of how 15 shabbily we treat our living heroes was Marshall McLuhan, who richly earned iconic status. He maintained his poise amid the customary slaughter dished out to our most thoughtful writers by the butchers who pass for book reviewers in these frosty latitudes (while becoming the dahling of New York's literati). But it didn't bother him. "I experience a great deal of liberty here in Canada," McLuhan once told me. "I wouldn't get that in the States, because I'm taken quite seriously there. The fact that Canadians don't take me seriously is a huge advantage. It makes me a free man."

McLuhan was wise enough to realize that being a hero in 16 Canada is an existential state with a shorter shelf life than boysenberry yogurt. We have little talent for excess and no patience with anyone who believes that heroism is worth achieving, except perhaps by inadvertence. There is a vague but valid link between our heroes and our weather, which remains Canada's most essential reality. Our frigid climate reflects the selectivity of how we pick our heroes: Many are cold, but few are frozen.

UNDERSTANDING DETAILS

1. According to Gray, why are we so "hero-poor"? Does Newman agree with her position?
2. Gray and Newman both use many examples of individuals or groups in their essays. Identify the individuals or groups that are mentioned by both Gray and Newman. Are their views of people or groups consistent?
3. According to Newman, how do countries other than Canada select and recognize their heroes? What is Gray's view?

ANALYZING MEANING

1. In what key respects do Gray and Newman agree about Canadian heroes? What are the significant differences in their positions?
2. Gray and Newman have both written biographies about a variety of Canadian figures. Based on the arguments they make in their essays and what you know about the subjects of their books, would they classify their subjects as heroes?
3. Gray and Newman make different, although not necessarily contradictory, arguments about the nature of heroes and symbols in Canada. Whose view is closer to your own? Explain.

DISCOVERING RHETORICAL STRATEGIES

1. What rhetorical strategies have Gray and Newman each used in their essays in addition to persuasion?
2. Gray and Newman both use many examples to support the points they are making in their respective essays. Which examples do you find most effective? Why?
3. Characterize the tone of each of the essays. How does each author establish this tone?

MAKING CONNECTIONS

1. Compare the views of Canada expressed by Gray and Newman with those of Janice Gross Stein ("Developing a National Voice"). On what points do they agree about the essential nature of Canada? On what points do you think they would disagree?
2. In what respects does Steven Heighton's essay "Elegy in Stone" support the points that Gray and Newman are making?

IDEAS FOR DISCUSSION/WRITING

Preparing to Write

Write freely about a person you view as a hero. What makes that person heroic? Do others also see that person as heroic? In what ways is that person's heroism recognized? Does that person see himself or herself as a hero? Why or why not?

Choosing a Topic

1. Gray points to our currency as evidence of the lack of national symbols. Write an essay in which you assess how well the current currency reflects a representative set of national symbols.
2. Choose a particular award and nominate your candidate. You might focus on an award in your school or community; an industry award such as the Juno Awards for Canadian music or the Academy Awards for movies; or an international organization award such as the Nobel Prize for Literature, Peace, or Science. Select the individual who you believe is the most deserving recipient and write your nomination piece, giving the selection committee plenty of specific examples that set your candidate apart from the other contenders and demonstrate why he or she is the obvious choice.
3. Write an essay in which you outline how Canada should treat its heroes, motivating all Canadians to participate in making this happen.

WEBSITES

www.schoolnet.ca/greatquestions/e/bio_q5_gray.html
Read the Great Canadian Questions biography of Charlotte Gray.

www.nlc-bnc.ca/9/2/p2-0105-07-e.html
Read about the writing of Gray's most recent biography of E. Pauline Johnson.

www.schoolnet.ca/greatquestions/e/bio_q5_newman.html
Read the Great Canadian Questions biography and bibliography of Peter C. Newman.

www.nlc-bnc.ca/2/6/index-e.html
Heroes of Yore and Lore: Canadian Heroes in Fact and Fiction.

www.schoolnet.ca/greatquestions/e/tools_4_0.html
Submit an entry to the Dominion Institute's Great Canadian Questions essay competition.

CHAPTER 10

DOCUMENTED ESSAYS

Reading and Writing from Sources

We use sources every day in both informal and formal situations. We explain the source of a phone message, for example, or we refer to an instructor's comments in class. We use someone else's opinion in an essay, or we quote an expert to prove a point. We cite sources both in speaking and in writing through summary, paraphrase, and direct quotation. Most of your instructors will ask you to write papers using sources so they can see how well you understand the course material. The use of sources in academic papers requires you to understand what you have read and to integrate this reading material with your own opinions and observations—a process that requires a high level of skill in thinking, reading, and writing.

Defining Documented Essays

Documented essays provide you with the opportunity to perform sophisticated and exciting exercises in critical thinking; they draw on the thinking, reading, and writing abilities you have built up over the course of your academic career, and they often require you to put all the rhetorical modes to work at their most analytical level. Documented essays demonstrate the process of analytical thinking at its best in different disciplines.

In the academic world, documented essays are also called *research papers*, *library papers*, and *term papers*. Documented essays are generally written for one of three reasons: (1) to **report**, (2) to **interpret**, or (3) to **analyze**.

The most straightforward, uncomplicated type of documented essay **reports** information, as in a survey of problems that children have in preschool. The second type of documented essay both presents and **interprets** its findings. It examines a number of different views on a specific issue and weighs these views as it draws its own conclusions. A topic that falls into this category would be whether children who have attended preschool are more sociable than those who have not. After considering evidence on both sides, the writer would draw his or her own conclusions on this topic. A documented essay that **analyzes** a subject presents a hypothesis, tests the hypothesis, and analyzes or evaluates its conclusions. This type of essay calls for the most advanced form of critical thinking. It might look, for example, at the reasons preschool children are more or less socially flexible than non-preschool children. At its most proficient, this type of writing requires a sophisticated degree of evaluation that forces you to judge your reading, evaluate your sources, and ultimately scrutinize your own reasoning ability as the essay takes shape.

Each of these types of documented essays calls for a higher level of thinking, and each evolves from the previous category. In other words, interpreting requires some reporting, and analyzing draws on both reporting and interpreting.

In the following paragraph, a student reports, interprets, analyzes, and uses sources to document the problem of solid waste in the United States. Notice how the student writer draws her readers into the essay with a commonly used phrase about America and then questions the validity of its meaning. The student's opinions give shape to the paragraph, while her use of sources helps identify the problem and support her contentions.

> "America the Beautiful" is a phrase used to describe the many wonders of nature found throughout our country. America's natural beauty will fade, however, if solutions to our solid waste problems are not discovered soon. America is a rich nation socially, economically, and politically. But these very elements may be the cause of Americans' wastefulness. Americans now generate approximately 160 million tons of solid waste a year—$3\frac{1}{2}$ pounds per person per day. We live in a consumer society where *convenience, ready-to-use,* and *throwaway* are words that spark the consumer's attention (Cook 60). However, many of the products associated with

these words create a large part of our problem with solid waste (Grossman 39). We are running out of space for our garbage. The people of America are beginning to produce responses to this problem. Are we too late? A joint effort between individuals, businesses, government industries, and local, state, and federal governments is necessary to establish policies and procedures to combat this waste war. The problem requires not one solution, but a combination of solutions involving technologies and people working together to provide a safe and healthy environment for themselves and future generations.

Reading and Writing Documented Essays

Reading and writing documented essays involves the skillful integration of two complex operations: research and writing. Reading documented essays critically means understanding the material and evaluating the sources as you proceed. Writing documented essays includes reading and understanding sources on the topic you have chosen and then combining this reading with your own conclusions. The two skills are, essentially, mirror images of one another.

How to Read Documented Essays

Preparing to Read. You should approach a documented essay in much the same way that you approach any essay. First, take a few minutes to look at the preliminary material for the selection: What can you learn from scanning Barbara Ehrenreich's essay ("The Ecstasy of War") or from reading the synopsis in the Rhetorical Table of Contents? What does Marilyn Dahl's title prepare you to read? And what questions do you have about "the ecstasy of war" before you read Ehrenreich's essay?

Also, you should learn as much as you can from the authors' biographies: What is Kilpatrick's interest in Winnie-the-Pooh's origins? What biographical details prepare us for his approach to this topic? Who was the original audience for Ehrenreich's essay? What is Dahl's background? Does she have the proper qualifications to write about the depiction of disabled people by the media?

Another important part of preparing to read a documented essay is surveying the sources cited. Turn to the end of the essay, and look at the sources. What publications does Kilpatrick draw from? Are these books and magazines well respected? Do you recognize any of the authorities that Dahl cites?

Last, before you read these essays, try to generate some ideas on the topics so you can participate as fully as possible in your reading. The Preparing to Read questions will get you ready for this task. Then, try to speculate further on the topic of the essay: What is the connection for Ehrenreich between war and ecstasy? What does this relationship tell us about human nature in general? What do you want to know from Dahl about disabilities and the media? Why do you think this topic has become such a major social issue?

Reading. As you react to the material in this chapter, you should respond to both the research and the writing. Record your responses as you read the essay for the first time: What are your reactions to the information you are reading? Are the sources appropriate? How well do they support the author's main points? Use the preliminary material before each essay to help you create a framework for your responses to it: Who was Dahl's primary audience when her essay was first published? In what ways is the tone of her essay appropriate for that audience? What motivated Kilpatrick to publish his examination of the source of Winnie-the-Pooh? Do you find it convincing?

Your main job at this stage is to determine the author's primary assertion (thesis statement), note the sources the author cites to support this thesis, and begin to ask yourself questions about the essay so you can respond critically to your reading. In addition, take a look at the questions after the selection to make certain you are comprehending the major ideas of the essay.

Rereading. As you reread these documented essays, take some time to become aware of the difference between fact and opinion, to weigh and evaluate the evidence brought to bear on the arguments, to consider the sources the writer uses, to judge the interpretation of the facts cited, to determine what the writer has omitted, and to confirm your own views on the issues at hand. All these skills demand the use of critical-thinking strategies at their most sophisticated level.

You need to approach this type of argument with an inquiring mind, asking questions and looking for answers as you read the essay. Be especially conscious of the appeals (logical, emotional, and ethical) at work in the essay (see Chapter 9), and take note of other rhetorical strategies that support each author's main argument.

Also, be aware of your own thought processes as you sort facts from opinions. Know where you stand personally in relation to each side of the issues here.

For a list of guidelines for the entire reading process, see the checklists on pages 17–18 of the Introduction.

How to Write Documented Essays

Preparing to Write. Just as with any writing assignment, you should begin the task of writing a documented essay by exploring and limiting your topic. In this case, however, you draw on other sources to help you with this process. You should seek out both primary and secondary sources related to your topic. **Primary sources** are works of literature, historical documents, letters, diaries, speeches, eyewitness accounts, and your own experiments, observations, and conclusions; **secondary sources** explain and analyze information from other sources. Any librarian can help you search for both types of sources related to your topic. Make sure you take time to assess the relevance and credibility of the sources you find.

After you have found a few sources on your general topic, you should scan and evaluate what you have discovered so you can limit your topic further. Depending on the required length of your essay, you want to find a topic broad enough to be researched, established enough so that you can find sources on it, and significant enough to demonstrate your abilities to grapple with ideas and draw conclusions. The Preparing to Write questions can help you generate and focus your ideas.

Once you have established these limitations, you might try writing a tentative thesis. At this point, asking a question and attempting to find an answer are productive. But you should keep in mind that your thesis is likely to be revised several times as the range of your knowledge changes and as your paper takes different turns while you research and write. Then, decide on a purpose and audience for your essay.

Once your tentative thesis is formed, you should read your sources for ideas and take detailed notes on your reading. These notes will probably fall into one of four categories: (1) *summary*— a condensed statement of someone else's thoughts or observations; (2) *paraphrase*—a restatement in your own words of someone else's ideas or observations; (3) *direct quotations from sources*; or (4) *a combination of these forms*. Be sure to make a distinction in your notes between actual quotations and paraphrases or summaries. Also, record the sources of all your notes—especially of quoted, summarized, and paraphrased material—that you may need to cite in your essay.

As you gather information, you should consider keeping a "research journal" where you can record your own opinions, interpretations, and analyses in response to your reading. This journal should be separate from your notes on sources. It is the place where you can make your own discoveries in relation to your topic by jotting down thoughts and relationships among ideas you are exposed to, by keeping a record of sources you read and others you want to pursue, by tracking and developing your own ideas and theories, and by clarifying your thinking on an issue.

Finally, before you write your first draft, you might want to write an informal working outline for your own information. Such an exercise can help you check the range of your coverage and the order and development of your ideas. With an outline, you can readily see where you need more information, less information, or more solid sources. Try to be flexible, however. This outline may change dramatically as your essay develops.

Writing. Writing the first draft of a documented essay is your chance to discover new insights and to find important connections between ideas that you may not be aware of yet. This draft is your opportunity to demonstrate that you understand the issue at hand and your sources on three increasingly difficult levels— literal, interpretive, and analytical; that you can organize your material effectively; that you can integrate your sources (in the form of summaries, paraphrases, or quotations) with your opinions; and that you can document (that is, cite) your sources.

To begin this process, look again at your thesis statement and your working outline, and adjust them to represent any new discoveries you have made as you read your sources and wrote in your research journal. Then, organize your research notes and information in some logical fashion.

When you begin to draft your paper, write the sections of the essay that you feel most comfortable about first. Throughout the essay, feature your own point of view and integrate summaries, paraphrases, and quotations from other sources into your analysis. Each point you make should be a section of your paper consisting of your own conclusion and your support for that conclusion (in the form of facts, examples, summaries, paraphrases, and quotations). Remember that the primary reason for doing such an assignment is to let you demonstrate your ability to synthesize material, draw your own conclusions, and analyze your sources and your own reasoning.

A documented paper usually blends three types of material:

1. *Common knowledge, such as the places and dates of events (even if you have to look them up).*

   Example: Neil Armstrong and Edwin Aldrin first walked on the moon on July 20, 1969.

2. *Your own thoughts and observations.*

   Example: Armstrong and Aldrin's brief walk on the moon's surface was the beginning of a new era in the U.S. space program.

3. *Someone else's thoughts and observations.*

   Example: President Richard Nixon reacted to the moonwalk in a telephone call to the astronauts: "For one priceless moment in the history of man all the people on this earth are truly one— one in their pride in what you have done and one in our prayers that you will return safely to earth."

Of these three types of information, you must document or cite your exact source only for the third type. Negligence in citing your sources, whether purposeful or accidental, is called *plagiarism*, which comes from a Latin word meaning "kidnapper." Among student writers, plagiarism usually takes one of three forms: (1) using words from another source without quotation marks; (2) using someone else's ideas in the form of a summary or paraphrase without citing your source; and (3) using someone else's paper as your own.

Avoiding plagiarism is quite simple: You just need to remember to acknowledge the sources of ideas or wording that you are using to support your own contentions. Acknowledging your sources also gives you credit for the reading you have done and for the ability you have developed to use sources to support your observations and conclusions.

Documentation styles vary from discipline to discipline. Ask your instructor about the particular documentation style he or she wants you to follow. The most common styles are the Modern

Language Association (MLA) style, used in humanities courses, and the American Psychological Association (APA) style, used in behavioural sciences and science courses. (See any writing handbook for more details on documentation formats.)

The internet is a newer source of information for your research papers. Electronic sources include online journals and magazines, CD-ROMs, software programs, newsletters, discussion groups, bulletin boards, and e-mail. But, just as with sources in more traditional media, not all electronic sources are equally accurate and reliable. Based on your topic, you need to exercise your best judgment and get your instructor's help in assessing the most useful online sites for your purposes. If you use electronic sources in any of your papers, remember that you have two goals in any citation: (1) to acknowledge the author and (2) to help the reader locate the material. Then you should check the MLA or APA home pages for their current guidelines for online documentation: The URL for the Modern Language Association is **www.mla.org**, and for the American Psychological Association, **www.apa.org**.

Even though documentation styles vary somewhat from one discipline to another, the basic concept behind documentation is the same in all disciplines: You must give proper credit to other writers by acknowledging the sources of the summaries, paraphrases, and quotations that you use to support the topics in your documented paper. Once you grasp this basic concept and accept it, you will have no trouble avoiding plagiarism.

Rewriting. To rewrite your documented essay, you should play the role of your readers and impartially evaluate your argument and the sources you have used as evidence in that argument. To begin with, revise your thesis to represent all the discoveries you made as you wrote your first draft. Then, look for problems in logic throughout the essay; you might even develop an outline at this point to help evaluate your reasoning:

- Are the essay's assertions clear?
- Are they adequately supported?
- Are other points of view recognized and examined?
- Does the organization of your paper further your assertions/ argument?
- Have you removed irrelevant material?

Next, check your documentation style:

- Is your source material (either summarized, paraphrased, or quoted) presented fairly and accurately?
- Have you rechecked the citations for all the sources in your paper?
- Do you introduce the sources in your paper when appropriate?
- Are your sources in the proper format according to your instructor's guidelines (MLA, APA, or another)?

Then, proofread carefully. Finally, prepare your paper to be submitted to your instructor:

- Have you followed your instructor's guidelines for your title page, margins, page numbers, tables, and abstracts?
- Have you prepared an alphabetical list of your sources for the end of your paper?

Any additional guidance you may need as you write and revise your documented essays is provided on pages 29–30 of the Introduction.

Student Essay: Documentation At Work

The following student essay uses documented sources to support its conclusions and observations about the effect of internet use on language. First, the writer sets the context of how common internet use is among teens. He then goes on to discuss the ways in which language is modified to suit the requirements of online communication and the negative effects of these shortcuts. Finally, this student writer ends his paper with his own evaluation of the situation and the potential problems created. Throughout the essay, the student writer carefully supports his principal points with summaries, paraphrases, and quotations from other sources. Notice that he uses the MLA documentation style and closes the paper with an alphabetical list of "Works Cited."

Language for a New Age

About 73% of teens between the ages of 12 and 17 access the Internet (<u>Lenhart et al</u>.). While these teens continue to develop their reading and writing skills, they are being exposed to the undisciplined, chaotic, and fast-paced World Wide Web. These

Citation (MLA format)

Background information

young surfers not only crave to connect faster to the Internet, they also want to communicate faster while on the Internet. They don't realize that, in their passion for speed, they may inhibit the development of their communication skills by inventing non-standard spellings, avoiding punctuation, and expressing emotion in new ways.

Student's first conclusion

Many of today's teenaged net heads may never become effective spellers because they frequently invent spelling while using instant messaging. Instant messaging is used to send a message to a friend who is online at the same time (Lenhart). The writer keys a brief message, sends it off, and it arrives almost immediately at its destination. Instant messaging is an extremely easy system to use, and its speed is unmatched for communicating among friends, even better than the much-revered e-mail system. Some teenagers converse simultaneously with several other instant messagers (Wood). If writers attempted to observe the conventions of standard written Canadian English, they would lengthen reply time and defeat the reason for instant messaging. The Internet generation has created a growing set of nonstandard spellings to increase their communications speed: *l8r*, for example, stands for "See you later"; *brb* stands for "Be right back" (Wood). Each message usually stands on its own line. Notice the absence of punctuation marks (and even capitalization). Keystroking the full statement seems too time consuming. As the list of these abbreviations continues to grow, and more teenagers accept them as normal, what effect will this have on their schoolwork and their ability to write standard Canadian English? (College students have been overheard discussing if proper spelling is *even necessary* on a Web page.) These nonstandard creations may become a common feature of online communication and may lead members of the so-called real world that does not appreciate, understand, or condone the use of these time-saving codes to judge such writing harshly: A reader who doesn't know computer speak simply sees errors when reading *btw, imho,* or *rofl* (for "by the way," "in my humble opinion," and "rolling on the floor laughing").

Paraphrase of secondary source

Common knowledge

Paraphrase of secondary source

Examples from secondary source

Student's opinion

Saving time by eliminating punctuation keystrokes may hurt more than a writer's intelligibility. Writers (or keyboarders, as time moves on) punctuate to express themselves clearly (Rogers 313). But consider this statement Bernard sent during an instant messaging session: "ok kev will be the spokes peron im way to into not thinking ting thru before acting" (Hupe). Some of the mistakes can be attributed to missed keystrokes, but where is the

Paraphrase of secondary source

Supporting example; quotation from secondary source

punctuation? Some readers may have trouble deciphering that Bernard was trying to say that another friend would represent Bernard during an online game. The writer omitted the punctuation; the reader had trouble understanding the message. Bernard is not alone. Enter just about any one of the growing numbers of chat rooms, or try instant messaging, and you will note this trend to omit punctuation. <u>Teenagers are being exposed to non-standard or non-existent punctuation, yet they must punctuate conventionally in school and while dealing with the world beyond the Internet</u>. Students might be excused for asking, If it's acceptable online, why is it not acceptable off line?

Common knowledge (margin note)

Are prolific users of instant messaging also limiting their capacity to write effectively about their emotions by inventing speedy but ineffective ways to convey feelings? It is challenging to communicate strong feelings in person let alone to someone that may be sitting in front of a monitor in an Internet café in another country, someone who can see only the typed words we send them. Instant messagers have handicapped themselves by not using proper punctuation or spelling to write clearly. Now innovators on the Internet have created simple pictures, *emoticons*, to show feelings. :) conveys a happy feeling. :(signifies a sad feeling. ;) is a conspiratorial wink. These symbols are used to communicate the tone that is lost when writers don't effectively use spelling and punctuation to set off certain words to create the desired effects within the writing. Amanda Lenhart and her colleagues report that many teenagers use the Internet for serious communication, including beginning or ending relationships and discussing important topics like depression and disease. Unlike the telephone, the text-based messaging of the Internet does not convey tone as easily as the human voice, so unless writers carefully craft messages to communicate tone in their writing, all the other person gets is words on a screen. <u>Expressing emotions is an important part of writing, and letting spelling and punctuation fall by the wayside will mean readers will not understand how their correspondents are feeling</u>.

Student's second conclusion / *Paraphrase of secondary source (facts)* / *Student's opinion* (margin notes)

People need to communicate to create a sense of community. When teens who make the Internet a big part of their life invent new spellings of common words and phrases, avoid the use of punctuation, and attempt to communicate their feelings with simple emoticons, they may be hampering their development of sophisticated writing skills. Critics of the educational system

Student's opinion (margin note)

Common
knowledge wonder why students are not learning to write skillfully. <u>Is it</u> Paraphrase
of
secondary
source
(opinion) <u>possible that the very computers and Internet access provided to</u> <u>help teenagers learn may be counterproductive (Quince)</u>? Students see one set of standards on the chalkboard, and then they are sent off to use a tool that fails to enforce and may even contradict the conventions. What message does this send students? Computers Student's
final
remarks have become a fact of life. As computers become faster, as the push intensifies to communicate faster, can people interact through the Internet without obliterating the conventions of standard written Canadian English that ensure that an English-speaking writer can send a message from a college dorm in Canada and be confident an English-speaking reader at an open access computer lab in China will understand it? Will readers be :) or :I (Pettrey)?

Works Cited

Hupe, Bernard Joseph. Personal conversation with Dave Kendell. 3 Oct. 2001.

Lenhart, Amanda, et al. "Teenage Life Online: The Rise of the Instant-Message Generation and the Internet's Impact on Friendships and Family Relationships." Survey Report. *Pew Internet & American Life.* 20 June 2001. 19 Feb. 2002 <http://www.pewinternet.org/reports/toc.asp?Report=36>.

Pettrey, William. "Emoticons." *MSN Messenger Services.* 14 Apr. 2002 <http://pages.yahoo.com/nhrp?o=williampettrey&p=msn.html&pos>.

Quince, Peter. "A Critique of Computers." Rev. of *High Tech Heretic,* by Clifford Stoll, and *Let Them Eat Data,* by Chet Bowers. *Resurgence* 205 Mar. /Apr. 2001. 10 Apr. 2002 <http://resurgence.gn.apc.org/issues/quince205.htm>.

Rogers, Douglas B. *Write of Way: Essay Strategies and Readings.* Toronto: Prentice Hall, 2002.

Wood, Chris. "A Mania for Messaging." *Maclean's* 13 Nov. 2000. 3 Feb. 2002 <http://www.macleans.ca>.

Some Final Thoughts on Documented Essays

The essays that follow offer vigorous exercises in critical thinking. They use a combination of the three different types of persuasive appeals we studied in Chapter 9 (logical, emotional, and ethical) and draw on a wealth of rhetorical modes that we have studied throughout the book. In the first essay, Barbara Ehrenreich illustrates the Modern Language Association documentation style as she uses sources to support her thesis that people do not have a natural instinct to kill. The second essay, by Marilyn Dahl, examines the role the media play in our societal images of disability; its use of sources illustrates the American Psychological Association documentation style. The third essay, by Ross Kilpatrick, makes the case for Canadian roots for A.A. Milne's character Winnie-the-Pooh. As you read these essays, be aware of the combination of appeals at work, the various rhetorical modes the authors use to further their arguments, and the way each author uses sources to support the topics within the argument.

Documented Essays in Review

Reading Documented Essays

Preparing to Read

- What assumptions can you make from the essay's title?
- Can you guess what the general mood of the essay is?
- What is the essay's purpose and audience?
- What does the synopsis in the Rhetorical Table of Contents tell you about the essay?
- What can you learn from the author's biography?
- Can you guess what the author's point of view toward the subject is?
- What are your responses to the Preparing to Read questions?

Reading

- What are your initial reactions to the essay?
- What is the author's main assertion or thesis?
- What sources does the author cite to support the thesis?
- What questions do you have about this topic?
- Did you preview the questions that follow the essay?

Rereading

- How does the author use facts and opinions in the essay?
- Are the sources the writer cites valid and reliable?
- Are the sources cited in the essay respected in the field?
- Does the author interpret facts accurately?
- Has the author omitted any necessary information?
- What are your responses to the questions after the essay?

Writing Documented Essays

Preparing to Write

- What are your responses to the Preparing to Write questions?
- What is your purpose?
- Who is your audience?

Writing

- Do you have a thesis statement?
- Do you use both primary and secondary sources in your essay?
- Have you organized your material effectively?
- Have you avoided plagiarism and cited your sources correctly?
- Do you use the appropriate documentation style?

Rewriting

- Are the essay's assertions clear? Are they adequately supported?
- Are other points of view recognized and examined?
- Does the organization of your paper further your assertions/argument?
- Have you removed irrelevant material?
- Is your source material (whether summarized, paraphrased, or quoted) presented fairly and accurately?
- Have you rechecked the citations for all the sources in your paper?

- Do you introduce the sources in your paper when appropriate?
- Are your sources in the proper format according to your instructor's guidelines (MLA, APA, or another)?
- Have you followed your instructor's guidelines for your title page, margins, page numbers, tables, and abstracts?
- Have you prepared an alphabetical list of your sources for the end of your paper?

BARBARA EHRENREICH

The Ecstasy of War

Barbara Ehrenreich (1941–) is a respected author, lecturer, and social commentator with opinions on a wide range of topics. After earning a B.A. from Reed College in chemistry and physics and a Ph.D. from Rockefeller University in cell biology, she turned almost immediately to freelance writing, producing a succession of books and pamphlets on a dazzling array of subjects. Early publications examined student uprisings, health care in America, nurses and midwives, poverty, welfare, economic justice for women, and the sexual politics of disease. Her recent books include *The Worst Years of Our Lives: Irreverent Notes from a Decade of Greed* (1990), an indictment of the 1980s that was described by *The New York Times* as "elegant, trenchant, savagely angry, morally outraged, and outrageously funny"; *Blood Rites: Origins and History of the Passions of War* (1997); and *Nickel and Dimed: On (Not) Getting By in America* (2001). Ehrenreich is also well known as a frequent guest on television and radio programs, including *The Today Show, Good Morning America, NightLine, Canada AM*, and *Crossfire*. Her many articles and reviews have appeared in *The New York Times Magazine, Esquire, The Atlantic Monthly, The New Republic, Vogue, Harper's*, and *The Wall Street Journal*. She has been an essayist for *Time* since 1990. Ehrenreich, whose favourite hobby is "voracious reading," lives in Syosset, New York.

Preparing to Read

Taken from *Blood Rites: Origins and History of the Passions of War* (1997), the following essay analyzes the psychology of war. Its citations and bibliography illustrate proper MLA (Modern Language Association) documentation form. As you prepare to read this article, take a few minutes to think about aggression in society today: Do you think aggression plays a significant role in North American society? In other societies? What do you think is the origin of aggression? In your opinion, what role does aggression play in war? In everyday life? How do you react to aggressive behaviour? How do people you associate with react to aggressive behaviour?

" *S*o *elemental is the human need to endow the shedding of blood with*   1
some great and even sublime significance that it renders the intel-
lect almost entirely helpless" (Van Creveld 166).

Different wars have led to different theories of why men   2
fight them. The Napoleonic Wars, which bore along with them
the rationalist spirit of the French Revolution, inspired the
Prussian officer Carl von Clausewitz to propose that war itself is
an entirely rational undertaking, unsullied by human emotion.
War, in his famous aphorism, is merely a "continuation of policy ...
by other means," with policy itself supposedly resulting from
the same kind of clearheaded deliberation one might apply to a
game of chess. Nation-states were the leading actors on the stage
of history, and war was simply one of the many ways they
advanced their interests against those of other nation-states. If
you could accept the existence of this new superperson, the
nation, a battle was no more disturbing and irrational than, say,
a difficult trade negotiation—except perhaps to those who lay
dying on the battlefield.

World War I, coming a century after Napoleon's sweep   3
through Europe and northern Africa, led to an opposite
assessment of the human impulse of war. World War I was hard
to construe as in any way "rational," especially to that generation
of European intellectuals, including Sigmund Freud, who survived
to ponder the unprecedented harvest of dead bodies. History
textbooks tell us that the "Great War" grew out of the conflict
between "competing imperialist states," but this Clausewitzian
interpretation has little to do with the actual series of accidents,
blunders, and miscommunications that impelled the nations of
Europe to war in the summer of 1914.[1] At first swept up in the
excitement of the war, unable for weeks to work or think of
anything else, Freud was eventually led to conclude that there is
some dark flaw in the human psyche, a perverse desire to destroy,
countering Eros and the will to live (Stromberg 82).

So these are, in crude summary, the theories of war which   4
modern wars have left us with: That war is a means, however
risky, by which men seek to advance their collective interests
and improve their lives. Or, alternatively, that war stems from
subrational drives not unlike those that lead individuals to
commit violent crimes. In our own time, most people seem to
hold both views at once, avowing that war is a gainful enterprise,
intended to meet the material needs of the groups engaged in it,

and, at the same time, that it fulfills deep and "irrational" psychological needs. There is no question about the first part of this proposition—that wars are designed, at least ostensibly, to secure necessaries like land or oil or "geopolitical advantage." The mystery lies in the peculiar psychological grip war exerts on us.

In the 1960s and '70s, the debate on the psychology of war   5 centered on the notion of an "aggressive instinct," peculiar to all humans or only to human males. This is not the place to summarize that debate, with its endless examples of animal behavior and clashes over their applicability to human affairs. Here I would simply point out that, whether or not there is an aggressive instinct, there are reasons to reject it as the major wellspring of war.

Although it is true that aggressive impulses, up to and   6 including murderous rage, can easily take over in the heat of actual battle, even this statement must be qualified to take account of different weaponry and modes of fighting. Hand-to-hand combat may indeed call forth and even require the emotions of rage and aggression, if only to mobilize the body for bursts of muscular activity. In the case of action-at-a-distance weapons, however, like guns and bows and arrows, emotionality of any sort can be a distinct disadvantage. Coolness, and the ability to keep aiming and firing steadfastly in the face of enemy fire, prevails. Hence, according to the distinguished American military historian Robert L. O'Connell, the change in the ideal warrior personality wrought by the advent of guns in the fifteenth and sixteenth centuries, from "ferocious aggressiveness" to "passive disdain" (119). So there is no personality type—"hot-tempered," "macho," or whatever—consistently and universally associated with warfare.

Furthermore, fighting itself is only one component of the   7 enterprise we know as war. Wars are not barroom brawls writ large, or domestic violence that has been somehow extended to strangers. In war, fighting takes place within battles—along with much anxious waiting, of course—but wars do not begin with battles and are often not decided by them either. Most of war consists of *preparation* for battle—training, the organization of supplies, marching and other forms of transport—activities which are hard to account for by innate promptings of any kind. There is no plausible instinct, for example, that impels a man to leave his home, cut his hair short, and drill for hours in tight formation.

As anthropologists Clifton B. Kroeber and Bernard L. Fontana point out, "It is a large step from what may be biologically innate leanings toward individual aggression to ritualized, socially sanctioned, institutionalized group warfare" (166).

War, in other words, is too complex and collective an activity to be accounted for by a single warlike instinct lurking within the individual psyche. Instinct may, or may not, inspire a man to bayonet the first enemy he encounters in battle. But instinct does not mobilize supply lines, manufacture rifles, issue uniforms, or move an army of thousands from point A on the map to B. These are "complicated, orchestrated, highly organized" activities, as social theorist Robin Fox writes, undertaken not by individuals but by entities on the scale of nations and dynasties (15). "The hypothesis of a killer instinct," according to a commentator summarizing a recent conference on the anthropology of war, is "not so much wrong as irrelevant" (McCauley 2).

In fact, throughout history, individual men have gone to near-suicidal lengths to avoid participating in wars—a fact that proponents of a warlike instinct tend to slight. Men have fled their homelands, served lengthy prison terms, hacked off limbs, shot off feet or index fingers, feigned illness or insanity, or, if they could afford to, paid surrogates to fight in their stead. "Some draw their teeth, some blind themselves, and others maim themselves, on their way to us" (Mitchell 42), the governor of Egypt complained of his peasant recruits in the early nineteenth century. So unreliable was the rank and file of the eighteenth-century Prussian army that military manuals forbade camping near a woods or forest: The troops would simply melt away into the trees (Delbrück 303).

Proponents of a warlike instinct must also reckon with the fact that even when men have been assembled, willingly or unwillingly, for the purpose of war, fighting is not something that seems to come "naturally" to them. In fact, surprisingly, even in the thick of battle, few men can bring themselves to shoot directly at individual enemies.[2] The difference between an ordinary man or boy and a reliable killer, as any drill sergeant could attest, is profound. A transformation is required: The man or boy leaves his former self behind and becomes something entirely different, perhaps even taking a new name. In small-scale, traditional societies, the change was usually accomplished through ritual drumming, dancing, fasting, and sexual abstinence—all of which serve to lift a man out of his mundane existence and into a new, warriorlike mode of being, denoted by special body paint, masks, and headdresses.

As if to emphasize the discontinuity between the warrior and the ordinary human being, many cultures require the would-be fighting man to leave his human-ness behind and assume a new form as an animal.[3] The young Scandinavian had to become a bear before he could become an elite warrior, going "berserk" (the word means, "dressed in a bear hide"), biting and chasing people. The Irish hero Cuchulain transformed himself into a monster in preparation for battle: "He became horrible, many-shaped, strange and unrecognizable," with one eye sucked into his skull and the other popping out of the side of the face (Davidson 84). Apparently this transformation was a familiar and meaningful one, because similarly distorted faces turn up frequently in Celtic art. 11

Often the transformation is helped along with drugs or social pressure of various kinds. Tahitian warriors were browbeaten into fighting by functionaries called Rauti, or "exhorters," who ran around the battlefield urging their comrades to mimic "the devouring wild dog" (Keeley 146). The ancient Greek hoplites drank enough wine, apparently, to be quite tipsy when they went into battle (Hanson 126); Aztecs drank pulque; Chinese troops at the time of Sun Tzu got into the mood by drinking wine and watching "gyrating sword dancers" perform (Griffith in Sun Tzu 37). Almost any drug or intoxicant has served, in one setting or another, to facilitate the transformation of man into warrior. Yanomamo Indians of the Amazon ingest a hallucinogen before battle; the ancient Scythians smoked hemp, while a neighboring tribe drank something called "hauma," which is believed to have induced a frenzy of aggression (Rolle 94–95). So if there is a destructive instinct that impels man to war, it is a weak one, and often requires a great deal of help. 12

In seventeenth-century Europe, the transformation of man into soldier took on a new form, more concerted and disciplined, and far less pleasant, than wine. New recruits and even seasoned veterans were endlessly drilled, hour after hour, until each man began to feel himself part of a single, giant fighting machine. The drill was only partially inspired by the technology of firearms. It's easy enough to teach a man to shoot a gun; the problem is to make him willing to get into situations where guns are being shot and to remain there long enough to do some shooting of his own. So modern military training aims at a 13 transformation parallel to that achieved by "primitives" with war drums and paint: In the fanatical routines of boot camp, a man leaves behind his former identity and is reborn as a creature of the military—an automaton and also, ideally, a willing killer of other men.

This is not to suggest that killing is foreign to human nature   14 or, more narrowly, to the male personality. Men (and women) have again and again proved themselves capable of killing impulsively and with gusto. But there is a huge difference between a war and an ordinary fight. War not only departs from the normal; it inverts all that is moral and right: In war one *should* kill, *should* steal, *should* burn cities and farms, should perhaps even rape matrons and little girls. Whether or not such activities are "natural" or at some level instinctual, most men undertake them only by entering what appears to be an "altered state"— induced by drugs or lengthy drilling, and denoted by face paint or khakis.

The point of such transformative rituals is not only to put   15 men "in the mood." Returning warriors may go through equally challenging rituals before they can celebrate victory or reenter the community—covering their heads in apparent shame, for example; vomiting repeatedly; abstaining from sex (Keeley 144). Among the Maori, returning warriors could not participate in the victory celebration until they had gone through a whaka-hoa ritual, designed to make them "common" again: The hearts of slain enemies were roasted, after which offerings were made to the war god Tu, and the rest was eaten by priests, who shouted spells to remove "the blood curse" and enable warriors to reenter their ordinary lives (Sagan 18). Among the Taulipang Indians of South America, victorious warriors "sat on ants, flogged one another with whips, and passed a cord covered with poisonous ants, through their mouth and nose" (Métraux 397). Such painful and shocking postwar rites impress on the warrior that war is much more than a "continuation of policy ... by other means." In war men enter an alternative realm of human experience, as far removed from daily life as those things which we call "sacred."

Notes

1. See, for example, Stoessinger, *Why Nations Go to War*, 14–20.
2. See Grossman, *On Killing*.

3. In the mythologies of the Indo-European tradition, Dumézil relates, thanks "either to a gift of metamorphosis, or to a monstrous heredity, the eminent warrior possesses a veritable animal nature" (140).

Works Cited

Davidson, Hilda Ellis. *Myths and Symbols in Pagan Europe: Early Scandinavian and Celtic Religions.* Syracuse, NY: Syracuse UP, 1988.

Delbrück, Hans. *The Dawn of Modern Warfare.* Vol. 4 of *History of the Art of War.* Lincoln: U of Nebraska P, 1985.

Dumézil, Georges. *Destiny of the Warrior.* Chicago: U of Chicago P, 1969.

Fox, Robin. "Fatal Attraction: War and Human Nature." *The National Interest* (Winter 1992/93): 11–20.

Grossman, Lt. Col. Dave. *On Killing: The Psychological Cost of Learning to Kill in War and Society.* Boston: Little, Brown, 1995.

Hanson, Victor Davis. *The Western Way of War: Infantry Battle in Classical Greece.* New York: Knopf, 1989.

Keeley, Lawrence H. *War Before Civilization: The Myth of the Peaceful Savage.* New York: Oxford UP, 1996.

Kroeber, Clifton B., and Bernard L. Fontana. *Massacre on the Gila: An Account of the Last Major Battle Between American Indians, With Reflections on the Origin of War.* Tucson: U of Arizona P, 1986.

McCauley, Clark. "Conference Overview." *The Anthropology of War.* Ed. Jonathan Haas. Cambridge: Cambridge UP, 1990, 1–25.

Métraux, Alfred. "Warfare, Cannibalism, and Human Trophies." *Handbook of South American Indians,* vol. 5. Ed. Julian H. Steward. New York: Cooper Square Publishers, 1963, 383–409.

Mitchell, Timothy. *Colonizing Egypt.* Berkeley: U of California P, 1991.

O'Connell, Robert L. *Of Arms and Men: A History of War, Weapons, and Aggression.* New York: Oxford UP, 1989.

Rolle, Renate. *The World of the Scythians.* Berkeley: U of California P, 1989.

Sagan, Eli. *Cannibalism: Human Aggression and Cultural Form.* New York: Harper and Row, 1974.

Stoessinger, John G. *Why Nations Go to War.* New York: St. Martin's Press, 1993.

Stromberg, Roland. *Redemption by War: The Intellectuals and 1914.* Lawrence: U of Kansas P, 1982.

Sun Tzu. *The Art of War.* Trans. Samuel B. Griffith. London: Oxford UP, 1971.

Van Creveld, Martin. *The Transformation of War.* New York: Free Press, 1991.

UNDERSTANDING DETAILS

1. What do you think Ehrenreich's main purpose is in this essay?
2. According to Ehrenreich, what is the difference between hand-to-hand combat and fighting at a distance?
3. What does Ehrenreich say are the various components of what we call "war"?
4. In what ways do some cultures ritualize the transformation from regular citizen to warrior? Give three examples.

ANALYZING MEANING

1. Do you believe war can ever be emotionless and rational, like "a difficult trade negotiation" (paragraph 2)?
2. What do Clifton B. Kroeber and Bernard L. Fontana mean when they say "It is a large step from what may be biologically innate leanings toward individual aggression to ritualized, socially sanctioned, institutionalized group warfare" (paragraph 7)?
3. Why is "the hypothesis of a killer instinct" "not so much wrong as irrelevant" to the "anthropology of war" (paragraph 8)?
4. Are you convinced by this essay that "In war men enter an alternative realm of human experience, as far removed from daily life as those things which we call 'sacred'" (paragraph 15)?

DISCOVERING RHETORICAL STRATEGIES

1. Who do you think is Ehrenreich's main audience? How did you come to this conclusion?
2. The author begins her discussion of war with different "theories of why men fight them [wars]" (paragraph 2). Is this an effective

beginning for what Ehrenreich is trying to accomplish? Explain your answer.

3. What information in this essay is most persuasive to you? What is the least persuasive?

4. What tone does the author establish by citing frequent statistics and referring to other sources in her essay?

MAKING CONNECTIONS

1. Compare and contrast Ehrenreich's insights on the psychology of war with Stephen King's theories on "Why We Crave Horror Movies." How do their ideas support one another? How do they contradict each other?

2. Compare Ehrenreich's use of examples with those of Marilyn Dahl ("The Role of the Media in Promoting Images of Disability").

3. In a conversation between Ehrenreich and Steven Heighton ("Elegy in Stone") about the glorification of war in American society, on what points would they agree and disagree? Give examples.

IDEAS FOR DISCUSSION/WRITING

Preparing to Write

Write freely about aggression in general: Why do people fight? Why do countries go to war? What are some ways in which people take out their aggression? Have you ever noticed people fighting just for the sake of fighting? When is aggression acceptable? When is it unacceptable?

Choosing a Topic

1. Ehrenreich claims that "even when men have been assembled, willingly or unwillingly, for the purpose of war, fighting is not something that seems to come 'naturally' to them" (paragraph 10). Do you agree or disagree with this statement? Explain your reaction in a clearly reasoned argumentative essay. Cite Ehrenreich's selection whenever necessary.

2. In the last paragraph of her essay, Ehrenreich suggests that warriors often have to go through rituals to return to their civilizations. Use Ehrenreich's article as one of your sources; then

read further on such transformations. Next, write a clear, well-documented argument expressing your opinion on a specific transformation. Organize your paper clearly, and present your suggestions logically, using proper documentation (citations and bibliography) to support your position.

3. Use additional sources to study the circumstances of a war you are familiar with. Then, referring to Ehrenreich's explanation of "the anthropology of war" (paragraph 8), write a well-documented argument explaining the causes and effects of the war by discussing or analyzing in depth the consequences you have discovered.

WEBSITES

lnf.uoregon.edu/notable/ehrenreich.html
Read an interview with Barbara Ehrenreich.

www.ffrf.org/fttoday/april2000/ehrenreich.html
This site features an essay by Barbara Ehrenreich entitled "My Family Values Atheism."

MARILYN DAHL

The Role of the Media in Promoting Images of Disability—Disability as Metaphor: The Evil Crip

Marilyn Dahl (1931–) is a western Canadian nurse educator originally from Broderick, Saskatchewan, and now retired and living in Port Coquitlam, B.C. After graduating as an R.N. in 1953 from the Victoria Hospital School of Nursing in Prince Albert, Dahl practised nursing in a variety of settings until 1977. During this time she was married, had three children, wrote a hospital teaching video, and also wrote and produced a weekly children's television program in Medicine Hat from 1967 to 1969. Dahl then returned to school at the University of British Columbia to get her B.Sc.N. in 1979. In the 1980s Dahl worked as an instructor at the Douglas College Faculty of Nursing and became a consumer advocate for the disabled in 1980. In 1985 she assumed the position of president of the Canadian Hard of Hearing Association and three years later became the vice-president of the International Hard of Hearing Federation. Dahl completed her M.A. at Simon Fraser University in 1988 with a thesis looking at how disabled role identity is culturally produced in Canadian society. Her many publications include *Caring for the Patient Who Is Hard of Hearing* (1979). This essay appeared in the *Canadian Journal of Communication* in 1993.

Preparing to Read

Before reading this article think about how disabilities are portrayed by the media. Brainstorm a list of movies, television shows, and books that include characters with disabilities. What disabilities do these characters have? Is the disability the focus of the story or is it an incidental characteristic? How are these people with disabilities portrayed? What do you know about the characters apart from their disabilities?

It is a commonly held theory that one cannot legislate attitude 1 change. One can legislate behavioural change and hopefully changes in attitude will follow. Attitudes, beliefs, and misconceptions of society constitute a major barrier for people with disabilities. Attitude change can follow on heightened awareness, increased contact, and increased meaningful communication between disabled and non-disabled people. Although personal interaction is the most effective medium for conveying the personal experience of disability, the mass media can be an effective vehicle for bringing about greater understanding, and a consequent gradual change in public perceptions, of people with disabilities.

Disability as a Metaphor

A review of our cultural forms of expression provides evidence 2 of the metaphoric role of disability which is deeply ingrained in our social values. It has been a convention of all literature and art that physical deformity, chronic illness, or any visible defect symbolizes an evil and malevolent nature and monstrous behaviour (Sontag, 1978). A summary look at literary distortions of handicapping conditions illustrates this point: Captain Hook (in *Peter Pan*) is intentionally an amputee with a prosthesis; Shakespeare links Richard III's hunchback to his evil lust. Somerset Maugham uses Philip's clubfoot (in *Of Human Bondage*) to symbolize his bitter and warped nature.

Occasionally a type of reaction formation is invoked and the 3 literary association to disability is instead quite sentimental. Hans Christian Andersen depicts The Little Lame Prince in maudlin tones, and some other childhood tales use the stereotype of the selfless dwarf, or the blind seer. Occasionally the protagonist copes nobly with a disability but even then it is depicted as a "curse" to bear. Cyrano de Bergerac with his grotesque nose and Quasimodo with his hunchback are remarked not for their deformity but because they are both deformed and good (as though one precludes the other). Rarely does there appear an average or ordinary person whose disability is incidental.

We are both repelled and intrigued by the cripple as 4 metaphor. Children's classics are particularly graphic and concrete in this regard. Villains are always ugly and deformed in some manner, heroes and heroines are possessed of beauty and grace. Fellini used freaks and disabilities to cue people to respond with revulsion and disgust to his film characters. Disney frequently promoted disability as metaphor. More recently, Hollywood has tended to sentimentalize the disabled with stock movies of two-dimensional characters who "learn to cope" and "live happily ever after." The deaf (*Voices*), the blind (*Ice Castles*), and quadriplegics (*The Other Side of the Mountain*) have all been treated within this formula. Film and television have also employed the metaphor of the disabled as helpless victim. Roughing up a cripple or a blind man is a device used to show a villain as a particularly evil person. At times television has tended to transform the metaphor by endowing the disabled person with superhuman characteristics, such as the Bionic Man; while in *Ironside*, the paraplegic was given a brilliant mind (Bird, Byrd, & Allen, 1977).

Research into the relationship between physical attractiveness   5
and crime in the various media found that physical ugliness and physical differences are often associated with media depictions of violence and crime (Needleman & Weiner, 1974). Horror movies make free use of this strategy. Gardner & Radel (1978), who analyzed American newspapers and television for references to disabled people, found that about one half of the items portrayed the disabled as dependent persons. A tenth of the items portrayed the disabled as being in some way deviant: "strange, antisocial or bizarre." Only about one quarter of the items portrayed the disabled as persons capable of independent living and of contributing to society. Cartoons and comic strip captions are also important carriers of prejudicial and discrimina-tory language and images of evil cripples. Words such as "stupid moron," "idiot," "crazy," are common jargon in strips such as *Beetle Bailey*, and the various "animal" comic strips. Everyday words which refer to specific conditions have become standard-ized as curse words, and stereotypes of conditions are reinforced (Weinberg & Santana, 1978).

In spite of these trends, there have been some changes in   6
American plays and films, which today present more sympathetic and romanticized views of the disabled. Gussow (1979) labelled the phenomenon "the time of the wounded hero." Some of the examples are *The Elephant Man* (congenital deformity), *Wings* (stroke), *Whose Life Is It Anyway?* (paralysis), and *Children of a Lesser God*. There have been more recent attempts to portray the disabled as "incidental" characters, neither hero nor victim. A policeman in a wheelchair on *Cagney and Lacey* portrayed an average role. The elderly, the ugly, the obese are seen more often as "normal." Marlee Matlin, as assistant district attorney in *Reasonable Doubts*, attempts to show a deaf person filling a professional role in much the same way as a hearing person. Made for television films in the 1980s have portrayed sensitive

and realistic stories of schizophrenia and Alzheimer's victims. *L.A. Law* portrays a mentally handicapped man in a sensitive way, and has a lawyer who wears a hearing aid.

Effects of Media Selectivity in Describing Disability

The media promote certain images of the disabled by selectively covering certain events and ignoring others. Dr. Kenneth Jernigan, president of the National American Federation of the Blind, reported that reporters invited to a press conference on a highly political topic, ignored the political topic and wanted instead to photograph and report on the various walking aids, lead dogs, and other stereotypical symbols of blindness (Bogden & Biklen, 1977). In covering the Terry Fox story, the media focused on the "dying hero" and the medical model of illness, ignoring the counter-ideology issue of environmental pollution from nuclear fallout over the area where Fox was born in the 1950s, and its relationship to causes of cancer (Harrison, 1985). 7

The selective coverage of disability has led to the creation of "heroes by hype." The power of the media in manipulating public response is seen in the media coverage of the disabled marathoners who in the 1980s were a uniquely Canadian phenomenon (Graham, 1987). While many marathoners crossed Canada for causes, it was only the young, attractive men with dramatic visual disabilities (Fox, Fonyo, and Hansen) who received orchestrated backing and media coverage. Promoters and handlers "packaged" the young man and directed the programs and publicity en route. A star was created. Increased coverage pressured corporations and politicians to be seen giving generously to the hero's cause. An exception was the "W5" program (CTV, 1987), which presented the misgivings held by disabled people themselves about what "disabled as superstar" portrays to the public. 8

The *Disability Network* (TVOntario) presents lifestyles of people with disabilities, but most disabled people would prefer to be shown as part of the average population. The Bay's advertising flyer recently featured a model in a wheelchair, McDonald's ads have included people with different types of disabilities (King, 1992). These ads are the exception rather than the rule. Advertisers do not seem to think in terms of disabled people as customers—drinking beer, brushing their teeth, or buying a car. One particularly onerous depiction of disability 9 remains a television regular: fund-raising telethons. The model for this is the Jerry Lewis Telethon which presents an alliance of business, high status public persons and service providers, plus a disabled child who is helpless and appealing. The images equate disability with childlike behaviour and an infantile condition, a minor role, while the healthy normal star has the spotlight, status, and prestige. Helping the disabled becomes entertainment (Dahl, 1987).

The mass media perpetuate stereotypes of disability through   10
their portrayals of characters. But there is no evidence that the mass media have any major effect on manipulating the attitudes and opinions of their audience. Researchers state that it is difficult to discover what are the precise effects of the media on public opinion. It is possible that attitudes and opinions change dramatically as a result of what is seen or heard. There are indications of selective perception of what is viewed, namely that audiences tend to identify with that which reinforces their existing beliefs. On the whole it appears that "the potential of the mass media to create false impressions ... is tempered by the tendency of the public to neglect the mass media in favour of other sources of understanding social reality" (Howitt, 1982, p. 179). Some speculation is in order, however, on the effect of negative stereotyping on the disabled themselves, especially children with disabilities. "Self-identity is formed by what is communicated through the media as well as by interpersonal acts" (Gumpert & Cathcart, 1982, p. 13). To see oneself labelled and cast always in the role of the villain, helpless dependent, or victim is not an enviable fate.

Creating an "Average" Typification of the Disabled

Although there are no specific data showing attitude change in   11
response to media communication, people tend to believe that the manner in which characters are portrayed is important. Characters presented on screen are sociocultural stereotypes designed to appeal to the majority of viewers, and reflect widely held values (albeit mostly American). It seems apparent that the repeated presentation of images in an acceptable and palatable manner will result in those images becoming a typification of everyday existence. The media are efficient in implanting new information and contributing new ideas and values, where they are not in conflict with strongly held views. The effect of mass

communication on society is often more a contributory than a sole effect (Schramm, 1973). "Media images, however, can help to shape the meanings we find directly in the situation and what we discover in the actual situation can influence the way we look at the media" (Kelly, 1981, p. 167).

The CRTC recognized the influence of broadcasting on 12 viewers in its 1986 policy statement: "Broadcasting is ... a powerful medium to reinforce [sex-role] stereotyping and can be equally powerful to correct it." Since 1979, the Treasury Board, the Advertising Management Group, the CRTC, and CBC have developed policies on the elimination of sexual stereotyping and cultural stereotyping. The CRTC called for self-regulation by the industry in regard to policy implementation. Guidelines are monitored by the CRTC, the industry, and consumer groups such as Mediawatch and Evaluation/Medias (in Quebec). The CRTC report (December, 1986) indicated that some sensitization to the issue of sex-role stereotyping had occurred, but significant reductions in such stereotyping had not been achieved. No separate set of guidelines exists with respect to persons with disabilities; such guidelines are included under regulations prohibiting discrimination. In 1990 the Department of Secretary of State, Canada, published two reports: *Worthless or Wonderful* includes recommendations on elimination of social stereotyping of disabled persons, modelled on the guidelines for sex-role and cultural stereotype elimination; *A Way With Words* (1990) provides guidelines and appropriate terminology for the portrayal of persons with disabilities.

We have moved somewhat away from the disabled as hero 13 or victim but we are still a long way from a normal depiction of disability. Disabled people could be depicted as living and working in a variety of situations, with a diverse range of responsibilities, and not necessarily overcoming great odds to achieve their status. The mass media affect public opinion and public perception of social reality by their ability to create typifications. Careful use of terminology and visual images of the disabled can gradually create a more acceptable and realistic typification of people with disabilities as "average" people.

References

Bird, E.K., Byrd, P.D., & Allen, C.M. (1977). Television programming and disability. *Applied Rehabilitation Counselling*, 8(1), 28–32.

Bogden, Robert, & Biklen, Douglas. (1977). *Handicapism*. Mimeographed paper, Social Policy Corporation, New York.

CRTC. (1986). *Sex role stereotyping in the broadcast media* (Policy Statement). Ottawa: Supply and Services Canada.

CRTC. (1986). *Sex role stereotyping in the broadcast media* (Report on Industry Self-Regulation). Ottawa: Supply and Services Canada.

Dahl, Marilyn. (1987). *The cultural production of the disabled role identity in contemporary Canadian society*. MA thesis, Simon Fraser University, Burnaby, BC.

Fiedler, Leslie. (1978). *Freaks, myths and images of the secret self*. New York: Simon & Shuster.

Gardner, J.M., & Radel, M. (1978). Portrait of the disabled in the media. *Journal of Community Psychology*, 6, 269–274.

Graham, R. (1987, January). On the road. *Saturday Night*, 102(1) 16ff.

Gumpert, Gary, & Cathcart, Robert. (1982). *Inter/media: Interpersonal communication in a media world*. New York: Oxford University Press.

Gussow, Mel. (1979, April 15). The time of the wounded hero. *The New York Times*, 11, 1–2.

Harrison, Deborah. (1985). The Terry Fox story and the media: A case study in ideology and illness. *Canadian Review of Sociology and Anthropology*, 22(4), 496–514.

Howitt, Dennis. (1982). *The mass media and social problems*. Oxford: Pergamon Press.

Kelly, John. (1981). *A philosophy of communication and culture*. London: Centre for Study of Communications and Culture.

King, Marsha. (1992, February 20). Companies doing the right thing. *The Province*, p. C9.

Needleman, B., & Weiner, N. (1974). *Faces of evil: The good, the bad and the ugly*. Mimeographed paper, Oswego State College Department of Sociology, New York.

Schramm, Wilbur. (1973). *Men, messages and media*. New York: Harper & Row.

Secretary of State. (1988). *A way with words: Guidelines and appropriate terminology for the portrayal of persons with disabilities.* Ottawa: Minister of Supply and Services.

Secretary of State. (1988). *Worthless or wonderful: The social stereotyping of persons with disabilities.* Ottawa: Minister of Supply and Services.

Sontag, Susan. (1978). *Illness as metaphor.* New York: Farrar, Strauss & Giroux.

Weinberg, Nancy, & Santana, Rosina. (1978, November–December). Comic books: Champions of the disabled stereotype. *Rehabilitation Literature,* pp. 11–12.

UNDERSTANDING DETAILS

1. According to Dahl, in what way does the mass media make life difficult for people with disabilities?
2. What does Dahl see as likely to cause attitude change regarding people with disabilities?
3. Why does Dahl not support fund-raising telethons for disabilities?

ANALYZING MEANING

1. Is Dahl optimistic or pessimistic about the current portrayal of people with disabilities by the mass media? Explain.
2. What is Dahl's attitude toward disabled marathoners such as Terry Fox, Steve Fonyo, or Rick Hansen?
3. Summarize the categories that Dahl establishes to organize portrayals of people with disabilities. Add one original example to each category.

DISCOVERING RHETORICAL STRATEGIES

1. From what you know about the source of this essay and the writer, describe Dahl's audience. Is this the same group that she usually addresses? How do you know this?
2. In this article is Dahl reporting, interpreting, or analyzing? How do Dahl's sources and statistics help advance her argument?
3. What main rhetorical modes does Dahl use to state her case? Give examples of each.

MAKING CONNECTIONS

1. Dahl contends that stereotyping can be diminished through changing the images that people see in the media, and that legislation can promote the changes in these images. How would Cecil Foster ("Why Blacks Get Mad") react to Dahl's position on the importance of the images that people see in the media? What is your position on this issue?
2. Imagine that Dahl is having a conversation with Wayson Choy ("I'm a Banana and Proud of It"), Barbara Kingsolver ("Life Without Go-Go Boots"), and Laura Robinson ("Starving for the Gold") about the effect of appearance. On what points would the four writers agree? On which would they disagree?

IDEAS FOR DISCUSSION/WRITING

Preparing to Write

Write freely about language and disability. What connotations are there to words like *maimed, crippled, handicapped, physically challenged, differently abled, disfigured,* or *disabled*? Which words are acceptable? Which ones are not? What associations do you have with the terms "retarded," "feeble-minded," and "moron"?

Choosing a Topic

1. In a letter to the organizers of one of the fundraising telethons for disabilities, explain the negative effects of their well-intentioned actions and encourage them to stop holding their telethon.
2. Dahl refers to the depiction of disabilities in fairy tales. In a well-documented essay, explore the portrayal of evil or bad characters in fairy tales. To what extent are disabilities used to reflect negative roles?
3. Using both primary and secondary sources, research the effects of including people with disabilities in advertisements. Write a well-documented essay in which you examine both the direct and indirect outcomes of this approach to advertising.

WEBSITES

www.protocol.gov.bc.ca/protocol/prgs/obc/1993/1993_MDahl.htm
Dahl was a 1993 recipient of the Order of British Columbia.

www.csc-scc.gc.ca/text/pblct/forum/e062/e062e.shtml
Read an article by Marilyn Dahl for the Canadian government entitled "Under-Identification of Hearing Loss in the Canadian Federal Inmate Population."

ROSS KILPATRICK

Winnie-the-Pooh and the Canadian Connection

Professor of classics at Queen's University in Kingston, Ontario, Ross Kilpatrick has particular interests in Greek drama and Roman poetry. In addition to serving as president of the Ontario Classical Association in the early 1980s and as the Canadian Regional VP on the Committee for Promotion of Latin, Kilpatrick is the author of several scholarly books including *Sir Charles G.D. Roberts' Orion and Other Poems: Text and Commentary* (1999), and two books on Horace's *Epistles*.

Preparing to Read

In this essay, which originally appeared in the *Queen's Quarterly*, Kilpatrick examines the source of the famous character Winnie-the-Pooh. Before you begin reading, think about Winnie-the-Pooh. Are you familiar with the character Winnie-the-Pooh? Where have you encountered this character? In your mind's eye, what does Winnie-the-Pooh look like? Where does Winnie-the-Pooh come from? Whose creation is Winnie-the-Pooh? What other characters do you associate with Winnie-the-Pooh?

Lately, there have been increasingly strident claims by both 1 British and Americans for ownership of Christopher Robin's original plush toys: Pooh, Kanga, Eeyore, Tigger, and Piglet. Since 1947 they have resided in the United States, most recently in the New York Public Library. "The Brits have their head in a honey jar if they think they are taking Pooh out of New York City!" declared an irate congresswoman. But as Charles Gordon noted in a recent column on the subject in the *Ottawa Citizen*: "Canadians, notoriously unconcerned about their own history, don't associate Pooh with Canada, perhaps because they never visit White River, perhaps because they watch the news on CNN."[1]

Canadians are reminded frequently on national television 2 (and by Canada Post, which issued four commemorative Winnie-the-Pooh stamps in 1996) that a bear cub dubbed "Winnie" who would later captivate the five-year-old Christopher Robin Milne at the London Zoo had originally come from White River, Ontario, in 1914. She had been bought at the station from a trapper by Lieutenant Harry Colbourne, a native of Winnipeg and a veterinarian, who was on his way overseas with the Fort Garry Horse. Winnie served as mascot of the 2nd Canadian Infantry Brigade in England until it embarked for France, when she was left in the care of the London Zoo. She remained there, a great favourite of young and old, until she died in 1934. Bronze statues of Winnie with Lieutenant Colbourne can be seen today in London and Winnipeg, and Walt Disney presented one of Winnie to the town of White River.

There is little doubt, however, that American claims to ownership of Pooh have some deep roots. 3

> Our Teddy Bear is short and fat
> Which is not to be wondered at.[2]

In A.A. Milne's poem "Teddy Bear" (1924) Pooh was celebrated as "Teddy," an attribution with a history dating back to Mississippi in 1902. In November of that year, President Theodore Roosevelt had drawn the line at shooting a wretched bear, cornered by dogs, stunned by a blow to the head from a rifle-butt, then tied up for him to bag during a hunt arranged for his visit there to arbitrate a boundary dispute with Louisiana. That sportsmanlike gesture by the famous outdoorsman-politician was immortalized by *Washington Post* artist Clifford K. Berryman in his famous front-page cartoon of 16 November 1902: "Drawing the line in Mississippi." The actual denouement of the affair was rather less flattering to the great man.[3] 4

Soon after that, toy manufacturer Morris Michton of Brooklyn, New York, obtained permission to use the president's nickname for his company's line of plush bears. "Teddy Bear" would soon become universally a term of great affection. Bear classifications by date, manufacturer, type, and country of origin are now all part of world-wide collecting, complete with its encyclopedias and websites. Pooh, for instance, is classified as a Farnell "Alpha Bear" (a line manufactured during the '20s), and was purchased by Mrs Milne at Harrods in 1921.[4] 5

In England, the Teddy Roosevelt connection became less clear, of course, but the popularity of King Edward VII helped fuel the "Teddy" craze. In Milne's poem "Teddy Bear," Pooh's *alter ursus* is saluted by the king of France: 6

But is it Mr. *Edward* Bear?
And Teddy, bowing very low,
Replied politely, "Even so!"

The heroic conclusion of *The House at Pooh Corner* sees Pooh   7
dubbed by Christopher Robin as "Sir Pooh de Bear, most faithful
of all my Knights."[5]

For all the Teddy Bear's acculturation in England as an icon   8
of King Edward, however, Theodore Roosevelt's original bear
connection was certainly not forgotten. The president's arrival
in London in 1910 to attend the king's state funeral was celebrated
in *Punch* (11 May 1910) in a cartoon by J.L.C. Boon, "A Suggested
Precaution."

This cartoon certainly implies an enduring interest in   9
Berryman's *Washington Post* cartoon of eight years earlier. And
not two months before (23 March 1910) a *Punch* cartoon by L.
Ravenhill represented Teddy Roosevelt, with his son Kermit,
about to bag even the Sphinx as a unique specimen of desert
fauna!

On 29 June 1910 *Punch* also published a poem by W.H.   10
Ogilvie, "The bear garden that I love." It begins:

The house is full of Teddy bears;
They creep upon me unawares;
They catch my feet upon the mat
And make me think I've squashed the cat;
I sit upon them during meals
And shiver at their long-drawn squeals;
I find them in my bed at night,
But luckily they never bite.

These three items would have been approved by the assistant   11
editor of *Punch*, none other than A.A. Milne. "Teddy Bears" and
"Teddy's Bears" were evidently a source of professional
amusement to the future author of *Winnie-the-Pooh* well before the
First World War, when Milne took a leave of absence from *Punch*
to serve in the Royal Warwickshire Regiment. (On his discharge
in 1918 he resigned as assistant editor to become a full-time
writer.)[6]

"As a child Milne had clearly enjoyed fantasy literature about   12
animals." Paula Connolly cites Milne's own *Autobiography* for
his great affection for Reynard the Fox and Uncle Remus, and
the stories in *Aunt Judy's Magazine*: "... here was a magic which

children, from generation to generation, have been unable to resist." Milne gave full credit to those authors for his own "laurels" as a children's writer. The boys' authors he read included W.H.G. Kingston, Robert Louis Stevenson, and Richard Jeffries.[7]

But there is one eminent young people's nature-writer conspicuously absent from this list: New Brunswick–born poet, essayist, and novelist Charles G.D. Roberts (later Sir Charles, 1860–1943).[8] Already a distinguished poet, Roberts had made a name for himself in North America and England, beginning in 1896, in the tradition of his contemporary Jack London, with a succession of successful nature novels. In 1907, in fact, he found himself (along with writers Jack London, Ernest Thomas Seton, and William V. Long) embroiled in a lively public debate with President Theodore Roosevelt, whose stern views about such "Nature Fakirs" among the literary fraternity were publicized through an interview with Edward Clark (and Roosevelt's own subsequent article) in *Everybody's Magazine*. Roosevelt took issue with Roberts on one detail of his short story, "Night Trail" (1907), in which he has a single lynx rout a pack of wolves: "Now the thing is so utterly ridiculous that any man who knows both the wolf and the lynx loses patience."[9] The affair even inspired a delicious cartoon by T.E. Powers in the *New York Evening Journal* of 24 May 1907, sending up the whole nature writers establishment. 13

For his part, Roberts entered the fray with relish, insisting that the president was confusing the *Lynx Rufus* with *Lynx Canadensis*, and the Western Timber Wolf with the Eastern Brush Wolf. When all the silliness settled down, however, the president and Roberts became warm friends, and Roosevelt revealed that he was a great admirer of Roberts' poetry. 14

Roberts lived in England and on the Continent from 1907 to 1924 (and like A.A. Milne he enlisted in the British army at the outbreak of war). Prior to and during that period he published some two dozen nature books, novels, and short stories, some of which were also serialized in magazines in England and the United States. Those publications began with *Earth's Enigmas*, in 1896, and ended in 1936 with *Further Animal Stories*. One particularly popular collection was entitled *Babes in the Wild*. Appearing in serial form in 1908 and 1909 in the US, and again in 1912 and 1913, it was issued in book form in 1912 by Cassel & Co. in England, and by Macmillan in the US (under the title 15

Children of the Wild). After the war it was twice reissued by Dent & Son, in 1920 and 1921, the latter retaining the original illustrations by Paul Branson. (And it would be re-issued yet again in 1928.)

One of the stories in *Babes in the Wild* rings familiar to Pooh   16
fans. Teddy Bear finds himself alone in this world after his mother and sister are caught in a trap. Hunting for berries, he tumbles into a deep depression or bowl, where he smells "the warm delectable smell of honey" coming from "a small hole near the top of [a] dilapidated old [maple] tree." From his mother he had certainly learned of bees' hot tempers, but—

> ... being a bear of great decision, he lost no time in wondering what he had better do. The moment he had convinced himself that the honey was up that tree, up that tree he went to get it. ... Most cubs, and some older bears, would have relinquished the adventure at this point; for as a rule, it takes a wise old bear to handle a bee-tree successfully. But Teddy Bear was no ordinary cub, let me tell you, *— or we would never have called him 'Teddy'.* ... [words in italics appear only in the serialized US version]
>
> Hauling himself up softly from branch to branch, he made no more noise than a shadow.

Teddy is eventually driven back down the tree by the bees'   17
assaults,

> ... swinging down from branch to branch, whining and coughing and spluttering, and squealing all the way. From the lowest branch he slid down the trunk, his claws rearing the bark and just clinging enough to break his fall.
>
> As soon as Teddy Bear had got rid of his assailants he clawed down through the leaves and twigs and moss ... till he came to the damp cool earth. Ah, how he dug his smarting muzzle into it, and rooted in it, and rubbed it into his ears and on his eyelids. ... And his glossy fur was in a state of which his mother would have strongly disapproved. But his twinkling eyes burned with wrath and determination.

He goes up the tree again slowly and deliberately, pulls away   18
"a strip of rotten wood" and gorges himself to bursting while the bees scurry to save what they can of their precious honey.

> Then, very slowly and heavily, grunting all the time, he climbed down the bee-tree. ... He just waddled over to a nook between the

roots of the nest tree, curled up his sticky nose between his sticky paws and was soon snoring.[10]

On Christmas Eve of 1925, the *Evening News* published a new 19
bear story for children by A.A. Milne, entitled "Winnie-the-Pooh." (The following year it was to appear as the first chapter of Milne's famous book of the same name.) It was also read over the wireless at 7:15 p.m. on Christmas Day "from all stations" by Donald Calthrop. E.H. Shepard had not been available to collaborate as illustrator for that original newspaper version, so J.H. Dowd was commissioned to provide the pictures.

As the first chapter in Milne's book, *Winnie-the-Pooh*, the 20
story begins:

> In Which
> We Are Introduced to
> Winnie-the-Pooh
> and Some Bees,
> and the Stories Begin.

We immediately meet an "Edward Bear" bumping down the 21
stairs behind a Christopher Robin, and are transported to Hundred-Acre-Wood. Pooh finds an "open place in the middle of the forest, and in the centre of the place is a large oak-tree, and, from the top of the tree, there came a loud buzzing noise."

Pooh doesn't smell the honey, however. He hears the bees— 22
and he is not driven from his perch by painful stings, but simply falls to the ground when a branch breaks—right into a prickly gorse-bush—"he brushed the prickles from his nose."[11]

Pooh collects Christopher Robin (who has brought a gun 23
and a blue balloon); then he goes "to a very muddy place that he knew of, and rolled and rolled until he was black all over ..." The balloon ruse to fool the bees into thinking that the muddy bear is a black cloud in the sky fails, of course, and Christopher Robin has to fire his pop-gun to bring Pooh back to earth clear of the bees.

Roberts had supported himself during his stay in England 24
and the Continent (1907–1924) by writing nature stories for the *Windsor Magazine* and various periodicals in the United States. While there is no direct evidence that he knew A.A. Milne, it seems very likely that he would have. Milne's fondness for stories for young people would have attracted him to Roberts' work, and "Teddy Bear's Bee-Tree" had appeared in *Saint Nicholas*

Magazine (New York) in 1913 in addition to its appearance in the various editions of *Babes in the Wild*. Milne's prominence as a writer and editor of *Punch* would have placed him in the same circles as Roberts, himself a member of the Authors' Club and Poets' Club in London. They both shared an interest in the views of Teddy Roosevelt. (Roberts was in New York in 1902 when the Berryman cartoon appeared, at the time when Milne was at Cambridge as editor of *Granta*.) The "Punchian" humour of the Roberts-Roosevelt tiff of 1907 (especially the Powers cartoon) would not have escaped Milne as editor of *Punch*.

So this charming tale is perhaps more Canadian than either   25
of the feuding parties in New York or London would care to admit. Pooh's namesake, a Northern Ontario black bear named "Winnie" (after her first owner's hometown of Winnipeg), was the flesh-and-blood bear that captivated Christopher Robin and his father at the London Zoo. And the plot of the very first chapter of *Winnie-the-Pooh*—in which a hungry bear climbs a tree in the woods "silent as a shadow" to steal honey from angry bees, falls to the ground, rolls in mud, and tries again—is the creation of a New Brunswicker, Sir Charles G.D. Roberts. Of course, we will have to accept with true Canadian tolerance that, unlike Roberts' "Teddy Bear" of "great decision," this *Pooh* of ours is but "a bear of very little brain," and must, more discreetly than valorously perhaps, forgo his honey till it comes safely in a jar.

Notes

1. Charles Gordon, *Ottawa Citizen*, 11 March 1998.

2. A.A. Milne, *When We Were Very Young*, illustrated by E.H. Shepard (London: Methuen, 1924).

3. The hunt was extensively covered in the press. See the *New York Times* for 14, 15, 19 November 1902. The true story of how the president "refused to make an unsportsmanlike shot" is given on page 1 of the *Washington Post* of 15 November. The exhausted bear had been run down and trapped in a water-hole by the dogs. Holt Collier jumped from his horse and dazed it with a blow from his rifle-butt, whereupon it was tied to a tree: "When the President arrived he would neither shoot it nor permit it to be shot. 'Put it out of its misery,' said he to Mr. Parker, and the latter ended its life with his knife."

4. See Pauline Cockrill, *The Teddy Bear Encyclopedia* (London: Dorling Kindersley, 1993), p. 50; C.R. Milne, *The Enchanted Places* (London: Eyre Methuen, 1974), p. 77.

5. A.A. Milne, *The House at Pooh Corner*, illustrated by E.H. Shepard (London: Methuen, 1928), p. 177.

6. A.A. Milne, *Autobiography* (New York: E.P. Dutton, 1939), pp. 249–67; Ann Thwaite, *A.A. Milne—His Life* (London and Boston: Faber and Faber, 1990), pp. 153–93.

7. Paula T. Connolly, *Winnie-the-Pooh and The House at Pooh Corner: Recovering Arcadia* (New York: Twayne, 1995), pp. 5–7; A.A. Milne, *Autobiography* (New York: E.P. Dutton, 1939), p. 44.

8. See two biographies: Elsie M. Pomeroy, *Sir Charles G.D. Roberts: A Biography* (Toronto: The Ryerson Press, 1943) and J.C. Adams, *Sir Charles God Damn: The Life of Sir Charles G.D. Roberts* (Toronto: University of Toronto Press, 1986).

9. Edward B. Clark, "Roosevelt and the Nature Fakirs," *Everybody's Magazine*, 16 (1907), pp. 773–4. Other pieces on this subject were Theodore Roosevelt, "Nature Fakers," *Everybody's Magazine*, 17 (1907), pp. 427–30, and Edward B. Clark, "Real Naturalists on Nature Fakers," *Everybody's Magazine*, 17 (1907), pp. 423–7. For a recent study of Theodore Roosevelt and bears, see Anne Innis Dagg, "Prestige, Power, and the Naming of Bears," *Queen's Quarterly*, 104/1 (Spring 1997), 97–106.

10. Charles G.D. Roberts, *Babes in the Wild* (London: Cassel, 1912), pp. 140–54.

11. A.A. Milne, *Winnie-the-Pooh*, illustrated by E.H. Shepard (London: Methuen, 1925), p. 9. (The book was published in the same year by Dutton in New York and by McClelland & Stewart in Toronto.) This investigation was inspired by an earlier article in this journal by my Queen's colleague Dr. Donald H. Akenson: "Winnie-the-Pooh and the Jesus Seminar," *Queen's Quarterly*, 104/4 (Winter 1997), 645–58.

UNDERSTANDING DETAILS

1. Where did Winnie come from? How did Winnie get to the London Zoo? In what ways are Canadians frequently reminded of Winnie-the-Pooh's Canadian origins?
2. Where does the term *teddy bear* come from?
3. What is the American claim to Winnie-the-Pooh?

ANALYZING MEANING

1. In paragraph 1, Kilpatrick quotes Charles Gordon suggesting a reason why Canadians don't associate Winnie-the-Pooh with Canada. What is Gordon's position? Do you agree with him? Why or why not?
2. Explain the connection between A.A. Milne and Charles G.D. Roberts.
3. Why are there claims to Winnie-the-Pooh from three different countries? What is the value in this association with the Winnie-the-Pooh character?

DISCOVERING RHETORICAL STRATEGIES

1. Who do you think is Kilpatrick's main audience? How did you come to this conclusion?
2. What tone does the author establish by referring to other sources in his essay?
3. What information in the essay is most persuasive to you? Least persuasive?

MAKING CONNECTIONS

1. Compare and contrast the way in which Kilpatrick uses examples and documentation in his argument with the use of these elements by Marilyn Dahl ("The Role of the Media in Promoting Images of Disability") or Barbara Ehrenreich ("The Ecstasy of War").
2. In "The Babar Factor," Evan Solomon focuses on the importance of children's stories. Imagine a conversation between Solomon and Ross Kilpatrick about the role of children's literature in our society. On what points do you think these two men would agree? Are there areas where you think they might hold differing points of view?

IDEAS FOR DISCUSSION/WRITING

Preparing to Write

Write freely about stories you remember from your childhood. What characters stand out in your memory? Do you remember Charlotte the Spider, Anansi the Spider, Peter Rabbit, or Babar the

Elephant? Why do so many children's stories feature animal characters that are personified? What makes these characters memorable?

Choosing a Topic

1. Think of a children's book or series of books that have experienced particular popularity (e.g., the Harry Potter books). Write a documented essay in which you examine the extent of the popularity and the reasons for it.
2. Kilpatrick contends that A.A. Milne was influenced by Charles G.D. Roberts. Think of an individual (musician, athlete, writer, film director, architect, visual artist) who has been influenced in his or her field by someone else. Write an essay in which you show the effect of the influence on your individual.
3. Where does influence stop and plagiarism or theft begin? Write an essay in which you clearly define the line between the two.

WEBSITES

www.queensu.ca/quarterly
Kilpatrick's essay comes from the *Queen's Quarterly* journal.

qsilver.queensu.ca/classics/KAAMS2.htm
Kilpatrick is a director of the Kingston Association for Archaeology and Mediterranean Studies.

www.pooh-corner.com/pooh.html
A short history of Pooh and Winnie.

CHAPTER 11

ESSAYS ON THINKING, READING, AND WRITING

In each of the preceding chapters, we have examined a single rhetorical mode in order to focus attention on how writers use that pattern to organize their thoughts. In this final chapter, three essays on the topics of thinking, reading, and writing use a combination of rhetorical modes at work in each selection.

Our primary purpose in this text has been to show how thinking, reading, and writing work together as fine machinery to help all of us function as intelligent and productive human beings. Our introduction discusses the relationship of thinking, reading, and writing; the text itself illustrates the crucial interdependence of these skills; and this last chapter concludes the book by presenting essays on such related topics as understanding the writing process, jargon, and passion for language. These essays are intended for you to read and enjoy. Let your mind run freely through the material as you recall in a leisurely way what you have learned in this text. The essays bring together the theoretical framework of this text as they illustrate how thinking, reading, and writing inform each other and work interdependently to make meaning. And they integrate the rhetorical patterns in such a way that each essay is a blend of the various rhetorical modes discussed in the preceding chapters—a perfect summary of the topics and strategies you have been working with throughout this text.

MARGUERITE ANDERSEN

Passion for Language

Language is my passion. I have no patience for those who 1
mumble, use empty phrases and fill words, lack energy,
character and emotion in their speech. In my opinion, all of this can
be remedied through good training and, above all, through an
acquisition of knowledge coupled with attention to everyday
experience, through reading, of course, which is the basis of my
passion. In other words, I am interested in language performance
based on competence, to use Chomsky's terms.

It sounds like an arrogant position, yet I do not like to 2
perceive myself as being part of an elite. But language is what
allows me to speak and to write, state my thoughts, my feelings
and give form to my imagination. How could linguistic ability not
be important to me? I possess three languages, English, French,
and German. Why have I opted for French in my professional
life, as a university teacher and as a writer? I believe it has to do
with what the French call *le mot juste*, which must be used to
express oneself clearly. I love searching for the right word; I read
dictionaries while eating breakfast or sitting in the bathtub. But
of course speech is not just a question of words. According to
Wittgenstein the meaning of a word is linked to the way we use
it in the language.

Then there is the question of truth, political or personal. Here 3
again, I look for clarity. A simple analogy: I have never lived in
a basement apartment. Maybe I was just lucky; my places have
always been filled with light. I love to wake up in the morning
feeling the sun on my face. I am one of those indoor plants that
thrive when there is light. I am always searching for clarity; I
love to hear it in people's speech, discover it in works of literature.

As a young woman, I wanted to become an actor. Today, I 4
say to myself that I did not pursue that dream because it was
not that intense. I don't know. Rather than speak the words of
others, I maybe prefer to use my own words. With passion!

NATALIE GOLDBERG

The Rules of Writing Practice

For fifteen years now, at the beginning of every writing work- 1
shop, I have repeated the rules for writing practice. So, I will
repeat them again here. And I want to say why I repeat them:
Because they are the bottom line, the beginning of all writing, the
foundation of learning to trust your own mind. Trusting your own
mind is essential for writing. Words come out of the mind.

And I believe in these rules. Perhaps I'm a little fanatical 2
about them.

A friend, teasing me, said, "You act as if they are the rules to 3
live by, as though they apply to everything."

I smiled. "Okay, let's try it. Do they apply to sex?" 4

I stuck up my thumb for rule number one. "Keep your hand 5
moving." I nodded yes.

Index finger, rule number two. "Be specific." I let out a yelp 6
of glee. It was working.

Finger number three. "Lose control." It was clear that sex 7
and writing were the same thing.

Then, number four. "Don't think," I said. Yes, for sex, too, I 8
nodded.

I proved my point. My friend and I laughed. 9

Go ahead, try these rules for tennis, hang gliding, driving a 10
car, making a grilled cheese sandwich, disciplining a dog or a
snake. Okay. They might not always work. They work for writing.
Try them.

1. *Keep your hand moving.* When you sit down to write, 11
whether it's for ten minutes or an hour, once you begin, don't
stop. If an atom bomb drops at your feet eight minutes after you
have begun and you were going to write for ten minutes, don't
budge. You'll go out writing.

What is the purpose of this? Most of the time when we write, 12
we mix up the editor and creator. Imagine your writing hand as
the creator and the other hand as the editor. Now bring your
two hands together and lock your fingers. This is what happens
when we write. The writing hand wants to write about what she

did Saturday night: "I drank whiskey straight all night and stared at a man's back across the bar. He was wearing a red T-shirt. I imagined him to have the face of Harry Belafonte. At three A.M., he finally turned my way and I spit into the ashtray when I saw him. He had the face of a wet mongrel who had lost his teeth." The writing hand is three words into writing this first sentence— "I drank whiskey ..."—when the other hand clenches her fingers tighter and the writing hand can't budge. The editor says to the creator, "Now, that's not nice, the whiskey and stuff. Don't let people know that. I have a better idea: 'Last night, I had a nice cup of warmed milk and then went to bed at nine o'clock.' Write that. Go ahead. I'll loosen my grip so you can."

13   If you keep your creator hand moving, the editor can't catch up with it and lock it. It gets to write out what it wants. "Keep your hand moving" strengthens the creator and gives little space for the editor to jump in.

14   Keep your hand moving is the main structure for writing practice.

15   2. *Lose control.* Say what you want to say. Don't worry if it's correct, polite, appropriate. Just let it rip. Allen Ginsberg was getting a master's degree from Columbia University. Back then, they were doing rhymed verse. He had a lot of practice in formal meter, and so forth. One night, he went home and said to himself that he was going to write whatever he wanted and forget about formalities. The result was "Howl." We shouldn't forget how much practice in writing he had prior to this, but it is remarkable how I can tell students, "Okay, say what you want, go for it," and their writing takes a substantial turn toward authenticity.

16   3. *Be specific.* Not car, but Cadillac. Not fruit, but apple. Not bird, but wren. Not a codependent, neurotic man, but Harry, who runs to open the refrigerator for his wife, thinking she wants an apple, when she is headed for the gas stove to light her cigarette. Be careful of those pop-psychology labels. Get below the label and be specific to the person.

17   But don't chastise yourself as you are writing, "I'm an idiot; Natalie said to be specific and like a fool I wrote 'tree.'" Just gently note that you wrote "tree," drop to a deeper level, and next to "tree" write "sycamore." Be gentle with yourself. Don't give room for the hard grip of the editor.

18   4. *Don't think.* We usually live in the realm of second or third thoughts, thoughts on thoughts, rather than in the realm of first thoughts, the real way we flash on something. Stay with the first

flash. Writing practice will help you contact first thoughts. Just practice and forget everything else.

Now here are some rules that don't necessarily apply to sex, 19 though you can try to apply them to sex if you like.

5. *Don't worry about punctuation, spelling, grammar.* 20

6. *You are free to write the worst junk in America.* You can be 21 more specific, if you like: the worst junk in Santa Fe; New York; Kalamazoo, Michigan; your city block; your pasture; your neighborhood restaurant; your family. Or you can get more cosmic: free to write the worst junk in the universe, galaxy, world, hemisphere, Sahara Desert.

7. *Go for the jugular.* If something scary comes up, go for it. 22 That's where the energy is. Otherwise, you'll spend all your time writing around whatever makes you nervous. It will probably be abstract, bland writing because you're avoiding the truth. Hemingway said, "Write hard and clear about what hurts." Don't avoid it. It has all the energy. Don't worry, no one ever died of it. You might cry or laugh, but not die.

I am often asked, "Well, isn't there a time when we need to 23 stop our hand moving? You know, to figure out what we want to say?"

It's better to figure out what you want to say in the actual 24 act of writing. For a long time, I was very strict with myself about writing practice. I kept that hand moving no matter what. I wanted to learn to cut through to first thoughts. Sure, you can stop for a few moments, but it is a tricky business. It's good to stop if you want, look up and get a better picture of what you're writing about, but often I don't stay there. If I give myself a little gap, I'm off for an hour daydreaming. You have to learn your own rhythm, but make sure you do some focused, disciplined "keeping the hand moving" to learn about cutting through resistance.

If you learn writing practice well, it is a good foundation for 25 all other writing.

When I was young, I played tennis. My arm wasn't very 26 strong, and I was impatient. I was so eager to play, I held the racquet up higher on the grip than I was supposed to in order to compensate. Unfortunately, I got used to using the racquet this way. I was a fine tennis player, but no matter how much I played, there was just so far I could improve, because I never mastered one of the important basics: the proper grip on the racquet.

I use this as an example for writing practice. Grow com- 27
fortable with it in its basic form before you begin to veer off into
your own manner and style. Trust it. It is as basic as drinking
water.

Sometimes an interviewer asks me, "So writing practice is 28
old hat? Have you developed something new?"

And I say, "It would be like a Zen master teaching you 29
meditation one year and the next year saying, 'Forget compassion.
Standing on our head is what's in.'"

The old essentials are still necessary. Stay with them under all 30
circumstances. It will make you stable—something unusual for
a writer.

Speak English, Dammit:
Why Has Jargon
Become the Language of Business?

In his 1946 essay "Politics and the English Language," George   1
Orwell wrote that language, "becomes ugly and inaccurate
because our thoughts are foolish, but the slovenliness of our language makes it easier for us to have foolish thoughts." Spent any
time in the new economy crossword puzzle? Things are definitely
doubleplusungood.

The language of business is fast becoming a kind of torture   2
chamber for plain English. Clear, comprehensible words enter;
horrifically disfigured and unrecognizable phrases stumble
out: management bandwidth; acquisition lockdown; mind-
share; stickiness; point of contact; vector; push back; tear
down; granularity. Please somebody, stop them before they
neologize again.

Business has always had buzzwords, and this isn't the first   3
time diction or intention have been obscured by sloppy verbiage.
In his 1978 book, *The Jargon of the Professions*, Kenneth Hudson
noted that "Business is subject to two quite different linguistic
pressures. On the one hand, there is the never-ending search for
the new, even more arresting phrase ... and on the other, the
wish to tone words down, to make them less dangerous, less
precise, less likely to blow up in the face of the person who uses
them." This has never been truer than it is today: in 1978, business
was still largely conducted in English; these days, it's done in a
kind of impenetrable Esperanto. The worst examples of e-lingo
combine what Hudson described, at once impressing people
with their futurism ("vortal") while insulating the speaker from
actually having an opinion that might later prove unpopular or
incorrect.

Language is the filter through which we describe reality, but   4
when it comes to dot-com-speak, unreality is the result. What
do words like reskin or envisioneer really mean, beyond proving

that the person saying them has found the time to skim through
Fast Company?

The problem is less the existence of jargon, which can act as   5
verbal shorthand between like-minded professionals, than the
proliferation of nonsense jargon, words that appear to have no
clearly defined meaning. This inflated language strives to make
the ordinary extraordinary, or, as Orwell put it, "give an
appearance of solidity to pure wind." Both of which are good
descriptors for the new economy, where an entire lexicon has
emerged to help obscure the fact that most web-based enterprises
are still in the widget business—sorry, "clicks-and-mortar." Sadly,
Internet start-ups are often too harried trying to become the
beneficiary of the IPO fairy to find the time to question their
most cherished words and phrases.

Given an uncritiqued column inch, some writers are   6
producing a mile of meaningless prose, best witnessed in the
recent and buzz-ridden book, *Funky Business*. Swedish authors
Jonas Ridderstrale and Kjell Nordstrom brag about their funky
bald heads and black leather pants to reinforce their funky,
revolutionary theories about business. To prove their rather
intriguing theory that "talent makes capital dance," and in lieu of
case studies and statistics, they create words like infomediaries,
heart share, staminacs, prosumption, heterarchical and hyphen-
ation. After reading about CDOs (chief destruction officers) or
phrase after phrase like "funky leaders are creators of chaos as
much as originators of order," one cannot help but recall Orwell's
dystopic *Nineteen Eighty-Four*. Phrases like "war is peace,"
"freedom is slavery" and "ignorance is strength" require nearly
the same mental gymnastics to unpack as the "funked up"
assertion that "total innovation requires ignoring and listening to
the customer."

Normally, when a business word or phrase crosses over into   7
popular culture, it acts as a eulogy. But despite Edward Norton's
world-weary "Do you want me to deprioritize my current reports
until you advise of a status upgrade?" in *Fight Club*, and the
occasional Dilbert pot-shot, e-lingo continues to thrive. The Jargon
Watch column in *Wired* magazine ends up legitimizing the
problem rather than ridiculing it.

Then again, maybe the Web is self-governing enough to solve   8
the problems it generated. There are sites devoted to Lingo Bingo,
e-lingo dictionaries (**www.polarisconsulting.com**) and the web

economy bullshit generator (WEBG), provided by **www. dack.com**. The WEBG randomly combines the most common nonsense words to create uniquely meaningless phrases of unintentional hilarity: implement integrated niches; exploit granular eyeballs; streamline vector convergence. When a Java applet sounds as bleeding-edge as a real person, perhaps it's time to declare e-lingo, like Latin, a dead language.

CREDITS

of the Canadian Journal of Communication Inc. • Gwynne Dyer, "Flagging Attention." Originally appeared in *enRoute* (July 1999), pp. 23–25. Reprinted with permission of the author. • Barbara Ehrenreich, "The Ecstasy of War," from *Blood Rights: Origins and History of the Passions of War* by Barbara Ehrenreich. Copyright © 1997 by Barbara Ehrenreich. Reprinted by permission of Henry Holt and Company, Inc. • Will Ferguson, "The Sudbury Syndrome." Excerpt from *Why I Hate Canadians* by Will Ferguson. Copyright © 1997 by Will Ferguson. Published in Canada by Douglas & McIntyre Ltd. Reprinted by permission of the publisher. • Joe Fiorito, "Breakfast in Bed," from *Comfort Me With Apples*, published by Nuage Editions. Reprinted by permission. • David Foot, "Boomers Dance to a New Beat," originally published in *The Globe and Mail*, (Jan. 9, 1998). Reprinted by permission of David Foot, Professor of Economics, University of Toronto, and co-author of *Boom, Bust & Echo: Profiting from the Demographic Shift in the Twenty-first Century*. • Cecil Foster, "Why Blacks Get Mad." Originally appeared in *Chatelaine*, November 1992. Reprinted by permission of the author. • Malcolm Gladwell, "Is the Belgian Coca-Cola Hysteria the Real Thing?" Originally appeared in *The New Yorker* (July 1999). Reprinted by permission of the author. • Natalie Goldberg, "Rules of Writing Practice," from *Wild Mind: Living the Writer's Life* by Natalie Goldberg. Copyright © 1990 by Natalie Goldberg. Used by permission of Bantam Books, a division of Random House, Inc. • Charlotte Gray, "Heroes and Symbols," from "Great Canadian Questions." *The Dominion Institute*. <www.greatquestions.com>. 1999. Reprinted with permission. • Steve Heighton, "Elegy in Stone," from *Admen Move on Lhasa* copyright © 1997 by Steven Heighton. Reprinted by permission of House of Anansi Press Inc. • Tomson Highway, "What a Certain Visionary Once Said." Copyright © 1992 by Tomson Highway. Reprinted by permission of the author. • Lawrence Hill, "Don't Call Me That Word." Essays. *Lawrence Hill*. <www.lawrencehill.com>. September 2002. Reprinted with permission of the author. • Monte Hummel, "A Passion for the Environment: Two Accounts," *Queen's Quarterly* 107/1 (Spring 2000), pp. 66–67. Reprinted with permission of the author. • Dave Kendell, "Language for a New Age," *The Call Magazine*. <http://www.callmagazine.com>. September 2002. Reproduced by permission of the author. • Ross Kilpatrick, "Winnie-the-Pooh and the Canadian Connection, " *Queen's Quarterly* 105/4 (Winter

INDEX OF AUTHORS AND TITLES